Faith-Based Diplomacy ▣ Trumping Realpolitik

Faith-Based Diplomacy

▣ Trumping Realpolitik ▣

EDITED BY

Douglas Johnston

OXFORD
UNIVERSITY PRESS

2003

OXFORD
UNIVERSITY PRESS

Oxford   New York

Auckland   Bangkok   Buenos Aires   Cape Town   Chennai
Dar es Salaam   Delhi   Hong Kong   Istanbul   Karachi   Kolkata
Kuala Lumpur   Madrid   Melbourne   Mexico City   Mumbai   Nairobi
São Paulo   Shanghai   Taipei   Tokyo   Toronto

Copyright © 2003 by Oxford University Press, Inc.

Published by Oxford University Press, Inc.
198 Madison Avenue, New York, New York 10016

www.oup.com

Oxford is a registered trademark of Oxford University Press

Library of Congress Cataloging-in-Publication Data
Faith-based diplomacy : trumping realpolitik / edited by Douglas Johnston.
    p. cm.
  ISBN 978-0-19-516089-5
  1. Religion and international affairs. 2. Religion and politics. 3.
Ethnic conflict—Religious aspects. 4. War—Religious aspects. I.
Johnston, Douglas, 1938–
  BL65.I55 F345 2003
  291.1'787—dc21   2002009488

9 8 7 6 5 4 3 2

Printed in the United States of America
on acid-free paper

War is a stern teacher—THUCYDIDES

In tribute to Abraham Vereide
and the spirit of his work

Foreword

When one thinks of religion's role in world history, violent confrontation is usually one of the first images to emerge. History is replete with illustrations of the divisive role that religion has played, as is today's contemporary world. In the numerous conflicts of identity that are currently raging in such places as the Balkans, the Middle East, Africa, and South Asia, one invariably finds a religious dimension. While religion is clearly central to so much of the strife that is taking place, it is also being looked at as an instrument of peace. The contribution of this book is that it sees religion not as something to overcome or ignore, but as an important part of conflict resolution and the promotion of peace.

In the following pages, Dr. Douglas Johnston and his team of eminent scholars examine how the peacemaking tenets of key religions can be brought to bear in five ongoing conflicts around the world. This effort represents an important step in acknowledging religion as a defining element in international security and in recognizing the largely untapped potential of a new form of diplomacy characterized by the authors as "faith-based diplomacy." Faith-based diplomacy speaks to the heart, mind, and spirit of the combatants—to those things that they hold most dear—not simply to the intellectual or material issues that dominate the practice of *realpolitik*. In so doing, it provides a transcendent capability that, under the right circumstances, can resolve differences where all else has failed.

While the factors addressed by traditional methods of diplomacy and statecraft are important, they are often insufficient in and of themselves to ensure peace on a lasting basis. They tend to underestimate the underlying grievances of the disputants, as has typically happened in the Middle East peace negotiations. Time and again, agreements like those hammered out at Camp David, Oslo, and Sharm al-Shiek have had many believing, or at least hoping, that peace might finally be within reach for this troubled region. Subsequent events have shown the emptiness of such hopes, as the fury of the second Intifada and the predictable reactions to it rage unchecked.

Although these courageous, yet unsuccessful, attempts at peace addressed key issues and brought initial agreement between opposing leaders, they overlooked the most vital aspect of the confrontation—the hearts and minds of the Israeli and Palestinian peoples. Neither side was prepared for peace, regardless of whatever agreements have been crafted and agreed to by their respective leaders. The approaches taken to date have not effectively addressed the deep-seated emotional wounds—the fear, hatred, and yearning for revenge—that dominate the outlook and attitudes of most Israelis and Palestinians. This same phenomenon holds true as well for scores of other conflicts across the globe. Until such scars are satisfactorily addressed at the grass-roots level, there is little chance that peace will ever take hold and almost no chance that it will last if it does.

At some point, the conflicting parties must sit down together and take an honest look at their respective histories, searching within to understand the reasons for their rage and that of their adversaries. Then they need to muster the courage to take the necessary steps to escape the bonds of that rage. This is where faith-based diplomacy can play a critical role. By capitalizing on the reconciling aspects of religious faith—what some would call the true face of religion—one can, under the right conditions, overcome the wounds and facilitate a process of forgiveness and reconciliation.

In responding to the longer term challenges of September 11, 2001, it seems clear that military action alone will not be adequate to the task; nor will our normal reactive mindset to world events serve us well. Religion is a powerful force in the lives of people and a strong foundation for many societies. It is thus striking that religion is often ignored by diplomats and policymakers. The stakes are simply too high to continue in this vein. What is needed is an effective strategy of cultural engagement that incorporates religion as a tool for preventing problems from reaching the crisis stage. This book does an exemplary job of pointing the way toward constructing such a strategy.

Lee H. Hamilton is Director, Woodrow Wilson International Center for Scholars and Former Chair, Foreign Affairs Committee, U.S. House of Representatives.

Preface

Realpolitik as commonly understood and referred to by most foreign policy experts has been the term of art to describe the practice of power politics based on a tough-minded, realistic view of the political, economic, and security factors that dominate any given situation. Typically, this concept has not included a sophisticated understanding of the larger religious and philosophical values that influence the actors, nor has it offered its disciples access to the kind of spiritual engagement that can sometimes be useful in the diplomatic search for solutions. If nothing else, the events of September 11, 2001, have exposed the limitations of the realist approach and the rational-actor model of decisionmaking that has served as its altar.

This purposeful exclusion of elements that clearly play a central role in some situations has left foreign policy practitioners with an inadequate frame of reference for dealing with the problems of communal identity that currently plague the global landscape in the form of ethnic conflict, tribal warfare, and religious hostilities. It is no small irony that this historical exclusion was never itself the product of rational analysis but rather a predictable outgrowth of dogmatic secularism. The question then becomes which of these two positions comes closest to the "real" meaning of realpolitik, dogmatic self-limitation or a rational willingness to see the world whole?

Just as a trump suit outranks all other suits in certain card games, so too do religious factors outrank those relating to realpolitik in some conflict situations. And like a trump card, faith-based diplomacy is "a key resource to be used at the opportune moment" (American Heritage Dictionary). The title of this book is thus intended to convey a dual meaning: (1) to signify the end of a period of narrow power politics in which religious factors have intentionally been excluded from the policymaker's calculus, and (2) to suggest a new goal for realist politics that provides a greater capability for understanding and dealing with the full range of human imperatives through its strategic inclusion of religious considerations.

At the beginning of the last millennium, Christianity and Islam were locked in mortal combat over their mutual claims to the Holy Lands. A thousand years later, the venue has changed, but little else. Why is it that these two monotheistic faith traditions, which share so much in common theologically, tend to talk past one another at best or, alternatively, resort to conflict to settle their differences? Something is missing; and that "something" is what this book is largely about—not only as it affects the West's interaction with Islam but its ability to interact with other religions as well.

To a considerable extent, Western policymakers have let their dedication to a vigorous separation of church and state become an excuse for failing to comprehend—and understand how to deal with—the worldview of Islam (in which no such separation exists). It is also the case that since the Enlightenment, Western decisionmaking has been all but devoid of religious content. Both realities have contributed to an inability to communicate across the divide that currently separates the religious world of Islam and the quasi-secular world of the West. The problem is thus one not so much of religious rivalry as of not speaking the same language. Islam speaks the language of integration (of politics and religion), while the West speaks the language of separation. Even the same words can have different meanings. When Westerners use the term "secular," for example, Muslims hear "Godless," while what was intended is "freedom to worship as one pleases."

Without undermining the Western separation of church and state, this book suggests a way to bridge the gap across religious boundaries through the practice of "faith-based diplomacy," a form of diplomacy that blends religious insights and influence with the practice of international politics. This activity, which is explained in chapter 2, is not something that governments can control—their political agendas would ipso facto compromise the integrity of such initiatives—but is something that they can reinforce and build upon to good effect under the right circumstances.

One of the more able faith-based diplomats on the world scene today is Pope John Paul II, who has been cited by none other than Mikhail Gorbachev as having been responsible for the fall of communism in Eastern Europe. His celebrated trip to Poland, while it was under Soviet rule, clearly set that process in motion and left a mark that will never be forgotten. In the following chapters, eminent scholars from key religions establish important guideposts that can help point the way for faith-based intervention in five ongoing and highly intractable conflicts.

The challenge of harnessing religion's transcendent qualities in the cause of peace is formidable and not for the faint of heart. Not only is this work intellectually and emotionally draining, but it involves significant risks as well. A number of spiritually-inspired peacemakers have paid the ultimate price for their efforts: Mahatma Gandhi, Anwar Sadat, and Martin Luther King, Jr., to mention a few of the better known. Despite the risks, and as September 11, 2001, so dramatically illustrates, spiritual engagement is a challenge that we ignore at our peril. Only time will tell if we are up to the task.

Acknowledgments

The strength of this book, like that of its literary antecedent, *Religion, the Missing Dimension of Statecraft*, lies in the collaborative nature of its development. Numerous individuals contributed in one way or another to the synergy that was sought and hopefully achieved. Beyond the world-class religious scholars who authored individual chapters, a formidable array of other scholars and practitioners vetted and discussed the initial drafts of those chapters. While it seems unlikely that any single participant would claim to be in total agreement with the final product that ultimately emerged, all will find some reflection of their respective contributions incorporated where appropriate. Those who offered such insights and suggestions include the following:

Dr. Amr Abdalla
Mr. Karu Abewickrama
Dr. Imad-ad-Dean Ahmed
Ms. Sharmin Ahmed
Dr. Richard Arndt
Professor Katni Bajpai
Dr. Jonah Blank
Dr. Zahid Bukhari
Mr. Maharagama Dhammasiri
Dr. Ahmed El-Bashir
Mr. Hashim El-Tinay
Mr. Rajmohan Gandhi
General Fabian Agalong Guem
Dr. Milos Ivanis
Mr. James Jatras

Ms. Rajika Jayatilake
Mr. Prem Shankar Jha
Dr. Rajesh Kadian
Dr. Arthur Keys
Mr. Naren Kumarakulasingam
Ambassador Samuel Lewis
Mr. Joseph Montville
Dr. Ghulam Nabi Fai
Dr. Deepa Ollapally
Dr. Mustapha K. Pasha
Mr. Gerald Powers
Dr. Khalid Qazi
Dr. John Richardson
Dr. Nedzib Sacirbey
Dr. Abdul Aziz Said

Mr. Vijay K. Sazawal	Dr. David Smock
Dr. Howard Schaffer	Dr. Max Ticktin
Ambassador Teresita Schaffer	Fr. Alexander Webster

Both singly and collectively, these participants deserve the gratitude and appreciation of prospective readers. Equally deserving is Richard Ruffin, Vice President for Preventive Diplomacy of the International Center for Religion & Diplomacy and Executive Director of Initiatives of Change (U.S.), who co-chaired the seminars at which these chapters were discussed.

I am personally grateful to Stanton Burnett for his uncommon insights on the limitations of realpolitick and to Abdulaziz Sachedina and Abubaker al-Shingieti for their valuable observations on Islam. Jonathan Eastvold, Darin Hamlin, Joe Mata, Kate Diaz, and Mike Van Hall deserve enormous credit for their insightful research on various aspects of the substance; and I would be remiss if I failed to acknowledge the support of my wife, Janean, whose unfailing encouragement provided inspiration throughout. Finally, hats off to the Smith-Richardson Foundation for providing the financial support that made it all possible in the first instance.

To you, the reader, we are all grateful for your willingness to peruse this work with an open mind. The current level of national and international violence suggests a strong need for more effective approaches to relating with one another across geographic, political, economic, and religious divides. Experience has shown that past tendencies toward isolation only lead to paralysis, whereas engagement makes possible the creation of new dynamics and the likelihood of forward movement. Although this book's advocacy for a new kind of engagement may evoke a degree of skepticism among those wed to the old style of realpolitik, it is our hope that it will stimulate debate and cause readers to think in new directions.

Why new directions? As noted by Philip Jenkins, Distinguished Professor of History and Religious Studies at Pennsylvania State University, in the October 2002 issue of *The Atlantic Monthly*, "the twenty-first century will almost certainly be regarded by future historians as a century in which religion replaced ideology as the prime animating and destructive force in human affairs, guiding attitudes to political liberty and obligation, concepts of nationhood, and, of course, conflicts and wars"("The Next Christianity," p. 54). To the extent there is any truth to this prediction, the challenge will be formidable indeed. So too must be our resolve, if we are to meet it.

Contents

III Closure

Contributors

Dr. R. Scott Appleby is professor of history at the University of Notre Dame and is director of the University's Joan G. Kroc Institute for International Peace Studies. He also served for six years as director of Notre Dame's Cushwa Center for the Study of American Catholicism. Dr. Appleby is the author of *The Ambivalence of the Sacred: Religion, Violence and Reconciliation,* a study of religious peacebuilding for the Carnegie Commission on Preventing Deadly Conflict. His book *Fundamentalisms Observed* won the 1991 American Association of Publishers award for best book in religion and philosophy, and the series he coedited on global fundamentalisms won the 1996 Award for Excellence in the Study of Religion of the American Academy of Religion.

The Reverend Canon Brian Cox is rector of Christ the King Episcopal Church in Santa Barbara, California, senior vice-president for Dispute Resolution Training of the International Center for Religion & Diplomacy (ICRD) in Washington D.C., president of the Reconciliation Institute of Santa Barbara, and adjunct professor of law at Pepperdine University School of Law in Malibu, California. His involvement with international reconciliation work began in 1984, when he spent several months in South Africa on a teaching sabbatical. In 1990, he founded the European Reconciliation Fellowship, which focused on the work of faith-based reconciliation with political and religious leaders in east central Europe. His present work with the ICRD focuses on reconciliation training in Sudan and Kashmir.

Dr. Khaled Abou El Fadl is the Omar and Asmeralda Alfi Distinguished Fellow in Islamic Law at the UCLA School of Law. He has lectured on Islamic law in the United States, Europe, and the Middle East and has acted as arbiter and expert witness in a variety of legal cases involving Islamic law. He has written numerous articles in academic journals and is the author of *The Authoritative and Authoritarian in Islamic Discourses*. Dr. Abou El Fadl has worked with the Lawyers' Committee for International Human Rights and is on the advisory board of Human Rights Middle East Watch.

Dr. Ainslie T. Embree is professor emeritus of history at Columbia University, where he founded the University Seminar on Modernization and Change in South and Southeast Asia. He is a member of the Kashmir Study Group, a nongovernmental body that seeks to resolve the tensions between India and Pakistan over Kashmir. Dr. Embree's most recent books include *Imagining India: Essays on Indian History* and *Utopias in Conflict: Religion and Nationalism in India*. He has received numerous honors and awards, including the Tannenbaum Award as well as various university awards for teaching excellence.

Rabbi Marc Gopin is visiting associate professor of international diplomacy at the Fletcher School for Law and Diplomacy of Tufts University. In addition, he serves as senior associate in the Preventive Diplomacy Program at the Center for Strategic and International Studies. He has been a consultant for the World Bank, the Embassy of Israel, Moral Re-Armament, and the Forgiveness Institute. He has written numerous publications and directed a number of presentations on conflict, religion, and development. Rabbi Gopin has also received the Nachum and Anne Glatzer Endowed Prize for excellence in Judaic scholarship.

Dr. Douglas M. Johnston Jr. is president and founder of the International Center for Religion & Diplomacy. He has served in senior positions in government, business, the military, and academia, including six years at Harvard, where he taught international affairs and was founder and first director of the university's Executive Program in National and International Security. His most recent assignment was as executive vice-president and chief operating officer of the Center for Strategic and International Studies. He is principal author and editor of *Religion, the Missing Dimension of Statecraft* (Oxford University Press, 1994) and *Foreign Policy into the Twenty-First Century: The U.S. Leadership Challenge* (CSIS, 1996).

Dr. Sulayman S. Nyang teaches in (and has chaired) the Department of African Studies at Howard University. In addition to his teaching, he has held the position of deputy ambassador of the Gambian Embassy in Jeddah,

Saudi Arabia. He is author of *Islam in the United States of America* and has contributed more than a dozen chapters to various other books.

Dr. H. L. Seneviratne is professor of anthropology at the University of Virginia, where he focuses on the themes and social processes arising from Buddhist social contexts. Dr. Seneviratne received his Ph.D. from the University of Rochester and has published "Kingship and Polity in Buddhism and Hinduism" and "Identity and the Conflation of Past and Present" in *Social Analysis,* among others.

Dr. David A. Steele is director of the Religion and Conflict Resolution Project at the Center for Strategic and International Studies, where he has developed and implemented an interreligious conflict resolution training program in the former Yugoslavia. He received his doctor of ministry degree at Andover Newton Theological School and his Ph.D. in Christian ethics and practical theology at the University of Edinburgh. He served as a pastor for fourteen years in the United Church of Christ and has published "Cooperative Conflict Resolution" and "The Lessons of Kosovo for U.S. Foreign Policy" in the *Northwestern Journal of International Affairs.*

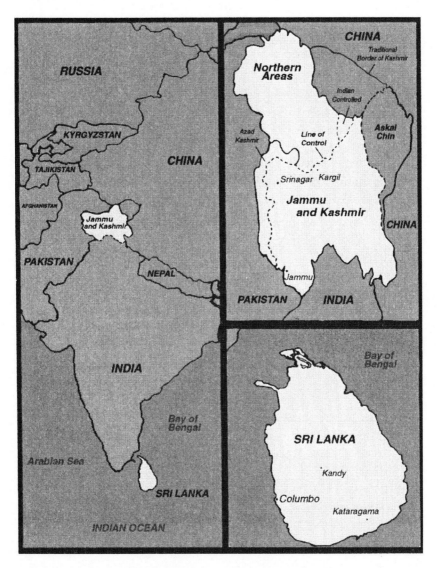

Kashmir and Sri Lanka in their regional context.

The Balkans.

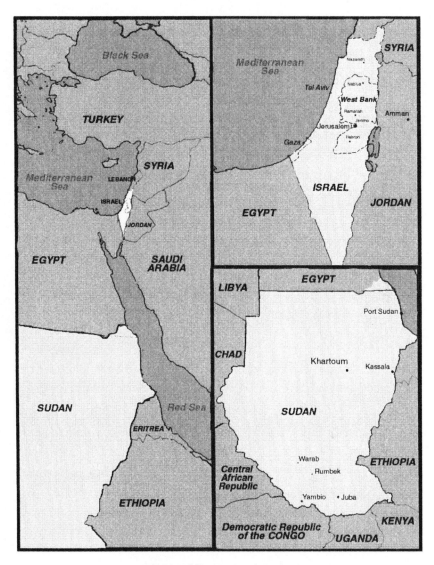

The Middle East and Sudan.

I

Faith-Based Diplomacy

I *Douglas Johnston*

Introduction
Realpolitik Expanded

There never was a time when, in my opinion, some way
could not be found to prevent the drawing of the sword.

—ULYSSES S. GRANT

As the attacks on the World Trade Center and the Pentagon so powerfully
remind us, the greatest threat facing the world today is the prospective marriage of religious extremism with weapons of mass destruction. Massive
amounts of money will be spent in the months and years ahead to defend
against this threat, with the bulk of it going to counter symptoms and far
less to addressing cause. The time has come—indeed, is long overdue—for
taking concrete steps to inspire religious activity in more helpful directions.
As the renowned religious scholar Huston Smith has noted, "the surest way
to the heart of a people is through their faith."[1]

Background

Since the founding of the republic, American diplomacy has essentially
placed religion beyond the bounds of critical analysis. In recent years, however, the global resurgence of religious militancy and influence has begun to
force a reappraisal. As a practical matter, U.S. foreign policy began to acknowledge this with the establishment in 1998 of the State Department's
Office of International Religious Freedom and the later assignment of military chaplains to that department's Bureau of Democracy, Human Rights,
and Labor. Yet another manifestation of this new awareness was a recent
training program for Navy, Marine Corps, and Coast Guard chaplains in
religion and statecraft, an initiative designed to enhance the conflict-
prevention capability of the sea-service commands.

Although such measures show a growing awareness of religion's political
importance, religious imperatives have yet to be incorporated as a major
consideration in U.S. foreign policy. They should be. Religion is central to

much of the strife that is taking place in the world today.[2] Whether it is the root cause of a conflict, as it appears to be in the Middle East, where there are competing religious claims for the same piece of territory, or merely a mobilizing vehicle for nationalist and ethnic passions, as has typically been the case in the Balkans, religion's potential to cause instability at all levels of the global system is arguably unrivaled.

In all likelihood, religion's importance will only continue to increase in response to the perceived threat to traditional values posed by economic globalization and the uncertainties stemming from rapid technological change.[3] To undervalue these realities in the formulation of U.S. foreign policy is to tempt the gods, so to speak.

Past reluctance to consider religious factors has not been without its costs. The U.S. failures in Iran, Lebanon, and even Vietnam were due, at least in part, to the fact that policymakers simply did not fully understand or respond effectively to the religious dynamics of the situation. In the case of Iran, the president and top policymakers in Washington were caught unaware by the Islamic revolution.[4] They should not have been. State Department reports at the time noted that the Ayatollah Khomeini had emerged as the most outspoken critic of the government, that the shah's Islamic opponents were in a strong position, and that the shah's days were probably numbered.[5] These observations were effectively suppressed at higher levels by a combination of dogmatic secularism and economic determinism.

It is entirely possible that greater recognition of the religious dimension may not have significantly altered the outcome in any of these situations. Had the religious factors been properly considered, however, the improved ability to anticipate and react could conceivably have spared the United States untold embarrassment in Iran (and the embassy staff in Tehran some 444 days of anguish). The same can also be said for Lebanon (and the loss of 241 U.S. Marines).

This deep-seated tendency to ignore the religious dimension continues to play out on a number of fronts. South Asia, for example, is replete with ethnoreligious challenges that are being dealt with along traditional secularist lines. Muslims and Hindus in Kashmir stare nervously at one another through the crosshairs of their rifle sights or, more ominously, their nuclear delivery systems—ever susceptible to the flames of nationalism and religious unrest. In Sri Lanka, the tenets of Buddhism have been perverted to justify a stream of military atrocities between the Buddhist majority and the Tamil separatists. Then there is Indonesia, an immense archipelago straddling a number of the world's vital shipping lanes. Once thought a rock of stability, it is currently wracked with religious violence so severe that some fear the country's outright disintegration. Further to the west, the predictable consequences of Sudan's colonial legacy continue to play out in a nineteen-year struggle for power and resources between the predominantly Arab and Islamic north and the largely Christian and African traditionalist south.

In the same vein, Muslims and Jews confront one another in the Middle East over their mutual religious claims to Jerusalem, while terrorists find ongoing inspiration to ply their deadly trade. Here, the West was taken aback in July of 2000 when Yasser Arafat, chairman of the Palestinian National Authority, rejected an offer by Israeli prime minister Ehud Barak to relinquish to Palestinian control 90 percent of the West Bank, all of the Gaza Strip, and some outlying areas of Jerusalem. On the face of it, the Israelis were offering the Palestinians more than they had any reason to hope for at the time and, in any event, all that Israel could have conceivably given in light of its domestic political climate. Indeed, Barak was pilloried by Jewish commentators in both the American and Israeli press for having gone too far. Yet Arafat turned him down. Apparently there were several sticking points, among which was the final status of Jerusalem, a topic replete with religious implications that were underappreciated in the West and over which Arafat was obviously not empowered to negotiate. A year and a half later, Barak's successor, Ariel Sharon, broke off negotiations with Arafat altogether, accusing him of not doing enough to stem the violence. Even here, the religious dynamics may have been more than Arafat could handle. The question then arises: If Arafat cannot negotiate on topics of religious significance, who can? Clearly, religious authorities need to be involved, and the sooner the better, if peace is ever to take hold.

Without the earlier bipolar confrontation of the Cold War to suppress historic religious antagonisms, religion has become too critical to vital Western interests to permit its continued marginalization in the policymaker's calculus. In an age of economic interdependency, high-tech weaponry, and international terrorism, foreign policy practitioners can no longer afford to treat the religious dimension as a geopolitical orphan. The consequences of the West's longstanding inability to deal with religious differences and demagogues who manipulate religion for their own purposes will only grow more serious with the passage of time.

It is also likely that existing doctrines of nuclear and conventional deterrence will become increasingly moot (as might traditional diplomacy) in the wars of identity that are already beginning to plague the twenty-first century.[6] In short, it is time to give religion its just due as a defining element of national security. While it is to this larger task that this book is devoted, it is focused more specifically on how the reconciling aspects of religious faith can be brought to bear in operational settings through the practice of faith-based diplomacy.

In the chapter on Kashmir, for example, Hindu scholar Ainslie Embree examines the ways in which religion, and specifically Hinduism, can be used to initiate a values-based dialogue that could ultimately lead to reconciliation between the warring parties. In similar manner, Buddhist scholar Professor H. L. Seneviratne explores how each of the several different expressions of Buddhism in Sri Lanka could be engaged to steer the civil conflict in that island nation toward a peaceful and lasting resolution. Rabbi Marc Gopin, in turn, makes a compelling case for why religious leaders should be included in the Middle East peace process and cites a range of scriptural resources from Judaism that could be brought to bear in ameliorating that conflict.

On yet another front, David Steele draws on his extensive involvement in training religious clergy and laity in the Balkans to illustrate how the peacemaking tenets of Christianity can be usefully applied to promote reconciliation between ethnic groups and prevent the further outbreak of conflict in Bosnia and Kosovo. Toward this end, healing historical wounds and addressing the various techniques (and spiritual basis) for resolving disputes receive major emphasis.

Finally, Islamic scholars Khaled Abou El Fadl and Sulayman Nyang assess the potential of Islamic law to transform the long-running conflict in the Sudan. In so doing, they examine how Qur'anic teachings on conciliation, justice, arbitration, and commitment to moral community can be utilized to help resolve tensions between Sudan's Islamic and Christian communities. Further, they point to the Prophet Muhammed's conciliatory attitude toward non-Muslims with whom he was in conflict and cite a number of precedents from Islamic jurisprudence in making a compelling case for why the dictates of conflict resolution should carry the same normative weight in disputes with non-Muslims as they do with Muslims.

In the concluding chapter, Scott Appleby, a widely respected religious scholar, provides comparative insights on the potential contributions of these religions to the resolution of longstanding political problems. In the process, he offers important observations on what will be required to support the successful practice of faith-based diplomacy in today's geopolitical context.

Fighting Fire with Fire

Just as setting a controlled fire is often an effective counter to an out-of-control fire, so too can religious reconciliation be an effective instrument for dampening the flames of religious fanaticism. The divisive influence of religion has long been recognized; its more helpful aspects have not. This began to change, however, with the publication in 1994 of *Religion, the Missing Dimension of Statecraft*, a book that led the way for others that followed in exploring the potential contribution of faith-based initiatives to international peacemaking.[7] It did so by demonstrating through a series of geographically diverse case studies how, under the right circumstances, religious or spiritual factors—ranging from the temporal power of the church to the efforts of spiritually motivated laypersons operating on the basis of their personal faith—can be brought to bear in helpful ways to prevent or resolve conflict, while advancing social change based on justice and reconciliation.

In making the case for integrating religious considerations into the conduct of U.S. foreign policy, the authors of the earlier book had two target audiences in mind: (1) the U.S. Foreign Service Institute (which trains junior and senior foreign service officers in the fine points of diplomacy), where it quickly became required reading, and (2) colleges, universities, and seminaries, many of which have now incorporated it into their graduate or undergraduate curriculums. The book itself has received favorable reviews in numerous journals and periodicals (including *Foreign Affairs*, the *New York Times*, the *Washington Post*, and the *Financial Times* of London), and is now in its twelfth printing and second foreign language translation. It was also cited in 1999 by *Sapio* (Japan's equivalent to *Time* magazine) as one of the ten most important books to read in preparing for the twenty-first century.[8]

Why all the interest? Much of it has been due to the coincidence of the book's publication with the collapse of the bipolar international system and the concurrent emergence of ethnic conflict and other problems of communal identity. Weak states that were once stabilized by aid from NATO or the Warsaw Pact were suddenly abandoned to deal with their own internal conflicts. The cultural and religious dynamics of these conflicts, in turn, are exceeding the bounds of the rational-actor model of decisionmaking to which traditional diplomacy has long been tied.[9] In such a context, the juxtaposition of religious reconciliation with official or unofficial diplomacy appears to offer greater potential. As the book implies, it will no longer suffice to pursue the zero-sum-game approach of the past. What is needed is a form of diplomacy that can uncover and deal with the deeper sources of conflict by rebuilding relationships and making concessionary adjustments wherever possible.[10]

Because of the enthusiasm with which *Religion, the Missing Dimension of Statecraft* was received, a felt need arose among several of the book's collaborators to start living the challenge. Accordingly, a new Preventive Diplomacy Program was put in place at the Center for Strategic and International Studies, the Washington-based think tank that had sponsored the seven-year project which led to the book's publication. Five years later and out of that same impulse, the International Center for Religion & Diplomacy (ICRD) was established. Conceived as an instrument for practicing faith-based diplomacy, the Center actively intervenes in difficult situations where communal conflict threatens or already exists. In addressing such problems, the Center bridges the religious and political spheres to facilitate collaborative approaches that will be effective and lasting. The following initiative, while not yet complete, is illustrative of this approach.

The ICRD's first undertaking has been the difficult and highly complex situation in the Sudan, where civil war has raged between the north and south for the past nineteen years (the second such prolonged conflict since Sudan achieved independence from the British in 1956). Through its work with the Christian and Muslim communities in the north, including the government of Sudan, the Center has inspired inter-religious reconciliation that would not have otherwise taken place. Perhaps the most far-reaching initiative in this regard was a meeting between Muslim and Christian religious leaders and scholars that the Center convened in Khartoum in November of 2000. The purpose of the meeting was to address the religious aspects of the conflict and those religious issues that are contributing to social tensions more generally.

Although the Khartoum meeting had incendiary potential in light of the deep grievances involved, it produced a genuine breakthrough in communications between the two communities and yielded seventeen consensus recommendations that collectively point the way to interreligious cooperation in the areas of human rights, education, employment, and humanitarian assistance. Once these recommendations are fully implemented, they will enhance religious freedom and lead to a fairer treatment of Muslims and non-Muslims alike.

The meeting's successful outcome was largely a result of the faith-based nature of the undertaking. The Sudan Council of Churches served as a co-ponsor of the event, and each day of the four-day meeting began with prayer as well as readings from the Bible and the Qur'an. This was preceded by an informal prayer breakfast each morning at a nearby hotel for the international participants and local Muslim and Christian religious leaders (on a rotating basis). Finally, the facilitating team included several members who attended for the sole purpose of praying and fasting throughout for the success of the deliberations. These activities provided a transcendent dimension that helped inspire the participants to rise above their personal and religious differences and work together for a common good.

On a related note, it is important to understand that many Muslims feel uncomfortable, if not resentful, when having to work with secular constructs. Secularism is simply not what they are about.[11] Their goal instead is to integrate their politics with their religious faith in constructing a community on earth that will be pleasing to Allah. Thus, they are far more comfortable when operating within a spiritual framework, even when it involves faiths other than their own.

To help provide such a framework in the Sudan, the ICRD engaged in a faith-based dialogue with the government of Sudan over the eighteen months leading up to the meeting. This involved numerous one-on-one conversations with top-level officials, not only in relation to the meeting (securing their willingness to host the event and to give serious consideration to any recommendations that emerged) but also with regard to other steps toward peace that should be taken. These discussions were largely of a real-politik nature—persuading them why it was in their own best interest to take whatever step was being suggested—but laced with helpful references to the Qur'an, the Prophet Mohammed, and Jesus (most Christians have no idea how deeply Islam reveres the figure of Jesus).[12] This dialogue with Muslim leaders was an essential ingredient in the mix of factors that contributed to the meeting's success.

In Kashmir, where the ICRD has been working for the past two years, a core group of 15 young Kashmiri Muslims has been formed, who are totally committed to promoting faith-based reconciliation. All of them are leaders in their community and some once held high positions in the militant movement, until they grew disillusioned with the dead-end effects of violence. They are actively taking initiatives to reconcile longstanding differences with the Hindu Pandits[13] and are living illustration of the degree to which Muslims respond to faith-based interventions.

The Challenge Ahead

Among the reasons this kind of work is so important is the urgent need to engage the Muslim world more effectively. A purely military response to the events of September 11, 2001, for example, will only expand the pool of future terrorists and ultimately drive the United States toward a police state as it seeks greater security in an increasingly insecure world. The price of freedom is cultural engagement—taking the time to learn how others view the world, to understand what is important to them, and to determine what can realistically be done to help them realize their legitimate aspirations. Because Islamic law emphasizes faith-based interactions rather than those among states, logic suggests that one of the more effective ways to engage Islam would be through a new form of diplomacy that effectively brings to bear the transcendent aspects of religious faith in addressing the secular obstacles to peace.[14] The operational premise is that reconciliation born of spiritual conviction can break the cycle of revenge that typically characterizes identity-based conflicts.

It is to examine this new diplomacy and its potential application to intractable situations across a range of religions that this book is dedicated. With this forward-looking and multireligious orientation, it thus becomes the natural sequel to *Religion, the Missing Dimension of Statecraft*.

NOTES

1. Huston Smith, *The Illustrated World's Religions: A Guide to Our Wisdom Traditions* (San Francisco: HarperCollins, 1994), p. 13.

2. "The World at War, January 1, 2001," *Defense Monitor*, Center for Defense Information vol 30, no. 1 (January 2001).

3. As the universal aspects of globalization clash with cultural mores, there is an accompanying tendency to hide behind religious exclusivism. But even that provides limited refuge because of the polarization that the same universalism is causing between religious moderates and extremists.

4. David, Charles-Philippe, Mary Ann Carol, and Zachary A. Selden, *Foreign Policy Failures in the White House: Reappraising the Fall of the Shah and the Iran-Contra Affair* (Lanham, Md.: University Press of America, 1993), p. 51.

5. *National Security Archive*, "Iran: The Making of U.S. Policy, 1977–1980" (Alexandria, Va.: Chadwyck-Healy, 1990), pp. 2–9 IR 03561.

6. Douglas Johnston, "Religion and Culture: Human Dimensions of Globalization," in *The Global Century: Globalization and National Security*, ed. by Richard L. Kugler and Ellen L. Frost. (Washington, D. C.: National Defense University Press, 2001), p. 676.

7. David Smock, "The Third Annual Perlmutter Lecture on Ethnic Conflict, Religion, and International Peacemaking," *Foreign Policy Research Institute Wire* 9, no. 4 (March 2001), note 4.

8. "Shoso Club: Why Japanese Politics Is Stagnated," *Sapio* (November 26, 1999), p. 81.

9. The rational-actor model assumes that national leaders, when facing a problem, will collect all relevant information, determine and prioritize the interests at stake, identify and assess the alternative courses of action available, and decide how to respond according to a logical analysis of which alternative will maximize their returns.

10. Douglas Johnston and Cynthia Sampson, eds., *Religion, the Missing Dimension of Statecraft* (New York: Oxford University Press, 1994), p. 333.

11. Since the conception of secularism was an outgrowth of the metaphysical debates surrounding the Reformation, a case can be made that the imposition of secular constructs in a non-Western context can be as narrowly sectarian as would be attempts to impose a particular religious template on Westerners. A similar argument was made by Murad Hoffman in a panel presentation on "Islamic Vision for the Twenty-First Century" at a conference on "America, Islam, and the New Millennium" cosponsored by the Center for Muslim-Christian Understanding and the United Association for Studies and Research, April 26, 2000, Washington D.C. This parallelism is also dealt with at some length in John Milbank, *Theology and Social Theory: Beyond Secular Reason* (Cambridge, Mass.: Blackwell, 1993).

12. A case in point relates to the Prophet Mohammed's exercise of forgiveness and opposition to retribution following the Muslims' return to Mecca in 630 AD.

13. Because of violence stemming from the Islamic militancy that took root in Kashmir in 1989 (in reaction to the heavy-handed tactics of Indian security forces), the Kashmiri Pandits (Hindus) vacated their homeland in the Kashmir Valley and moved to refugee camps near Jammu.

14. Faith-based diplomacy should be viewed as a complement to traditional diplomacy—to be called into action when the normal tools of diplomacy are inadequate to address the problem.

Faith-Based Diplomacy
and Preventive Engagement

The twenty-first century will be religious or it will not be at all.

—ANDRE MALRAUX

The contemporary global resurgence of religion is a development that con-
travenes one of the most controversial theses in the history of social science:
that with modernization and "progress" there would be "a gradual, persis-
tent, unbroken erosion of religious influence."[1] This secularization thesis
provided one of the major principles on which the eighteenth-century philosopher Auguste Comte founded the field of sociology—which, he pre-
dicted, would eventually supplant religion as the future source of moral
judgments.[2]

Quite often, the reaction against Western modernization is framed in
religious terms.[3] This is a valid characterization when one considers the
modern, secularized, and rather compartmentalized approach to life standing
in sharp contrast to and threatening the organic mixture of religious, political,
and socioeconomic values and actors in so-called traditional societies. In
addition to whatever institutional interest may exist on the part of religious
authorities to preserve their prominent social role, the strict division between
the sacred and the secular observed in the West is a relatively recent inno-
vation—and is foreign to much of the rest of the world. As Boston University sociologist Peter Berger has pointed out, the current surge of academic interest in religion is based on "an upside-down perception of the
world":

> The notion here was that so-called fundamentalism (which, when all
> is said and done, usually refers to any sort of passionate religious
> movement) is a rare, hard-to-explain thing. But in fact it is not rare at
> all, neither if one looks at history, nor if one looks around the con-
> temporary world. On the contrary, what is rare is people who think

otherwise. Put simply: The difficult-to-understand phenomenon is not Iranian mullahs but American university professors.[4]

To the extent that religion is used as the legitimation for all aspects of life and—to borrow Robert Bellah's phrase—"as a cultural gyroscope . . . [that provides] a stable set of definitions of the world . . . [and] of the self,"[5] threats to any aspect of the established order pose a potential threat to the religious groundings of the society as a whole. The often-cited example of the Inquisition accusing Galileo of heresy for his scientific progress is a case in point.[6] As pointed out by Tedd Robert Gurr in *Minorities at Risk: A Global View of Ethnopolitical Conflicts* (1993), empirical studies reveal that "religious cleavages are at best a contributing factor in communal conflicts and seldom the root cause."[7] However, even in those cases where religion is not a core factor in a conflict, its prominence in some societies leads many to perceive that it is.[8] Consequently, it is often necessary to address a conflict's religious aspects in order to move toward a just and peaceful settlement consistent with each side's religious imperatives.

A major reason for the West's indifference to these imperatives has been the tendency of many Western scholars and policymakers to continue dealing with the world through the same reductionist political and economic paradigm that served them well during the Cold War. In the years leading up to the Iranian revolution, the one recorded suggestion within the Central Intelligence Agency that it might make sense to monitor the complex and volatile religious situation in Iran was scornfully rejected as "sociology"[9]— "a term," Edward Luttwak writes, "used in intelligence circles to mean the time-wasting study of factors deemed politically irrelevant."[10]

A New Awakening

There is reason to hope that significant change may be on the way. As Martin Marty notes in his introduction to *Religion, Ethnicity, and Self-Identity: Nations in Turmoil*, many policymakers "have grown in their awareness of the religious factor in war and peace."[11] The U.S. Foreign Service Institute—the training arm of the Department of State—now requires its students to take religion into account as a force to be reckoned with in the political sphere.

This new awareness, however, will not necessarily ensure a predictable outcome in every situation. At first glance, the NATO decision to continue the bombing of Serbia on Orthodox Easter in 1999—despite ardent pleas from the Orthodox Church not to—would appear to be yet one more example of the West's indifference to religious considerations. That decision, which apparently resulted from the NATO commander's concern that if the bombing were halted for even a day, it might prove impossible to get the Allies to reengage, was taken only after an intense debate in which the religious aspect was fully discussed. Whatever the wisdom of the decision, the Serbs were quick to point out that the only others to have bombed them on this holy day were the Germans in World War II. It is a choice they will never forget.[12]

A more recent example of this nature was the U.S. decision to continue the bombing in Afghanistan during Ramadan (in response to the terrorist attacks on the World Trade Center and the Pentagon). Leading up to Ramadan, there was considerable hand-wringing in U.S. policymaking circles and the media over the long-term impact that continued bombing would have on world opinion, particularly among Muslims. The concern was well placed; only in this instance, historic precedence suggested a greater room to maneuver.

The first consideration to be taken into account in such situations is understanding the significance of the religious celebration itself. Ramadan, like the observance of Lent for Christians, is a time when Muslims seek a closer relationship with God through a spirit of sacrifice and self-discipline. During the month-long observance, adherents do not eat, drink, smoke, or engage in sexual relations during daylight hours. By the same token, the good that is achieved through this observance can be offset if the observer lies, commits slander, denounces someone behind their back, swears a false oath, or falls prey to greed or covetousness.

As for engaging in military action during this period, it becomes instructive to examine how Muslims themselves have dealt with the same issue. During the Iran-Iraq war, for example, both sides fought through Ramadan every year of the conflict (although Saddam Hussein once offered a cease-fire to observe Ramadan, only to have it rejected by the Ayatollah Khomeini). In 1973, Egypt and Syria attacked Israel during Ramadan. While commonly referred to in the West as the Yom Kippur War, among Muslims it is known as the Ramadan War. Finally, in 630 AD, Mohammed himself conquered the holy city of Mecca during Ramadan. While none of the foregoing should be viewed as constituting a free license to do as one pleases, it does provide a helpful context for determining how to deal with such questions.

The paradigm shift that is evolving as a result of religion's enhanced role relates in part to the fact that a religious authority's support for or opposition to a conflict is often an influential factor in determining its outbreak or its conclusion. Among the attributes that give religious leaders and institutions sizeable influence in peacemaking, four stand out:

1. A well-established and pervasive influence in the community
2. A reputation as an apolitical force for change based on a respected set of values
3. Unique leverage for reconciling confliction parties, including an ability to rehumanize relatiohships
4. The capability to mobilize community, national, and international support for a peace process.

Most important, religions possess a transcendent authority for their followers that is the envy of most temporal leaders. Secularization theory's basic weakness is its assumption that ordinary decisions in public life should not be shaped by one's view of ultimate reality (i.e., issues of metaphysics). As this theory has begun to erode in many parts of the world—often because of people's inability to deal with the strains of life apart from such a perspective[13]—religion has recovered much of its salience.[14]

The significance of this religious resurgence has not been lost on nationalist demagogues. While issues of realpolitik and economic advantage may be sufficient to convince political leaders and other elites to go to war, a more compelling reason is often needed to motivate those who will be asked to put their lives on the line for their country. Religion is one of the more effective vehicles in this regard, for it alone provides a vision of reality that transcends temporal and terrestrial life and thus inspires people to make the ultimate sacrifice. Conversely, few influences are more effective in discouraging people from starting a war than a declaration on the part of religious authorities that such activity will provoke divine disapprobation. Once war has erupted, however, it becomes difficult, if not impossible, for religious reason to prevail. That aside, when temporal and eternal authorities clash on issues of major importance, the temporal often lose.[15] Although there is a long way to go before the international system realigns itself to accommodate religion's increasing role, the slavish devotion to secularism and to the rational-actor model of the past is clearly on the wane.

Religion, as is becoming increasingly apparent, is a double-edged sword. It can cause conflict or it can abate it. But even in those instances where a particular religion may be viewed as part of the problem (to the extent that it is either central to a conflict or has allowed itself to become a mobilizing vehicle for nationalist or ethnic passions), that religion will include within the core of its tradition extensive teachings that encourage neighborly concern and the betterment of humanity. These teachings, irrespective of current practice, represent valuable belief structures for countering sectarian tendencies and providing a basis for resolving intractable problems.

A Need for New Tools

Although moral warrants for peacemaking exist in the theologies of all major world religions, their development and articulation have been inadequate, despite the increasing need to apply religious principles and instruments to the practical work of conflict prevention and resolution. Ways must be found to use religion as a positive force in resolving problems of communal identity that are proving beyond the reach of traditional diplomacy, such as ethnic conflict, tribal warfare, and religious hostilities. It was to address this need that seven eminent scholars were engaged to determine how the peacemaking tenets of key world religions can be brought to bear in ongoing conflicts in which those religions are actively involved.

The religions and settings chosen—Hinduism in Kashmir, Buddhism in Sri Lanka, Judaism in the Middle East, Christianity in the Balkans, and Islam in the Sudan—share little in common either with respect to the nature of the conflict that is taking place or the degree to which religion is involved in the conflict. To the extent that they differ, they provide a tapestry of insights into the potential of faith-based diplomacy to make a difference in difficult situations. Before examining the operational possibilities, though, it may prove instructive to examine the concept of faith-based diplomacy itself—what it is and how it is practiced.

A New Diplomacy

Faith-based diplomacy, while conceptually new to the field of international relations, is a form of Track II (unofficial) diplomacy that integrates the dynamics of religious faith with the conduct of international peacemaking. As such, it is more about reconciliation than it is conflict resolution. The peace that it pursues is not the mere absence of conflict but rather a restoration of healthy and respectful relationships between the parties. While faith-based intermediaries believe that diplomacy and the international system should be morally grounded (as do many secularists), they also understand the need for pragmatism in their pursuit of reconciliation.

The reconciliation sought by faith-based diplomats causes them to seek:

1. Unity in diversity through active acceptance of the pluralistic nature of life itself in terms of race, gender, ethnicity, and culture
2. The inclusion of all parties in any final solution, including one's enemies wherever possible
3. The peaceful resolution of conflict between individuals and groups (consistent with the principles of just war theory)
4. Forgiveness as a prerequisite for restoring healthy relationships
5. Social justice as the appropriate basis for a right ordering of relationships

Among the transcendent aspects of faith-based diplomacy, one might expect to find the Buddhist concept of "critical tolerance," in which the other party is given the benefit of the doubt; Hinduism's emphasis on tolerance and absorption, as reflected in Gandhi's approach to overcoming hostility by befriending one's enemy; and the similar admonition of Jesus to love one's enemy and turn the other cheek, as reflected in the Quaker and Mennonite approaches to peacemaking. Implicit in the foregoing is an emphasis on nonviolent approaches to conflict resolution and a broader array of roles than those normally associated with traditional diplomacy—from impartial observer to message carrier to advocate to activist—all of which derive from an unquestioned moral authority.

The New Diplomat

The faith-based diplomat is one whose actions are informed by five characteristics. First, there is a conscious dependency on spiritual principles and resources in the conduct of peacemaking. This is perhaps the most significant way that faith-based diplomacy departs from the rational-actor model of decisionmaking. Faith-based practitioners call into play a range of spiritual tools that are unavailable to their secular counterparts: prayer, fasting, forgiveness, repentance, and a wealth of helpful and often inspiring references from sacred scriptures. This is in contrast to intermediaries who embrace a religious faith but for whom it plays no meaningful role in their practice of statecraft (and complementary to those for whom it does, however discrete that role may be).

The second characteristic of faith-based practitioners is that they operate with a certain spiritual authority. All intermediaries face the need to establish legitimacy with the parties to a conflict, and theirs is derived in one of two ways: either through their ties to a credible religious institution or through the trust evoked by a personal spiritual charisma. The intervention of the

Vatican in the 1978 confrontation between Chile and Argentina over their mutual claims to the Beagle Islands was an application of institutional authority in which the temporal power of the church was invoked to prevent two Catholic countries from going to war. On the other hand, the role played by Cardinal Jaime Sin in securing a peaceful transfer of power in the Philippines from the Marcos to the Aquino regime in 1986 was an illustration of charismatic authority in action.

The third quality is a pluralistic heart. Faith-based diplomats with a pluralistic heart are firmly rooted in their own religious traditions, but they understand and respect the essence of other traditions. They do not seek common ground by reducing faith to its lowest common denominator but by appealing to those from different traditions on the basis of the peacemaking warrants that exist within their respective theologies. By the same token, faith-based practitioners can lose their credibility if they fail to appreciate the profound and irreconcilable differences between religious traditions. Intermediaries who adopt an approach that all religious traditions are fundamentally the same will risk offending the adherents of other faiths.

The fourth characteristic is a transcendent approach to conflict resolution. This, once again, is where religious faith introduces a logic that is absent in secular diplomacy. Faith-based intermediaries may be well-trained in the disciplines of conflict analysis, negotiation, mediation, and diplomatic communications, but they recognize perhaps more fully than their secular counterparts that there are limits to human understanding. Accordingly, they look to their sacred texts to inform them not only about human nature and behavior but about the spiritual dimensions of human existence and how those can be tapped where all else fails. The same sensitivity also enables them to discern the religious subtext underlying many identity-based conflicts, something frequently missed by secular-minded policymakers and diplomats. For example, the unfamiliarity of Western policymakers with the relevance of theological concepts to the motives of others has at times led to policy proposals or actions that are inherently offensive to Muslims.

The final quality of faith-based intermediaries is their ability to persevere against overwhelming odds. Their motivation to be reconcilers and peacemakers stems from a deep sense of religious calling. Christian peacemakers, for example, take seriously Jesus' teaching in the Sermon on the Mount, "blessed are the peacemakers, for they shall be called the children of God." Muslim peacemakers are reminded in the Holy Qur'an that the heart or essence of the Abrahamic tradition is not holy war but peace, social justice, and reconciliation. Because the faith-based peacemaker's perseverance is divinely inspired, it tends to be more lasting in nature than that of those who pursue peace strictly as a profession (although some of them may be similarly motivated and resolute). It is the same inspiration that has led religious intermediaries to put their lives on the line in such places as Nicaragua, Mozambique, Bosnia, Northern Ireland, South Africa, and Kashmir.

Faith-Based Peacemaking

Just as there are multiple traits that characterize faith-based diplomacy and multiple dimensions to the reconciliation that it pursues, so too are there different modes of intervention in this kind of peacemaking. Among others, four particularly stand out. First, there is the offering of a new vision, in which the diplomat encourages the parties to embrace a new reality and a new relationship with one another. Each of the major world religions contains a set of moral principles to govern human relationships. Sometimes an appeal to those principles that are held in common can create a transcendent dynamic for overcoming the secular obstacles and moving toward reconciliation. Professor Harvey Cox of the Harvard Divinity School speculates that one reason Jesus' words touched Mahatma Gandhi so deeply may be that they evoked associations with his very Hindu conviction that even the bitterest enemies can be reconciled if they can be led to see the situation differently.[16]

It is possible for reconciliation itself to constitute a central element in the moral vision of a particular community or nation-state, quite apart from whether or not that community or state is embroiled in conflict. In deeply divided societies emerging from violent conflict, it is particularly important that the concept of reconciliation become firmly anchored and constitute a permanent center of gravity for all sides. Without a fresh moral vision, the past remains unhealed and can cause even greater harm in the future. Imparting such a vision becomes particularly important when intervening with heads of state or leaders of ethnic communities, since a key aspect of effective leadership is the very ability to convey a sense of vision. A good illustration of this approach was the initiative taken by the Moral Rearmament movement in bringing French and German leaders together following World War II in order to reconcile their differences on a personal level. This process effectively prepared the way for the later establishment of the European Coal and Steel Community.

A second mode of intervention is building bridges, a task that involves the development of tangible and intangible connections between diverse groups so that they can communicate their respective needs and aspirations more effectively. Bridge-building assumes a pluralistic vision for a community and provides the framework for forging unity out of diversity. When bringing people together in this manner, faith-based intermediaries look to spiritual principles and traditions as a basis for establishing common ground. The Quakers are among the best at building such bridges.

A third mode involves healing conflict, usually through mediation. Here the goals are threefold: to bring an end to the hostilities, to resolve the issues underlying the conflict, and to restore the relationships. People of faith place as much, if not more, value on relationships as they do on negotiating a successful settlement. Through spiritual conversations with the parties to a conflict, a faith-based intermediary is able to penetrate the heart and uncover the deeper interests and values that can form the basis for a lasting settlement of the conflict. The Mennonite role and that of the Moravian Church in securing peace between the Sandinista regime and the East Coast Indians of Nicaragua in the 1980s is a good example of this kind of intervention.

Yet another mode of intervention focuses on healing the wounds of history. These are normally the result of events in the collective institutional memory of an identity-based community, the recollection of which brings a sense of pain and suffering and inhibits the healthy development of that community. Until these wounds are effectively addressed, they inevitably give rise to the stereotyping and demonizing of those who caused the wounds. This, in turn, can adversely affect relationships into future generations. So long as one or both parties remain captive to a wounded history, they will be unable to reach beyond their bitterness and sense of injustice. Faith-based diplomats are among the best-equipped to deal with such situations. There are resources within religious traditions that can enable adherents to (1) reflect on their history in a redemptive manner, (2) bring meaning and dignity to the suffering, and (3) hold out the promise of genuine healing.

New Applications

In which specific situations is faith-based diplomacy appropriate? Whether or not one agrees with Samuel Huntington's thesis that future conflict will take place at the fault lines between cultures and civilizations, there are any number of scenarios in which faith-based intervention could work in the opposite direction. The first such possibility is a conflict in which religion is a significant factor in the identity of one or both communities. The long-standing dispute between India and Pakistan over Kashmir is representative. The tensions in Kashmir have stubbornly endured over half a century and three major wars. Of even greater concern, the situation is seen by geopolitical strategists as the most likely flashpoint for the world's first nuclear exchange.

To what extent does religion play a role in this conflict? Religious persuasion is a key ingredient in the nationalist identities of the Kashmiri Muslims, the Hindu Dogras of Jammu, the Kashmiri Pandits, the Buddhists of Ladakh, and the Sikhs of the Punjab. In general, Kashmiri Muslims envision an independent Kashmir or accession by Pakistan, whereas Dogras, Sikhs, and Buddhists insist on remaining with India.

To what extent can religion play a role in resolving the conflict? Because faith and politics are inseparable in Islam, a secular approach to peacemaking, which might work for the Hindus, is all but inconceivable to a practicing Muslim. Hence intermediaries who operate within a religious framework or who can integrate political and theological concepts may be the best-equipped to develop creative solutions to the problem.

The second scenario in which faith-based intervention can work is a conflict situation in which religious leaders can be mobilized to facilitate peace. One such conflict is Sudan's bitter civil war, which, while multidimensional in nature, includes religion as a significant factor. While the Sudanese constitution speaks of being a "nation under God" and avoids any reference to being an Islamic state, the practice on the ground is quite different. Christians experience discrimination in the sharing of power and distribution of resources and are made to feel like second-class citizens under *Shari'ah* (Islamic law). As mentioned in the introduction, a meeting of religious leaders and scholars was convened in November of 2000 to address the religious aspects of the conflict. The meeting was devoted to building relationships, establishing common ground, discussing perceptions of the conflict, and developing creative options for consideration by the government and appropriate opposition groups.

Of the seventeen recommendations that emerged, three of the more far-reaching have been or are being implemented: (1) joint reconciliation training for Christian and Muslim leaders; (2) formation of an independent interreligious council to help resolve differences between the two communities and to facilitate interreligious cooperation in the cause of peace; and (3) establishment of an independent human rights center to monitor and promote human rights throughout the country.

As of this writing, three other recommendations that relate to the conflict are also moving forward: (1) involving religious leaders in the peace process (in any deep-seated conflict in which religion is a significant factor, as it is in the Sudan, the Middle East, and elsewhere, giving religious leaders a feeling of ownership in the peace process is one of the more effective ways to ensure that any political settlement that emerges will have grass-roots support); (2) providing freedom of movement for religious leaders to perform their duties in the zones of conflict; and (3) protecting holy sites on both sides from destruction or desecration. Most of this has taken place at a time when normal diplomatic relations between Sudan and the United States were for all intents and purposes nonexistent.

A third situation in which faith-based approaches can be usefully brought to bear is where there has been a protracted estrangement between two major religious traditions in a conflict that transcends national borders. The concept of a "civilizational dialogue" was first suggested by President Mo-hammed Khatami of Iran in 1997 and has since gained currency in the minds of many international relations scholars and practitioners. President Khatami appeared to be thinking particularly about establishing such a dialogue between the Islamic world and the Christian West. Most of today's conflicts that include a religious dimension involve a confrontation between these two missionary faiths. Indeed, there are innumerable historical and contemporary examples of hostility, misunderstanding, and disrespect between these traditions.

The spiritual core of both traditions, if called into account, would support strong interreligious cooperation. It is ironic that it wasn't until the seventeenth century and the influence of philosophers such as John Locke that tolerance began to take a firm hold in the West.[17] Prior to then, Christianity was markedly intolerant of other faiths, and Islam was clearly more tolerant. The early Islamic stance on tolerance is reflected in the charter granted by the Prophet Mohammed to the Christians of Najar near the end of his life:

> To the Christians of Najar and the neighboring territories, the security of God and the pledge of his Prophet are extended for their lives, their religion, and their property—to the present as well as the absent and others besides; there shall be no interference with the practice of their faith or their observance; nor any change in their rights or privileges; no bishop shall be removed from his bishopric; nor any monk from his monastery; nor any priest from his priesthood; and they shall continue to enjoy everything great and small as heretofore; they shall not oppress or be oppressed. . . .[18]

Another manifestation of this tolerance is the fact that Jews under Muslim rule in Moorish Spain lived unpersecuted and fared far better than they did in Christian Europe.

It was also in the seventeenth century that the political decline of Islam began, eventually culminating in the demise of the Ottoman Empire following World War I. Over the same period, the impact of Western colonialism and other factors caused Islam to become increasingly defensive and intolerant. These trends have now reached the point where a Christian in the West can freely convert to Islam without jeopardizing any of his or her personal freedoms, whereas a convert from Islam to Christianity may face the death penalty in some Muslim countries (despite the Qur'anic admonition that there be no compulsion in religion). As the English scholar Christopher Catherwood so aptly puts it,

> freedom and Islam are not historically incompatible. If the West discovered tolerance at the end of the seventeenth century, Islam can *rediscover* it in the twenty-first. If this evolutionary retrenchment in Islam makes the task of religious peacemaking more difficult, it also makes it more urgent.[19]

A fourth possibility that is particularly well suited to faith-based diplomacy is third party mediation in conflicts where there is no particular religious dimension present. The role played by the lay Catholic community of St. Egidio in settling the long-running civil war in Mozambique is an excellent example of this kind of involvement.[20] The Quakers and Mennonites often get called on to play this kind of role as well because of their respective track records as peacemakers and the trust which that conveys. They bring with them no political agenda; only their concern for the human suffering involved.

Finally, there are those situations in which the forces of realpolitik have led to an extended paralysis of action, as has been the case in Cuba for a number of years. Here, the pope's visit in January of 1998 had enormous political and religious ramifications for that island-nation. In addition to meeting privately with Fidel Castro, he conducted public masses in Havana and four provincial capitals, during which he sharply criticized the regime's policies on religious freedom, political prisoners, state-monopolized education, and abortion. By the same token, he condemned the U.S. embargo and its effects on the Cuban people.

The fact that Castro not only absorbed the criticism but promoted the visit in the first instance by granting paid leave for workers to attend the masses and by agreeing in advance to public, uncensored broadcasting of the pope's speeches has caused some observers to speculate that the occasion may have constituted a personal catharsis for this "godless" communist ruler in relation to his religious roots. (Castro was raised as a Catholic and educated by the Jesuits, and his mother still practices the religion.) Moreover, it appears that a personal bond may have formed between the two men as a result of an earlier visit to the Vatican by Castro in November of 1996.

Following the papal visit, Castro freed more than 100 political prisoners in response to the pope's request and promised to evaluate the cases of hundreds of others. The visit also prompted a comprehensive review of U.S. policy by American decisionmakers that resulted in a resumption of humanitarian flights to the island, permission for Cuban exiles in the United States to send money to their families in Cuba, an easing of restrictions on the sale of medical supplies, and a visit by 40 U.S. businessmen, lawyers, and scholars to Havana to explore trade and investment opportunities once the embargo is lifted. Two years later, the U.S. Congress passed a law allowing the sale of U.S. products to Cuba on a humanitarian basis.

Although the U.S. embargo remains in effect, there is increasing pressure from within Washington and beyond to have it lifted. None of these developments would have taken place had it not been for the pope's faith-based intervention.

Preventive Engagement

Although much has been written about various aspects of conflict prevention, little thought has been given to the cultural dimension. Before addressing this particular facet, though, a review of some of the generic challenges and opportunities associated with the concept of prevention itself may be useful.

There are numerous reasons why conflict prevention is preferable to crisis response, all of them quite compelling. High on the list is the fact that prevention is inherently more cost-effective. This holds true for protagonists and external actors alike. As calculated in a recent Carnegie Commission study, the costs to the international community of intervening in seven major conflicts in the 1990s were estimated to be on the order of $200 billion. This contrasts with an estimated $70 billion that would have been required for effective preventive action.[21] One can only speculate on what the long-term benefits could have been of investing the $130 billion difference in poverty reduction and sustainable development.

As obvious as the benefits of prevention are, the reasons why they are so difficult to achieve are equally straightforward. To mention only a few:

- First, prevention requires thinking beyond the crisis of the immediate—always a challenge, even under the best of circumstances.
- Second, it is inherently difficult to prove the effectiveness of prevention. (How does one prove with certainty the reason that something did not happen; and how often does one see politicians investing in

the present to avoid greater spending in the future, when they may no longer be in office?)

- Finally, there is the overriding problem of mustering the political will to take action. A recent case in point—for several years, the West lamented the likelihood that the tinderbox of Kosovo would ignite at any time, yet did next to nothing to prevent it. Of course, NATO was absorbed in Bosnia at the time, which points to another related problem: the difficulty of addressing more than one crisis at a time.

The problem runs even deeper, however, as evidenced by the substantial cuts of the recent past in the U.S. foreign affairs budget—at a time when the world was becoming increasingly interdependent and when the United States needed to become even more engaged diplomatically.

All this is by way of saying that prevention is something that doesn't come naturally in a democracy where outright crisis is the normal prerequisite for intervention. While there is every reason to hope that preventive action in the political and economic spheres will one day rival the emphasis now being placed on pre-emption by military planners in the global war against terrorism, the cultural dimension is no less deserving of comparable, if not higher priority, treatment. To give it its just due, however, new approaches that are not yet in place will be required.

In many respects, preventive engagement is about cultural engagement, and as Samuel Huntington has pointed out, religion is the defining element of culture.[22] Wherever one looks in the world today—Kashmir, Chechnya, Nigeria, Indonesia, Sri Lanka, Sudan, the Middle East—one often finds a religious dimension to the conflict. That being the case, it becomes important to assess how the positive influence of religion might be brought to bear in an effective strategy of preventive engagement. In considering this challenge, three mutually reinforcing possibilities come to mind: enhancing the State Department's capabilities in matters of religion, utilizing existing military assets to achieve new ends, and capitalizing on the contributions of nongovernmental organizations (NGOs).

Religion Attachés

Consideration of religious factors within U.S. foreign policy would be considerably enhanced by the creation of a new religion attaché position within the Foreign Service. These attachés would be assigned to those missions in countries where religion has particular salience in order to deal more effectively with complex religious issues. The attaché's principal function would be to establish relationships of trust with local religious leaders and groups in order to understand better and deal more effectively with the religious imperatives of any given situation. In the process, the attachés would gain added insights into new developments in this critical arena at both the grass-roots and national levels and become attuned to concerns that local religious leaders may have across a spectrum of interests, ranging from actions that the West may be taking or contemplating to schemes of local or national demagogues who may be seeking to manipulate religion for their own political ends.

It is estimated that a cadre of 30 such attachés could satisfy the global need at an annual cost of ten million dollars.[23] In view of the vast sums being spent to address the symptoms of terrorism, devoting ten million dollars to causal factors is not much to ask. The greater challenge will be finding the people with the necessary skills to hold such a post. Among other qualifications, the prospective attaché would need to understand how religious faith inspires action and be conversant in the relevant local languages and dialects (religious leaders often do not have the same command of English that is normally found among government officials with whom other foreign service officers regularly interact). He or she would also need to be sensitive to and capable of interpreting religious motives and priorities.

Naturally, there are any number of concerns that arise with the creation of a new position; but in this particular case, they all appear quite manageable.[24] Suffice it to say, the added insights that would accrue to policymakers from the informed contributions of religion attachés could significantly enhance the nation's conflict prevention capability.

Military Chaplains

Another formidable asset in the quest to enhance prevention is the chaplaincy of the military services. Military chaplains serve at the cutting edge of U.S. involvements overseas and are thus uniquely positioned to be helpful on an ongoing basis. Further, their multifaith experience coupled with their considerable interpersonal skills are attributes that are particularly well suited to the complex challenges of engagement. Finally, they are a resource-in-being, with a longstanding religious mandate (which both avoids the battle of the budget and finesses any concerns about separation of church and state).

With appropriate training, the role of military chaplains could be expanded to include peacemaking and conflict prevention. Through their personal interactions with local religious communities and selected NGOs with which they come in contact, they would be able to develop a grass-roots understanding of the religious and cultural nuances at play in any given setting and, at times, possibly provide a reconciling influence in addressing misunderstandings or differences with these communities. Perhaps more importantly, they could advise their commanders on the religious and cultural implications of command decisions that are either being taken or that should be taken.

It is important that the chaplains' expanded functions relating to faith-based diplomacy not be allowed to undermine their primary task of providing spiritual counsel to the men and women of their commands. This will be a fine line to walk; but in the U.S. European Command, which encompasses some 89 countries in Europe, Africa, and the Middle East, chaplains are already serving as a bridge to other military and civilian communities. Thus, in addition to their ongoing function of addressing human casualties after conflict has erupted, they could become an important tool in preventing its eruption in the first instance.[25]

The NGO Contribution

Another prospective contributor to an effective preventive engagement strategy is the NGO community and the kinds of informal diplomatic and problem-solving capabilities that it can bring to bear in addressing problems before they reach crisis proportions. When dealing with the religious sphere, NGOs bring resources to bear that governments would be hard pressed to match. For example, the work that the World Conference on Religion and Peace does in coordinating the peacemaking efforts of church leaders around the world certainly falls into this category, as do the efforts of the lay Catholic community of St. Egidio with governments and church leaders in resolving conflicts and providing humanitarian relief, also on a global basis.

Yet another example of a germane prevention capability that Western governments would find difficult to emulate is the approach used by one NGO in which multi-skilled, interreligious action teams are deployed to trouble spots where conflict threatens. These teams are composed of individuals who have secular skills relevant to the problem(s) being addressed and who collectively reflect the same mix of religious faiths as those with whom they are working on-scene. That way, the local parties involved can feel reassured that someone on the team understands their religious sensitivities, including related cultural issues that affect their sense of dignity and self-worth.[26]

There are many other NGOs that have relevant prevention capabilities as well, capabilities that can be called into action under the right circumstances. In addition, religious and spiritual leaders from around the world are currently in the process of establishing a World Council of Religious Leaders, an independent body that will seek to provide the spiritual resources of the world's religious traditions to "assist the United Nations and its agencies in the prevention, resolution, and healing of conflicts and in the eradication of their causes."[27]

The assets are many and collectively constitute a matrix of capabilities which, under the right circumstances, can be brought to bear in synergistic combinations to forestall the outbreak of conflict. Preventive engagement is thus about developing tailored strategies—faith-based and secular alike—to pre-empt or address problems before they become crises. Through engaging religion as part of the solution, it is also about providing a new and potentially effective capability for addressing identity conclicts that exceed the grasp of traditional diplomacy.

Looking Ahead

The intent behind each of the following chapters is not to provide a blueprint for dealing with particular conflict situations or to describe future directions these conflicts may take but rather to establish an intellectual and spiritual framework for examining the possibilities, suggesting available points of entry, and recommending approaches that could prove helpful.[28] Every conflict situation is unique and is often as much a function of personalities as of circumstances. Finally, an attempt is made to draw conclusions about the commonalities and differences that exist between religions and their respective outlooks on peacemaking and reconciliation.

NOTES

1. Anson Shupe, "The Stubborn Persistence of Religion in the Global Arena," in *Religious Resurgence and Politics in the Contemporary World*, ed. by Emile Sahliyeh (Albany: SUNY Press, 1990), p. 19.

2. Rodney Stark and Laurence Iannaconne, "A Supply-Side Reinterpretation of the 'Secularization' of Europe," *Journal for the Scientific Study of Religion* 33, no. 3 (1994), p. 249.

3. For a good discussion of this point, see Mark Juergensmeyer, *The New Cold War: Religious Nationalism Confronts the Secular State* (Berkeley: University of California Press, 1993).

4. Peter L. Berger, "Secularism in Retreat," *National Interest* 46 (winter 1996–97), p. 3.

5. Robert N. Bellah, "Epilogue: Religion and Progress in Modern Asia," in *Religion and Progress in Modern Asia*, ed. by Robert N. Bellah (New York: Free Press, 1965), p. 173.

6. Another crucial lesson to glean from this example is that quite often a seemingly

religious issue is not really religious at all, despite the initial reservations of the religious authorities and the eagerness of reactionary demagogues to paint it as such. Serious theological study of social change is thus essential to strip away the religious veneer on issues that are easily exploited to motivate people to violence.

7. "Only eight of the forty-nine militant sects in the study are defined solely or mainly by their religious beliefs. . . . The other sectarian minorities also have class identifications, such as the Catholics of Northern Ireland and Turkish immigrants in Germany, or nationalist objectives, such as the Palestinians in Israel's Occupied Territories and the Moros in the Philippines. The driving force of the most serious and protracted communal conflicts in the Middle East is not militant Islam but the unsatisfied nationalist aspirations of the Kurds and Palestinians." Tedd Robert Gurr, *Minorities at Risk: A Global View of Ethnopolitical Conflicts* (Washington, D.C.: U.S. Institute of Peace, 1993), p. 317.

8. As R. Wallis and S. Bruce note, when "culture, identity, and self-identity are challenged by a source promoting either an alien religion or rampant secularism and that source is negatively valued," then religion quite often becomes the rallying point for resistance against it. R. Wallis and S. Bruce, "Secularization: The Orthodox Model," in *Religion and Modernization*, ed. by S. Bruce (Oxford: Clarendon Press, 1992), pp. 17–18.

9. James E. Bill, *The Eagle and the Lion: The Tragedy of American-Iranian Relations* (New Haven: Yale University Press, 1988), p. 417.

10. Edward Luttwak, "The Missing Dimension," in *Religion, the Missing Dimension of Statecraft*, ed. by Douglas Johnston and Cynthia Sampson (New York: Oxford University Press, 1994), p. 12.

11. Martin Marty, Introduction to *Religion, Ethnicity, and Self-Identity: Nations in Turmoil*, ed. by R. Scott Appleby and Martin Marty (Hanover, N.H.: University Press of New England, 1997), p. 10.

12. Douglas M. Johnston, Jr., "Religion and Foreign Policy," in *Forgiveness and Reconciliation: Religion, Public Policy, and Conflict Transformation*, ed. by Raymond G. Helmick, S.J. and Rodney L. Petersen (Philadelphia: Templeton Foundation Press, 2001), p. 118.

13. W. Miles, "Political Para-Theology: Rethinking Religion, Politics, and Democracy," *Third World Quarterly* 17, no. 3 (1996), p. 525.

14. Indeed, as reflected in a recent Gallup poll, 95 percent of Americans say they believe in God or a universal spirit, and 48 percent say they had talked about their faith in the workplace in the past twenty-four hours. Michelle Conlin, "Religion in the Workplace," *Business Week*, November 1, 1999, pp. 152–53.

15. For an excellent philosophical discussion of the importance of religion in social order, see Leszek Kolakowski, "The Revenge of the Sacred in Secular Culture," *Modernity on Endless Trial* (Chicago: University of Chicago Press, 1990), pp. 63–74.

16. Douglas Johnston and Cynthia Sampson, eds., *Religion, the Missing Dimension of Statecraft* (New York: Oxford University Press, 1994), p. 271.

17. Christopher Catherwood, *Why the Nations Rage: Killing in the Name of God*, rev. ed. (Lanham, Md.: Rowman and Littlefield, forthcoming).

18. Yusaf al-Qaradawi, *Non-Muslims in the Islamic Society* (Indianapolis: American Trust, 1985), p. 7.

19. Catherwood, *Why the Nations Rage: Killing in the Name of God*.

20. The final breakthrough to peace in 1994 evolved from the Community's recognition that it would have to do something to resolve the conflict if the humanitarian

assistance it was providing was to have any useful effect. Accordingly, its members set out to win the trust of both sides, taking initiatives that governments would never consider: escorting individual guerrillas to their first dental appointments; buying them their first spectacles. In short, through rehumanizing the situation and winning trust on a personal level, they were able to persuade the two sides to come together to negotiate their differences.

It took ten rounds of talks before an agreement was reached to end the war. During this process, it became apparent to these religious peacemakers that if they were successful in their efforts to halt the fighting, they would not have the wherewithal to monitor a cease-fire agreement or to guarantee fair multiparty elections. Accordingly, in the ninth round of talks they invited diplomats from Italy, the United States, Portugal, France, and the United Nations to participate as official observers. In the tenth round, they officially passed the baton to these diplomats, who, in turn, brought the resources of their respective nation-states (and the UN) to bear in overseeing the signing of the peace agreement, monitoring the cease-fire, and guaranteeing fair elections.

Today there is peace in Mozambique under a democratically elected government, with an economy that, until recent natural disasters, was on the rebound and outperforming the rest of the continent—all because official diplomacy was able to reinforce and build on the trust developed by a religious third party. Cited in Johnston and Sampson, *Religion, the Missing Dimension of Statecraft,* pp. 328–29.

21. Kofi A. Annan, introduction to *Prevention of Armed Conflict, Report of the Secretary-General* (New York: UN Dept. of Public Information, 2002), pp. 1–2.

22. Samuel P. Huntington, *The Clash of Civilizations and the Remaking of World Order* (New York: Simon and Schuster, 1997), p. 42.

23. Douglas M. Johnston, "The Case for a Religion Attaché," *Foreign Service Journal* (February 2002), p. 36.

24. Ibid., pp. 37–38.

25. Douglas M. Johnston, "We Neglect Religion at Our Peril," *Naval Institute Proceedings* (January 2002), p. 52.

26. This approach is being pioneered by the Washington-based International Center for Religion and Diplomacy.

27. *Charter of World Council of Religious Leaders: An Outcome of the Millennium World Peace Summit* (Bangkok, Thailand: June 2002), p. 1.

28. Because the breadth of discovery varies among authors, a disclaimer is in order. The mandate for each of the authors of Part II was to explore how the peacemaking tenets of the religion in which the particular author has an established expertise might be strategically applied to an ongoing conflict in which that religion is centrally involved. Some authors held to that assignment, while others went a bit further in exploring the imperatives of whatever other religions might be involved in the conflict in question. Quite apart from whether or not a specific religion's subordinate contribution to a particular conflict has been examined, its dominant role in another conflict has been the subject of in-depth analysis by a world-class scholar from that religion who is clearly qualified to conduct such an inquiry. Again, what is being sought in each of the cases is not a definitive solution to an intractable problem based on a comprehensive analysis of the relevant factors but rather an illustration of how faith-based diplomacy can be applied in any given conflict, regardless of the prevailing religious context.

II

Applications

3   *Ainslie Embree*

Kashmir
Has Religion a Role in Making Peace?

In 1947, as the British Empire began divesting itself of its colonies, the Indian sub-continent was divided into two independent countries, India and Pakistan. The new nation of Pakistan was intended to serve as a homeland for Muslims who were uncomfortable with the idea of living in an independent, predominately Hindu India. Most Kashmiris assumed that Kashmir, a predominately Muslim area lying along the line of partition, would go to Pakistan. However, when the Hindu maharajah of Kashmir hesitated in acceding to either Pakistan or India, conflict broke out over the issue of joining Pakistan. There is some dispute as to whether the hostilities were precipitated by Pakistanis invading from across the border or by Muslim Kashmiris, aided by tribesmen from Pakistan. Either way, the maharajah agreed to cede control to India (in October 1947) in exchange for Indian military assistance to contain the conflict. Pakistan refused to recognize this accession and campaigned to reverse the situation. These events evolved into a bitter dispute between India and Pakistan that lasts into the present and has led to two major wars along the way. Many geopolitical strategists consider this confrontation the most likely flashpoint for the world's first nuclear exchange, thus earning Kashmir the title of the "world's most dangerous place."

The aim of this chapter is to explore the potential applicability of the peace-making tenets of Hinduism to the longstanding conflict in Kashmir,[1] a conflict that has brought untold misery to the people of Kashmir and strained relations between the nations of India and Pakistan to the breaking point. Because the use of force has failed to achieve the aims of any of the principal parties involved, it is written with the conviction that any change in the destiny of the region will require a fundamental change in the attitudes of everyone involved. While "Track II" discussions by various unofficial groups working behind the scenes have proven somewhat useful—especially in keeping the channels of communication open—they have not been able to develop a plan for peace that commands any kind of widespread backing.

Faith communities of the region—the missing dimension of statecraft—appear to offer some hope for facilitating healing and reconciliation in this otherwise intractable situation. Traditional diplomacy, on the other hand, has through its neglect of religious factors "rendered the West ineffective both in dealing with religious differences and in combating demagogues who adeptly manipulate religious labels to their own purposes."[2] The wounds of the people of Kashmir, which are grievous, will not be healed, however, by the crying of "Peace, Peace," as at the Millennium Summit of Religious and Spiritual Leaders at the United Nations in August 2000, but by a long and arduous process of dialogue, followed by good-faith negotiations.

Running counter to this assertion that religion can and should play a creative role in bringing peace to Kashmir is the conclusion, reluctantly arrived at, that many adherents of Hinduism and Islam, the two dominant religions of South Asia, now use religion to justify the conflict. This is not to say that religion is the cause of the conflict, only that the two are intertwined at every stage. All religions have a vision of a good society of which they are in a sense the guardians; and when this vision is denied by adversaries, their adherents often resort to violence to preserve it.[3] This is due partly to their interpretation of their own religion but even more potently to their interpretation of that of their adversaries. Fanaticism is routinely ascribed to the adherents of Islam in the Indian press (and in that of the West as well), just as alleged brutalities of Indian soldiers in Kashmir are often coupled in the Pakistani press with their identification as Hindus.

Membership in a religious community often gives one a sense of belonging, of identity, but it also provides a basis for identifying those from other communities as enemies. This is an attitude that has become known in India as communalism and that, while long present as an element of modern political life, has since 1989 become a defining factor in the conflict in Kashmir. The frustration and fear that are so palpably present in Kashmir today have their roots in social and economic conditions that could have been ameliorated by secular political remedies. When these were lacking, the answer was found in religious communalism, which offered "a readily available solution by legitimizing the violence that is born of hatred and despair."[4] In Kashmir, as in Indonesia, Sudan, Palestine, and Northern Ireland, the use of religious vocabulary in justifying political solutions has corrupted both religion and politics.

Kashmir is often used as a kind of shorthand for Jammu and Kashmir, one of the largest of the five hundred or so quasi-independent princely states that formerly existed within the framework of Great Britain's Indian empire.

Most of these princely states were merged fairly peacefully into one of the two new states, India and Pakistan, within the years immediately following independence in 1947. Jammu and Kashmir, however, was the tragic exception. After forty years of the area being a subject of heated dissension between India and Pakistan, a virtual civil war broke out there in 1989. The state is now divided into five principal regions that differ in geography, demography, and history. The first three are controlled by India: Ladakh, Jammu, and the Kashmir Valley. In Ladakh, where the majority of the sparse population lives in the arid and remote regions of the Karakoram Mountains and the upper Indus River valley, about half of the people practice a variant of Tibetan Buddhism and the remainder are Muslims. Jammu, which is an extension of the Panjab (Punjab) into the foothills, has a population that is two-thirds Hindu and one-third Muslim. The Kashmir Valley has a population of about four million, about 90 percent of which is Muslim. Conflict has generally focused on control of the Kashmir Valley and its surrounding mountains, although bitter fighting has taken place in the Doda district of Jammu, in the Kargil district of Ladakh, and in the ill-defined region of the Siachen Glacier.

The Kashmir Valley is famous for the beauty of its towering mountain ranges surrounding a fertile valley of lakes and streams; and Kashmiris are fond of quoting from a poem attributed to the Mughal emperor Jahangir (1569–1627) that "if there is a paradise [*firdaus*] on earth, it is this, it is this, it is this." A contemporary Kashmiri poet, playing on that same image, has written a long poem entitled, with bitter irony, *Firdaus in Flames*. That paradise, he says, is lost in the ashes that the "flames leave behind in the valley, as they consume blood and bridges, life and hope, past in the present." Much of that past that is being destroyed in the present is inextricably bound up with religion. At the end, the poet suggests that weapons be piled for a bonfire celebration and that Hindus and Muslims, "watchers of divine grace," get ready to heal the wounds of the valley.[5]

Kashmir has been described by one geographer as "a half closed ecosystem, opening up slowly in space and across time," with the fertile and well-cultivated valley cut off by high mountains.[6] Although isolated by its mountain walls, Kashmir throughout history has maintained trade and cultural ties with Iran, Central Asia, Tibet, and China, which have resulted in a rich mix of Hindu, Buddhist, and Islamic influences. The combination of religion, language, history, and geography, in turn, has helped to create in the Valley a unique culture of assimilation known as "kashmiriyat."[7]

The fourth and fifth regions of the former princely state are controlled by Pakistan. Azad Kashmir, or Free Kashmir as it is known by Pakistan, is a narrow territory that was formerly part of the Jammu region until Pakistan occupied it in 1947. It has a population of about two million people, almost wholly Muslim. The fifth region, the Northern Territories, is mountainous and arid; it is occupied by approximately 750,000 people, the majority of whom are Muslim. It is from bases in these areas, India alleges, that Pakistan has been supplying weapons and fighters—many from Pakistan itself, as well as other Islamic countries—to wage war against India in neighboring Kashmir, Ladakh, and Jammu. To the west of Azad Kashmir lies the barren region of Aksai-Chin—not a part of Jammu and Kashmir—which is claimed and effectively occupied by China. India, it must be emphasized, claims the whole of Jammu and Kashmir, a claim stemming from India's accession of it in 1947 from the Hindu ruler of the state.[8] For the Muslim communities in Pakistan and Kashmir, this action of a Hindu ruler turning over a state with a majority Muslim population to "Hindu" India, without any consultation with its people, provides the symbolic source of the conflict for Pakistanis and most Kashmiris.

Any sensible person recognizes that peace in Kashmir would benefit India and Pakistan, as well as Kashmir. Since 1989, when the current wave of violence began, police have documented 33,854 killings, of whom 19,781 were civilians, 11,757 were militants, and 2,316 were members of the Indian security forces.[9] These tabulations, however, are too precise and bureaucratic to be accepted by peace groups either in India or Kashmir, who believe that probably twice as many have died and that many of those listed as "militants" were often innocent people killed by the security forces.

Thousands of refugees have left their homes out of fear of either the militant groups, referred to as terrorists by the Indian government and as freedom fighters by their own partisans, or the measures adopted by the Indian authorities to combat the violence. The uprising has led to a breakdown of much of the civil structure, including educational institutions, medical services, and the legal system. While in this chapter, as in all discussions of the dispute, one must turn inevitably to India and Pakistan as both its authors and victims, Kashmir must remain central to the discussion; for, as a poignant headline in a Kashmiri newspaper once put it, "home is where the heartbreak is."[10]

Beyond this human suffering, the violence in Kashmir has been an enormously costly struggle for the government of India, as it has consumed immense resources that could have been better spent in alleviating deep-seated social problems. The same is true of Pakistan, a state on the verge of economic collapse, where the economy and the direction of government policies have both been distorted by the priority given to Kashmir. While the economic price has undoubtedly been much greater for the Indian government than for Pakistan, the effect has been far more debilitating on Pakistan than on India. Beyond any economic and psychological costs, though, the fact that both states are armed with nuclear weapons raises the stakes immensely, particularly when one notes that these two protagonists have gone to war three times in the past fifty years and came close to all-out war again in the summer of 1999 and in the spring of 2002. All of this underlined former President Clinton's assertion, which was angrily rejected by India's political leaders, that South Asia is the world's most perilous region.[11]

There are at least four reasons why the religious communities of the subcontinent, especially Hindu and Muslim, could play a positive role in remedying the situation in Kashmir. First, because religious considerations are inextricably interwoven with the conflict, religious leaders have the wherewithal to influence events. Second, all religions of South Asia are grounded in values that emphasize human dignity and compassion. Third, the respective religious communities have a constituency of the faithful that could be motivated to demand an end to conflict. Fourth, throughout their histories, Hinduism and Islam have expressed some of their greatest creativity and vitality through the spiritual traditions of Bhakti and Sufism,[12] both of which lie outside the bounds of conventional orthodoxy but each of which holds important principles in common with the other, principles that could help bridge the differences that underlie the conflict.

Beyond the subcontinent, religious communities of the world should feel a moral compulsion to become involved in the search for peace in Kashmir as well. The sufferings of the people of Kashmir are reason enough for involvement, but the linkages between religion and the conflict add a further dimension, the need to examine with serious concern the relationship of religion to war and violence. By the same token, this chapter will attempt to demonstrate how interreligious dialogue can enhance political negotiations and become a positive force for peace.

The distinction between dialogue and formal political negotiations is significant and important to understand. The nature of political negotiations was succinctly described by Richard Holbrooke, widely regarded as one of America's most skillful negotiators, when he retired from his post as United States ambassador to the United Nations. Negotiating, he said, is like jazz: "you're improvising on a theme, and the theme has to be your goal." Paraphrasing Henry Kissinger, another famous negotiator, he said that you do not go into diplomatic negotiations unless your chances of success are 85 percent, because negotiating is a zero-sum game, and if you lose, "your loss is a setback for national prestige and a gain for your adversaries."[13] This is a reasonable characterization of the attitudes that guided recent negotiations in Bosnia and Palestine. This zero-sum-game approach, while perhaps useful in some situations, was what led to the blood-filled partition of India following the negotiations over independence between Jawaharlal Nehru and Muhammad Ali Jinnah in 1946.

In contrast to diplomatic negotiations, a process of dialogue does not begin with a win-lose mindset but rather a win-win approach in which reconciliation is sought between the adversaries. Dialogue is often defined as "seeking mutual understanding and harmony"; few would claim that such an attitude has characterized the behavior of the protagonists in the meager negotiations that have taken place thus far in Kashmir. What is needed for peace in Jammu and Kashmir, and for the region as a whole, is a dialogue in which both official and unofficial representatives of the groups concerned participate. It is only after such a dialogue has taken place that negotiations can be expected to bear fruit.

As with any peace process, one must search out and travel roads that are often difficult to traverse. The rest of this chapter is divided into five sections that examine different aspects of the terrain, keeping in mind the fundamental need for dialogue. The first section explores the role of religion in South Asian public policy. The second section sets forth in summary form the relevance of religion's values and practices to peacemaking in the South Asian context. The third section examines the realities of the conflict, noting how frequently religion becomes an explanation and excuse for violence. The fourth section identifies those issues that are central to the conflict, including the aspirations and fears of the principal actors—Kashmiri, Indian, and Pakistani—and noting how religion shapes many of the issues. The fifth section, building on the positions advanced in the previous four, offers suggestions that may provide the basis for a dialogue that can lead to healing and reconciliation.

Religion in Public Policy

In examining a possible ameliorating role for religion in the Kashmir conflict, it is essential to keep in mind that the conflict is rooted in the nature and commitments of the two national movements that brought independence to the Indian subcontinent in 1947 and the ways these commitments have developed since then. To explicate these in detail would require a history of the subcontinent for the past century, but for present purposes a brief summary of how the development of the two movements relates to religion and public policy as they affect Kashmir must suffice. The function of religion as it has influenced public life in the two movements is dramatically different. One of the movements—usually, if somewhat misleadingly, identified with the totality of Indian nationalism—was embodied in the Indian National

Congress, founded in 1885. Under its many able leaders, of whom Jawaharlal Nehru (1889–1964) and Mahatma Gandhi (1869–1948) were the best known and most influential after 1920, India became an independent state in 1947.

The other nationalism expressed itself through the Muslim League, which was founded in 1906 but did not become an important force in Indian public life until the late 1930s, when it came under the able leadership of Muhammed Ali Jinnah (1875–1948). Jinnah brought political meaning to the vague but appealing idea of Sir Muhammad Iqbal (1873–1938), the most famous Indian Muslim literary figure of the twentieth century, that the Muslims of India should have a homeland on the subcontinent where they would be in a majority. In Europe, Iqbal argued, religion had been a private affair, divorced from the state, but in Islam there was no such bifurcation of the spiritual and temporal, no separation of church and state. In Islam, Iqbal insisted, matter, including the state, "is spirit realising itself in space and time."[14] Jinnah's transformation of this poetic ideal into an argument for a specifically Muslim state, minus much of Iqbal's mystical religious nationalism, was presented in a speech to the Muslim League in March of 1940. In what is now regarded as the foundation document for the establishment of Pakistan, Jinnah said that the Muslims of India wished to live in a society where they could "develop to the fullest our spiritual, cultural, economic, social, and political life in a way that we think best and in consonance with our ideals and according to the genius of our people."[15] The tragedy of the subcontinent is that although Nehru and Gandhi shared the same ideals, they were interpreted very differently through the filters of religion and politics in their respective parties, the Muslim League and the Indian National Congress. What Jinnah called an "honorable and peaceful solution" was rejected by the Congress and became the prelude to the horrendous bloodbath of Partition, of which the violence in Kashmir is a continuing legacy.

After independence was granted in 1947, the Indian National Congress remained the ruling party in India for the next forty years and, despite recent electoral setbacks, is still an important actor in Indian political life. The place it assigned to religion in public policy both before and after independence is, however, now under serious challenge from those who question the definition enshrined in the preamble to the Constitution that India is a "secular" state. This designation masks the contradictions that mirror the complexities of Indian history, all of which are directly related to attempts to realize a peaceful settlement in Kashmir, especially those that involve initiatives from the faith communities. Although the word "secular" did not actually find its way into the Constitution until an amendment incorporating that language was passed in 1976, two proponents of the concept had championed it as essential to the social and political health of the country during the constitutional debates of 1948–49. B. R. Ambedkar, the law minister, noted that all that "the secular state means is that the Parliament shall not be competent to impose any particular religion upon the rest of the people." Nehru as prime minister gave the concept more positive content by noting that it meant complete freedom and equality for all religions, providing "an atmosphere of tolerance and cooperation."[16]

Essentially what secularists like Ambedkar and Nehru were saying was that religion, as it found expression in confessional communities, would have no role in defining Indian nationalism or in the formation of public policy. In stark contrast to this is the pervasiveness of religious belief and practice in Indian life, memorably expressed in the personal life and public ideology of Mahatma Gandhi. Most of the political leaders recognized that the diversity of religions in India, and the historical experiences associated with them, meant that they could not be used to unite the people; and the unity of India then, as now, was an overriding concern. The national leaders were convinced that the various religious communities were, in fact, sources of division that threatened national unity. It is likely that the majority of opinionmakers in India—journalists, academicians, politicians, businesspeople—would have given general assent to Nehru's proposition that "the cardinal doctrine of modern democratic practice is the separation of the state from religion" and that the idea of a religious state "has no place in the mind of the modern man."[17] With this definition of modernity, Nehru was excluding Jinnah and his Muslim homeland, as well as quite a few members of the Indian National Congress.

Nehru, then, would almost certainly have given an uncompromisingly negative answer to the question posed in the title of this chapter. As he and other Indian nationalists struggled to create a united nationalist movement to win India's freedom, they saw religion as obscurantism and bigotry, a reactionary force working to prevent needed change. In 1928, his father, Motilal Nehru, one of the great figures in the nationalist movement, declared that the association of religion and politics had been good for neither: "Religion has been degraded, and politics has sunk into the mire. Complete divorce of one from the other is the only remedy."[18]

Another visionary, however, offers a telling rejoinder to these expressions of hope for a public sphere in India from which religion would be excluded. Those who say that religion has nothing to do with politics, Mahatma Gandhi insisted, are only showing how little they know of either religion or politics. Gandhi deplored Hindu-Muslim antagonism, but he was convinced that it was utterly wrong to suppose one could or should extract religion from the context of Indian public life, for it was inextricably intertwined with every aspect of Indian culture. He was always careful, however, to give religion an inclusive character, covering all varieties of Indian religious experience. The religion that many Indian intellectuals feared was, he insisted, the lifeblood of Indian life; and his solution was not to rid politics of religion but to permit what he considered religion's true expression: love, compassion, tolerance, and nonviolence.[19]

The consequences of Gandhi's appeal to true religion as a solvent for the increasing conflict between Hindus and Muslims are not easy to assess. There can be little doubt that his message of nonviolence and his insistence on the inherent truth of all religions moved the nationalist movement for many years away from the violence that might have engulfed it; yet it is equally true that the very terminology, such as *ahimsa*, nonviolence, and *satyagraha*, the power of truth, that he used with such telling effect to build a mass movement was conspicuously drawn from Hinduism. While appealing to a Hindu constituency, the identification of nationalism with Hindu culture alienated Muslim leaders, most notably Jinnah. Although Gandhi left Delhi in despair at the time of Partition as a whirlpool of hatred engulfed North India, he later returned to continue advocating nonviolence. In the end, a Hindu who thought Gandhi was too favorable toward Muslims assassinated him.

In recent years, the role of religion in public policy has become a central issue in Indian social and political life because of the growing power of Hindu nationalism, which directly affects the search for peace in Kashmir. Detractors have always raised dissenting voices against Gandhi's reading of India's past as pacific and nonviolent, as well as Nehru's notion that secularism was the only viable paradigm for Indian civil society. These voices have only grown stronger as Hindu nationalists argue that both are false readings of Indian culture and religion.[20]

In the early stages of nation-building, the concept of a secular state seemed a reasonable solution to the problems created by India's religious diversity. This eventually led to the insertion of a clause on religious freedom into the Indian Constitution. The wording of this clause rejects a special role for Hinduism, even though it was the religion of the vast majority of the population and was intertwined with every aspect of Indian culture. Religious freedom in India is defined in part 3, "Fundamental Rights," articles 25 to 30 of the Constitution as adopted in 1949, and is mandated very succinctly in article 25(1): "all persons are equally entitled to freedom of conscience and the right freely to profess, practice, and propagate religion." In 1976 the clause in the preamble to the Constitution that had declared that India was a "Sovereign, Democratic Republic" was amended to read that it was a "Sovereign, Socialist, Secular, Democratic Republic." The articles on religious freedom and the addition of the word "Secular" to the preamble resonate with the history of India both before the coming of independence in 1947 and since.

Nehru and other like-minded leaders saw secularism as a creative force, which while permitting religious freedom, prevented it from interfering in the great task of nation-building. Secularism, he said, meant more than the free play of all religions: "it conveys the idea of social and political equality."[21] In other words, secularism was to define Indian nationalism. In a thoughtful study of the Indian constitution, the American scholar Granville Austin has suggested that Nehru had fallen into a semantic trap by enlarging secularism's meaning.[22] This vision of the secular state as a just, egalitarian society, with its emphasis on unrestricted religious freedom, seemed to be a denial of the old loyalties of Indian society to family, caste, and traditional religious values. Religion as a fundamental component of Indian national life seemed to many to be sidelined.[23]

It was this perception that Nehruvian secularism was an attack on the traditional Indian way of life that gave rise in the 1980s to the potent force of Hindu nationalism. This phenomenon, which in retrospect was probably the most important social movement of the twentieth century in India, continues to grow in power and social dynamism as the new century begins.[24] Because it stands in opposition to the liberal, secular tradition enshrined in the Indian constitution, Hindu nationalism must be taken into account if religion is to play a constructive role in bringing peace to Kashmir.

Nationalism has been defined as the congruence of power and culture, and this fairly accurately describes what has been happening in India during the past fifty years.[25] In other words, the national culture, in which religion is a vital element, has become intimately identified with national politics. Kashmir, with its claims for autonomy based on its own history and culture, poses a particular challenge to Hindu nationalism: while this movement sees the unity of India grounded in a Hindu culture that embraces all of India, Kashmiris see the denial of autonomy as a threat to the continued existence of their own culture.

Many organizations have promoted this convergence of power and culture known as Hindu nationalism, but undoubtedly the most powerful has been the Rashtriya Swayamsewak Sangh (RSS).[26] While the RSS was founded in 1925, it moved to a central position in Indian life only after the coming of independence, when it began to seek agreement and recognition that India was a specifically Hindu nation. In so doing, the RSS has denied that it is either a religious or a political organization. Instead it asserts that it is a cultural one, for Hinduism, by definition, is a culture that includes religion but is not confined to it.[27] The constitution of the RSS indicates how thin the dividing line is between religion, culture, and politics when it declares its aim: "To eradicate differences among Hindus; to make them realize the greatness of their past; to inculcate in them a spirit of self-sacrifice and selfless devotion to Hindu society as a whole; to build up an organized and well-disciplined corporate life; and to being about the regeneration of Hindu society."[28]

Elaboration of the idea that India is culturally and historically a Hindu nation is known as *Hindutva*, and the use of "Hindu" as equivalent religious and cultural designations is especially important among Hindu nationalists. One of their leading spokesmen, M. S. Gowalkar, declared that Hindus had built a great civilization, a great culture, and a unique social order and the name *Hindu* "has been associated with us in our history and tradition for so long that it has now become our universally accepted and adored name."[29] In another statement, he defined with brutal frankness his views, which have unfortunately penetrated deeply into Indian life, on the place of Muslims, Christians, and other non-Hindus: they "must entertain," he declared, "no idea but the glorification of the Hindu race and culture."[30] This is, of course, extremism, but in modified versions it explains to a considerable extent why Kashmir, with its militant Muslim challenge, remains, as the title of a book on the Kashmir problem puts it, "a secular crown on fire."[31]

The RSS has become a major player in Indian life for a number of reasons. First, its core membership consists of well-disciplined cadres working for what they regard as the regeneration of Hindu society. From this small group, working in at least semisecrecy, have come numerous organizations to serve the aims of the RSS, including trade unions, youth groups, print media, and the Vishva Hindu Parishad (World Hindu Council), a leading promulgator of Hindu nationalism and a defender of the Hindu way of life.[32] The cadres of the RSS have had the most impact, however, in the establishment of political parties. The first of these was the Jan Sangh, which had considerable support in the late 1950s but was soon replaced by the Bharatiya Janata Party (BJP). By 1997, the BJP had become the major opposition party in power, and then in 1998, in alliance with other parties, it formed the national government. All of its major figures, including the prime minister Atal Bihari Vaypayee and his chief lieutenant L. K. Advani, were trained in the cadres of the RSS.

The manifestos and statements by the BJP's political leaders have stressed three commitments that have deeply troubled Muslims, Christians, and many liberal Hindus. All three are very complex issues and can only be briefly mentioned here. The first is for a universal civil code of personal law, replacing the special provisions for Muslims relating to such matters as marriage, adoption, divorce, and inheritance. The second is the building of a temple to the god Rama on the site of the Babri Masjid mosque in Ayodhya, which was destroyed by a Hindu mob in 1992. The third, of special importance for the Kashmir crisis, is the amendment of article 370 of the Constitution, which gives Kashmir a special status of autonomy.

An early attempt to integrate Kashmir into India by giving it a greater measure of autonomy than that enjoyed by any other Indian state, article 370 can be seen on one level as a strictly legal arrangement; it met some of the political demands of the state for autonomy in most matters (except defense, foreign affairs, and communications), but there was always a sense that this status was a recognition that, unlike any other state in the Indian union, Kashmir had a majority Muslim population. Hindu nationalists especially resented Kashmiri laws that forbade other Indians from buying land there and saw this as a symbol of "pandering" to Muslims. Hindu nationalists saw article 370 as inviting movements of secession, not only in Kashmir but throughout the rest of India as well; furthermore, they viewed it as an encouragement for Indian Muslims to look toward Pakistan.[33] Religious groups, especially Hindu ones, could be of enormous help in the process of reconciliation in Kashmir by opposing any move to amend article 370 and by supporting the resolutions of the Kashmir legislative assembly asking for greater autonomy.

Religions of South Asia

To provide a summary account of religion in South Asia is to hear the rustle of the wings of departing angels. As Mark Twain noted when he entered Bombay harbor, India is "the home of a thousand religions and two million gods."[34] Basavanna, a poet who lived in South India in the twelfth century, complained: "Gods, gods, there are so many, there's no place left for a foot"; and in the fifteenth century the poet Kabir made a comment that is often echoed in India at the beginning of the twenty-first century: "The Hindu says Ram is the Beloved, the Turk [the Muslim] says Rahim. Then they kill each other."[35] It is interesting to note that Kabir identifies the Muslims of India with the ethnic origin of the Central Asian conquerors, even though the vast majority of Muslims in India, like himself, had come from Hindu origins.

A description of "lived religion," a term often used to indicate contemporary beliefs and practices, is what is being attempted here, in contrast to textual studies of the foundational documents of religious systems. Having said that, it is nonetheless obligatory to undertake that most difficult of tasks, indicating how one is using the term "religion." A simple definition must suffice here to delimit those aspects of human experience under discussion.

"Religion" as used in this chapter connotes a fusion of memories and experiences around symbols that are regarded as possessing transcendent powers. Such shared impressions unite people into a community. By the same token, just as religion fulfills the vital function of giving identity and meaning to people through a sense of belonging to a community, it can also promote disunity through emphasizing separation and difference from other communities. This definition says nothing about the validity of any particular religious belief, only that religion is an ineradicable part of culture. Religion is not, then, a self-sufficient entity but is embedded in the historical processes that shape and respond to all human creativity.

The term "Indian religions" is frequently used to refer to those systems of beliefs and practice whose origins and development through the centuries have been identified with the Indian subcontinent, in contrast to those systems that have been brought to India from areas outside the subcontinent. The four religious traditions indigenous to the subcontinent are Hinduism, Buddhism, Jainism, and Sikhism, while the systems that are thought of as non-Indian, having originated outside the subcontinent, are Islam, Christianity, and Judaism. These three are often contrasted with Indian religion as "Semitic" or "Abrahamic" because of common origins and belief patterns. All of them, however, have roots in India that go back at least a thousand years, so they are in no sense "new" or "un-Indian." Furthermore, all of these religions, indigenous and nonindigenous, originated in some part of the Asian continent.

Westerners, and some Indians, often argue that Hinduism is not a religion but many forms of belief and practice loosely linked together. However, students of contemporary religion in India make a strong case for showing that in fact certain well-known features have been dominant in South Asian religion for the last thirty centuries.[36] In Indian contemporary discourse, moreover, "Hindu" and "Hinduism" are used by Hindus themselves, not only in English but also in Indian languages. The term "Hindu" is used, in the Indian constitution, not only for Hindus but also for Jains, Buddhists, and Sikhs, although this usage was later rejected by the Sikhs. However dubious it may be to apply the term "Hinduism" to ancient India, by the beginning of the twentieth century it had become accepted in social and political discourse.

The four Indian indigenous religions share in common, though with many variations, certain assumptions that distinguish them from the nonindigenous groups.[37] One of these assumptions is an acceptance of the idea of reincarnation, or *samsara*, the cycle of existence. This is the belief that all living things will die and be reborn again in some form. A second common assumption is a belief in *karma*, or the idea that all actions—mental, emotional, as well as physical—have consequences that lead to rebirth. One's destiny proceeds from one's karma; thus, one's destiny is not subject to fate or the will of a deity but instead to one's own actions. A third core belief is embodied in the concept of *dharma*, or the moral obligations that come with birth. "Dharma" is often used by Indians as equivalent to what Westerners would call religion. Dharma signifies both the way things are and the way they should be. According to this belief, good people are the ones who fulfill their dharma; and people will turn for guidance to those who are seen to possess it. In the context of facilitating meaningful dialogue on Kashmir, dharma becomes a key to action. The fourth shared value is *moksha*, translated as salvation or liberation. This term denotes the sense of being freed from the cycle of birth and rebirth. Finally, all Indian religions, but especially Hinduism, emphasize that there are many levels of *satya*, or truth, which depend upon the intellectual, moral, and spiritual capacities of the person concerned.

To engage Hinduism in the search for peace and healing in Kashmir, the concepts of dharma and truth will be particularly important and could provide a context for meeting with Islam and the other religions of India. Dharma, in a very important sense, defines India's civic culture through its emphasis on order and adherence to traditional values. Mahatma Gandhi saw it as a unifying factor in Indian society and urged that it "be offered to the world . . . as the best remedy against heartless greed and competition."[38]

These five assumptions are, it must be stressed, not at all religious beliefs in the sense of being creedal statements that an adherent accepts for inclusion within a group; instead, these are part of a worldview, that seems to have prevailed throughout the subcontinent from very ancient times. This worldview gives depth and meaning not only to the adherents of the indigenous religions but often to members of all religions imbued with the Indian ethos.

An expression of "lived religion" that is vital to the Hindu tradition itself is the great tradition of Bhakti, or devotional religion. Bhakti, or the intense emotional devotion to a particular deity characterized as a relationship of love, is what many Hindus, both now and in the past, understand to be true religion. Where it intersects theologically with the Sufi tradition of Islam, Bhakti may represent an effective path to authentic dialogue on the conflict in Kashmir.

Hinduism is not the only religion of India that must be party to the search for peace in Kashmir; Islam is the religion of approximately 300 million people in India, Pakistan, and Kashmir. Within this vast population there is great diversity, which renders it difficult to envisage any kind of common Islamic cause with regard to the future of Kashmir. A brief summary of the status of Islam in the three regions suggests the complexity of the situation and why one will need to examine each region separately to assess how Muslims might contribute to an inclusive process of dialogue and negotiation.

An important point to acknowledge in facilitating a dialogue on Kashmir is to recognize that Muslims in Kashmir, as in the rest of India, are not recent converts, as is often portrayed by Hindus. Indeed, Muslims have been an integral part of the fabric of Indian society for many centuries. This constitutes a significant hurdle because of the deeply entrenched belief that Indians were made to accept Islam or face death by the Turks and other conquerors. Although some of the Turkish invaders who were Muslim by religious affiliation did engage in forced conversion at the urging of religious leaders, there is no evidence to suggest that this practice was widespread. This is as true in Kashmir as it is elsewhere.

Surprisingly little is known about the process of religious change that did take place, although it must rank as one of the more significant transformations in Indian history. Conversion is often misunderstood as a personal decision based on a spiritual experience leading to a deliberate, conscious break with old ways of thinking and behavior. This is a misleading reading of the practice of Islam in Kashmir, where Hinduism and Islam, especially in their manifestations in the Bhakti and Sufi traditions, mingle in a unique way. Religious identity for both Hindus and Muslims was most often expressed in new social identities and patterns of devotion.

An important explanation for the spread of Islam in Kashmir, as elsewhere in India, is likely to be found in the activities of Sufis, or Muslim mystics, who played a vital role in creating an Islamic society in Kashmir beginning in the thirteenth century.[39] It was through the Sufis, rather than through the *ulama*, or scholars trained in traditional learning and theology, that Islam became the religion of Kashmir. They were responsible for translating Islam to the new culture and making it accessible to non-Hindus. One scholar of the period sums up this process by suggesting that the great Sufi shrines became important urban centers because the Sufis "worked with characteristic missionary zeal for the acceptability of the new regime at the base level of their local jurisdiction." Their good deeds, spirituality, and ascetic lifestyle attracted multitudes around them, narrowing the differences between the alien and the indigenous and "leading to the emergence of a synthetic cultural pattern."[40]

In looking at the religiosity of Pakistan, one finds that while it appears remarkably homogenous and lacking the religious diversity of India, there are divisions within its Muslim population that have great political significance. The Sunnis constitute about 77 percent and the Shi'as about 20 percent of the Muslim community. Considerable financial support is provided to the Sunnis from Saudi Arabia and to the Shi'as from Iran, much of which goes to support religious schools, or *madrassas*. It is from these schools, particularly the Sunni, that the militants in Kashmir recruit their members (as did the Taliban in the recent past). As is frequently reported by Western journalists and scholars, the young men from these schools see themselves as fighting a jihad, or holy war. For them, the Kashmiri struggle for independence is increasingly seen as an Islamic movement to bring all of Kashmir under Pakistan's control.[41]

The term *jihad* comes freighted, as Islamic scholars complain, with a double burden of Western and Hindu misinterpretations. The term is often misused in attacking Islam, partly because of ignorance and partly by design in an attempt to demonize Islam for political reasons. Islamic scholars insist that the word denotes "struggle" and "endeavor," which can be interpreted to mean warfare against the enemies of Islam, as in the injunction in the Qur'an "to fight them until there is no persecution and the religion is God's; then if they give over, there shall be no enmity save for evildoers"(2:193). However, *jihad* is most commonly used to describe the internal struggle within each individual against one's own evil inclinations or against the evils of one's society. The latter usage is the one most employed in Sufi writings.

Muslim scholars argue that not all wars in which Muslims fight are jihads; on the contrary, only those that are fought in self-defense or to help fellow Muslims who are threatened by an enemy qualify for this description. These scholars further maintain that war should only be made against unbelievers if they are persecuting the faithful.[42] Numerous passages in the Qur'an, as well as in the *hadith* (sayings of the Prophet), confirm these interpretations. Another point that scholars of Islam emphasize is the importance that Islam places on keeping a contract: "you have made it with Him and not merely with your fellow men."[43] Young fighters often quote this verse, pointing out that in breaking its promise to hold a plebiscite in Kashmir, India had brought God's wrath upon itself.[44]

India's criticism of Pakistan as being responsible for a jihad in Kashmir gained new strength with the announcement by the governments of India and Russia in the summer of 2000 that they now had a common purpose in fighting Islamic terrorism—the Indians in Kashmir and the Russians in Chechnya. In a joint statement from Delhi, Indian and Russian leaders said that they were convinced that "a transfer of the center of international terrorism to this region has taken place, and we intend to coordinate the efforts of all agencies to combat international terrorism."[45] India has also received indications of support against alleged Islamic terrorism from the United States and Israel.[46] It is against this backdrop that requests for

Muslim leaders in India, Pakistan, and Kashmir to engage in dialogue with Hindus, or with Christians, must be placed. If Hindus accept without dissent their government's interpretation of Islam, no serious dialogue can take place. To refuse to see that Muslim values on war and peace are rooted in valid moral interpretations, based on sacred scripture, is to end communication altogether.

Religion and Conflict in South Asia

This section will attempt to provide a sensing of the extent to which the conflict is perceived to be rooted in religion by India, Pakistan, and Kashmir, all places where perception reigns supreme. A poignant point in time in this regard was in the spring and late summer of 2000, a time when religious loyalties seemed to have become the driving force for political action, or at least were continually invoked as the basis and explanation for such action. This was a time of disappointed hopes, when new initiatives for peace foundered amid senseless massacres while India and Pakistan hurled accusations of perfidy at one another, including thinly veiled hints of resorting to nuclear war. Subsequent hints relating to more recent provocations haven't been so veiled, but a case can be made for why future initiatives toward peace and understanding will hinge upon the events of that earlier period and how they continue to be interpreted by the protagonists.

The term "communalism" is the pejorative shorthand used in India for attitudes and practices that have colored political life for the past eighty years and are now especially prominent in the Kashmir conflict. T. N. Madan, a social scientist of Kashmiri origin, has succinctly defined it as the use of religion as a significant means of mobilizing people for secular objectives, notably the acquisition of power.[47] Newspaper headlines translated this cool language of social science into violent reality in the spring and summer of 2000 when they reported "Hindu Pilgrims Slain in Kashmir Massacre." The article went on to relate how Muslim militants opened fire on some of the thousands of Hindu pilgrims on their way to the holy cave at Amarnath, where the god Shiva is worshiped.[48] The militants who carried out the attack insisted they were angry not with the Hindu pilgrims, but with the largest of the many militant Muslim groups, the Hizbul Mujahideen, for having promised a unilateral cease-fire with the Indian government.

Such attacks are often described as "senseless," with violence having become an end in itself, but this is a serious misreading of the situation. These acts of terror are born out of desperation and an awareness that the militancy is not making headway against the power of the Indian government. Those who carried out such attacks justify them on the grounds that the Indian security forces have brutalized the Muslim people of Kashmir through torture, killings, and rape; for them, retaliation is the only recourse against the vast forces of the Hindu Indian government. When the foreign minister of Pakistan suggested that the massacres had been carried out by renegade groups at the behest of the Indian security forces to malign the Muslim Kashmiri freedom fighters before the international community, his suggestion was rejected with scorn by the Indian government but was given credence in some Kashmiri circles.[49] The temper of the times was further indicated when K. S. Sudarshan, head of the RSS, the most important of the Hindu nationalist organizations, declared that the killing of the Hindu pilgrims by Muslim militants made clear the need for "yet another epic war—between Hindus and non-Hindus" and was part of the "emerging clash of civilizations against the Semitic religions."[50] For their part, the militants called for a renewed jihad against Hindu India over Kashmir.[51]

Other news items recounted a depressing sequence of events in succeeding months. One of the most savage attacks, seemingly motivated by religion, took place on March 20 in the village of Chattisinghpora, where "the massacre of 35 innocent, unarmed and uninvolved Sikhs caused universal outrage."[52] This incident has special relevance for religion both as a cause of conflict and as a possible transforming agent, for as the story unfolded, it was clear that the massacre was symptomatic of the conflict. At first, the reports suggested that this was clearly a religiously motivated attack by Muslims against Sikhs. However, according to M. Y. Tarigami, a respected member of the Jammu and Kashmir legislative assembly, when he visited the village shortly after the massacre, people in the village as well as many other people in the Valley were convinced that the killers were actually from the Indian security forces. This allegation was made, he said, because the Indian army had lost all credibility and the people were willing to believe almost any accusation made against them. A Sikh religious leader from Panjab, known for his strong views against the Indian government, worsened the situation when he claimed that the Sikhs had been killed by Indian security forces in order to defame Pakistan. Hindu nationalist politicians, from the other direction, denounced the killers as Muslim terrorists. Summarizing the charges and countercharges, a journalist concluded that the religious right had no one to blame but themselves for the hatred that the killings had stirred up.[53] Listening to accounts of the massacre and reading interpretations of it, it is difficult to dissent from this judgment.[54]

Religion and the Aspirations of Kashmir, India, and Pakistan

The motivations and aspirations of the participants in the conflict in Kashmir are deeply rooted in their understanding of the history of the area, which lies not so much in what actually happened as in how Indians, Kashmiris, and Pakistanis interpret the past. Everywhere in South Asia the interpretation of the past is of immense importance, but what can best be called the contemporaneity of the past is present to an extraordinary degree in the conflict in Kashmir. The events believed to have happened in the past are understood not just to have influenced social developments through the centuries but also to be contemporaneous with the present. Not surprisingly, the religion of the rulers and of the classes that once had power is almost always seen as the decisive factor. To reiterate the point made before—and it is arguable that this is not the case—religion is increasingly seen as the controlling factor. Relatively isolated, Kashmir was never for very long under the control of any of the great empires that were established in the Indian heartland; but under successive rulers, who had usually come from the outside, it developed a rich cultural tradition even when its people were oppressed. The truth seems to be that its rulers, whatever their religion—Hindu, Muslim, Sikh—frequently exploited the people whether or not they shared a common religion.

To speak in any detail of how the history of religion in Kashmir coincides with its political history would be a voluminous undertaking; so a succinct picture of the religiopolitical milieu will be attempted through a summary of the principal historical events that have transpired since 1846. That year the British defeated the Sikh rulers of the Panjab, who had added the Kashmir Valley and Ladakh, the Tibetan Buddhist territory to the north, to their territories. At that time, the actual boundaries of all this territory were quite unknown, and the British, having never exercised any authority in the region and having no wish to do so, sold it for one million pounds sterling to Gulab Singh, the Hindu ruler of Jammu.

The majority of Singh's new subjects were Muslim peasants and artisans, and from them he had to extract the taxes to pay the British for the kingdom he had bought and to maintain his government. The official document, the Treaty of Amritsar, spells out the conditions of the sale. While there was no demarcation of the boundaries of Kashmir, the treaty declared that Kashmir was to belong "forever, an independent possession, to Maharaja Gulab Singh and the heirs male to his body."[55]

It is on these words in the treaty that the government of India bases its claim that Kashmir was the Maharaja's private estate, which he was free to do with as he pleased, as he did when he signed it over to India in 1948. This replay of one of the grubbier moments in imperial history, the selling and buying of an entire population, continually resonates throughout the Kashmir conflict. The famous Indian poet of Kashmiri descent, Muhammad Iqbal, mentioned earlier in connection with the foundation of Pakistan, captures what many people in the valley think when they remember the sale of Kashmir to Gulab Singh: "Each hill, each garden, field. Each farmer too they sold / A nation for a price, that makes my blood run cold."[56]

The Kashmiri Muslims are center stage in the story of oppression. However, another group that has suffered is the small Hindu community of Brahmans, known as Pandits, who number around 200,000. Only perhaps 5,000 remain in Kashmir, the rest having fled in fear of persecution and harassment by the militants since the most recent uprising in 1990. Under Hindu rule since the middle of the nineteenth century, the Kashmiri government contained a disproportionate representation of Pandits in all branches of government service. Many of them, such as the Nehru family, held high positions in India. That this favored position of the Kashmiri Hindus was resented by Kashmiri Muslims is understandable, but both the Hindu and Muslim Kashmiris insist that there was little religious prejudice as such, at least before the militancy began. Both stress the commonalities they shared in Kashmiri culture and social relations and argue that it is only after the outbreak of militancy and the harsh response of the Indian security forces that social identities as Hindu and Muslim became sources of antagonism. As will be noted later, Kashmiris of both communities acknowledge the fusing of the Bhakti and Sufi traditions in Kashmiri culture, and this suggests a possible pathway to healing and reconciliation.

At the same time, one should not overlook the fact that by the 1930s, members of the Muslim majority had begun in a guarded way, since they could not do it openly, to express their resentment of the preferential treatment that they believed was given by the maharajah's government to Hindus. Sheikh Abdullah (1905–82), who became the great leader against the maharaja's rule, tells of how, as a young boy, he asked his mother why, since they were in the majority and contributed most of the revenues to the Maharaja, the Muslims were oppressed and the Hindus treated so well. When her answer was "God is the ultimate ruler," he replied, "Then why is this injustice meted out only to the Muslims of Kashmir?"[57] A senior member of the maharaja's council, Sir Albion Banerji, made the same point in 1927 when he reported that the Muslim population was "absolutely illiterate, labouring under poverty . . . and governed like dumb driven cattle."[58]

When the uprising began in 1990, the militants took revenge on Pandits, characterizing them as supporters of the maharaja's oppressive regime, and survivors tell tales of rape, murder, and looting.[59] Many of them fled the Valley and are living in wretched refugee camps in Jammu, while others have gone to India, the United States, Canada, and England. Like almost everything about Kashmir, this migration of the Pandits has generated conflicting explanations. One is that these Kashmiri Hindus, holding important posts in the bureaucracies both in Delhi and Jammu and Kashmir, persuaded the central Indian government, on the grounds that the Kashmir Valley was falling into chaos, to assume direct control of the state of Jammu and Kashmir, replacing its elected chief minister and legislature with rule by an appointed governor.[60] A second explanation, widely believed in Kashmir, is that when the uprisings became serious in 1990, Jagmohan, the governor, who was pro-Hindu and anti-Muslim, encouraged the Pandits to leave. His intention, according to some Kashmiri Muslims, was to gain support from Hindu nationalists in India by spreading stories of Muslim atrocities forcing Kashmiri Hindus to flee. Whatever the truth of such stories, they point to the alienation of the Kashmiris from India. Thus, the Pandits must be participants in any dialogue about resolving the conflict, not only because of the injustice they have suffered but also because of their place in Kashmiri culture and religion.

The major Indian concern in Kashmir is the preservation of the territorial unity and integrity of India. Enshrined in the preamble of the Constitution and in many of its most important articles and amendments, the unity of India has been the central commitment of all political parties since the coming of independence, just as it was of the nationalist movement in the preindependence movement.[61] This insistence on the identity of territory, nationality, and religion as defining the unity of India underlies much of the unrest in Kashmir. The trauma of Partition in 1947 remains for many Indians a catastrophic tragedy, and the fate of Kashmir is intimately linked with the assertion that there must be no further vivisection of the Motherland.

Pakistan's goals and aspirations for its involvement in Kashmir are quite clearly the product of its understanding of the history of the region. Contrary to many journalistic accounts that speak of India and Pakistan both claiming Kashmir, Pakistan does not make a territorial claim for the area in the same way that India does. At the United Nations in 1948, Pakistan's case was presented by Sir Zafrulla Khan almost wholly in religious terms, arguing that Pakistan became involved in Kashmir not to gain territory but to protect the Muslims there from massacres by the Indians and the army of the Hindu maharaja.[62] It was, to use a current phrase, humanitarian intervention. This remains Pakistan's case and is the basis of the strong emotional appeal that is made to the people of Pakistan and the justification used for the support it gives to the militants in the form of arms and training facilities. A subsidiary aim of Pakistan in giving assistance to the militants is probably using them, as many Indians assert, in a proxy war to weaken India. However, it is always the religious element of helping free Kashmiri Muslims from Hindu India that is stressed in Pakistan; and the importance of this as a controlling factor can scarcely be doubted.

As for the aspirations of the Kashmiris, one of the great problems in a search for a solution to Kashmir's problems is that the people do not know what either the Indians or the Pakistanis really want for the Valley beyond the defeat of the other.[63] The Kashmiris of the Valley, who have suffered the most from the conflict, find it difficult to be specific on how they see their political future because they are painfully aware that outsiders, Indians and Pakistanis, are determining their future. This, incidentally, is one reason why Kashmiris do not seem to resent the significant role that foreign militants have played in the uprising and why they so often express a desire for American involvement. Kashmiris who know the history of their troubled valley are aware that its fate has too often been decided by outsiders. It is important to note that the conflict is seldom referred to in Kashmir as a civil war or revolution, for it has neither a readily identified leader nor a clearly defined aim. There is no Castro, no Ho Chi Minh, no Gandhi, and certainly no George Washington to define goals and provide a rallying point for action.

A very wide range of opinions are expressed by Kashmiris on the subject of their political future, but most observers who have recently visited the Valley agree that three general sets of attitudes tend to dominate the thinking of Kashmiris who are not directly involved in the militancy. First, Kashmiris are alienated from India because of what has amounted, in their eyes, to oppression by the enormous Indian army of occupation. Alienation is also a product, however, of the very high rate of unemployment among the educated young people, who fault India for doing nothing for the economy. This dislike of India does not mean, however, that it is balanced by a liking for Pakistan, which many Pakistanis believe to be the case. In private conversations and in the print media, Pakistan is blamed for supplying the weapons to militant groups, whether from within Kashmiri society or from outside, that have made possible the continuation of the conflict. These militants, it is widely recognized, have no hope of defeating the Indian armed forces. However, they are able to maintain a level of violence against the Indian security forces that is sufficient to invite reprisals, which, in turn, inflict punishment on the civilian population. The militants also attack elements in Kashmiri society that refuse to support them, are suspected of cooperating with the Indians, or are simply trying to remain neutral.

Another common expression, even from some militants and former militants, is a desperate yearning for peace and return to normalcy. Most disturbing in many ways is the assertion by a number of well-informed people that the Indian government has deliberately sought to mask the depth of opposition to India by using religion to accentuate contrived distinctions and portraying the conflict as a communal problem. The Indian government, one former militant argued, presents the Kashmir problem as a conflict of Muslim militants against Hindus to win support at home for its repressive policies in Kashmir. The Indians were following, he alleged, the technique of "divide and conquer" used by their British predecessors.[64]

Although Kashmiris may not formulate very specific political plans for the future, nonetheless, from conversations, the print media, and political statements, recurring themes emerge with reasonable clarity. One is *azadi*, the second is human rights, and a third is reconciliation between religious communities in Jammu and Kashmir. The term "azadi" seems to have as many meanings as the English word "free": liberated, emancipated, or freedom of action. Moreover, "azadi" carries the weight of two demands for Kashmir as well as for India and Pakistan: for self-determination and, inextricably related to it, for autonomy. Both are part of the vocabulary of people everywhere struggling for radical political change; and everywhere in the subcontinent, not least in Kashmir, religious identification and ethnicity are very intertwined. Self-determination and autonomy, while political aspirations, also carry the moral and religious overtones that Gandhi had in mind when he said that political independence is meaningless without control over one's personal and private existence.[65] Yasin Malik, a former Kashmiri militant leader, is not the only militant who has spoken of Gandhi with great respect, to the embarrassment of Indian officials. Shabir Shah, a fiery leader who has spent much of his life in Indian jails, has also been outspoken in his admiration for the Indian leader. Many Indian politicians, one suspects, would agree with Robert Lansing, Woodrow Wilson's secretary of state, when he remarked on the danger of Wilson's famous declaration of the right to self-determination: "Will it not breed discontent, disorder, and rebellion? What a calamity that the phrase was ever uttered! What misery it will cause."[66]

The right of self-determination raises in Kashmir, as elsewhere, the issue of the right of secession and, almost inevitably, the right to use violence against the state. In Kashmir, India sees that violence in religious terms as Islamic terrorism, while those engaged in it see themselves as fighting for freedom and liberation, not just for secular freedom but also for righteousness against evil. In this way, religion legitimizes the violence. As Mark Juergensmeyer, a noted religous scholar, has argued in a number of penetrating studies, that stimulation to violence may lie close to the center of power of all vital religious experience.[67]

Paths to Healing and Reconciliation through Dialogue

The four preceding sections have been, in effect, an analysis of how and why religion has been involved in the Kashmir conflict. This was a necessary prelude to suggesting, as this section will attempt, how the religions of the subcontinent can help advance the process of healing and reconciliation. While some faiths, notably Christianity, have historically been concerned with questions of war and peace between states, others have not. On the Indian subcontinent, Islam has had a peculiarly complex relationship with the state on these questions, whether under Muslim or non-Muslim control. Hinduism and the various other forms of Indian religions have not been very concerned with such questions either theoretically or practically.[68]

While the life and career of Mahatma Gandhi may seem to contradict this statement, Gandhi's principal concern, as he always insisted, was focused on the true meaning of freedom for India.[69] He made this point early on in a letter to a European correspondent who, assuming that Gandhi was a pacifist in the Tolstoy fashion, expressed bitter disappointment that he had supported the British war effort during the First World War. The correspondent further complained that Gandhi had subordinated the essential needs of humanity to those of India.[70] In the dark months at the end of Gandhi's life, however, when the likelihood of war between India and Pakistan became a reality, he retreated from conventional political negotiations and insisted that the proper way to proceed was through strategic nonviolence, that is, "to recognize that the technique of unconquerable nonviolence of the strong has not been discovered as yet."[71]

While there does not appear to be much hope for bringing Gandhi's "technique of unconquerable non-violence" to bear on the conflict in Kashmir, a process of dialogue is available, and it is consonant with Gandhian thought and indeed with the fundamental teachings of the great religions. The great Jewish philosopher Martin Buber best conveys the distinction between dialogue and negotiation in his statement that true "dialogue expresses an essential aspect of the human spirit, when we listen and respond to one another with an authenticity that forges a bond between us."[72] No serious dialogue has yet been attempted in this sense, for the halfhearted and insincere negotiations instituted by the governments and militant groups can hardly be classed as dialogue, although some nonofficial groups have made credible attempts.[73]

If Buber's sense of dialogue is to be the basis for fruitful negotiations, then it must be characterized by three features.[74] First, all parties must commit to treating one another as equals and abstaining from all forms of coercion. So far, India has resolutely refused to discuss Kashmir with Pakistan, with or without the participation of Kashmiris. The distinction between negotiation and dialogue was sadly illustrated during the summer of 2000, when the powerful militant group Hizbul Mujahideen offered to negotiate with the Indian government. In spite of the offer, the government summarily rejected such a proposal because of the Hizbul's demand that Pakistan be a party to the negotiations.[75]

The second requirement for authentic dialogue is the ability of participants to respond with empathy, to walk in the other's shoes. To understand how far apart all of the concerned groups are on this issue, it is only necessary to read newspapers, watch television, listen to political speeches, and, above all, to talk to the common man and woman. Although Indian officials insist that the Kashmir problem is a bilateral dispute about boundaries, unfortunately it is much more. As a Kashmiri writer grimly put it, "the clash of civilizations will become a reality in the Indian subcontinent."[76] Thus, to ignore the aspirations and urges of the people of Kashmir and Pakistan is to deepen the conflict between Hindus and Muslims.

The third requirement for substantive dialogue is that it "must be concerned with bringing forth people's most deep-rooted assumptions."[77] This does not mean determining the basis for other's arguments in order to undermine them but rather placing them alongside one's own assumptions in order to understand the basis of dialogue. The etymology of the word "dialogue" is suggestive: *dia* in Greek means to see through; dialogue should help us to see through the meaning of our own assumptions and those of others. The unwillingness both to examine one's own assumptions and those of others was demonstrated in the summer of 2000 when the Kashmiri legislative assembly passed a resolution urging a greater measure of autonomy. A corresponding unwillingness to consider dialogue was shown when the Indian government refused even to discuss the resolution, for to have done so would have required a recognition of the religious issues underlying the resolution. One concern was that it would give the Muslim majority in Kashmir bargaining advantages over the Hindu minority. Another issue was that Hindu nationalists saw the demand for greater autonomy as a move toward secession by Muslims wishing to destroy the Indian Union. From their side, Muslim leaders in Pakistan and Kashmir saw the Indian government's action as one more rejection of the rights of Kashmiris because they were Muslims.[78]

Hope for peace in Jammu and Kashmir, and for the whole region, resides in the beginning of a dialogue in which different levels of representation of the groups concerned will participate. So far, however, it appears that the religiously oriented groups in the subcontinent who could contribute to this process have been committed to ideological positions that preclude dialogue. But here one must note an exception. While somewhat bizarre, it is relevant in indicating the strange complexities of the situation insofar as the religious communities are concerned.

The Indian media in the summer of 2000 carried accounts of the Shankaracharaya of Puri, Swami Adhokshayananda, holding talks with leaders of the Hurriyat, an umbrella group for various militant factions in Kashmir, in an attempt to bring about peace. The Shankaracharya is the head of a great religious center at Puri, a city in Orissa famed for its temples, who by virtue of his office holds a high place among Hindu religious figures. He is often referred to by journalists as "the Hindu pope"; but, given the nature of Hinduism, this is quite misleading. Ironically, and on a somewhat amusing note, just as there were antipopes in the fourteenth century claiming the papal office, so too at the present time are there three rival claimants for the office of Shankaracharya in Puri. The office was supposedly founded in the eighth century of the current era by the great philosopher Shankarachayra, who is credited with defending Hinduism against attacks by other religious groups.[79] In the same spirit, holders of the office emphasize that the function of the office is to propagate Hinduism and to defend it against attacks from other religions.

The newspaper accounts that the Shankarachayra of Puri was engaged in negotiations with the Hurriyat leaders drew instant condemnation from his rivals and many other Hindus who saw this as a traitorous dealing with the Muslim enemies of India and of Hinduism. The media accounts drew an immediate response from Swami Madhwashram, widely acknowledged to be the true Shankaracharya, who denounced Adhokshayananda as an impostor and said that he himself would have nothing to do with mediating a peace with the Muslim leaders of the Hurriyat.[80] As a result of his foray into politics, Swami Adhokshayananda was arrested by the police in Puri. After news of the arrest spread, his followers gathered outside the court where they protested that his talks in Kashmir with the Hurriyat leaders proved that his aim was to restore peace in the entire country.[81]

The Hindu nationalist groups in India, principally the Vishva Hindu Parishad (VHP) and the RSS, have strenuously opposed any concession toward autonomy in Kashmir. Their argument has been that such a move poses a threat to the territorial integrity of the nation, but their constituents' pervasive hostility toward Muslims has weighed at least equally in the balance. Girilal Jain, a well-known newspaper editor, has cogently argued that Nehru and Western-educated elites in India accepted the territorial argument because they knew how deeply religious sentiments run in Indian life. The continued Indian presence in Kashmir has been defended in terms of national integrity because the political elite has not been ready to acknowledge how integral to national life Hinduism is. Thus, defense of India's claims for Kashmir on political grounds has served as a "substitute for Hindu cultural self-assertion."[82] Those committed Hindu groups who equate making concessions to the Kashmiris with being antinational will make interfaith dialogue on Kashmir more difficult. Nonetheless, it is essential that they be represented from the outset in such a dialogue, along with representatives of groups that differ sharply from them.

In Pakistan, there is a somewhat analogous situation. There, the Jama'at-i-Islami, the organization that claims to speak for authentic Islam in the national context of Pakistan, is utterly opposed to the official Indian position that Kashmir is an integral part of India. For the Jama'at, the struggle in Kashmir is indeed a jihad in line with the classical struggle to defend believers against unbelievers. While it has not been successful in winning seats in electoral politics, the Jama'at has succeeded in making Islam a subject of intense debate so that no party, including the military, can ignore its religious influence with students and the lower and middle classes. A careful student of the movement has summarized its position in Pakistan succinctly and accurately: "the numbers do not undermine the argument that the Jama'at has emerged as a powerful force through the use of emotive symbols and slogans, discipline, hard work, and the use of violence."[83] Those who would support a genuine process of dialogue over Kashmir, that is, for a process that might move toward a solution radically different from that supported by the Jama'at, would find strident opposition from this group. Prospective supporters for dialogue are more likely to be found in the beleaguered human rights groups and among those individuals—principally journalists, academicians, and lawyers—who espouse a modernist version of Islam.

In Kashmir itself, the Jama'at has been consistent in its support of militant leaders, whether they are native Kashmiris or foreigners supported by Pakistan, who insist that the whole of the former state of Jammu and Kashmir belongs to Pakistan, not because it has any territorial claim but because it is the rightful home of Muslims, especially those oppressed by unbelievers. This is almost certainly not the position of the majority of Kashmiri Muslims, according to most observers, including Indian journalists and scholars.

The task of those seeking dialogue will be to identify responsible religious groups who have the courage to take the initiative. This will require uncommon courage, for such leaders will be targeted for assassination by groups hostile to peace. One person frequently mentioned who might play such a role is the young Mirwaiz Maulvi Umar Farooq, who holds a special position in Kashmir as a revered hereditary religious leader. His family claims descent from Sheikh Hamadani, the famous fourteenth-century Sufi who is credited with the conversion of Kashmir to Islam. In addition, there are many people of piety and learning who would be willing to enter into genuine dialogue if it seemed to promise peace.

However, genuine dialogue can only begin when one starts with a recognition that compromise, coexistence, and mutual respect are fundamental; and this is the arena where religions can make a real contribution to peace. There are many commonalities where a basis for dialogue can be found, but there are three that offer particular hope. Two are concepts that have immediate practical ramifications, and the third relates to the way religion finds personal and social expression.

The first of the concepts is truth. This refers to an objective understanding of reality and how it is apprehended. The second is the term "dharma," or ethical behavior, from the Hindu tradition. The third is the devotional or mystical expression of religion, as found in Sufism in Islam and Bhakti in Hinduism. All three cause dynamic tension both within their own faith communities and in relation to outside groups, but all three to one extent or another will be fundamental to any genuine dialogue where participants can listen to one another and respond with authenticity. Before this can occur, however, each faith tradition must accept the fact that the others hold fundamental positions that are antithetical to their own. This is one of the greatest hurdles the religions of the Indian subcontinent will have to overcome as they seek to promote dialogue between warring secular groups, who will only be too quick to say, "Physician, heal thyself." Listening, learning, and accommodating are attitudes now sadly lacking in all of the religious groups concerned with Kashmir. However, at the same time, there are values and beliefs in each of these religions that can be brought into play.

While stressing the concept of truth as one of the fundamental values of the religions of South Asia that can undergird the search for peace, one must recognize that a dialogue must first occur between religions on what is meant by truth. A concept of truth is surely a fundamental feature of any religious system, and it is on this point that those who speak for Hinduism at the present differ most sharply from those who speak from within Islam, Christianity, or Judaism. One Hindu view, usually attributed to Ram Mohan Roy (c. 1774–1833), is that all religions have a common core of truth that can be discovered by diligent searchers who are willing to discard distortions, accretions, and corruptions that have crept into all religions through the centuries. Swami Vivekananda (1863–1902), in his famous speech to the World Parliament of Religions in 1893, went even further when he declared that all religions are true and that such aspects of Hinduism as the worship of idols and the caste system were good for those who need them. Here he was echoing his master, Ramakrishna, who said that people like Roy wanted to hear only one note of music when they could be listening to many notes, "producing a sweet and melodious harmony."[84] This understanding of truth in modern Hinduism has been aptly summarized by the Hindu scholar Arvind Sharma: "All the various religious forms represent diverse paths to the one Truth, paths that are all in some degree valid."[85]

This irenic reading of Hinduism would seem to be the most suitable meeting place with the other religious traditions that constitute India's diversity, but in practice it is working out very differently. The declaration that all religions are true has become a dogmatic statement that condemns as bigots those religions of India, notably Islam and Christianity, that make universal claims for what they regard as their core truth. As noted earlier, Hindu nationalism condemns Islam and Christianity as antinational religions that in their claims for truth deny the truth of Hinduism, the true expression of Indian culture. Another response has been to attack Christians for their activity in seeking converts; such attacks have often taken the form of church burnings and attacks on pastors. The pope has also been a special target, not just by Hindu nationalists but by some liberal secularists, because of statements he made on a visit to India to the effect that he prayed for the conversion of all Asia. The astonishing fact was not so much the venom of the attacks but that anyone was surprised that the pope believed that his church possessed the keys of the kingdom. The issue was succinctly expressed by a revered Indian religious figure, Sant Shri Aasaramji Bapu, when he said: "Conversion is wrong and should be stopped."[86] Another famous Hindu leader, Sri Mata Amritanandmayi, or "Amma," made a touching plea for peace and social justice at the Millennium World Peace Summit but stressed that it was harmful to think of religions as having different understandings of truth.[87]

An argument for the possibility of dialogue between religious groups with strong, differing beliefs was given eloquent expression by a Jewish leader speaking of dialogue with Christians. Noting irreconcilable theological differences between Jews and Christians, the statement stresses that dialogue must motivate one "to think someone else's thoughts and to feel someone else's feelings." It ended by noting that when the differences between the faiths were recognized, understood, and accepted as not subject to change, people could then work together against war, persecution, poverty, human degradation, and misery.[88] With some such understanding of the irreconcilable interpretations of truth by Hindus, Muslims, and Christians, it would be possible for the faith communities to draw on their spiritual resources to seek peace in Kashmir. They could become, in the words of the poet, "watchers of divine grace" to heal the wounds of the Valley.

The second area of commonality between the great religions of the subcontinent is ethical behavior, subsumed in Hinduism under the term "dharma" and in Islam under God's law for humankind. According to an ancient scripture, dharma, which has been translated as duty, law, obligation, proper action, and right behavior, "is the foundation of the whole universe."[89] This surely is in keeping with Islamic conceptions of the good life, although Muslims would phrase this as obedience to God's will or obeying his law. Law in this sense includes the law administered by the ruler and the courts, as well as all moral action.

Dialogue on what dharma and God's law means for Kashmir would not be easy, but it could signal a new beginning to the end of violence. Would it be conceivable, however, to think of a dialogue on the meaning of dharma and Islamic law and ethics that included representation from India, Pakistan, and Kashmir? The great problem here is the relationship of Hinduism and Islam with the states in which they are situated, for it is difficult in either country for religious groups effectively to oppose the government. But what about the huge Muslim population of India? This, one would suppose, would have a decisive voice in any dialogue on Kashmir. However, the position of Muslims in India, especially now with the rising tide of Hindu nationalism, is such that it is unlikely that they can take any position that will seem to be critical of the government's actions in Kashmir.

In January 1948, when the Kashmir crisis was just beginning, there was a meeting of the All-India Muslim Conference. Deputy Prime Minister Sardar Patel, who was widely regarded as pro-Hindu and anti-Muslim, asked the delegates: "Why did you not open your mouth on the Kashmir issue?" He meant by this that he was disappointed they did not lend their support to the Indian position against Pakistan. According to A. G. Noorani, an eminent constitutional lawyer and political commentator, Indian Muslims got the point: "Repeated and vehement declaration of support for government policies on Kashmir and other issues has been regarded as a test of their loyalty." To do otherwise leads Muslims to being denounced as antinational and pro-Pakistan. However, as Noorani argues, if Muslims are to play a role in national life, they must be willing to join with Hindus of vision and goodwill and show that "India, democratic and secular, is more than a country worth living *in*. It is a country worth living *for*."[90] It would be a difficult task for Muslim religious leaders to join with their Hindu counterparts to demand that the Indian government enter into sincere dialogue with the militants and Pakistan. This dialogue would most certainly have to include the most prominent Hindu leaders of the VHP, the Divine Life Society, the Chinmaya Mission, and the Ramakrishna Mission if true progress is to be made.

The active involvement of Indian Muslims advocated by leaders like Noorani, however, does not have the unqualified approval of other Muslim leaders. Maulana Wahid Khan, of the Islamic Centre in New Delhi, has had considerable influence on Indian Muslims because of his piety and learning. He is also well regarded in the Hindu community as a moderate voice. When asked what he thought could be done to bring peace to Kashmir, his answer was that peace had a price that people were not willing to pay. That price, according to Islam, was an acceptance of the status quo. His argument for this surprising answer was that changing the status quo, as people of all factions were attempting to do in Kashmir, would lead inevitably to violence. As a self-proclaimed Islamic state, Pakistan had only two options: one was to accept the decision made by the Kashmir maharaja and the second was to declare war on India to rescue the Muslims from the control of the Hindus. The kind of proxy war it was fighting in Kashmir was not an acceptable option in Islam, he insists, and the militants had no right to make war, for the waging of war was a prerogative of the state alone. Gandhi's method of showing resentment through nonviolence was, however, within Qur'anic ordinances.

On one level, this form of Islamic social quietism may point the way toward peace in Kashmir. It may also be an example of what a Muslim journalist diagnoses as an absence of self-confidence that leads the Indian Muslim to retreat into "sullen isolationism which breeds its own tendency towards confrontation with the majority community."[91]

In Pakistan, the situation for Muslim leaders is very different. They have frequently been in the forefront in condemning the government for following policies that were against Islamic law. Unfortunately, there does not seem to be any evidence of the ulama critiquing the government's involvement in Kashmir except for denouncing it for not giving more support to the militants.[92] This is not, however, the whole story, for there are courageous individuals like Asma Jahangir, the prominent civil rights lawyer, who has argued that one of the great needs of Pakistan is to end the intrusion of religion into politics.[93]

The area where the two great religions of the subcontinent might meet in genuine dialogue is through the great forms of devotional religion, Bhakti in Hinduism and Sufism in Islam. Both in the past were prominent in Kashmir and continue to remain so. There is a large and controversial literature on the commonalities of these two forms of religious expression with one another and with mysticism in general; and some attempts to find common historical origins have, unfortunately, not helped the cause of dialogue even when they were intended to be irenic.[94] While Bhakti and Sufism share an emphasis on the search for unity with the divine, the respective understandings of Ultimate Reality in Hinduism and Islam are so different as to make difficult the kind of dialogue envisioned here. However, Bhakti and Sufism can find common ground in their mutual practice of seeking a personal and emotional relationship with the divine.

A modern scholar of Sufism has argued, with copious citations from their writings, that the Sufis directed their attention toward the creation of a social order free from dissension and conflict. He relates that "in love, faith, toleration and sympathy, they found the supreme talisman of human happiness."[95] While this is a reading of history by a believer deeply committed to the idea that the spirit of Sufism has worked throughout history to heal the divisions between Hinduism and Islam, it finds confirmation in current practice, as well as in the vast corpus of Sufi and Bhakti literature.

Bhakti found its most notable expression in the songs of poets who expressed the love they felt for the deity whom they worshiped and from whom they received the joy of personal communion. This poetry speaks of "the trials of life in society, the hollow shell of the body, friendship, betrayal, beauty, birth, death, and the pains and exaltations of love."[96] Many of these poet-saints, as they are often called, were women. One of these was Lalla (c. 1335–c. 1376), a Kashmiri Brahman who had a profound influence on both the Bhakti and Sufi traditions and demonstrated through her teachings ways in which they could be brought together. For example, she once said that "a real man is he who fears God, and there are not many such men about." However, when she met the Muslim saint Sayyid Ali Hamadani, she exclaimed, "I have met a man, I have met a man." In turn, a Muslim saint-poet, Sheikh Nur-ud-din (1377–1438), exclaimed, "That Lalla—She was indeed an avatar of ours. O God, grant me the self-same boon."[97] Her poetry exemplifies an important function of the Bhakti tradition: through a devotion to one's Lord that renounced all other loyalties, one could inwardly defy many of the conventions of caste, class, and gender, while outwardly conforming to them. Some of the poet-saints were from the lowest castes, suggesting that Bhakti provided a safety valve for the frustrations and restrictions that society imposed and made it possible for people to accept the insights of other traditions.

A sympathetic Indian Muslim scholar, Rasheeduddin Khan, speaks for many interpreters of Sufism and Bhakti when he insists that both traditions emphasize love, tolerance, and accommodation as the essence of the good and enlightened person.[98] He argues that the Sufi saints were popular heroes who fraternized with different communities, upheld the rights of the common man and woman, and actively dissented against the tyranny of the sultans and feudal aristocracy. One Sufi, Shaikh Abdul Quddus (d.1537), asked a question that is peculiarly relevant for the search for dialogue: "Why this meaningless talk about the believer, the Kafir, the obedient, the rightly guided, the misdirected, the Muslim, the pious, the infidel, the fire worshipper? All are like beads in a rosary."[99]

Kabir, another poet-saint mentioned earlier who lived in the fifteenth century, has been claimed by both Hindus and Muslims—the former as a follower of Bhakti and the latter as a Sufi. In modern times, both have argued that Kabir's life and work demonstrate the unity of the two great Indian faiths in their common emphasis on devotional religion. There are pitfalls, however, of which one must be aware before claiming Kabir as an early apostle of Hindu-Muslim unity. In his teachings, Kabir specifically denies the truth of either Hinduism or Islam: in his view, both are radically false in their theological statements and in their social practice. In his own time, there was plenty of evidence of the narrow-minded intolerance that, in his understanding, characterized both religions. He was asserting, as many of the great saints of the Sufi and Bhakti traditions did, that the truth was beyond both religious creeds; or as a modern commentator puts it, the only poems suggesting all religions are the same are those in which "they are denigrated in the same breath," as when he declares:

> If the mosque is the place where god resides,
> Then who owns the rest of the land?
> Ram lives in images and holy locations?—
>   Then why has no one ever found him there?
>   Hindus, Muslims—where did they come from?
>   Who got them started down this road?[100]

Ultimately, he insisted that both Hinduism and Islam expressed themselves in belief systems and ritual practices that divided them and which often led to violence against one another and their own coreligionists. This is a reminder that Hinduism and Islam, in all their diversities, are the keys to both violence and peace in the Indian subcontinent. In one of his poems, Kabir tells of his fruitless attempt to get people to understand that the "pious Hindus, rule-followers," and the Muslim teachers, "reading their books and teaching their pupils techniques," know nothing of the Truth:

> They are all deluded!
> Whatever I say, nobody gets it.
> It's too simple.[101]

In making such claims, the great poet-saints of the Bhakti and Sufi traditions proclaim a message of universalism that cuts across the boundaries of nationalism, caste, religion, and gender. While the influence of Bhakti devotionalism on the development of Sufism is not clear, it is reasonably certain that the Sufis played a major role in the acceptance of Islam by many Hindus. Especially in Kashmir, devotional religion was a synthesis of Hindu mysticism, grounded in the unique developments that had taken place there of Saivism (Bhakti worship of the Hindu deity Siva), Buddhist influence, and Sufism.[102] According to Kashmiri Muslims, the reality of kashmiriyat is rooted in Sufism, and it is this grounding that makes the political struggle worth the effort.

Historically, Islam in Kashmir, at least in its Sufi form, is for the most part far from strict orthodoxy. This is illustrated by the story of the Timurid prince Mirza Haidar Dughlat, who invaded Kashmir in 1541 and found that the people, although nominally Muslim, were heretics. "Many of the people of Kashmir," he wrote, "I brought back to the true faith whether they willed it or not, and many I slew. A number took refuge in Sufism, but were not true Sufis."[103] Obviously, there was no dialogue based on the commonalities of Bhakti and Sufism in 1541. These commonalities of Bhakti and Sufism nonetheless offer the potential for a dialogue that might lead, along with the application of other religious resources, to healing and reconciliation in Kashmir at the beginning of the twenty-first century.

To continue a metaphor used earlier, the detours taken in the five sections of this chapter were largely journeys through the past. In the language of the poem *Firdaus in Flames*, quoted at the beginning of this chapter, the past has been consumed by the present. The challenge now is to promote dialogue by commandeering the peacemaking tenets of the religions of South Asia.

In light of the preceding discussion, two questions remain. First, how will the process of dialogue begin? It would be presumptuous for an outsider to suggest a method, a timetable, or an agenda beyond the reiterated insistence on a dialogue in Buber's sense. It is quite conceivable that the Indians with their great military superiority could, as the ancient Briton said of the Roman invasion of his land, "make the world a desert and call it peace"; but there is, happily, evidence that this approach has repelled many Indians. Will dialogue begin with a meeting of individuals, known for their piety, learning, and dedication, who are committed to finding a way to peace in

Kashmir? Will they then move out to reach ordinary believers to constitute a grass-roots movement? Srivatsava Goswami, an erudite, urbane scholar whose family supports a vibrant Krishna temple in Vrindaban, argues rather persuasively that religious leaders must carry on a dialogue with civil society about such issues as Kashmir. He adamantly holds that good leadership, not a grass-roots movement, is the key to dialogue.[104] Such leadership is a feature of both Hinduism and Islam, religions in which charismatic figures have revitalized both communities, often through the marriage of politics and religion.[105] High-quality leadership is, of course, a need in all movements, but in India there is always the memory of Gandhi as the leader who combined total religious commitment with continuous dialogue with the civil authorities. While there do not appear to be any Gandhis on the horizon in India, Kashmir, or Pakistan, his example remains available for all.

Within Islam, leaders who combined religious commitment with political success were less prominent on the all-India scene than were their Hindu counterparts; for Jinnah and other Muslim leaders of the Pakistan movement were not committed to a personal religious vision of a good society as was Gandhi. There were, however, modern charismatic Muslim leaders who had considerable effect on a smaller canvas, notably leaders of the Tablighi Jama'at, a movement that revitalized large segments of Islamic life through "articulating goals and utilizing modes of argumentation from within the historic tradition."[106] However, this movement deliberately withdrew from political activity. The other great Islamic movement, the Jama'at-i-Islami, has actively opposed many of the peace initiatives made so far by the Indian government and groups of Kashmiri militants.

Two recent academic studies, although having little direct reference to core religious values, indicate how faith communities interacting with civic life can help facilitate the healing process in communal conflicts. One of the studies was conducted after the author had been overwhelmed by the emotional intensity he encountered while studying the violence in Kashmir. This led him to ask why there were few outbreaks of violence in some Indian cities while in others it had been endemic. He concluded that a key factor in determining whether or not Hindus and Muslims would live together peacefully relates to the existence or absence of civic associations in which members of both communities are active participants. This associational contact was far more important than the mere fact of members of both faith communities living in the same locality but without such relationships.[107]

The second study looked at the presence or absence of violence in a number of princely states, and came to a different, but somewhat similar, conclusion. What was important, the study found, was that areas were peaceful where there was a strong communal culture, either Hindu or Muslim, that privileged one community with dominant political and social power but where the other community, even if it was in the numerical majority, did not provoke communal confrontation.[108] Both of these studies have peculiar relevance for Kashmir where political and other forms of power before 1947 had been largely in Hindu hands, but where there had been significant associational connection between the communities. This gradually broke down by 1989, giving way to violence on the part of both the militant Kashmiris and the Indian security forces.

What the scholars were saying in 2002, Mahatma Gandhi had said in a different idiom in 1920 when he remarked that politics were encircling Indian society like the coil of a snake, crushing its life. In order to wrestle with that snake, he had been experimenting, he explained, by introducing religion into politics. What he had in mind was, on one level, associational actions, dramatically exemplified by his support for the Khilafat movement, the struggle by Muslims in India to oppose the British actions against the Ottoman Empire at the end of the First World War. On another level, he sought to bring religion into politics through grounding political action in what he regarded as the fundamental values of the Hindu tradition, namely truth, nonviolence or *Ahimsa,* and *Dharma* or social action. Incorporation in the political process of these three religious values coupled with associational civic relationships could set the stage for the kind of dialogue that is so desperately needed for peacemaking and peacekeeping in Kashmir.

The second question left to be answered is also problematic: May there emerge as part of the peace process a place for individuals and groups from outside the national boundaries of the countries involved in the conflict? This an issue of great sensitivity in India, where any kind of foreign interest or involvement in the Kashmir issue has been discouraged by the government and treated in the media as a meddling in India's internal affairs. This has been true for such human rights groups as U.S.-based Amnesty International and Human Rights Watch. This has not been the case in Pakistan or Kashmir, where such groups, rightly or wrongly, are seen as sympathetic to the Kashmir cause. India, along with China and Indonesia, has been vigorous in insisting that different cultures have their own views of human rights that are not always consonant with those of the West. The role of international faith communities in India is related to this controversy over the universality of values. This has been dramatized in recent years by hostility toward Christians as well as toward Muslims on the grounds that they represent a foreign intrusion. This was also true, as noted earlier, in the extraordinary furor created by the pope's visit to India in 1999.

The role of international faith communities in the Kashmir dispute relates to an issue that will be of increasing importance in the future, namely, the right of humanitarian intervention by governments in the internal affairs of other states when there have been gross human rights abuses. Beyond the concern of nations not to trespass on the sovereignty of other nations, many faith communities will insist on the moral right of human beings everywhere to be concerned with the plight of other humans irrespective of national boundaries. Any dialogue on Kashmir will have to give serious attention to these issues, for as a careful study by the Council on Foreign Relations pointed out, the very concept of intervention on humanitarian grounds "is simultaneously an appeal to conscience and a caution to judgment."[109]

After fifty-two years, Kashmir is still the stubborn reality in determining relations between India and Pakistan. When India went to the UN Security Council with a complaint against Pakistan in January of 1948, they charged that nationals of Pakistan were getting aid from the government of Pakistan in an invasion of Kashmir, which was part of India. If Pakistan did not stop this assistance, the government of India's representative warned, India might feel compelled to enter Pakistan to take military action against the invaders.[110] The United Nations sent various representatives to India and Pakistan hoping to prevent such an action, but they failed in the larger issue of finding a solution for a lasting peace. The words of one of the representatives, Frank Porter Graham, underline the crucial role that religion could play in solving the crisis:

> The light of faith and the fires of the inner spirit . . . were lighted
> among Asian, African and Mediterranean people for all peoples. . . .
> With their two-fold heritage of faith in the Moral Sovereignty, which
> undergirds the nature of man and the universe . . . these peoples may
> again give a fresh lift to the humane spirit of people everywhere.
> They might in these shadowed years transform with high faith and
> good will the potential forces of bitterness, hate and destruction . . .
> towards peace for all peoples on earth as the God-given home of the
> family of man.[111]

Graham, a wise, religious man, who was very experienced in the ways of the world, would have given a resoundingly affirmative answer to the vital question: Has religion a role in peacemaking?

Conclusion

Confronted by the brutal violence in Kashmir, one has to ask, in Graham's words, what are the lights of faith and the fires of the inner spirit within

Hinduism that can give religion a role in peacemaking in Kashmir? The primary burden is necessarily upon Hinduism, because it, in all of its complexity and contradictory varieties, defines the religious heritage of the vast majority of the billion people of India, the overwhelmingly dominant political, military, and economic power of South Asia. While all religious groups have contributions to make, Hindus as the dominant community need to facilitate the process.

Toward this end, Hindu leaders could initiate confidence-building measures to promote a faith-based dialogue with Pakistan and Kashmir. Celebrating the roles of Sufism and Bhakti, through honoring the people and places associated with their influence on kashmiriyat, would be one way to capitalize on the significant potential that these traditions have to offer for badly needed understanding and goodwill. Further, appealing to the shared values of the two religious movements in both official and unofficial discussions might create space for increased political maneuverability.

This is an arena in which nongovernmental organizations could make a significant contribution as well. For example, an NGO-inspired grass-roots faith-based reconciliation movement is currently gaining momentum in Kashmir.[112] This initiative, which focused first on young Kashmiri Muslim leaders, is now in the process of reconciling young Hindu and Muslim leaders with one another and, in turn, equipping them to do the same in their own communities. Providing political and financial support for the newly established Institute for Reconciliation in Srinagar, which serves as a resource for the movement, would also be a helpful contribution.

In addition, Hindu leaders should encourage intercommunal participation in governmental and nongovernmental civic associations, thereby strengthening frayed communal bonds. By the same token, leaders of all faiths need to seek common social goals that are consonant with their respective core values.

If the dispute over Kashmir is to be resolved, increased space for dialogue and political maneuverability between the parties will be essential. It is only through such dialogue that one will be able to develop the kind of trust needed to facilitate a breakthrough. Hinduism can make a real contribution in this regard. Indeed, the progress to date in developing faith-based reconciliation in Kashmir suggests that religion may in fact be the untried key that unlocks the door to peace.

NOTES

1. I am grateful to the members of the seminar on December 12, 2000, at the International Center for Religion and Diplomacy, all of whom contributed helpful comments on the original essay. I have corrected factual errors and taken into account

questions that were raised about my interpretations and opinions. None of these persons are responsible for any remaining errors or for the opinions with which they disagree. In addition to those who were present, Walter Andersen of the State Department generously provided written comments that were extremely helpful.

2. Douglas Johnston, "Religion and Culture: Human Dimensions of Globalization," in *The Global Century: Globalization and National Security*, ed. by Richard L. Kugler and Ellen L. Frost, 2 vols. (Washington, D.C.: National Defense University Press, 2001), p. 667.

3. Ainslie T. Embree, *Utopias in Conflict: Religion and Nationalism in Modern India* (Berkeley: University of California Press, 1990), pp. x–xi.

4. Embree, *Utopias in Conflict*, 132.

5. H. K. Kaul, *Firdaus in Flames* (New Delhi: Virgo, 1995), pp. 11, 173.

6. Moonis Raza et al., *The Valley of Kashmir: A Geographical Interpretation* (Durham, N.C.: Carolina Academic Press, 1978), vol. 1, p. ix.

7. Riyaz Panjabi, "Kashmir: The Bruised Identity," in *Perspectives on Kashmir: The Roots of Conflict in South Asia*, ed. by Raju G. C. Thomas (Boulder, Colo.: Westview Press, 1992), p 132.

8. For the controversy surrounding the legality of the accession, see Alastair Lamb, *Kashmir: A Disputed Legacy, 1846–1990* (Karachi: Oxford University Press, 1993), pp. 121–45 and Prem Shankar Jha, *Kashmir, 1947: Rival Versions of History* (Delhi: Oxford University Press, 1998), pp. 1–10.

9. Barry Bearak, "Kashmir: Lethal Decade," *New York Times*, Sept. 7, 2000, p. A6, "World Briefing."

10. Quoted in Lewis Simons, "Kashmir: Trapped in Conflict," *National Geographic*, August 1999, p. 3.

11. Judith Miller, "A Nuclear War Feared Possible over Kashmir," *New York Times*, August 8, 2000, p. 1.

12. Bhakti, which stems from the earliest Hindu scriptures, finds expression in an adherent's intimate relationship with God, who is predominantly worshiped as Vishnu or Shiva. Finding its basis in the Qur'an and *hadith* (sayings of the Prophet), Sufism emphasizes the unity of Allah and the relationship of love that exists between the believer and Allah, among other tenets.

13. "Era Waning, Holbrooke Takes Stock," *New York Times*, January 14, 2001, p. 8.

14. Sir Muhammad Iqbal, "Presidential Address" (All-India Muslim League, 1930), in *Speeches and Statements of Iqbal* (Lahore: Al-Manar Academy, 1948), pp. 3–36.

15. Ahmad, Jamil-ud-din Ahmed, ed., *Some Recent Speeches and Writings of Mr. Jinnah* (Lahore, India: M. Ashraf, 1946–47), vol. 1, p. 180.

16. Quoted in M. K. Sankhdher, ed., *Secularism in India: Dilemmas and Challenges* (New Delhi: Deep and Deep, 1922), p. 3.

17. Jawaharlal Nehru, *Independence and After* (New York: John Day, 1950), pp. 122.

18. Quoted in Mushirul Hasan, *Nationalism and Communal Politics in India, 1885–1930* (New Delhi: Manohar, 1991), p. 253.

19. M. K. Gandhi, *The Collected Works of Mahatma Gandhi* (New Delhi: Publications Division, Ministry of Information, Government of India, 1960), 59:401.

20. Muchkund Dubey, ed., *Communal Revivalism in India: A Study of External Implications* (New Delhi: Har-Anand, 1994), pp. 9–23.

21. Quoted in Granville Austin, *Working a Democratic Constitution: The Indian Experience* (New Delhi: Oxford University Press, 2000), pp. 557–58.

22. Ibid.

23. Peter van der Veer, *Religious Nationalism* (New Delhi: Oxford University Press, 1996), pp. 11.

24. There is a large literature on Hindu nationalism, among the most useful recent works are G. Aloysius, *Nationalism without a Nation in India* (New Delhi: Oxford University press, 2000); Christophe Jaffrelot, *The Hindu Nationalist Movement in Indian Politics, 1925 to the 1990s* (London: Hurst, Company, 1993); Peter van der Veer, *Religious Nationalism: Hindus and Muslims in India* (New Delhi: Oxford University Press, 2000); and John Zavos, *The Emergence of Hindu Nationalism in India* (New Delhi: Oxford University Press, 2000). Donald Eugene Smith, *India as a Secular State* (Princeton: Princeton University Press, 1963), remains the seminal work.

25. G. Aloysius, *Nationalism without a Nation in India*, p. 14.

26. Walter Andersen and Shridhar D. Damle, *The Saffron Brotherhood: The Rashtriya Swayamsevak Sangh and Hindu Revivalism* (Boulder, Colo.: Westview Press, 1987), is the most authoritative guide to the RSS.

27. V. D. Savarkar, *Hindutva: Who Is a Hindu?* (Bombay: Veer Savarkar Prakashan, 1969; 1 ed. 1923).

28. Quoted in Ainslie T. Embree, "The Function of the Rashtriya Swayamsewak Sangh: To Define the Hindu Nation," in *Accounting for Fundamentalisms*, ed. by Martin E. Marty and R. Scott Appleby (Chicago: University of Chicago Press, 1994), 619.

29. Ibid., p. 630.

30. M. S. Gowalkar, *We, or Our Nation Defined* (Nagpur, India: Bharat Prakashan, 1938), p 53.

31. Asghar Ali Engineer, *Secular Crown on Fire: The Kashmir Problem* (Delhi: Ajanta Publications, 1991).

32. Lisa McKean, *Divine Enterprise* (Chicago: University of Chicago Press, 1996), p. 26.

33. Arun Shourie, *Indian Controversies: Essays on Religion in Politics* (New Delhi: ASA, 1993), pp. 465–66.

34. Mark Twain, *Following the Equator* (New York: Dover, 1989), pp. 347–48.

35. Basavanna, in *Speaking of Shiva*, trans. by A. K. Ramanujan (Baltimore: Penguin, 1973), p. 84, and Kabir, *The Bijak of Kabir*, trans. by Linda Hess and Shukdev Singh (Berkeley: North Point Press, 1983), sabda 4.

36. David M. Knipe, *Hinduism: Experiences in the Sacred* (New York: HarperCollins, 1991), p. 2.

37. Charles F. Keyes, "The Study of the Popular Ideas of Karma," in *Karma: An Anthropological Inquiry*, ed. by Charles F. Keyes and E. Valentine Daniel (Berkeley: University of California Press, 1983), p. 3.

38. Quoted in Stanley Heginbotham, *Cultures in Conflict: Four Faces of Indian Bureaucracy* (New York: Columbia University Press, 1975), p. 50.

39. Bhakti and Sufism are discussed further hereafter.

40. H. M. Naqvi, *Agricultural, Industrial and Urban Dynamism under the Sultans of Delhi, 1206–1555* (New Delhi: Munshiram Manhorlal, 1986), p. 132.

41. Jessica Stern, "Pakistan's Jihad Culture," *Foreign Affairs* 79, no. 6 (November/December 2000), pp. 115–126.

42. Rudolph Peters, "Jihad," in *The Encyclopedia of Religion* (New York: Macmillan, 1987), pp. 88–91.

43. K. G. Saiyidain, *Islam, the Religion of Peace* (New Delhi: Islam and the Modern Age Society, 1976), p. 162.

44. Personal interview with interviewees who asked that their names not be used, Muzaffarabad, Azad Kashmir, August 12–13, 1998.

45. "India and Russia Agree to Create Strategic Alliance," *Washington Post,* October 4, 2000, p. A25.

46. "Israel Assesses Kashmir's Security Needs," *News India-Times* (New York), September 29, 2000, p. 1.

47. T. N. Madan, *Modern Myths, Locked Minds: Secularism and Fundamentalism in India* (Delhi: Oxford University Press, 1997), p. 273.

48. Luke Harding, "Kashmir Massacres," *Guardian (Manchester)*, August 3, 2000, p. 1.

49. Barry Bearak, "Massacres in Kashmir May Be Effort to Sabotage Peace Initiative," *New York Times*, August 3, 2000, p. A10.

50. Praveen Swami, "The Massacre at Chattisinghpora," *Frontline* (Chennai), April 14, 2000, p. 29.

51. "Peace in Kahsmir," editorial, *Herald* (Karachi), August 20, 2000, pp. 24–28.

52. Balraj Puri, "Alternatives to Violence in Kashmir," Commentary, *Economic and Political Weekly*, May 13–19, 2000, p. 1.

53. Swami, "The Massacre at Chattisinghpora," The name of the village is sometimes spelled Chitisinghpura.

54. For a detailed account by an American journalist, from a different point of view, see Barry Bearak, "A Kashmiri Mystery," *New York Times Magazine*, December 31, 2000, pp. 26–31.

55. C. U. Aitchison, *A Collection of Treaties, Engagements and Sanads* (Calcutta: Superintendent of Government Printing, 1892–93), 12:21:22.

56. Quoted in Victoria Schofield, *Kashmir in the Crossfire* (New Delhi: Viva Books, 1997) p. 49.

57. Sheikh Abdullah, *Flames of the Chinar: An Autobiography*, abridged from the Urdu by Khushwant Singh (New Delhi: Penguin, 1993), pp. 12–13.

58. Sir Albion Banerji, quoted in Schofield, *Kashmir in the Crossfire*, p. 100.

59. The events surrounding the migration of the Pandits from the Valley is one of the most controversial aspects of the Kashmir conflict. I am grateful for the detailed comments from others with opposing viewpoints, not only on this issue but also on all of the major problems. I especially thank Dr. Vijay K. Sazawal, the international coordinator of the Indo-Kashmiri Forum, who believes that the Pandits have been treated badly, and Dr. Ghulam Nabi Fai, executive director of the Kashmiri-American Council, who sees the Indian government as encouraging the exodus.

60. Pankaj Mishra, "Kashmir: The Unending War," *New York Review of Books*, October 19, 2000, p. 27.

61. Ainslie T. Embree, *India's Search for National Identity* (New York: Knopf, 1972), pp. 3–20.

62. Sisir Gupta, *Kashmir: A Study in India-Pakistan Relations* (New York: Asia, 1966), pp. 146–47.

63. Interviews with young Kashmiris in Azad Kashmir, August 12–13, 1998, and in Srinagar, August 15–20, 2000.

64. Personal interview with Nayeem Khan, Srinagar, August 20, 2000.

65. Gandhi, *Collected Works*, 35:294.

66. Quoted in M. H. Halperin and D. J. Scheffer, *Self-Determination in the New World Order* (Washington, D.C.: Carnegie Endowment, 1992), p. 17.

67. Mark Juergensmeyer. *The New Cold War: Religious Nationalism Confronts the Secular State* (Berkeley: University of California Press, 1993), pp. 33, and *Terror in the Mind of God: The Global Rise of Religious Violence* (Berkeley: University of California Press, 2000), p. 90.

68. Douglas Johnston, Jr., "Beyond Power Politics," pp. 5–6, and Harvey Cox et al., "World Religions and Conflict Resolution," in Johnston and Sampson, *Religion: the Missing Dimension of Statecraft*, pp. 266–81.

69. Judith M. Brown, *Gandhi: Prisoner of Hope* (New Haven: Yale University Press, 1989), pp. 320–21.

70. Quoted in Christian Bartoff, ed., *The Breath of My Life* (Berlin: Gandhi Information Centrum, 2000), pp. 26–29.

71. Quoted in ibid., p. 375.

72. Daniel Yankelovich, *The Magic Dialogue: Transforming Conflict into Cooperation* (New York: Simon and Schuster, 1999), pp. 14–15.

73. Kashmir Study Group, "The Kashmir Dispute at Fifty: Charting Paths to Peace," and "Kashmir: A Way Forward" (privately published, 1997–99).

74. Yankelovich, *Magic of Dialogue*, pp. 43–46.

75. *Times of India*, August 18, 2000, p. 1.

76. Syed Tassadque Hussain, "The Death of an Inchoate Dialogue," *Kashmir Times*, August 24, 2000.

77. Yankelovich, *Magic of Dialogue*, p. 44.

78. D. R. Goyal, "RSS-BJP Cold War," *Nation and the World* (New Delhi), September 1, 2000.

79. Professor J. E. Llewellyn of Southwest Missouri State University, in an as yet unpublished manuscript entitled "Festival of Discord: The 1998 Kumbh Mela in Hardwar" has given a lively and authoritative account of the rivalries among Hindu religious specialists.

80. M. I. Khan, "Puri Shankaracharya To Expose False Godmen,"; on-line, available at: *www.rediff.com*, July 6, 2000.

81. "Puri Seership Claimant Held," *Statesman Weekly*, Calcutta, July 22, 2000, p. 3.

82. Girilal Jain, "Secularism and Nehruism," in *Secularism in India: Dilemmas and Challenges* (New Delhi: Deep and Deep, 1992), p. 130.

83. Raffiuddin Ahmed, "Redefining Muslim Identity in South Asia," in Marty and Appleby, *Accounting for Fundamentalisms*, p. 699.

84. Stephen Hay, ed., *Sources of Indian Tradition*, vol. 2 (New York: Columbia University Press, 1988), pp. 23, 74, 71.

85. Arvind Sharma, "World Religions and Conflict Resolution," in Johnston and Sampson, *Religion, the Missing Dimension of Statecraft*, p. 270.

86. "Fanaticism Is Not Taught by Any Religion," *Times of India*, August 29, 2000, p. 15.

87. "Destroy the Mind's Nuclear Weapons: Amma," *News India-Times*, September 29, 2000, p. 40.

88. Peter Steinfels, "Beliefs," *New York Times*, September 23, 2000, p. A13.

89. Ainslie T. Embree, ed., *Sources of Indian Tradition*, vol 1 (New York: Columbia University Press, 1988), p. 217.

90. A. G. Noorani, "The Indian Muslims," reprinted in *Mainstream* (New Delhi), April 20, 1991, pp. 15–17.

91. Saeed Naqvi, *Reflections of an Indian Muslim* (New Delhi: Har-Anand, 1993), pp. 50–51.

92. Personal interviews with interviewees who asked that their names not be used, Islamabad, May 6–18, 1997, and in Azad Kashmir, August 12–13, 1998.

93. Amitav Ghosh, *Countdown* (Delhi: Ravi Dayal, 1999), p. 72.

94. Aziz Ahmad, *Studies in Islamic Culture in the Indian Environment* (Oxford: Clarendon Press, 1964), pp. 119–39.

95. Kaliq Ahmad Nizami, "Impact of Sufi Saints on Indian Society and Culture," in *Contemporary Relevance of Sufism* (New Delhi: Indian Council for Cultural Relations, 1992), p. 140.

96. John Stratton Hawley and Mark Juergensmeyer, *Songs of the Saints of India* (New York: Oxford University Press, 1988).

97. Braj B. Kachru, *Kashmiri Literature* (Wiesbaden: Otto Harrasowitz, 1980), p. 17.

98. Rasheeduddin Khan, "The Contemporary Relevance of Sufism in Building the Composite Culture of India," in *Contemporary Relevance of Sufism* (New Delhi: Indian Council for Cultural Affairs, 1993), p. 210.

99. Quoted in Kaliq Ahmad Nizami, "Impact of Sufi Saints on Indian Society and Culture," *Contemporary Relevance of Sufism*, p. 143.

100. Hawley, *Songs of the Saints of India*, 41.

101. Kabir, *The Bijak of Kabir*, sabda 4.

102. Peer Giyasud-Din, *Kashmir: Islam, Ideology and Society* (Jammu Tawi: Jay Kay Book House, 1994), pp. 4–8.

103. Quoted in Annemarie Schimmel, *Islam in the Indian Subcontinent* (Leiden: Brill, 1980), p. 48.

104. Interview with Srivatsva Goswami, Vrindabhan, August 25, 2000.

105. Convincing evidence is found in Hay, *Sources of Indian Tradition*, vol. 2, chaps. 2–6.

106. Barbara Metcalfe, " 'Remaking Ourselves': Islamic Self-Fashioning in a Global Movement of Spiritual Renewal," in Marty and Appleby, *Accounting for Fundamentalisms*, pp. 706–07.

107. Ashutosh Varshney, *Ethnic Conflict in Civil Life: Hindus and Muslims in India* (New Haven: Yale University Press, 2002), pp. 3–5.

108. Ian Copland, "The Construction of Muslim Identities in Princely North India: From Pluralism to Communal Assertion," seminar at Southern Asian Institute, Columbia University, September 23, 2002.

109. *Humanitarian Intervention: Crafting a Workable Doctrine* (New York: Council on Foreign Relations, 2000), p. vi.

110. United Nations Security Council Official Records, S/628, January 1, 1948.

111. United Nations Commission on India and Pakistan Documents, S/3984, Sixth Report of Dr. Frank Porter Graham, March 31, 1958.

112. The International Center for Religion & Diplomacy in concert with the Srnigar-based Kashmir Foundation for Peace and Developmental Studies has facilitated this movement over the past two years.

Religion and Conflict
The Case of Buddhism in Sri Lanka

Sri Lanka, formerly known as Ceylon, gained its independence from Britain in 1948. However, political and economic tension soon developed between the majority Buddhist Sinhala and minority Hindu Tamil communities. In the face of an expanding Sinhala ethnic nationalism, Tamil groups initially expressed their grievances through legally constituted political channels. The nationalist government elected in 1956 designated Sinhala as the only official language and created a department of cultural affairs. These hegemonic policies were further solidified in the new constitution of 1972, which accorded priority to Buddhism. Friction between the Sinhala majority and those who had now become the Tamil separatists finally erupted in violence in the early 1980s. Tens of thousands have subsequently died in an ethnic war that was only recently brought under control through a Norwegian-brokered cease-fire. There have been other cease-fires in the past, and considerable obstacles remain before a final peace agreement will be reached.

Buddhism, like any other great religion, is not one but many things. Therefore, to understand what contribution, if any, Buddhism has made toward the conflict in Sri Lanka and might make toward its resolution, it is first necessary to indicate what kind of Buddhism is being evaluated. For the purposes of this chapter, and at the risk of some oversimplification, Buddhism can be usefully understood as falling into one of three categories: (1) textual Buddhism, (2) syncretistic Buddhism, and (3) modern Buddhism. This chapter briefly examines each of these areas with a view to determining their relation to the conflict.

Textual Buddhism

The term "textual Buddhism" refers to the core of Buddhist doctrine as depicted in Buddhist scriptures. Buddhism, like all other great religions, has evolved through the centuries, and in the process produced a textual corpus and an extensive commentarial literature. It should come as no surprise, then, that such a complex body of literature with its myriad interpreters should contain varied and sometimes contradictory ideas and interpretations. Despite this, the core of Buddhism is both clear and undisputed. It is the doctrine of the Four Noble Truths, namely, that there is a problem, it has a cause, there is a solution, and there is a path to that solution.

This is a universalist doctrine that defines the problem of existence in general human terms and makes a solution available to any who wish to subscribe to it. There are no chosen people or a concept of the elect in Buddhism. It makes no distinctions on the basis of race, ethnicity, color, gender, geographic location, or any other sectional or parochial criterion. Thus, in its infancy in India, Buddhism defied the existing caste system, claiming that it is not by birth but by action that one becomes a noble person.

In his typology of world religions, the sociologist Max Weber considered Buddhism an "other-worldly asceticism."[1] He emphasized its goal-oriented focus and the rational means for achieving said goals insofar as nothing else was valued. He described Buddhism as apolitical and anti-political and underlined its rationality by calling it not a religion but a religious technology. He emphasized the point further by associating Buddhism with a class that is considered to have a high propensity toward rationality, namely, the schooled mendicant monks. This rational otherworldly goal orientation was further expressed in Buddhism's devaluation, indeed amused denigration, of ritual, a denigration that some Buddhist writers perfected into an art form.

Among the great religions, Buddhism with its fundamentals of nonviolence, compassion, moderation, replacement of ritual with ethics, denial of any meaningful external mystical agency, and enthronement of human effort as the only path to liberation is arguably the most tolerant and pacifist. Buddhist monastic rules, which also constitute a blueprint for the ideal Buddhist secular society, emphasize the importance of consensus or concord as the basis for conducting collective business and for meaningful and disciplined social organization. From these and other characteristics listed earlier, it is clear that textual Buddhism is not a factor in the conflict in Sri Lanka.

Syncretistic Buddhism

"Syncretistic Buddhism," on the other hand, refers to the system of beliefs and practices that actually exist in Buddhist societies, which is quite different from the Buddhism of the texts. Empirically viewed, syncretistic Buddhism

is the particular adaptation of Buddhist ideas to the preexisting mystical beliefs of a given Buddhist society, producing a culturally based Buddhism
unique to each Buddhist society, whether it be Sri Lanka, Burma, Thailand,
Vietnam, Cambodia, or Tibet. Max Weber again provides another way of
looking at these particular cultural or syncretistic Buddhisms. According to
Weber, religion as a humanly meaningful cultural artifact must serve two
needs: first the spiritual and ethical needs of the elites, and second the emotional religiosity of the masses. Popular religiosity requires magic or a savior
for the amelioration of physical and psychic distress that people experience
in everyday living. As would be clear from the preceding discussion, neither
is available in textual Buddhism. So if Buddhism were to have mass appeal,
which it obviously does since it has spread throughout the length and breadth
of Asia, there is only one explanation: textual Buddhism has transformed
itself to a form that caters to the emotional religiosity of the masses.

To put the case differently, textual Buddhism makes an analysis of the
human condition and suggests a remedy. It is a remedy that places the burden
of an individual's salvation squarely upon the individual believer. There is
no savior; one has to tread the path of liberation oneself. This is a difficult
task that is unappealing to all except a minority of disciplined professionals
who are willing to devote themselves full-time to the arduous task of achieving the goal. In contrast to this, religious concerns for the vast majority
involve divine intercession in psychic and physical distress in this world and
the promise of heaven in the hereafter. Buddhism transformed itself to provide for these needs by syncretistically accepting the preexisting forms of
religious belief and practice or making compromises in other ways. Thus in
the syncretistic Buddhism of Sri Lanka, the Buddha, far from being human,
as he insisted he was, has been elevated to the status of a superdeity, literally
called "the god of the gods" (*devatideva*).

Sri Lankan syncretistic Buddhism consists of a "pantheon," headed by
the Buddha as "god of the gods," with a hierarchy of national, provincial,
and local gods, planetary deities, and various other types of mystical beings.
In creating this pantheon, the syncretistic Buddhism of Sri Lanka has appro-
priated major Hindu gods, as well as a variety of ritual procedures from
Hinduism, which is the religion of the Tamil minority of Sri Lanka. The
Hindus in general consider the Buddha to be an incarnation of Vishnu, one
of the principal gods of the Hindu pantheon. In Buddhist temples, adjacent
to the Buddhist shrine, there is invariably a shrine for the deities who, as
just observed, are largely derived from Hinduism. Some Buddhists are devotees of some of the better-known Hindu shrines. Upper-class Colombo
Buddhists and Tamil Hindus sit together in Sai Baba worship and sing devotional songs together. Thus, far from being a factor in the conflict, as is

often imagined, religion can be seen as a point of harmony between the two groups. In some major festivals, such as the Asala festival in Kandy, the last capital of the kings, and in the major annual festival at Kataragama, Buddhist and Hindu devotees together experience camaraderie and ecstasy with no apparent alienation from one another. The same is true of the pilgrims visiting the sacred mountain Sri Pada, which is frequented not only by Buddhists and Hindus but by Muslims and Christians as well.

In considering syncretistic Buddhism, one needs to reach beyond the "religious" field, consisting of textually based Buddhism on the one hand and the worship of mystical beings on the other, to include broader worldviews and mythological spheres. In Sri Lanka, as indeed in most Buddhist polities, one finds a cluster of mystical ideas pertaining to Buddhism and kingship that must surely be considered an aspect of syncretistic Buddhism in this broader sense.

In some respects, the origins of this mystical relationship can be traced to the great Indian king Asoka (269–232 BCE), who reportedly felt remorse for the suffering caused by his many conquests. In his search for solace, he converted from Hinduism to Buddhism, and his newfound beliefs motivated him to establish a kingdom in which all religious traditions could live together in peace. His was the first attempt to use the Buddha's moral and spiritual teachings as an effective guide to public policy, an attempt that met with considerable success. This understanding and use of Buddhism was later exported by Asoka to Sri Lanka, where it gained popularity and contributed to religious tolerance and acceptance of ethnic diversity.[2]

In the case of the Theravada Buddhist societies of South and Southeast Asia, the symbiotic relationship between kingship and Buddhism was translated into (1) a triangular relationship between the king, the Sangha (order of monks), and the people as the underlying essence of the "Buddhist state," and (2) related to the preceding, a special alliance between the king and the Sangha, with the former supporting and protecting the latter and the latter legitimizing the former.[3] It can be argued then, that given such a sanctified tradition of intimacy between Buddhism and politics, monastic involvement in contemporary politics is a natural development. This presents some political problems, however, the most preeminent of which relates to ethnic conflict, which can well be understood as being rooted in this syncretistic religion.

The problem with this position needs to be elaborated with reference to the unsuspected ramifications and paradoxes to which it leads. Stanley J. Tambiah, one of the foremost exponents of the theory of the Buddhist polity, in his later works makes a clear distinction between the precolonial polity of Lanka and the postcolonial modern state of Sri Lanka.[4] The former was ethnically and religiously inclusivist and had mechanisms for absorbing in a peaceful and harmonious manner the periodic influxes of foreign ethnic and religious groups. The deep structural relationship between religion and the state, Sangha and king, that characterized the premodern polity had no adverse effect on ethnic relations, and indeed seems to have fostered salutary relations between the different groups. This contrasts with the modern state of Sri Lanka, which has proved incapable of inclusion and instead has evolved into an intolerant, exclusionist sociopolitical entity. The primary reason for this, in Tambiah's analysis, is the distinctive feature of the modern polity, with its centralization of authority upheld conceptually by the theory of the modern state, whose sovereignty is held to be indivisible and inalienable.

In contrast to the organic nature of precolonial Sri Lankan society, the centralized modern state, which Tambiah calls "the radial polity," has led to ethnic confrontation. The reason is not difficult to discern. Whereas in a noncentralized system, local communities can and do act with a degree of independence from the center, centralized systems can easily stifle independence, especially if the center is controlled by an ethnic, religious, linguistic, or other majority and local communities are comprised of minority populations.

Among those scholars commenting on the ethnic crisis in Sri Lanka, there are two clearly demarcated groups: the social scientists led by anthropologists on the one hand and historians and literary/linguistic scholars on the other. Whereas the former hold that the ethnic crisis is solely a contemporary phenomenon, the latter are of the view that it is rooted in history, which makes them rather strange bedfellows with Tambiah's early works. While there is no open admiration of Tambiah among these scholars, they have certainly taken over his ideas in defense of their hegemonic theory of the historicity of "the Buddhist state," quietly forgetting the inclusivism that is an integral part of that theory. Tambiah in his later works is quite unambiguous as to the roots of Sinhala Buddhist hegemony in the centralized modern state, made possible by the advent of British colonial rule—a hegemony culturally facilitated by a postcolonial Buddhist revival.

Modern Buddhism

Based on the foregoing, it would appear that neither textual Buddhism nor syncretistic Buddhism has contributed in any major way to the conflict. This then leaves modern Buddhism as the remaining category to be examined. In the new (or modern) Buddhism, one finds religion bound up with a movement of ethnic nationalism. The underlying rationale for this movement was national regeneration achieved through a program of social reform in which the Buddhist monk was to become the central actor. This amounted to defining a new, more powerful role for the monk, which, in turn, led to the emergence of a "Buddhist fundamentalism." It is in this fundamentalism that one finds the major "religious" impetus for the conflict.

Before proceeding further, it is important to clarify the use here of the term "fundamentalism," since it can be seen as having two distinct meanings. In conventional usage the term is derived from the historical and theological study of Christianity and refers to the adherence to orthodox beliefs, such as the inerrancy of scripture and the literal acceptance of the various creeds as fundamentals of Protestant Christianity. In contrast to this sense, in which the term refers to specifically Christian phenomena, the term has recently been used in reference to *any* religious extremism involving intolerance of other beliefs and their associated sociocultural structures and activities, often expressed in aggressive and violent form. In this new sense, religious fundamentalism is a general and largely modern phenomenon easily blending into ethnic, linguistic, regional, and other parochial sociocultural formations. It is, however, important to keep in mind that fundamentalism in this new sense carries with it the ideological position that what its proponents believe in, and militantly work for, is, in fact, no more than a restoration of a utopia allegedly embodied in the original message of the religion in question. It is in this recent sense of the term that contemporary Sri Lankan Buddhism can be said to exhibit traits of "fundamentalism."

The author of the monk's newly defined role mentioned previoiusly was the reformer Anagarika Dharmapala (1864–1933), the founder of and most influential figure in modern Buddhism. Born to a successful business family and educated in Christian missionary schools, Dharmapala was deeply moved by what he saw around him: the poverty and misery of the people, their lack of cleanliness and health habits, their illiteracy and intemperance, their entrapment in ritual and magical beliefs, which he considered primitive and non-Buddhist, and the absence of order in their lives. He attributed all of this to an alienation of the people from their own culture and traditions and their acceptance of what he considered to be Western vices: eating meat; consuming alcohol; gambling; merry-making; wearing foreign apparel; using foreign languages, including foreign names; and embracing foreign religions. These influences effectively pulled the people away from their moral life and natural industriousness.

Dharmapala imagined a past society, a glorious Buddhist utopia, in which the Buddhist monk was the central actor and everybody lived happy, prosperous, and morally pure lives. He further imagined that this lost paradise could be regained through a process of moral regeneration and rearmament and by restoring to the monk his former primacy in social life, of which colonialism had deprived him. This regenerated Buddhist utopia would be the same as the one lost to colonial rule, except for one major difference, namely, that economically it would approximate a modern industrial society of the West.

It is clear that this "ideal" society is a fusion of two elements. The first consists of an economic vision to be realized through rational means, for example, by educating young people in international languages and training them in industry, crafts, and modern ways of thought. The second element involves a vision of an ideal political and cultural order in which indigenous culture and morality are the preeminent determinants of value and behavior. It is a broad ideological framework within which all else is encompassed. After the electoral victory of the nationalist forces in 1956, this ethos of the nationalist elites was translated into national policy, with adverse consequences for the minorities.

Dharmapala found an enthusiastic response to these ideas in some of the younger monks, particularly student monks enrolled at the two major Buddhist monastic colleges, Vidyodaya and Vidyalankara, during the first decades of the twentieth century. These two colleges were identical in their curricula and organization and were descendants of the same scholastic tradition. In their political outlook, however, they turned out to be drastically different. Vidyodaya was the more conservative, adopting a realistic and pragmatic attitude of acceptance toward British colonial rule as the properly constituted authority. Vidyalankara, on the other hand, took a somewhat radical and antiimperialist stand. Although seemingly contradictory, both perspectives, the conservatism of Vidyodaya and the radical nationalism of Vidyalankara, derived from Dharmapala. More specifically, the Vidyodaya monks incorporated his economic agenda, and with it his more pragmatic and accommodating side, whereas the Vidyalankara monks adopted his ideological, cultural, and political agenda, with its exclusivist, darker side. Thus Dharmapala's army of regeneration consisted of two battalions of monks representing the duality of his agenda: the sober, accommodating "economic monks" of Vidyodaya and the exclusivist, hegemonic "ideological monks" of Vidyalankara.

Economic Buddhism

In the 1930s and the 1940s, the Vidyodaya monks attempted to put this idea of national regeneration into action in the form of a project known as *gramasamvardhana*, or rural development. Two features are notable in the concept of rural development put forward by these monks. First, it was free of ideology, in that it did not blame colonial rule for the distressed state of the peasant. Second, it was an activity of the economic sphere that was deemed to be independent of the political. Rural development in this sense was devoid of deliberately constructed issues of religion, language, culture, and ethnicity, which constitute the second part of Dharmapala's agenda. Three monks from Vidyodaya stand out as the most illustrious activists of this movement—Kalukondayave Pannasekhara, Hinatiyana Dhammaloka, and Hendiyagala Silaratana. It is as if these pioneers consciously separated the pragmatic and the ideological that were united in Dharmapala's thinking; they discarded the ideological while holding on to the pragmatic.

The greatest achievement of these monks was their clear and effective articulation of a doctrine of religioeconomic action that brings to mind Max Weber's "inner-worldly asceticism." As explained hereafter, in addition to Dharmapala's influence, the doctrine also derived from ancient developments in the Buddhist tradition. In his theory of the regenerated Sinhala-Buddhist society, Dharmapala had envisaged a hardworking peasantry, but the theory also envisaged a rigorous moral code that prohibited any form of mundane enjoyment. The people of Dharmapala's utopia were constrained to spend all of their leisure time in religious activity and meditation. According to Dharmapala, this exercise in honest and hard work coupled with an abnegating lifestyle would ensure happy rebirths and eventually nirvana. The pragmatic monks of Vidyodaya elaborated this doctrine with great skill and made it the theme of the "sermons" they delivered as they traversed the length and breadth of the country in the cause of rural development.

In taking upon themselves the economic dimension of the Dharmapalite agenda, the Vidyodaya monks also articulated another idea contained in Dharmapala's theory, namely, that the duty and role of the monk is to repay the laity's material support of the monks not with religious instruction and ritual services alone but with substantial contributions toward the improvement of life in this world, especially of those in need. This refers to a broad range of activities that include alleviating poverty, promoting health, providing better housing and adequate nutrition, resolving conflicts, eradicating crime, and practicing temperance. While some of this was part of the monk's traditional moral instruction to the laity, the difference lay in the fact that these were advocated as functional pursuits for improving *this* world as opposed to generating merit for the *next* world. These monks interpreted Dharmapala as advocating their involvement in the *this-worldly* welfare of the laity. This even included gifts of material goods to the laity, constituting a radical departure from the unidirectional flow of material goods from layman to monk that had been the historic hallmark of the relationship in the past.

Political Buddhism

As for the second or ideological part of the Dharmapalite agenda, the monks of Vidyalankara College built a nationwide organization in the 1940s for the pursuit of political ends. With the approach of the 1956 election, they intensified their activities and helped elect the new government. They subsequently lobbied hard to make Sinhala, the language of the majority, the only official language of the country and to create a department of cultural affairs that would in effect give Buddhism official status. These policies eventually took hold and were carried further when the new Constitution of 1972 accorded to Buddhism a "special place" and the Constitution of 1977 created a ministry of Buddhism. English was abolished not only as the official language but also as the medium of instruction in the schools. These developments clearly gave priority to the majority over the minorities.

Dharmapala's goal in empowering the monk was national regeneration. What has happened, however, is quite the opposite. The policies initiated by the nationalist government elected in 1956 have led to an alienation of the minorities and to economic stagnation. Related assaults on the autonomy of the public service and the judiciary, the denial of a free press, an erosion of professionalism and professional ethics, the dismantling of democratic institutions, and the violent call for a separate state have collectively led to a general breakdown of the social order. To be successful, any measures that are taken will need to address this fundamental, underlying alienation and not merely its external manifestations.

A Doctrinal Basis for Reconciliation

Although it is only the modern expression of Buddhism that has played a significant role in fomenting the ethnic crisis in Sri Lanka, all three expressions—the doctrinal, the syncretistic, and the modern—have a potential role to play in resolving the conflict. In the doctrinal arena, there are numerous ideas and assumptions that could form the basis for reaching an understanding between the conflicting parties. An important one, unique to Buddhism, is the emphasis on human effort as the path to liberation, as opposed to a reliance on divine assistance that characterizes all other major world religions. Another is the denial of "self" as an immutable entity that continues after this life, which equates to a powerful devaluation of individual identity and, in turn, ethnic (or any other) identity. Further, Buddhist universalism opens its path to all who wish to tread it rather than to any chosen group, thus supporting inclusiveness rather than exclusivism and a denial of equal rights.

The identification of volition with the essence of karma is yet another expression of universalism. The corollary of this is the elevation of ethics and moral action over ritual action. At yet a different level, there is a spectrum of more directly expressed ideas and values, such as the concepts of nonviolence, "loving kindness," generosity, equanimity, and the like. Buddhist monastic organization also provides two important values that are striking and relevant: decision by consensus and decentralization. Indeed, in Buddhism as in other religions, there is no shortage of ideas relating to social harmony, only the resolve to act on them. This then is the challenge: how to translate such ideas into action.

Religious Tolerance

Syncretistic Buddhism, as alluded to earlier, has incorporated deities as well as patterns of ritual and worship from Hinduism, the predominant religion of the Tamil minority. Buddhism and Hinduism, though philosophically divergent, have throughout the history of Sri Lanka been closely related at the level of popular worship. Official worship at the major Buddhist shrines is modeled on the pattern of Hindu ritual known as *puja*. As mentioned already, many Hindus participate in major Buddhist festivals such as the Asala pageant in Kandy, in which one major Hindu deity is served by Tamil Hindu priests.

This traditional inclusivism of syncretistic religion finds a modern counterpart in the increasingly cordial relations between the majority Buddhists and all minority religious groups—Hindus, Muslims, and Christians. Deriving from the councils of Vatican II, held between 1962 and 1965, the Catholic Church of Sri Lanka, to which the large majority of Christians belong, has developed an appreciation for the truths found in Buddhism (in contrast to its earlier attitude of intolerance). Further, it uses indigenous languages and customs in its liturgy and has redefined the function of the priest from sacred mediator to social and economic supporter of the parish. Buddhist customs and Sinhala, the language of the majority, are now considered aspects of indigenous culture that the Christians share with the Buddhists.

An interesting illustration of religious accommodation relates to the question of religious noise. Traditionally, Buddhism and Hinduism have rather noisy ceremonies, while the rituals of Christianity and Islam have been relatively quiet. Today, however, the equation has changed, at least in the case of Islam. With the ready availability of loudspeakers, the Muslim call to prayer in the cities is usually amplified. Buddhists make noise of their own in the chanting of texts (known as *pirit*) by monks, and other ritual proceedings that are also often amplified. Most ordinary people care little about such noise, which in any event is rampant in the cities, with endlessly honking vehicles, vendors hawking their wares, and sellers of lottery tickets shrieking through handheld amplifiers. While on some occasions in the past noise led to conflict, it is now no more than a subject of mock complaint, like the bad weather.

Every year, Buddhist, Hindu, Christian and Muslim devotees worship together at the great festival at Kataragama, and, during the four months from January through April, climb the 6,000-foot Adam's Peak together to pay homage to an imprint there that Buddhists believe to be the footprint of the Buddha, Christians believe to be that of Adam, and Muslims that of the Prophet. Moreover, they join together in witnessing the spectacle of the sun rising above the sea and mountains, interpreting the glorious illusion of the sun taking several dips in the sea before finally deciding to rise as the solar deity's own obeisance to the sacred footprint.

There are today channels of communication between some sections of Buddhist monks and the clergy of other faiths that did not exist two decades ago, a development that is reflected in an interfaith organization known as Pavidi Handa, the Voice of the Clergy. A key objective of this organization is to utilize religious harmony in facilitating a peaceful resolution of ethnic hostilities. The general atmosphere of religious tolerance and amity in Sri Lanka is particularly noteworthy when contrasted with the negative influence of religious factors in several of the world's other similarly intractable conflicts.

A Pragmatic Approach to Peace

Paradoxically, modern Buddhism, in which the seeds of the present crisis reside, is also a potential resource for achieving peace. It has a positive and creative aspect which, in turn, could help put the social order on a more reasonable path which in turn, could both help to facilitate a peace settlement and provide a broader framework within which such a settlement could endure. This aspect of modern Buddhism can be traced to Dharmapala's "pragmatic" side. While he clearly lays out the ingredients of a rational social order and how to achieve it, the formulation is entwined with his "ideological" side. The challenge then is to disentangle the two and retain the pragmatic while discarding the ideological. This is precisely what his three best-known disciples did (as described earlier). Their writings portray an ideal social order centered on a "rational man" whose life conduct is based on the principle of *ubhayalokartha*, or the "gaining of both worlds." This refers to a rational ordering of life based on the systematic pursuit of productive work within a religious and ethical framework. Such a pursuit will in this life bring success in the form of material wealth and happiness and in the next bring favorable rebirths and ultimately nirvana. While sound in theory, implementation of this approach in the form of "rural development" ended with meager success. This does not invalidate the theory; it merely suggests a need to apply it with greater insight so as to construct a broader structure of institutions and social relationships within which peace can take hold and flourish.

The Monk as a Conduit of Reconciliation

In addressing the immediate and pressing need for peace, what religious resources might one tap? A good place to begin is by examining the role that the monk himself can play within modern Buddhism. While two of the expressions of Sangha activism derived from modern Buddhism essentially failed—the rural development movement and the involvement of monks in nationalist politics—a third remains that holds some promise. This is the activism displayed by a small group of monks who emerged as critics of the government that was elected in 1977 and later deteriorated into de facto authoritarianism.[5] These monks, who showed a pragmatism reminiscent of the rural development monks of the early twentieth century, played an important role in the electoral defeat of the regime in 1994. During that campaign, they organized themselves into discussion groups and held town meetings in which they explained to the people the need for power-sharing with the minorities, an approach that will be key to any negotiated settlement of the conflict. These monks are now partnering with the clergy of other religions, especially Christian priests, in working toward peace. Their organization is the previously mentioned Pavidi Handa, the Voice of the Clergy, and their peace efforts have advanced to the point where they are meeting periodically with the Tamil rebels. These members of the clergy, both Buddhist and non-Buddhist, need to be supported and empowered so they can have a greater effect on the political process.

Thus far Buddhist public opinion has leaned in the opposite direction, reflecting a largely one-sided and confrontational attitude. What is needed is a respected Buddhist spokesperson who can articulate a convincing approach toward accommodation and justice that is based on the Buddhist principles of compassion and loving kindness. In short, Buddhists face the challenge of developing a process that will enable them to practice what they preach.

Buddhist scholars also have an important role to play. At present, most of them are content to support the Sinhala Buddhist majority. Those who are not and who are more objective in their assessments should enter into a constructive dialogue with their colleagues and persuade them to collaborate in a critique of past actions that have been injurious to ethnic relations. In other words, they need to help pave the way for a deeper understanding of their recent history and politics and to use that understanding to engage in an informed Buddhist activism. Enlisting the participation and support of respected Tamil scholars, who themselves need to break away from colleagues who are more given to propaganda than scholarship, would be highly valuable.

For some time now, international mediation has been considered a useful tool for facilitating peace. As of this writing, Norway is engaged in such an effort and appears to be meeting with some success. Mediation, however, need not be confined to international parties or political and diplomatic figures alone. Efforts should also be made to enlist the services of charismatic religious figures, both Buddhist and non-Buddhist, from within and outside the country. A good example of an outside charismatic figure who might be helpful is the Dalai Lama. The fact that the Dalai Lama represents Mahayana Buddhism, while the Sri Lankan tradition is Theravada, should not interfere, since there is a great deal of overlap in the principles on which each is based. In addition to specific individuals like the Dalai Lama, there are also knowledgeable and sophisticated communities of Buddhists in western Europe and North America whose goodwill could also be harnessed in the cause of peace.

It would also be helpful to expand the identification of Buddhism with groups beyond the Sinhala majority. Few are aware that Buddhism thrived among the Tamils of South India for another ten centuries after it had disappeared from its original home in North India (in about the seventh century). Popularizing this fact and highlighting the achievements of Tamil Buddhism, including the fact that Buddhaghosa, the great fifth century Buddhist commentator, was probably a Tamil monk, are other ways in which the scholarly community could help.

Religion and Business: Partners in Peace

Another untapped source of peacemaking is the business community. Business has a significant stake in peace, and the peace process could benefit from the same kind of creativity that many spiritually minded businessmen show in their work. Although the business community has periodically undertaken peace initiatives in the past, their efforts have been all but totally ignored by the politicians. This is unfortunate; future peace efforts could benefit enormously from their contributions.

In this connection, there is a direct linkage between religion and business that could also prove helpful. Buddhism in Sri Lanka arose partly in response to the transition from a pastoral to an industrialized economy, with the attendant growth of cities and a city culture. For the business elites of these early cities, the economically destructive sacrificial rituals of Hinduism were seen to be a waste. What they needed was a code of ethics conducive to disciplined enterprise, and that is what they found in Buddhism. Hence the patronization of Buddhism by business elites and its subsequent spread along the trade routes of the time. This spirit of early "Buddhist capitalism" should be resurrected and its principles disseminated as widely as possible through the media and the efforts of charismatic monks. This would amount to revisiting the approach of the early Vidyodaya monks, informed by whatever intervening lessons history has to offer.

Conclusion

It is instructive to note that where the economic is primary and based on a code of ethics, parochial considerations like ethnicity and linguistic or regional affiliation lose their grip and diminish in importance. As it is, ethnic conflict currently prevails as one of many expressions of a pervasive state of anomie that has seized the land. The moral underpinnings of Sri Lankan society have eroded to the point where law and order and the norms that govern civilized political competition have broken down. The country is in a major crisis that only a national consensus for peace can resolve. Thus far, partisan political gain has prevented the formation of such a consensus.[6]

Buddhist monks are uniquely placed to help in this situation. Today's educated monks define their role more in terms of "social service" than ritual service. Most of the people, however, look upon them as purely ritualistic. What better way for the monks to gain the credibility and image they seek than to take the lead in forging a national consensus for peace?

In addition to supporting nonviolent methods of conflict resolution, these monks could also take the lead in addressing the deep-seated wounds created by this longstanding conflict. Because of the conflict's brutal history, the excesses on both sides will probably need to be publicly acknowledged before healing can take place. At that point, the monks could then capitalize

on the peacemaking tenets of Buddhist theology in breaking the endless cycle
of violence and retribution. Forming a coalition around these activist monks
could be a critical ingredient in this process.

Amid the malaise in contemporary Sri Lanka, there is a body of intel-
ligent and cosmopolitan opinion that is capable of comprehending the problem in all of its dimensions, analyzing it in an intellectually coherent manner,
developing a viable solution that incorporates the peacemaking tenets of
Buddhism, educating the general public, and rallying its support in reconstructing society. Representative of this body of opinion are such organizations as the Voice of the Clergy and the Vibhavi Centre, the Social Scientists'
Association, as well as some nongovernmental organizations, and publications such as the weekly newspaper *Ravaya*. These institutions and organs
are deeply committed to the task of rebuilding society and have been working against all odds. They clearly deserve the moral and financial support of
the international community.

NOTES

1. The reference here and in the following paragraphs is to Max Weber, *Religion of
India* (Glencoe, Ill.: Free Press, 1958).

2. Harvey Cox, "World Religions and Conflict Resolution," in *Religion, the Missing
Dimension of Statecraft*, ed. by Douglas Johnston and Cynthia Sampson (New York:
Oxford University Press, 1994), pp. 272–73.

3. This is extensively documented in the literature dealing with Buddhist polities.
A particularly succinct early account is Trevor Ling, *The Buddha* (London: Temple
Smith, 1973). The best-known more recent expositions of the idea are the works of
Stanley J. Tambiah on Thailand. See especially *World Conquerer and World Renouncer*
(Cambridge: Cambridge University Press, 1976).

4. *Ethnic Fratricide and the Dismantling of Democracy* (Chicago: University of Chicago
Press, 1986); *Buddhism Betrayed?* (Chicago: University of Chicago Press, 1992).

5. For discussion of this critique, see H. L. Seneviratne, "Buddhist Monks and Ethnic Politics," *Anthropology Today* 17, no. 2 (April 2001), pp. 15–21.

6. An opportunity for this arose in the summer of 2001, with a section of the ruling
coalition breaking ranks and the government losing its parliamentary majority. The sense
of national emergency was enhanced when the Tamil Tigers bombed the only international airport, threatening the country with severe economic crisis. But in characteristic fashion, partisan politics prevailed, and the government opted to shore itself up
with support from the radical nationalist youth party, the Janata Vimulti Peramuna
(JVP), which opposes a peaceful dialogue with the Tigers, rather than reaching out to
the opposition, which in turn is to blame for not responding to what overtures were
made to it by the government.

5 *Marc Gopin*

Judaism and Peacebuilding in the Context of Middle Eastern Conflict

Following World War II, the British withdrew from their UN mandate of Pales-
tine, and the United Nations partitioned the area into a Palestinian state and the
new Jewish state of Israel, an arrangement to which Palestinians and the rest of the
Arab world strongly objected. In response to threatened or actual attack, the Israelis
subsequently defeated the Arabs in a series of wars, victories that ultimately exacer-
bated the conflicting claims to land and associated holy sites. The issues of the Pal-
estinian right-to-return (to their pre-1948 homes) and the final status of Jerusalem—
holy to Jews and Muslims alike—have been especially troublesome. Perhaps the
best chance for a peaceful settlement was dashed in 1995, with the assassination of
Israeli Prime Minister Yitzhak Rabin by a Jewish extremist. Soon thereafter, the
Israeli-Arab peace process slowly unraveled, leading in late 2000 to the beginning of
a second Palestinian intifada (uprising) that continues unabated to the present.

The situation in Palestine and Israel is deadly, dangerous, and tragic. The
lost opportunities of the peace process are too numerous to calculate. However, the single greatest failing has been the all-but-total neglect of human
needs on all sides, whether among the millions of poor Palestinians, the
isolated settlers, the angry and confused religious visionaries, the misguided
and desperate teenagers, or the average person—Jew or Arab—who lives in
fear of the violence at his or her doorstep. Had these immediate and long-
term needs played a significant role in the peace process, Palestine and Israel
would not be so radicalized today.

One could spend endless months deconstructing the political intrigues
on both sides that may have contributed to the violence. But the triggers
do not matter as much as the cultural and psychological despair that has
provided the gunpowder for those triggers. To undermine the cycle of violence and the debilitating interaction of politics, militarism, and religious

imperatives, one must focus on the human dimensions of the conflict. Although the injuries and needs of both sides are different, they are equally pressing.

In addressing this decades-long conflict, the emphasis should be on negotiating and relationship building, focusing on what can be agreed to by consensus, rather than bargaining over rules or principles that one knows the other party cannot accept. Thus one would begin from ground zero and proceed to a vision that incorporates the values on both sides. In this context, the distribution and use of land becomes a critical variable.

Relinquishing Land

If terrible crimes have been committed over land disputes, then the surrender of some of that cherished land should be a powerful way to transform the situation. However, it should also require acknowledgement of just how cherished that land is. Doing less dilutes the impact. For example, as Israel has relinquished territory that it perceived to be a part of its historical Holy Land, those secular, peace-oriented Jews who were willing to trade land for peace expressed little concern for this lost property, at least publicly. Religious Jews, on the other hand, felt deeply the loss of this ancient, sacred land and had no interest at all in giving it up. To avoid such a possibility, they have been commensurately less willing to face up to and admit the injustices that have been perpetrated on Palestinians. Their focus instead has been almost exclusively on what Palestinians, Arabs, and gentiles in general have done to them. Hence their use of any and all arguments to prevent the loss. On the other side, the loss of land has been every bit as traumatic for hundreds of thousands of Palestinians. It seems clear that the final status of the two states will ultimately require the surrender of aspirations on both sides at a deep cultural level.

When land is given up, or when the rights to land are relinquished, as the Jews must do with the West Bank and the Palestinians must do with Haifa and pre-1948 Israel, this sacrifice of land should be mourned, acknowledged, and honored in a fundamental way. The real heroes of this transformation from war to peace will be those who deeply cherish the land and feel that it was given to them by God but who are willing to give up a part of it out of a sense of justice and a commitment to peace. The most effective gestures of peacemaking are those that involve acts of genuine sacrifice. It is necessary to point this out because often the other side will have to make supreme sacrifices as well, and they must understand that the depth of sacrifice is mutual.

Restoring Dignity

Although the West has been long attached to the rational-actor mode of decisionmaking, it is important to recognize that formal ceremonies can solidify emotions and moments of transformation in ways that rational dialogue can rarely acheive. Although such ceremonies cannot replace negotiations over future relationships or security arrangements and the corresponding distribution of power and resources that must take place, they are nevertheless an indispensable tool of conflict transformation.

By the same token, rational negotiations and dialogue can do nothing for those who have been killed. In some respects, the memories of those lost in the struggle weigh on the survivors as a burden of indescribable pressure. Beyond the understandable urge for revenge, survivor guilt is a principal goad that motivates those who perpetuate conflict. The conflict is thus a way to keep alive the memory of the dead while assuaging the guilt of those who survive.

There is also a related problem with peacemaking, even the kind that seriously engages issues of justice and reparations. Nothing is so valuable to human beings as their lives and the lives of their loved ones. In deadly conflicts, these are losses that cannot be replaced. Therefore, there is a tendency in rational and even emotion-laden peace processes to ignore the dead. Monetary compensation for these deaths is rarely brought up and would seem inappropriate, if not obscene, in any event. Religious traditions, however, suggest the need to address this problem anyway.

The formal methods of address at burial sites seem worthy of serious consideration as part of a complete process of peacemaking in deadly conflicts, especially those that involve Jews, who have this aspect embedded in their cultural consciousness. It is embedded not only as something that may be expected when they are the victims but also, potentially, as something that they may be willing to do for victims of their own actions. What effect this could have in conflict resolution is difficult to predict, but it is definitely worth trying, especially in conflicts involving Jews. If done sensitively, this could be a decisive factor in moving reconciliation work to a new level of effectiveness.

Sharing Sacred Space

The sacralization of space is one of the most powerful phenomena in religious experience across the world. In polytheistic traditions, this experience of sacralization can have a rather diffuse quality. Since the sacred and actual deities can be located in numerous locations and objects, it could be argued that there is less intensity around exclusive ownership over particular sacred locations. The monotheistic vision of the world, on the other hand—up through and including Mohammed's conquests and the Crusades—has often expressed itself in a strong drive to create exclusive sacred space.

This is the principal Abrahamic contribution to the Arab-Israeli conflict, with disputed sacred space to be found everywhere. From the West Bank (as the former Judea and Samaria) for Judaism to the holiness of Jerusalem for all three faiths, the sacredness of the space is the subject and object of the dispute for millions of people. Furthermore, sacred space seems to become even more sacred as the conflict intensifies or as more and more "holy" sites, such as burial places, are discovered or rediscovered and become the object of jealous veneration.

It is therefore necessary to conceive of shared sacred space on many levels and involving different kinds of compromises: Jewish-Islamic-Christian compromises, secular-religious compromises, and intrareligious compromises. While some spaces on the Temple Mount need to be exclusive, there is no reason that others cannot be shared according to agreed-upon rules. Not only can this concept of sharing be justified and supported within the framework of existing religious doctrine but it could also help create bridges between religious traditions.

The concept of sharing space should accommodate the original emphasis of sacralization among the venerated monotheistic prophets of the Hebrew Bible, namely the moral preconditions governing the entrance to sacred ground.[1] One such condition, for example, could involve agreement by all parties to provide aid to the poor and those who suffer. Another condition might require all who enter the space to observe respectful and honorable modes of greeting and to subscribe to a moral/spiritual etiquette that has roots in all three Abrahamic traditions. All would project an attitude of respect for the property of others, especially lost property. All could also agree to the special treatment of animal and plant life in the sacred spaces, rules that are embedded in all religions and that could be utilized as a basis for cooperative healing. Thus, rather than a space of ultimate contention, shared sacred space could represent a disciplined paradigm for interreligious morality. In other words, what parties to the conflict might consider doing is to redefine hermeneutically, but in a very conservative and conserving fashion, the concept of sacred space, moving away from defining it exclusively in terms of sole ownership. This would be made easier by internalizing on both sides the monotheistic idea that ultimately everything belongs to God.[2]

These sacred rules of interpersonal engagement can or should have their counterparts in secular constructs and contracts that all would agree to abide by when on sacred ground. In short, the imposition of Abrahamic laws or principles of moral behavior on sacred sites could empower religious consciousness in a way that would make sharing an easier challenge.

Finally, this contractual commitment to shared sacred space could form the basis for a multireligious treaty and secular-religious treaty for governing the entire Holy Land region as sacred space. Now this would not satisfy those for whom its sacredness is only vouchsafed by exclusive ownership, or those who want to go further in disallowing any behavior contrary to traditional Jewish law or Islamic Shari'ah. In other words, it will not satisfy those with a messianic anticipation of theocracy and absolute control. But it will go a long way toward creating a new and integrated regional culture that can provide the conflicting parties with several critical needs: (1) it will acknowledge their territorial claims as at least partially legitimate, (2) it will give them a sense of dignity through their participation in constructing a civil society, and (3) it could bring healing to those who are caught in the middle of these cultural struggles.

Such an arrangement would require a new approach among fundamentalist visionaries on both sides for whom exclusive or coercive future visions take precedence over ethics. It means adopting a vision that will not appeal to everyone but that will include enough religious people from all sides to sideline the current rejectionist zero-sum mentality. In short, it will offer an alternative vision of sacred space that does not require exclusive ownership to be religiously fulfilling.

Shared Living Space and Memorialization

A changed vision of sacred space is only one challenge of peacemaking as it relates to land. The struggle for living space is less symbolic but far more at the heart of the conflict that has led to such enormous losses on both sides. The losses incurred from struggles over land are complicated by the disproportionality of those losses. Palestinians in the tens of thousands lost their actual homes, and Jews were the clear victors in terms of territorial gain. Jewish losses of home and family in Europe, with 90 percent of European Jewry annihilated, cannot be blamed on the Palestinians. And yet those losses are part and parcel of the struggle. These unfair asymmetries are a feature of countless interethnic wars around the world, where one party pays for the injustices done to another by yet a third party.

Past losses make the need for land acute in the minds of millions of

Jews, and these losses have been incorporated for thousands of years in Jewish prayers, long before Zionism appeared on the scene. But there are losses and needs on all sides, with many of them tied to the land.

The actual loss of life at specific locations is another critical way to think about the use of land for healing the past and building a different future. Museums and memorials are critical to a community's capacity to cope with its past. Mourning over lost life is very related to lost land because for many people, the land and life on the land are inextricably linked. Land is so contested in this conflict, however, that each and every attempt at memorialization will undoubtedly become a source of controversy. Nevertheless, paying such tribute should be pursued anyway, so long as it is done bilaterally. It is also possible that the associated controversy itself could be utilized for constructive purposes.

Consider the following: burying the dead, memorializing the dead, and mourning the dead are gestures that are entirely consistent with the Abrahamic traditions. Religious people, officials or laity, should jointly experiment with ways to lead their communities into an extended period of memorialization and mourning. This would focus on the loss of both life and land as a result of violence experienced in this and the last century by each religious community. However, it must be done in such a way that each community shares in the memorialization with the other communities. Numerous spaces need to be created for remembering, acknowledging, mourning, and committing to a different path.

Such an approach can be adopted by the public sector as well, but care must be taken to avoid cooption of the process by political considerations. For best results, it is necessary that these bilateral processes become widespread and diffuse. In this way the very nature of the experiment will regularly improve on itself as the wisdom of what works and does not work in a particular multicultural context grows with each exchange. The nature of these exchanges would differ, for example, if they took place between liberal, secular actors as opposed to taking place between the very religious on each side. It would differ still if one managed to arrange such a process between nationalistic elements, such as Jewish settlers on one side and Palestinian nationalists on the other.

How could this be done? Every recognized place that Palestinians have died violently at the hands of Jews, for whatever reason and without judgment or blame, could become a place of joint mourning, memorial, and commitment. Every recognized place that Jews have died at the hands of Palestinians, for whatever reason and in whatever circumstance, would become a place of joint mourning, memorial, and commitment. This would include sites of terrorist attacks, massacres, and violent confrontations of any kind. It would include Mahane Yehuda market in Jerusalem, for example; Deir Yassin, the corridor of the forced march from Ramallah in 1948, where a number of Palestinian villagers were massacred by Jewish irregulars; Hebron's burial place of the Patriarchs and Matriarchs, *meor'at ha-makhpelah*; the site of the Yeshiva where numerous Jewish students were slaughtered in a pogrom in 1929; as well as major scenes of battle in the various wars between the two sides. Unfortunately, there are multitudinous locations that could become candidates for such treatment.

This process would have to occur over an extended period of time, and it would also need to be executed exclusively on a bilateral basis. Memorialization should take place in close bilateral proximity wherever possible, both in terms of time and space. In other words, it would be best if memorials that were close geographically were joined by simultaneous or nearly-simultaneous ceremonies. Cemeteries where the victims are buried would constitute an equally suitable space for this reconciling process.

The degree to which each community is capable of expressing remorse, apology, or request for forgiveness at these sites where death occurred would represent a contribution to the healing process and a shift in the relationship. This is not to be de jure or expected but rather to come naturally for those communities or individuals who are prepared to engage in this way. Some accompanying form of acknowledgement, respect, and regret, however, is essential.

The rituals and statements or prayers that would be appropriate in these places would depend solely on the parties themselves and would be a function of what they deem to be appropriate. Minimally, there would have to be expressions of regret, if not acceptance of responsibility, as well as a commitment to a different future. The more these gestures are formulated in cultural and religious terms that bear the stamp of authenticity, the more effective they will be.

Anyone in this work must be prepared for the inevitable backlash. First of all, rejectionists will be inclined to violate sacred space out of a perceived need to remain true to the dead. Memorials often become contested spaces, as has been the case with Jewish memorials in Europe, which are subject to regular desecration. Memorials dedicated to the Jewish dead become an affront to anti-Semites or to those who, for religious reasons, feel that Jews simply should not exist. The dead have a way of heightening one's conceptualization of life, which is why cemeteries are such beautiful but vulnerable places.

A constructive approach to conflict resolution utilizes all pain and provocation to further the process of reconciliation. One of the more insidious causes of conflict is the illusion of nonconflict and the burial of crime. Memorials bring all of this into sharp relief, both symbolically and historically. The very backlash against these memorializations will be a good reminder to those who might otherwise become complacent and fall victim to the illusion that the work of peace, justice, reparation, and repentance is over simply because there is no overt violence. In addition to actively promoting these memorializations, religious leaders can also play an important role in official peace negotiations.

Involving Religious Leaders in the Peace Process

Since 1998 considerable effort has gone into translating the ideas expressed in this chapter into concrete actions. High-level, back-channel meetings have taken place between President Yasser Arafat, Israeli rabbinic leaders, and Palestinian sheikhs, all in order to forge religious relationships that could stem the tidal wave of violence that grips the Middle East—including, personally, several meetings with Arafat in order to work out a religious cease-fire to the Intifada, a concept that has received significant support from both sheikhs and rabbis.

The strategy associated with such a cease-fire would call for follow-on ceremonies that honor both Islam and Judaism and simultaneously call for nonviolent solutions to the conflict. The ultimate aim is to transform the role of religion in the struggle—from its current use by extremists to keep the conflict alive to making it an instrument of peace in bringing the two sides together.

Although this approach has received tacit approval from American officials, there have been no real attempts to encourage this kind of cultural peacemaking. On several occasions, the parties themselves, at the highest levels, have privately acknowledged the need for third parties, especially the United States, to pursue religious peacemaking as a parallel component of the official negotiations.[3] President William Clinton himself endorsed this kind of approach, yet American diplomacy has failed to make it even a minor priority.[4] The reasons for this reluctance remain a mystery, but further pressure is clearly in order.

Since September 11, 2001, efforts have been stepped up to win the support of leading Middle Eastern leaders for this kind of approach, along with that of significant third parties, such as the United Nations. Where this will lead remains to be seen, but there can be little doubt that a cultural and religious track must accompany or be a part of any future peace process, if that process is to have any chance of success. In sum, there are a number of cultural and religious resources in Judaism, which, if brought to bear thoughtfully and sensitively, could help inspire profound change in the Israeli-Arab conflict.

The parties to the conflict have behaved badly, and it is easy to trace the causes and effects of their brutality, callousness, and deception. It will be up to third parties (especially religious leaders) to guide them into a new relationship on an interpersonal basis, as opposed to continuing the endless bargaining of the few, marked by sophistication, cleverness, and ultimate irrelevance.

The deescalation plan proposed here encapsulates some of what has just been discussed and incorporates other reconciling elements of Jewish sacred scripture addressed in the appendix. Much more is needed, but if even some of what is recommended here is put into practice, it could help reverse the ongoing spiral of violence and point the way toward a new beginning.

CULTURAL DEESCALATION PLAN FOR ISRAEL AND PALESTINE

PREAMBLE

No political plan to resolve the Israeli-Palestinian conflict will be successful at this point in time, regardless of how rational it may be, unless there is a parallel effort to deescalate the rage and fear that is feeding the rejectionism and hardening of positions. One can speculate endlessly about which side deserves greater blame for the current state of affairs. Moving to a constructive approach, however, will require a bilateral set of actions that provides the leadership on each side with sufficient political space to move to a final settlement.

1. Involve Religious Leaders in the Peace Process

The advantages that religious leaders bring to a peace process have been summarized in chapter 2. Foremost among them are their moral authority and the organizational structure they have at their disposal. The important lesson to be drawn from past failed attempts at peacemaking is the need for Jewish and Muslim clerics to be an integral part of future negotiations in order to deal effectively with the religious issues that lie at the heart of the problem and which, in many ways, transcend the political, economic, and security considerations.

2. Restore the Sanctity of Holy Places

Gestures of regret, honor, and rededication should take place in all religious spaces that have been violated in Israel and Palestine in the recent past, including synagogues, mosques, and gravesites. These gestures should be bilateral, organized by interfaith organizations, and publicly endorsed by leading political and religious figures on both sides. Third parties, like the United States, would need to make clear to both sides that this activity is to be a priority consideration.

3. *Engage in Joint Mourning*

Loss of life is not only a human tragedy, it is a desecration of cultural and religious sensibilities. As such, mourning and joint expressions of regret can help reverse the cultural damage that has taken place.

4. *Support Injured Adversaries*

Efforts should be made to offer support to injured members of each community from the opposing community. This is already taking place in limited form, but, as with other such activities, it is receiving no support from the political leadership on either side. The effect of political endorsement could be dramatic.

5. *Develop Trust-Building Initiatives*

Both communities feel an overwhelming sense of fear with regard to the future. Fear, in turn, begets hatred and political intransigence. Efforts must be made to build trust that will address the wishes and intentions of the majority in each community. The majorities who have not participated in the violence and who do not condone an excessive use of force are generally silenced by the political leadership. Ways must be found to foster greater communication between these majorities. Once again, there has never been any pressure on the political leaderships to consider this an integral part of peacemaking. The endorsement of political leaders would thus generate the needed energy to strengthen and renew those limited efforts of this nature that already exist. The Israeli public needs to hear the fears of the average occupants of Palestinian towns, just as Palestinians need to hear Israeli fears, either directly or through the media. Each needs to understand the life situation of the other.

6. *Develop a Process for Restoring Justice*

It is difficult to overestimate the specter of injustice that accompanies this conflict. Whatever the composition of governmental or nongovernmental inquiries, it is essential that a just and fair evaluation be undertaken of what went wrong and who committed what excesses. If any international body manages to do this in an unprejudiced fashion, it will greatly help the process of recovery. The problem is that most bodies of inquiry will be swayed by their own feelings toward the various parties to the conflict and will not be sufficiently detached to provide an objective evaluation of the conflicting parties' behavior. With the appropriate objectivity, however, such a process would represent a healthy contribution to the peace process.

Most important, the justice claims and the rage emerging from a sense of injustice on the part of the average Palestinian must be acknowledged in the peace process. One cannot hope to move forward without a better venue than presently exists for channeling this rage. There are also a great number of people on the Israeli side who feel and claim a deep posture of injury because of injustices committed by the Palestinians and, more generally, the Arab world. The violation of human rights when a Palestinian's land is summarily taken is well recognized, as is the fact of their frequent mistreatment at the borders and the loss of innocent lives during Israeli military reprisals. What is less acknowledged is the violation of human rights that takes place when an innocent Jew is purposely blown to bits in his fruit market in Jerusalem. This too cries out for justice. If justice and human rights are not blind, then they will disappear like vapor. Consideration should be given to the establishment of an ongoing justice and reconciliation commission through which many of these issues can be addressed, and through which the losses of victims and their families can be properly acknowledged.

7. Combat Poverty

Abject misery drives this conflict, as it does so many others. Cultural and religious sensibilities are held hostage to the damage that human misery wreaks on individual and collective identities. It is critical to understand how the rejectionist politics on both sides receive their impetus from the deprivation of the poor.

Any peace process in the future should be accompanied by high-profile antipoverty measures that lead to immediate relief in the lives of the needy whose support will be vital to the long-term success of that process. Those antipoverty measures associated with the peace process to date have been abstract in nature and largely focused on infrastructure, with an accompanying penchant for corruption and further alienation of the population. Small loans to large numbers of people, for example, should be given priority over large loans to a few. Employment training should be available on some level for every young person. It is critical that such efforts be directly and publicly associated with the peace process. For far too long, the benefits of peace have been held for the end of the process. There is no longer any patience for this.

8. Restore Dignity

Human dignity has been the greatest victim to date of the Israeli-Palestinian conflict. The majority on both sides feel intuitively that their enemies and most of the world do not particularly value their existence. Too many Jews feel that the rest of the world will never understand their security needs because "they," the gentiles, have never valued Jewish life. Palestinians feel abandoned and humiliated by everyone, even by some of their own leaders.

There is no greater area of miscommunication between the two sides than that which exists on the issue of honor. Most Israeli leaders and citizens do not understand how important dishonor and humiliation are in this conflict and how much both serve to fuel the rage. They tend to think in pragmatic terms and do not understand why their adversaries refuse to consider otherwise seemingly fair alternatives put forward in the negotiating process. This is true in many conflicts where the side having the greater power and sense of normalcy dismisses violence for the sake of honor as irrational and irresponsible. Real conflict resolution and peacebuilding in many respects is a function of how well third parties help each side understand its blind spots, both with respect to its behavior and that of its adversaries.

9. Engage Religious Traditions in Transforming Relationships

Judaism, Islam, Christianity, and even Buddhism can help facilitate the kinds of ethical, psychological, and cultural transformations that will be needed to bring peace to the Middle East. For these religious traditions to exercise their full potential in reconstructing broken relationships, religious people will have to extricate themselves from bigoted interpretations of their traditions; and secularists will have to shed their instinctive antipathy toward organized religion and welcome religious peacemakers as allies. Religious healing of the kind suggested here is unavailable to standard diplomacy. It is past time that it be brought to bear in this most intractable of conflicts.

APPENDIX

Peacemaking Qualities of Judaism
as Revealed in Sacred Scripture

What will it take to restore lost dignity on both sides in the Middle East conflict? What will it take for rejectionists in the Jewish camp to feel that it is not by the gun that the value and dignity of Jewish life can be restored? What will it take for a Palestinian family and clan to recover their dignity?

What will restored dignity look like for those who have adequate resources and education but who have suffered the loss of property or a village that can never be recovered? What will it take for those in refugee camps who have nothing, and how much will they depend on an honest integration of cultural dignity and economic rights? What will it take to restore honor?

These are questions that should be posed to everyone involved about themselves *and* about others. Of course, in the actual dialogic moment it would be presumptuous and inappropriate to suggest to others what they need and do not need in order to recapture their dignity. That is not the intention. Rather, it is the empathetic psychology that needs to be stimulated. The exercise of anticipating the other's sense of dignity and of shame should be an integral part of preparing for meaningful dialogue.

Connecting individuals to their cultural moorings will help identify why and when they fight and why and when they make peace. If those cultural moorings provide ways of moving toward peace, then they may prove more effective in doing so than would an imposed peace process. If, on the other hand, those moorings tend to generate conflict, then one may be able to determine the cultural and psychological changes needed to support peace that would not otherwise be discernible through traditional theories of conflict. This holds true for large political or military events that may have nothing to do, on the surface, with religion or culture. Often the rituals, myths, and metaphors of a community—especially in a modern context— are buried in oblique spaces that are not supposed to affect public behavior. But they do.

The goal of this appendix is to uncover these deeper roots of conflict as they pertain to Judaism and the Jewish community and apply what can be learned to the challenges in Palestinian-Israeli relations over the coming decades. There are many interlacing subsets of this conflict, including the intermonotheistic, as well as the larger Arab-Israeli and Western-Arabic dimensions. Internal conflicts within the Palestinian and Israeli communities over the proper role of religion also weigh in the balance, as do internal psychological problems of the post-Holocaust Zionist community and the post-Catastrophe community of Palestinians.[1]

The role of religion in perpetuating the principal conflict hardly needs delineation: Hamas and Islamic Jihad, Jewish assassins, nationalist religious parties, aggressive seizing of land in the name of God, suicide–mass murder in the name of God, outside religious entities with vested interests in worsening the conflict, Jerusalem as an object of desire and conquest by all three religions, and holy sites as burgeoning reifications of conflict. But even more lies beneath the surface. It is essential, therefore, as an outgrowth of such analysis, to integrate the relevant cultural values of these communities into a deepened peacemaking process. This has yet to be attempted, and the consequence has been a superficial and fragile peace process that has not penetrated the moral consciousness and collective behavior of either side. This appendix addresses this task.

As an alternative to a tragically inadequate peace process, an integration of imagery, metaphor, and law and ritual that is both old and familiar can have a profound effect on peacemaking, as will be described hereafter. It provides a way for moving the hermeneutics into less violent expressions. But this is only a beginning and, by itself, insufficient.

Conflict, Injury, and Transformation

The capacity to transform old religious categories of exclusion or hatred is only one part of the challenge in building a new relationship between former enemies; but it is one that prepares the theological groundwork for an important transformation in the mindset of religious individuals and communities. Rereading tradition is a major social challenge for a religious community whose structural integrity depends on agreed-upon categories of meaning, as well as principles of inclusion and exclusion. But intertwined with this in a very complicated way are personal and collective injuries— the scars of conflict and violence. Scars endure not only because of "hard" offenses, like torture and the murder of loved ones, but also because of "soft" offenses, such as humiliation and disdain. All such scars involve losses that are either difficult or impossible to reconcile. The more one's psyche becomes wedded to these losses, and the more devoted one has been to lost objects of love and veneration, the more unacceptable it becomes to think of trading in one's condition of "perpetuated mourning" for economic compensation or some other comparable surrogate. In fact, this principled rejectionism should be honored by observers and interveners as a positive expression of moral principle—as destructive as that may be for peace in the short term. The more intense one's feelings for and devotion to those who have suffered or died, the more problematic, even obnoxious, will rational responses appear to be.

"Perpetuated mourning" is a state in which human beings find one way or another to keep old wounds open—to maintain an attachment to the loss by extending some state of affairs in which that loss is kept at the surface (in addition to the perpetuation of moral justifications for taking such a position). This is a vital way in which people keep what they have lost as close to home as possible. It is also a way to avoid the guilt of living well or happily as a group, which could easily be interpreted as a betrayal of those people and things that one has lost. Lost things can also include an idealized relationship with God in the distant past or a time of glorious sovereignty in some bygone era.

Religion and Community Formation

Organized religion plays an important role in perpetuated mourning. A significant percentage of Jewish prayer and ritual, for example, is dedicated to mourning past losses, beseeching God to forgive the sins that have led to those losses (understood and framed as "punishments"), and praying for punishment of the enemies who caused them. The biblical book of Psalms, shared by all three monotheistic religions, is replete with these kinds of prayers. For much of Jewish history, the images conjured by these ancient prayers had very real counterparts in the immediate experience of prejudice, cultural humiliation, or actual persecution.

It is no accident that, in effect, the Psalmist, traditionally King David, is the godfather of traditional Jewish prayer. The psalms attributed to David combine an intense and creative religiosity that offers the comfort of a personal and privileged relationship to God. It also entails an honest process of self-judgment, which is combined in subtle ways with a vivid re-creation of persecution at the hands of enemies. It sets up an existence wherein God is the only refuge and ultimate salvation for the righteous. This fit perfectly (or formed?) the Jewish penchant for strong self-criticism and drive to repentance, which merges in an artful way with a persecution consciousness.

The trouble with prayer, devotion, and the construction of universes of meaning that become deeply embedded is that they tend not only to explain the vicissitudes of life, and thus give comfort and reassurance, but also to *create* reality by forming the mindset of the adherent and thus making it difficult to change reality. This combination of making sense of reality by softening its blows and simultaneously creating a rigid pattern of interpretation is a constant in most theologies, east as well as west. Comfort in the discovery of meaning seems to always come at the price of rigid conformity to that very theology, which, at least sometimes, is perpetuating some form of self-imposed misery.

This kind of internalized mental structure of the world is so powerful that, in moments of tension and uncertainty, it may short-circuit creative possibilities for peace. It may fall back on the emotionally and philosophically familiar consciousness of persecution as an existential constant, expressed so powerfully in the old rabbinic adage: "It is a law (of the order of the world), Esau (gentiles) will always hate Jacob (the Jewish people)."[2]

There is no question, however, that, beyond the manufactured cultural character of mourning based on habit, there is a very real set of injuries that run very deep in communities that have suffered terrible losses over large spans of time. Understandably, formal and informal processes of mourning are the only ways that human beings have for coping with these kinds of losses.

Generally speaking, included in traditional mourning processes over such losses is a corresponding attribution of blame to traditional enemies. This is not always the case, however; and, in fact, religion does have in its cultural repertoire something unavailable to ethnonationalist thought. Often, perhaps too often, biblical religion holds the individual (as well as the religious community) accountable for his or her own troubles. Simple interpretations of biblical religion assume God to be both directly cognizant of and responsible for day-to-day tribulations. Thus, if God is both all-powerful and perfectly just, then human beings must be responsible for their own tragedies.

This can make people sick with internalized guilt for some unethical act or minor ritual that they failed to perform that supposedly resulted in some egregious loss such as the death of a loved one. While such guilt can become a brutal agent of control and psychological punishment, it can also lead to a level of self-examination for one's troubles that is totally absent in ethnonationalist psychology. The latter is nothing less than self-worship or narcissism and therefore cannot admit of basic flaws.

Patterns of Abrahamic Reconciliation: Act, Ritual, and Symbol as Transformation

Despite the difficulty with the aspects of religion and culture that demonize the outsider and hold him or her to blame for all problems, the fact is that religious cultures are very complex and paradoxical. The reservoir of possible religious reactions to conflict is much greater than one could imagine. A critical task, then, is to mine sources that give rise to other, countervailing hermeneutic possibilities and psychological reactions to the world. How then does Judaism teach people who are enemies to change as they confront one another?

Expanding Moral Boundaries

While many of the processes of change described hereafter are insightful and in many ways have much to teach modern conflict resolution theorists and practitioners, they also suffer from a variety of flaws. The biggest flaw by far, shared almost universally in all religions, is limiting the application of these insights and processes to problems within one's own community— such as the confrontation between those who conform to traditional *halakha/* Jewish law and those who do not—while suppressing them with respect to external enemies. The latter can include those who choose not to practice or believe, those who did but now reject it, those whose spiritual decisions about practice or belief differ from some human/religious authority structure that claims divine or historic sanction, or large groups that threaten or stand in the way of expanding or maintaining the temporal power of one's own religion.

This flaw has been singly responsible for the suffering and death of countless millions of people in the history of religion, and certainly in the history of the Abrahamic faiths. Needless to say, despite some restrictive and even violent religious laws and dogmas, there are countless religious adherents in history who were not responsible for either and who read their traditions within a mental framework of the deepest humanity. They either reread or selected the most humane paradigm of their tradition.[3] Nevertheless, the antisocial tendency in many religious texts, and the uses thereof to support violence, remains a principal challenge that cannot be denied. It is therefore the case that, as one examines the methods of interpersonal transformation, there is a contemporary need to negotiate and expand the boundaries of the moral universe of Judaism specifically as it addresses the ethics of conflict resolution and reconciliation.

What is less acknowledged and analyzed is how the extension of pro-social values to outsiders is often complicated and contradicted by the existential fears of the group. This is a very subtle and deadly challenge. With every effort to extend moral boundaries outward, there is a corresponding backlash that contracts the moral universe of a particular religious or cultural group. This is as true of the Jewish community as a whole as it is of sub-sectors such as the ultra-Orthodox *haredim*.

Forgiveness

In examining the hermeneutic foundations of pro-social engagement, conflict prevention, conflict resolution, and restoration of relationships, it is appropriate to begin with the concept and practice of forgiveness, since it plays such a fundamental, albeit complex, role in religious responses to conflict. There is no question that divine emulation, *imitatio dei*, is critical in Judaism. Emulation in terms of compassion has clear sources,[4] but emulation specifically in terms of forgiveness is not as universally known. But God as the principal source of forgiveness does become a paradigm for human beings in Judaism.

The standard emphasis of rabbinic Judaism rests squarely on forgiveness as embedded in a process of change that is initiated by the person who did something wrong. In this sense, crime, change, and forgiveness are embedded in the much larger practice and metaphysical reality of *teshuva*, which could be translated as repentance, returning, transformation, or restoration. Teshuva, the capacity to transform oneself or a community, is considered to be one of the most sublime elements of faith in a good, forgiving God. The fact that repentance can change a guilty verdict, and even sin itself, is a great blessing. Resh Lakish, one of the great rabbinic authorities of the Talmudic period, exclaimed: "Great is repentance, for it transforms intentional sins [*zedonot*] into sins of negligence or forgetting [*shegagot*]." And in another version: "Great is repentance for it turns intentional crimes into testimonies for a person's goodness."[5] This presumably means that the degree of evil in the crime is now matched by the heroic effort it took on the part of the sinner to change what he was like, which turns the previous crime into a testimony for the person's present goodness. The discrepancy between the two versions of Resh Lakish's aphorism is solved Talmudically by suggesting that the latter refers to someone who repents out of love, while the former is someone who repents out of fear.[6]

There is also an important rabbinic idea, which is critical for Jewish consciousness, that true repentance comes when the person stands again in the same place, with the same opportunity to do the crime, and then resists it.[7] This will be important later in terms of strategies for building trust between enemies, but for now it suggests some concern with whether processes of repentance or confessions of wrongdoing are really authentic unless there is some external manifestation of the process. In fact, the rabbis of the Talmudic period suggest that there are limits to the legitimacy of repentance. For example, if someone sins and repents three times, the fourth is not believed, he (or she) is not forgiven. But this last conclusion may reflect the legal/spiritual court system of the rabbis and how to handle repeat offenders. On a divine-human plane, there are numerous sources, both biblical and rabbinic, that suggest that the patience of God, and the willingness to accept *ba'ale teshuva*, people who repent, is infinite, an eternal feature of existence itself.[8]

There are several interacting themes of forgiveness at work in these sources. There is, as already stated, the idea of teshuva, repentance. There is *mehila*, which is the standard word for forgiveness; but there is also *seliha*, which is sometimes translated as pardon and sometimes as forgiveness. *Seliha* is translated in Psalm 130:4 as "the power to forgive."[9] There is also the metaphor of wiping away or blotting out sin[10] and the concept of atonement, *kapparah*. But it is the wiping away, the pardoning and forgiving, that is stressed in most prayers, both biblical and rabbinic. Suffering is considered an atonement for sin, but the praying person expresses hope for those paths of atonement that do not involve suffering. Finally, it should be emphasized that the prayers, both daily and for special occasions, stress that divine forgiveness is a perpetual activity and that this is an ongoing process between God and human being that literally requires permanent patience on the part of God.[11]

Another crucial phrase is *over al pesha*, the passing over or overlooking of sin, and *noseh avon*, literally carrying the burden of sin.[12] All of these divine qualities entail forgiveness, forbearance, patience, and a resistance to anger, in addition to the obvious quality of mercy in overlooking someone's guilt. God, in these texts, is the ultimate knower of sin. He knows just how guilty everyone is in ways that are far more expansive than the sins that the public occasionally witnesses. Thus the fact that God continues to sustain human beings, to nurture their bodies from moment to moment, knowing full well the extent of their failings, is seen as a perpetual commitment to mercy, forgiveness, and patience. God loves and sustains every living human body even as the same God is conscious at every moment of the failings of that body's occupant. This willingness to nurture at the very same time that one is cognizant of another's failure is the quintessential quality of a forgiving being. This theological foundation is critical to understanding what is hoped for in the personality of the human being who is called on to forgive those who have hurt him.

The rabbis characterize forgiveness as something that should come immediately if it is clear that someone is embarrassed by what he (or she) has done or if he feels guilty about it.[13] In fact, there is a surprising notion of a person having a right to forgiveness when he has clearly repented and is now living a decent life. He may even insist upon it.[14]

In all of these cases, forgiveness is seen as a kind of quid pro quo for the moral transformation of the person. In interpersonal terms, it involves a bilateral, formal process that also has internal elements. But it seems that the rabbis saw something in forgiveness that goes beyond a bilateral process. They said, for example, that anyone who cries at the death of a good person is forgiven for all his (or her) sins;[15] that a good, kind man who experiences the death of his child (1) is to be treated with the greatest possible compassion, and (2) all his sins are forgiven[16]; and that if even one person does authentic teshuva, repentance, it is enough to forgive the entire world (!).[17]

This last point is particularly astonishing, and it suggests that there is an independent power that forgiveness has on a metaphysical level that extends

well beyond a simple tit-for-tat of one sin, one repentance, and one forgiveness for that sin. But it is also clear that most of the emphasis of this
literature is on the responsibility of individuals who have hurt someone else,
or sinned against God, to initiate the process of change themselves, and only
then receive a response from the injured "other."

There is, however, an accompanying body of literature that suggests a
unilateral process whereby the pious individual who forbears the hurts of
others, who is patient with them, and who surrenders his (or her) own
principles, or at least overlooks his indignation and sense of being wronged,
is acting in a patient fashion, as God does. This is seen as classic *imitatio dei*.
Patience seems to be the key idea here. Vengeance, even if it is justified, is
seen as the opposite of this divine quality. This is where the ideas of *over al
pesha*, the divine quality of tolerating human sins, and *noseh avon*, God accepting human sinfulness and coping with it, come into play.[18]

There is an important interplay of several related concepts here. Arrogance, or "hardness of the face" (*azut panim*), which is considered the opposite of humility, characterizes someone who never surrenders. He (or she)
always stands in a hard way before people; he is vengeful. The vengeful
person never forgives his friends who have injured him. This, in turn, causes
conflict and hatred. The person who is perpetually angry cannot surrender
his own positions, and this too leads to revenge.

Several conclusions emerge. Forgiveness as a means of peacemaking
must be accompanied by cultivation of the kind of person who develops a
sense of humility in human interactions; who disciplines himself (or herself)
in patience for long periods of time; who avoids a "hard face" or arrogance
in his presentation of self to others, especially to enemies; who learns to
control his anger; and who is willing to surrender his positions sometimes,
even if he is in the right.[19]

Humility and Silence

Closely related to forgiveness are the often overlooked qualities of humility
and silence. If one were to choose the two ingredients that are missing most
from human relations in the Middle East, they would be humility and silence. Perhaps that is why so many young Israelis have turned to Eastern
religions and have welcomed with open arms the likes of the Dalai Lama
and Thich Nhat Hanh to Israel.[20] A possible explanation of young Israeli
interest in these religious leaders is that, on one level, it is difficult to imagine
anyone who would irk the religious establishments of monotheism more
than these Buddhist teachers. Most monotheistic leaders—Jewish, Muslim,
and conservative Christian—would consider these teachers idolaters in the

classical biblical sense. The opportunity to do something to spite a religious establishment that controls key parts of their lives is never lost on the youth in the Israeli culture wars.

On a deeper level, however, young people always help identify what is missing in a culture, what its greatest weaknesses are. A young person has not yet had to buy into the established culture formulated by adults, and therefore he or she becomes an important barometer of any tragic flaws that may exist. It is no surprise that these Buddhist teachers, who practice silence and repeatedly speak of humility and compassion toward all living things, are the leaders who would most attract young, disaffected Israelis in search of spiritual solace. This is what is missing in life for many people of this region. These young people are happy to respect and accept the more un-familiar and strange aspects of Eastern spirituality because the underlying gentleness, humanity, and antiargumentation are qualities that are lacking most in an environment that has made tension a cultural centerpiece.[21]

As far as silence is concerned, the ritual practices of Judaism are rather loquacious in comparison to Buddhism, for example. Prayer is communal and loud; study is the same. However, the biblical prophetic tradition is a tradition that is characterized as much by silent listening as long speeches. After all, most monotheistic prophets received their wisdom from silent med-itation in desert locations. Even more important are the actual prescriptive traditions about the wisdom of silence and listening.

Patience and Transformation

At this juncture, patience plays a key role in creating adequate space for healing to occur. Patience intimates a kind of self-sacrifice, and this is a characteristic that is particularly difficult for injured parties to embrace in conflict interactions. The self-sacrifice involves a temporary suspension of the demands of justice and a willingness to focus on the transformation of relationships in order to create a world in which the needs and demands of justice will be more fully realized. Patience is a temporary sacrifice of some of one's justifiable needs and demands in order to create a world in which those needs and demands will be more easily met by future genera-tions. On a deeper level, however, religious patience, especially as emulation of a divine being, suggests an expansion of one's perception of reality, a seeing of reality in terms of the future even more than from the perspective of the present or past.

Wisdom and experience seem to prove that individuals or groups of people will repudiate the worst of their behavior someday when confronted with the evidence. Without even requiring compassion for an enemy or self-sacrifice, the wisdom of long views of time suggests that violent actions of enemies are at least as destructive to themselves as they are to others. The long view of time, or patience, knows that those who act so horrifically as to be indistinguishable from monsters will someday have grandchildren who will recoil in horror when confronted with the evidence and will repudiate those actions, just as have a new generation of Germans, or Americans when confronted with what was done in Vietnam or to Native Americans. In so doing, the very permanence that so many enemies seek through genocidal fantasies of eliminating others, such as "a thousand-year Reich," will be drowned in their descendants' shame and wish to forget.

This long view of change requires enormous patience, but it is something that Judaism suggests is essential to processes of reconciliation. It requires building a relationship with future persons and a confidence that history proves time and again that those new persons will emerge and are emerging even as one expresses patience with their failures.

Jewish mystical tradition suggests a profound process of reconciliation involving forgiveness. A person should emulate God as the one who actively wipes away another's sin. A person should take it upon himself to wipe away the sin of his fellow human being, and by virtue of this personal involvement in improving the life of the other, helping him with his failings, the offender becomes too ashamed to then revert to his old behaviors in front of the one who has generously helped him. This aid includes engaging the other even to the point of absorbing insults.

Similarly, a human being, like God, should forbear the sin of his (or her) fellow human being. With an enormous investment of patience, he should actually nurture the other, as God does, even as the other fails, suffering through this with him. In so doing, he stays with "the other" person until the person is "repaired" and the sin is wiped out.[22] This has profound implications in terms of conflict resolution.

Forbearance and Mercy

The standard conflict resolution method of engagement involves bilateral processes of communication and negotiation. This requires, on a moral level, a subtle combination of two values, peace and justice, in which, for the sake of peace, one agrees to the first stages of engaging the enemy "other" in a nonviolent meeting. But, for the sake of justice, that engagement will not involve self-sacrifice to the point of self-abuse. And yet part of the process of helping someone to change in a religious sense may involve the acceptance of a certain amount of humiliation. This is only possible because there is an implicit calculation of ethical values, namely, that it is worth occasionally absorbing insults in order to reach a deeper level of relationship with the estranged "other."

Everyone at one time or another has done this with the people that he (or she) truly loves, a father, mother, child, or lover. In the context of conflict dynamics, one occasionally yields to awful treatment (especially when one knows that the person who is being abusive is going through a particularly traumatic time) that one would never accept from others, because of a higher goal or deeper relationship that is too precious to place at risk. One suffers occasional insults and views them as worth it if they will help someone to change whom one loves. Classic conflict resolution theory and psychology might suggest that none of these insults, large or small, should be tolerated. They certainly should not be buried or left unaddressed. But everyone does this—often—in order to preserve his most cherished relationships.

Few allow for this kind of sacrifice, however, for the sake of enemies that they do not know. Yet this may help explain the difference between those in a particular group that has been subject to serious violence who try to make peace and those in the same group who view their peacemaker brethren as traitors. The latter cannot comprehend the sacrificial element of peacemaking. It is also true that peace efforts are sometimes motivated by enlightened self-interest, including, for example, avoiding the mutual de-struction and waste of resources that often accompanies warfare. Or peace-makers sometimes rationally argue that the quest for security that justifies huge defense budgets could more appropriately be achieved through careful, verifiable cooperation. These arguments for peace do not really evoke anger among the rejectionists but rather accusations of naiveté.

Some other peacemakers, especially religious ones, have an unmistakable sense of care for the enemy. Because of a perceived sense of common hu-manity, or common origins in God, they apply to the enemy "other" a level of tolerance that most others reserve for family or loved ones.[23] How many have looked into the eyes of an enemy's small children and recoiled in horror at the prospect of injuring them? These peacemakers view the abusive be-havior of some in a group in the context of the overall humanity of that group, which, in turn, is deserving of some kind of caring relationship. In fact, the flaws of the "other" evoke empathy, because the flaws suggest a common humanity and also evoke a response to the need that the "other" has for aid and understanding. All of this makes perfect sense in normal bonds that develop between lovers, for example, even including the ways in which one invariably hurts those that one loves. Extending this attitude to the larger, injuring world, however, while sensible to some, is horrifying to others, who see such a response as an act of betrayal. Rage among the latter is often the result. The act of truly caring for an enemy group, while simultaneously caring for one's own (in other words, universal care) is the most difficult of all human challenges, requiring extensive psychological and spiritual training.

Honor and Shame

Interwoven with forbearance are the qualities of honor and shame, two moral and spiritual categories that are fundamental to Jewish ethics. They are so fundamental to proper human relations and to the character of God in Judaism that they seep into the style and content of countless classical texts. They are not ethical precepts; they are ways of being—critical components of a metaphysical intentionality to the universe that has placed the human being in the exalted and responsible role of caretaker. Therefore, violations of human dignity are not only ethical failures causing immense personal injury, they are affronts to God and the divine plan. Furthermore, because this way of thinking has such deep communal roots in the Abrahamic tradition, a personal affront to one human being is often seen as an affront to all of Judaism. In Judaism, an assault on the dignity of a Jew is an assault on a member of God's own people and on the image of God implanted in the human being.

Each community and each religious tradition embodies different historical memories, however, and different ways of interpreting issues of honor and shame. Therefore, when Arabs and Jews gather to attempt peacemaking in a more lasting way than mere political negotiation, they had better expect equally sensitive reactions to issues of honor and shame. They should also anticipate that active efforts to recover honor as a central axis of peacemaking will yield powerful results if pursued carefully and sensitively.

The most important point is that conversations about honor and shame may have certain beneficial results, but nothing can compare to carefully crafted gestures and symbols of honor, ways that enemies can convey honor to the humiliated "other." This is at the heart of peacemaking, and it is often completely overlooked by formal processes of peacemaking. Furthermore, rarely is there a conflict in which both sides, regardless of how many security or economic imbalances there may be, do not need and, indeed, crave gestures of honor and respect from the other side.

It is understandable how the inhabitants of Israel and the Palestinian lands have developed a culture of stress and argumentation. Few would pass judgment on how others cope with interminable violence, injustice, and fear. But it is possible to diagnose what is wrong on a deep cultural, psychological, and spiritual level, note how many are rebelling against this, and recommend future alternatives. It seems clear, from a religious point of view, that humility, silence, and the wisdom of listening that emerge from compassion have ample precedent in monotheistic literature, both as recommended moral behavior and as deeper religious experience.[24] This is not to disparage in any way Eastern resources on these matters but rather to indicate a path of cultural regeneration for the Middle East.

Throughout biblical and qur'anic literature, humility is a sine qua non of the human being's position before God.[25] It is a quintessential act of faith and in Judaism is even portrayed as a divine attribute to be emulated.[26] For all biblically based religions, the great prophet of the Bible, Moses, is described as the humblest of all men.[27]

The Peacemaker as Bridge

The true, disciplined peacemaker always acts as if he (or she) is the *bridge* between his community and the enemy community. Effectively, in halakhic/ Jewish legal terminology, he must be able to contain within himself countervailing *mitsvot*, divinely mandated deeds in Jewish tradition. He must seek to emulate all the divine characteristics mentioned earlier toward the enemy "other" but must also express all of the love for special family, for the Jewish family, that the biblical and rabbinic tradition requires. He must extend a helping hand to the suffering enemy, as Exodus 23 demands, while simultaneously expressing the special love of his people that the Torah expects.

As such, the peacemaker must discover a prosocial relationship with the enemy "other," while maintaining a caring relationship with his (or her) own group. Otherwise he is no longer a bridge and therefore no longer an effective peacemaker. That is why it is difficult to escape judgment of the enemy as morally evil in some way, because if a person's group identity means anything, then it must mean some sympathy for the group's pain and, therefore, moral outrage at the injuries that the other group has inflicted. That having been said, the values of compassion, patience, and overtures of friendship are at the heart of these biblical means of reaching out to the enemy, even as one judges him unfavorably. This is a difficult but not impossible path. It is no more difficult than the tortuous path of diplomacy taken by veteran mediators of the Oslo peace process, for example. It is simply a different kind of discipline, and it can be cultivated in a great many people, though clearly not in all or even in most. If even a quarter of the adversaries in the Palestinian-Israeli conflict had cultivated these qualities, much of the violence would probably have been avoided.[28]

From Repentance to Reconciliation

In examining Jewish approaches to reconciliation, a more detailed understanding of Jewish repentance and personal change becomes useful. As history has proceeded, there has been an effort on the part of numerous legal codifiers to collect and unify classical Jewish sources on any number of subjects, including repentance. In addition, various Jewish thinkers have developed a philosophy of repentance.[29]

One of the greatest Jewish legal minds and codifiers of all time was Maimonides (d. 1204). His codification of the procedures and basic elements of repentance contains significant insights into the process of change in relationships.[30] Maimonides' codification by no means represents the final word on the subject, but it was brilliant at eliciting all of the various strands of thought from the classical sources, strands that become very useful when dealing with damaged relationships.

Most prominent in the rabbinic notion of repentance is confession (*viduiy*), which contains within it the elements of specifying the wrong done, regret (*haratah*), and the commitment to a completely different future (*kabalah le-habah*).[31] This element of change is over and above—but never a substitute for—restitution, where restitution is called for by the law, as in injury or theft. A "complete" repentance is one in which the opportunity to commit the crime presents itself again and at this point the person resists. This proves that the repentance is not due to some external fear or loss of physical strength but rather to an authentic change of heart.[32]

There are other elements of repentance that are not as fundamental but that enhance the process. These include crying, the giving of charity, and public confession, in addition to private expressions of sorrow. There is also the notion of changing one's name as an expression of the idea that one is now an utterly new person. In addition, there is the concept of voluntary exile from one's home as a kind of penance for what one has done. Exile is considered so powerful a trauma that it becomes an additional atonement for the sin(s) in question.

There is an additional requirement to engage in a kind of appeasement in approaching the victim. In addition to restitution and repentance, there is a notion of the perpetrator making peace with the victim by way of approaching him (or her) and apologizing until the victim forgives (*piyyus*). If this did not work, there was also a tradition of the perpetrator bringing three friends and apologizing before them and the victim, and doing this up to three times with three different sets of people. Maimonides suggests this as a last resort. But Rabbi Hisda, in the Talmudic period, recommended this as a formal requirement of repentance, replete with a ceremony involving successive rows of three colleagues, on three separate occasions.[33]

Finally, the Talmud, as well as Maimonides, who was its later codifier, recommended a procedure for the most tragic—and most common—human injury, that is, when the victim is already dead. The perpetrator goes to the grave of the victim with ten people and confesses and asks forgiveness there.[34] If there is restitution due, it is given to the heirs, and if there are no heirs, then it is given to the court, which would presumably distribute it to the community in as just a way as can be conceived.

One of the great dangers of this process of *piyyus* is how heavily focused it is on words, words that may or may not reflect the inner feelings of the perpetrator. Thus the Talmud warns against those who do not mean what they say. This is a danger to any process based on words.[35] It does intimate that, although Jewish repentance has many elements that go beyond word to deed, it is unavoidable that the victim must at some point be willing to trust the words of the perpetrator. This is perhaps the most difficult step of all.

It should be noted finally that the Day of Atonement, the holiest day of the Jewish year, is a day completely devoted to repentance in the form of repeated confessions in great detail. It is also a day characterized by great physical deprivation in the form of fasting, among other things. This fasting character has an important element of offering one's body and one's self to God. It is a kind of human sacrifice, a total offering like the ancient *olah,* whole burnt offering—similar to what almost befell the Patriarch Isaac, but without the prospect of bloodshed.[36]

The metaphor of the death and sacrifice of the old for the creation of the new has powerful implications in terms of the psychology of reconciling with an enemy. Of course, in an enemy system, it would require a kind of mutual rebirth. This has many implications for the kind of rhetorical language that should be used by Jews and Arabs as they are moved toward symbolic ceremonies and mythic moments of transition.

There are some remarkable qualities of this process that suggest that teshuva (repentance) can be a profoundly healing element of social change. Indeed, some rabbis speak of repentance as something that brings healing to the world.[37] Confession, regret, and commitment to the future is a powerful antidote to the damage done to victims. It addresses the need that victims have for their story to be acknowledged as true. Thus, it speaks to memory, to one's basic sense of identity, to one's sense of justice, and, perhaps most important, to one's trust in a completely new future. The detailed confession is the most difficult to elicit, especially when the crimes have been committed in both directions, as has been the case in Israel, and when it may expose the perpetrator to criminal prosecution and restitution. That said, it is important to remember that it is best to take what one can get, even if it represents half a loaf. It may be more than enough to create peace and reverse the violence if one can elicit from the parties a general regret about past action and commitment to a different future. Detailed confession, however, may prove more elusive. Detailed confession has a powerful impact on healing rage and allowing victims, and perhaps even perpetrators or their community, to move on. Denial of the details has a way of festering for as long as people pass on the memory of the crime, which can be forever.

Efforts underway in Slovakia and a number of other places to create shared histories between enemy groups are in a certain sense a secular expression of the religious power of confession. But it is modulated to deal with the reality of conflicting histories and stories. At the end of the day, it is just as difficult to predict the prosocial spiral of healing moments as it is to predict the destructive spirals of violence. In the Israeli-Palestinian conflict, general admissions of past mistakes may very well elicit more detailed and more powerful expressions of regret on both sides.

Returning to the classical Jewish sources, "complete repentance" (*teshuva gemurah*), as mentioned earlier, involves having another opportunity to commit the crime but resisting the temptation to do so. This speaks to the justifiable distrust that the victims have for the words of the perpetrators. This is often an elusive circumstance of peace processes, inasmuch as security measures are normally taken to ensure that the violence cannot be repeated. Or, quite often, there is total defeat of one side, and the opportunity to commit the same crime is no longer available, as was the case in Nazi Germany. In such cases, much is gained in guaranteeing security for former victims, but something is also lost. Without a repeat of the circumstances, it is doubtful that genuine trust can be restored. That is a price worth paying in circumstances of deadly violence, but the power of teshuva gemurah should still be acknowledged as an important tool of conflict resolution.

The power of venting the deep emotions involved in injury through crying is self-evident. What is not as evident is how important it may be for people who have injured or been injured to witness one another's tears. Of course, the cultural variation regarding public displays of emotion is self-evident, but the Jewish sources here speak to the power of tears in reconciliation in the search for authenticity and trust and should not be taken lightly. How often have communities, which have been involved in terrible crimes, buried the tears of countless members who cry in private over the crimes that loved ones committed. But they never shared those tears with the victims or survivors! How can the victims know the inner life of these people, if the tears are not shared?

Charity and acts of kindness as a kind of penance are yet another way that Judaism recommends going beyond the word of repentance to the deed. It is also a vital way to combine peace and justice, essential dimensions of any conflict. This aspect was captured in a Jewish community Friday night prayer service in California, to which the non-Jewish public of Sacramento was invited.[38] This followed an unprecedented burning of three synagogues in that city, a situation that evoked a powerful governmental and private communal response. The event was packed with people of every religion, including a large contingent from a national Methodist convention that was taking place in the city at the same time. At one point, a woman went up to the podium who represented the local region of the Methodist church. She made a donation of $4,000 toward the rebuilding of the synagogue library. This evoked a gasp and tears from the Jews present as well as two minutes of applause. To at least one Jewish witness, it represented a complete reversal of history, a move beyond pious words of apology to an unprecedented—in his mind—effort of Christians to help Jews rebuild their *religious* lives. The Christian community was investing in the future life of the Jewish community, not just reacting with guilt to their death or suffering.

Changing one's identity is another possible form of repentance that occurs in various expressions of the Abrahamic traditions. In Judaism, the idea of changing one's name certainly begins with the founding Patriarch himself, whose name was changed by God from Abram to Abraham, according to the Genesis story.[39]

Voluntary exile as yet another form of repentance raises some interesting issues, especially where conflict and violence have occurred in a dispute over land. Place and identity are integrally related for most people on the planet. But exile has a way of putting the issue of identity in a different light. Exile in the Jewish tradition represents punishment, but it is also a means of purification, a way of learning humility, and a way of avoiding the idolatry associated with land or the abuse of land that led to the original exile of the Jews in 586 BCE. It is no exaggeration to say, in this regard, that massive abuse of a majority by a minority takes place only in the context of absolute dominance of a piece of land by the minority. Refugees are capable of many crimes, but not organized, massive abuse.[40]

Voluntary exile as a way of experiencing life differently was often practiced by the saints in Jewish history. Communal leaders or rabbis who were used to special treatment would voluntarily exile themselves for a time, thus experiencing a new and anonymous identity. It was a way of discovering humility and loosening their attachment to ego. The ego is intimately related to, and exaggerated in false ways by, attachment or overattachment to place and superior social position, the latter being a derivative of permanent place. In Buddhism, as in some rabbinic approaches to Judaism, it is this over-attachment to place, position, and ego that is seen to be the basis of all misery (*dukkah*), as Buddhism expresses it, or sin (*he'et*), as Judaism would phrase it. Exile heals this in providing a new perspective on ego and human attachments.

Finally, repentance expressed through *piyyus*, a unilateral process of approaching the person or group that one has injured with words of kindness and reconciliation, has obvious benefits; and the power of the rituals and acts such as those recommended by Rabbi Hisda, mentioned earlier, is also self-evident.

Conclusion

In sum, the sacred scriptures of Judaism contain a number of insights on qualities relating to peacemaking that could be applied in meaningful ways to ameliorate the conflict in the Middle East. Among these qualities are forgiveness, forbearance, patience, mercy, humility, friendship toward one's enemy, and individual (or collective) accountability that leads to a heartfelt self-examination of one's own contributions to the dispute. Either singly or collectively, a thoughtful application of these theological insights could go far to transform the conflict.

NOTES

Notes to Chapter 5

1. See Psalms 15 and 24 as examples of an entire literary genre of "entrance Psalms," which provide the proper conditions for entrance to the Temple. This suggests the possibility of an entirely new approach to sacred space. Entry may be viewed as not a right of any person or group but a privilege that is preconditioned. Thus it does not deny or even minimize the importance of sacred space, as modern liberal approaches might, but it does deny it as a *right* of anyone, as opposed to a *reward* for a moral existence. This puts everyone who claims ownership on notice and makes the moral preconditions primary. In the context of conflict over sacred space it almost necessitates conflict resolution as a precondition of entry, given the fact that it is almost impossible to carry on intractable, bloody conflicts and then enter the sacred space with clean hands, as the Psalms demand. From a just war point of view, this is especially true in modern warfare, where, in a bizarre reversal of history, civilians, women, and children are the primary victims (sometimes the primary targets) and soldiers are the most protected class of people in the civilizations in question. This is true of most interethnic warfare today.

2. Leviticus 25:23; Psalms 24:1, 50:12.

3. Private interviews.

4. Marc Gopin, *Holy War, Holy Peace: How Religion Can Bring Peace to the Middle East* (New York: Oxford University Press, 2002), p. 52.

Notes to Appendix

1. See Marc Gopin, *Between Eden and Armageddon: The Future of World Religions, Violence, and Peacemaking* (New York: Oxford University Press, 2000).

2. See Sifre Be'Ha'alotekha 11; Midrash Tanhuma (Warsaw ed.) Exodus 27. See also Midrash Tehilim 25:14, where Esau's hatred is actually justified as due to the loss of the birthright.

3. The Turkish consul in France, Yolga Namik, a Muslim who repeatedly challenged the Nazis, defended and saved four hundred Jews during World War II. In explaining the reason why he did this, he said, "Yes, thanks be to Allah, as you say, I am a Muslim. But that does not at all signify that I feel differently from you French, or Jews, or whoever. That didn't hinder me from saving Jews, on the contrary! It is the humane qualities in a person that are important. If a man is good, kind, God—be it the God of Allah, of Jews, of Christians, of other religions—God, then, will take you into His Paradise . . . it goes better for you if you begin at once to show love, to help one's fellow man." Marek Halter, *Stories of Deliverance: Speaking with Men and Women Who Rescued Jews from the Holocaust*, trans. by M. Bernard (Chicago: Open Court, 1998), p. 194. This is a remarkable book that is quite relevant to issues of healing old wounds, a subject that will be addressed later on. Notice here Yolga Namik's understanding of Islam: any good, kind person is accepted by Allah into Paradise, which makes the effort to help fellow human beings on earth the principal vehicle to Heaven. So according to this view, only the Nazis and those who helped them were the ones who would not enter Paradise.

4. Talmud Bavli (henceforth T.B.) 133b.

5. The last phrase is a translation of *zekhuyot* in this context only.

6. T.B. Yoma 86b.

7. Ibid.

8. See, for example, Malachi 3.7; Zechariah 1:7, and the important discussion in Ezekiel 18. On the rabbinic side, see the *Amidah*, the quiet standing prayer, of Yom Kippur; see under *Elokenu, ve'eloke avotenu, mehal*, in the standard Mahzor of Yom Kippur. This prayer is said every year on the Day of Atonement many times. It reflects the notion of continuous forgiveness in response to the need every year to "wipe away" the sins of the people.

9. *Tanakh: The Holy Scriptures* (Philadelphia: Jewish Publication Society, 1985).

10. This nuance is captured by the verb *maha*. See Psalm 51:3. It is also often associated with the washing away of sin.

11. Many texts, including Micah 7:18–20, emphasize the divine quality of infinite patience, *erekh apayim*. The daily standing prayer, the Amidah, refers to God as a *mohel ve'sole'akh*, a Being whose essential quality or name is Forgiver and Pardoner. This emphasizes that forgiveness is built into a permanent relationship between God, the individual, and the community.

12. See Micah 7:18; Proverbs 19:11.

13. T.B. Hagigah 5a; T.B. Berachot 12b.

14. Avot of Rabbi Nathan 40:5, statement of Rabbi Elazar ben Rabbi Yossi.

15. T.B. Shabbat 105b.

16. T.B. Berachot 5b.

17. T.B. Yoma 86b; *Otzar Midrashim*, Gadol u'Gedulah 6.

18. There seems to be a parallel structure of the moral human trait of *ma'aver al middotav*, occuring in early rabbinic literature (T.B. Ta'anit 25b), and the divine quality of *ma'aver al pesha*, the wiping away of sin. In both cases, divine and human, it involves a kind of surrender of justifiable indignation in order to achieve a higher moral goal of compassion and, above all, patience. See *Orhot Tzadikim* (n.d.; rpt. Jerusalem: Eshkol, 1946), chaps. 4, 8, 12.

19. *Orhot Tzadikim*, chaps. 4, 8, 12.

20. See Yair Sheleg, "From Yiddishkeit to Yeshivashram," *Ha'aretz*, September 29, 2000; Yair Sheleg, "Faith Healers," Ha'aretz, April 21, 2000.

21. It goes without saying that this is the *perception* of Buddhism in the West, or the way in which it has been presented and hermeneutically developed by great contemporary masters such as the Dalai Lama. There is plenty of conflict and pettiness in the history of organized Buddhism that could be comparable to monotheistic history. However, it is perhaps less bloody. This deserves a separate study.

22. Rabbi Moshe Cordovero, *Tomer Devorah* (New York: Feldheim, 1993), chap. 1, pp. 7–11. Cordovero continues (pp. 17–19) with the effectiveness of never perpetuating one's anger. Citing Exodus 23:5 on the biblical commandment to help one's enemy, he quotes T. B. Pesachim 113b, which suggests that the anger that one party feels to the other in this text is due to the fact that A witnessed B committing a crime, but does not have a second witness, and thus cannot bring B to justice. This makes A hate B. But the Bible instructs the believer to help this criminal with his burden anyway, as a gesture of love, in order to help B literally leave behind (a Midrashic rereading of the phrase *azov ta'azov* in the biblical verse) his sin. Thus, Cordovero applies this process of reconciliation even to those who one sees as violators of the norms of society or the norms of the Torah.

23. It would be interesting to do a study measuring what is normally referred to as "unconditional love," namely, the tendency to express strong levels of respect and love for loved ones even when they do things with which one profoundly disagrees. Do those who have a tendency to be peacemakers have a strong quotient of unconditional love for loved ones relative to the larger population? Is there an inverse proportionality, wherein those who have greater tolerance for enemy groups have less tolerance for their own immediate love relationships? What evokes in some the human capacity to care, even in the context of extreme disappointment, is quite relevant to the study of conflict resolution.

24. *Tractate Derekh Eretz Zuta* 1; *Avot of Rabbi Nathan* 15; For a representative collection of rabbinic approaches to humility, see Moshe Chayim Luzzatto, *The Path of the Just*, trans. by Shraga Silverstein (New York: Feldheim, 1969), chap. 22. There are numerous sources on silence and its relationship to understanding. See Midrash Rabbah (Margoliot ed.) Leviticus 16:5; Midrash Tanhuma (Warsaw ed.) *Va'ye'tseh* 6; Otsar Midrashim Alpha Beta d'Ben Sira, paragraph 19; Tractate Derekh Erets Zuta 7; T. B. Pesahim 99a.

25. See, for example, Qur'an 7:161; 57:16.

26. See Midrash Rabbah Deuteronomy 7:12; Midrash Tanhuma (Warsaw ed.), Bereshit 4, Vay'erah 8, Ki Tisah 15.

27. Numbers 12:3.

28. There are other religious values that involve the temporary suspension of judgment of others until one gets to truly understand them. This provides a vital space in the relationship that allows for open-minded listening and the prevention of rash judgments but that also does not require the surrender of one's values of justice. Ultimately, maintaining a sense of justice requires passing judgment on the actions of others. But if it is coupled with a temporary suspension, training in listening and empathy, then it is likely that one's sense of justice will become more nuanced and subject to compromise with the justice perspective of the enemy.

29. See, for example, Jonah Gerondi (d. 1263), *The Gates of Repentance* (New York: Feldheim, 1976). For a contemporary set of essays on repentance, see Pinchas Peli, *Soloveitchik on Repentance: The Thought and Oral Discourses of Rabbi Joseph B. Soloveitchik* (New York: Paulist Press, 1984).

30. Maimonides' Laws of Repentance is to be found in his *Mishneh Torah*, the Book of Knowledge. For an English translation and commentary, see *Maimonides, Mishneh Torah, Hilchot Teshuvah: A New Translation and Commentary*, by Rabbi Eliyahu Touger (New York: Maznaim, 1987).

31. Maimonides, *Mishneh Torah*, Laws of Repentance, 1:1.

32. Ibid., 2:1–6.

33. T.B. Yoma 87a.

34. Many texts exist in later Jewish history of prayers for the graveside. Several are dedicated to asking forgiveness of the dead. See, for example, *Siddur for the House of Mourning*, ed. by David Weinberger and J. J. Schacter (Brooklyn, N.Y.: Mesorah Publications and the Orthodox Union, 1995).

35. The problem of the use of the word for peacemaking is too large a topic to be dealt with here. This is treated more systematically in Marc Gopin, *Holy War, Holy Peace: How Religion Can Bring Peace to the Middle East* (New York: Oxford University Press, 2002).

36. Abraham had come within inches of sacrificing his only son, Isaac, to God, based on a divine test or command, as recorded in the book of Genesis. This is a pivotal Jewish story of test and sacrifice, and simultaneous repudiation of human sacrifice. But it is also the quintessential Jewish paradigm of ultimate offering of one's most precious possession to God.

37. T.B. Yoma 86a.

38. Personal letter from Alan Canton to the author, Sacramento, California, June 29, 1999, circulated by Leah Green and the Compassionate Listening Project.

39. Genesis 17:5.

40. Leviticus 26:34–35.

6 David A. Steele

Christianity in Bosnia–Herzegovina and Kosovo
From Ethnic Captive to Reconciling Agent

In the early 1990s, post-Tito Yugoslavia began to unravel along ethnoreligious lines. Slovenia, Croatia, Macedonia, and Bosnia & Herzegovina all declared independence in 1991-92. Under President Slobodan Milosevic, Serbia led various military efforts to unite Serbs in the neighboring republics into a "Greater Serbia." Although these efforts ultimately proved unsuccessful, fighting in Bosnia was especially intense, with Muslim Bosnians, Catholic Croatians, and Orthodox Serbs squaring off against one another and engaging to one degree or another in what came to be known as "ethnic cleansing." Finally, in late 1995, NATO peacekeepers restored order based on the U.S.-brokered Dayton Accords.

In 1999, Milosevic and the Serbs moved against the ethnic Albanians living in the once autonomous Yugoslav province of Kosovo, expelling thousands from their homes and forcing them to flee to refugee camps in neighboring Albania and Macedonia. This action provoked a strong international response, including the NATO bombing of Serbia and the stationing of NATO and Russian peacekeepers in Kosovo. To date, both Bosnia and Kosovo are being run by a NATO-led international coalition.

Extraordinary examples of cooperative, interfaith efforts at reconciliation exist among all the religious communities in Bosnia-Herzegovina and Kosovo.[1] In the most prominent postwar case, the leaders of the Serbian Orthodox, Roman Catholic, Muslim, and Jewish communities of Bosnia-Herzegovina publicly affirmed a statement of shared moral commitment and agreed to create a new interreligious council in their country in 1997. Together they condemned "acts of hatred based on ethnicity or religious differences," and they denounced "acts of revenge." They also resolved to create procedures for processing and verifying "complaints concerning human rights violations," which they deemed to be transgressions of divine, as well as human, law.[2] Three years later, all four leaders of this Interreligious Council of Bosnia-Herzegovina went to Kosovo in order to encourage their counterparts in that war-torn society to form a similar interfaith institution. In response to this initiative, Kosovo's Serbian Orthodox, Roman Catholic, and Muslim leaders formed their own Interreligious Council and joined their voices in condemning all violence, intolerance, and acts of retribution.[3]

These two examples of postwar collaboration are of historic importance. Not so long before, some of the religious leaders of these same faith communities had condoned aggressive war and ethnic division. The tendency of religion to deepen social cleavages, rather than unite the different ethnic peoples, in the former Yugoslavia has a long history. It can be traced, in part, back to the sixteenth- and seventeenth-century European political order whereby the people were expected to adopt the religion of the ruler. But it was also a result of the millet system of local control within the Ottoman Empire, in which the Turks, during their five hundred years of rule in the Balkans, gave local administrative authority to religious hierarchies in exchange for their loyalty to the sultan. In this way, religion inevitably molded social and political identity and, in turn, was shaped by political loyalties.[4]

Consequently, at the end of the twentieth century, when the forty-five-year communist experiment to delegitimize ethnoreligious identity failed, the door to a politicized religion was, again, opened in Yugoslavia. During the 1980s, certain factions within the various religious communities began to identify themselves with nationalist groups. Religious revival, affiliated with ethnic nationalism, was on the rise among Croatian Catholics, Kosovo Albanian Catholics, and Serbian Orthodox, resulting in increased ethnic tensions in Croatia, Herzegovina, and Kosovo. This recent revitalization of religious influence in the former Yugoslavia has been documented by surveys conducted by the Institute of Social Sciences in Belgrade, revealing that 84 percent of the country's adult population expressed a confessional identity by 1990. Some scholars have contended that this revitalized religiosity, together with the nationalist views held by some religious leaders, provided fertile soil for ethnopolitical mobilization.[5]

There has been great debate over the exact role played by each of the religious communities, especially in regard to their actions in Bosnia-Herzegovina and Kosovo. For the purpose of this chapter, which is focused on the role of Christianity in the Balkans conflict, the examination will be limited mostly to the Serbian Orthodox Church and the Roman Catholic Church. Have these churches been founts of ethnic hostility, contributing to the atmosphere that led to war? Or have they been agents of reconciliation, contributing to efforts to make or maintain peace? There have been rigorous denunciations accusing most of the main religious traditions of complicity, especially those in Bosnia-Herzegovina. These have been countered by denials by both indigenous and outside observers. The issue is certainly a complex one that necessitates looking beyond merely a recitation of the appropriate official statements on the part of either Serbian Orthodox or Roman Catholic hierarchies. One must also acknowledge when the unofficial statements of church leaders seem, at least in the eyes of their counterparts, to contradict official statements. In addition, one must examine the actions of church leaders, as well as local priests. In the end, one must evaluate to what degree the statements and actions of church leaders have contributed to the rise of ethnic hostility or to the pursuit of reconciliation. Furthermore, any examination of the role of the church in this part of the world must also examine the part played by religious identity in the resurgence of ethnic identity.

The purpose of this chapter, however, is not only to examine the role played, both negative and positive, by various actors within the Serbian Orthodox and Roman Catholic Churches in Bosnia-Herzegovina and Kosovo but also to examine the potential within the Christian tradition for effective future peacemaking and reconciliation efforts within both of these conflict-ridden societies. Therefore, the conclusion of this chapter is devoted to an application of Christian teachings on reconciliation and peacemaking to the present situation in Bosnia-Herzegovina and in Kosovo. In the conclusion, traditional Christian teachings on peace, reconciliation, and hospitality toward the stranger will be examined, which will then be followed by a demonstration of how both the indigenous churches and the wider Christian world community have begun to put these Christian principles into practice. Three basic peacebuilding roles—advocacy, mediation, and education—will be examined in a number of contexts: holding interfaith seminars for religious people, building indigenous interfaith institutions, supporting faith-inspired individuals, and moving beyond faith communities to influence the peacebuilding capacity of the wider society.

The Role Played by the Churches in Bosnia-Herzegovina

Both the Serbian Orthodox and the Roman Catholic churches have, since early in the war, issued statements expressing opposition to the armed conflict. Some of these statements have been joint proclamations. Patriarch Pavle of the Serbian Orthodox Church and Cardinal Franjo Kuharic of the Croatian Catholic Church met in Geneva on September 23, 1992, and issued a statement calling for an immediate end to all hostilities in Bosnia-Herzegovina, the closing of all prison camps, the cessation of ethnic cleansing, the condemnation of all criminals regardless of religious affiliation, the return of all refugees, and equal access to humanitarian aid. Furthermore, it was significant that these spiritual leaders, coming from Serbia and Croatia (lands that had stoked the flames of resurgent nationalism in Bosnia-Herzegovina), expressed regret that the head of Yugoslavia's Islamic Community, the reis-ul-ulema Jakub Selimosky, had been prevented from coming because of the siege of Sarajevo.[6] In November of that year all three religious leaders signed a statement containing the same points.[7]

Alongside the expressions of opposition to war and affirmations of concern for other ethnic groups, however, there has also been a darker side to the voice of the churches. Beginning in the early 1980s, many "unofficial" statements and actions by leaders within both churches served to enflame and legitimize armed conflict. Primarily, this was a function of the role played by religion in the identity formation of each community. Religion has long been the single most important defining factor in ethnic differentiation for Serbs, Croats, and other peoples in the region. The Serbian Orthodox Church was essential to the preservation of Serbian identity, and likewise the Roman Catholic Church was essential to the preservation of Croatian identity, as various foreign empires dominated the region.[8]

All too often the strong linkage between religion and ethnicity has greatly contributed toward blindness on the part of Christian people from both churches. Some people and groups within each of the churches have, out of a concern for the well-being of their own people, spoken and acted in ways that were perceived as a threat to others. Some of this has been fed by fears of victimization. Concern for the preservation of one's own church or ethnic group has too often nourished negative perceptions of, and actions toward, others. This has contributed toward the sacralization of one's own nationality and the development of an atmosphere of intolerance. As a result, some leaders in both churches legitimized the aspirations and underlying fears of their own ethnic group while nationalist politicians manipulated this religious sentiment in order to solidify their control over their own people and territory.

At the same time, it must also be recognized that other factors—cultural, political, economic, and military—played major roles in the escalation of violence in the former Yugoslavia. Moreover, religious leaders, emerging from decades of marginalization under communist rule, were understandably anxious to play a larger public role in societies that were searching for their traditional foundations. Finally, clergy understandably give pastoral priority to their own communities, speak out against human rights abuses against their people, and act as advocates for the legitimate defense of their people and customs.

However, the actions of many church people from both confessions went well beyond the outer limits of acceptability. First was the extensive support given in many ways to nationalist political parties. By making declarations, attending meetings, being available for photos, or lobbying for legislation, they advertently or inadvertently sanctified and legitimized questionable political actions and programs. This activity helped to foster unconditional adherence and overheated veneration for political frameworks in an attempt by the political leadership to present their own agenda as nonnegotiable and immune from dissent. Second, many clergy actively participated in the development and propagation of national myths and memories. Sermons, speeches, and religious media were used to reinforce enemy images of the "other" and to depict their particular church as the defender of the nation. The newly gained freedom of expression was too often used to sacralize a victimhood mentality within one's own confession, a mentality that maximized the rights demanded for oneself and minimized the abuses suffered by others at the hands of one's own group. Third, a segment of the clergy actively participated in military activity, blessing sordid military initiatives and actually taking up arms themselves. There is no case of disciplinary action being taken for such behavior within either of the churches. Finally, some clergy were involved in the formation of nationalist organizations.

While primarily addressing the role of Christian churches in Bosnia-Herzegovina, it is also important to at least note the role played by the Islamic community. Certainly there are links between ethnic Muslim and religious Muslim identity, though the origin of an officially recognized Muslim nationality in Yugoslavia is as recent as the early 1970s. The political influence of Islamic religious leaders in Bosnia-Herzegovina was also initially more limited than that of their Orthodox and Catholic counterparts. In the aftermath of tremendous Muslim suffering at the beginning of the war in the early 1990s, political advocacy on the part of religious Muslim leaders did increase. In post-war Bosnia-Herzegovina, their social and political influence is now much greater than it was at the beginning of the war in 1992. However, at no point could one accuse the Bosnian Muslims of supporting Islamic fundamentalism. Only a few foreign mujahedin have operated in Bosnia-Herzegovina and they have not been accepted by most of the Bosnian population. At the same time, Serbian and Croatian charges regarding the rise of Islamic fundamentalism in Bosnia abounded in the early 1990s.[9] Having countered the extreme argument, however, it is important to note that some, though not all, observers have claimed that a few leading Bosnian Muslim theologians, imams, and activists became increasingly radical, though not fundamentalist.[10]

The most controversial Islamic influence, however, came not from Islamic religious leaders but from some Muslim government officials, beginning with President Alija Izetbegovic and his Party of Democratic Action. In 1990, President Izetbegovic published the "Islamic Declaration," in which he called for the implementation of Shari'ah, Islamic law, although he specified that this must be done through democratic process.[11] In addition, another Islamic publication, distributed around Bosnia-Herzegovina in early 1992, entitled "The Declaration of Independence of the Islamic Republic of Bosnia and Herzegovina," called for one of the two houses of the Bosnian Parliament to be composed of "beys," or religious leaders from the Islamic community.[12] In response, many Serbs and Croats then charged the Izetbegovic government with attempting to inflate the number of voting Muslims in order to democratically elect an Islamic government in Bosnia-Herzegovina.[13] Visits by President Izetbegovic to Iran and Libya further fed Serbian and Croatian fears of Bosnia becoming part of a pan-Islamic federation, a vision also stated by Izetbegovic in his "Islamic Declaration."[14] Consequently, although the minister for religious affairs for the Bosnian government affirmed the right of people of all faiths to live together in peace,[15] a majority of the Serbian and Croatian population were understandably fearful of being led by a president who was on record as opposing interfaith coexistence.[16]

At the same time, there was a distinct difference in the roles played by religious leaders of the Muslim and Christian communities. Some leaders within both Christian churches fostered a social/political infrastructure that was both nationalistic and intolerant. Taduesz Mazowiecki, the UN human rights rapporteur in the Balkans, has accused Catholics in Herzegovina and Serbian Orthodox in Bosnia-Herzegovina of behaving nationalistically. Mazowiecki described the role of religion as structural and deliberate.[17] These negative nationalist tendencies were most apparent in locations where a given tradition was dominant, since it is there that the tradition sensed a threat to its "rightful place in society." Where a tradition was in the minority, it tended to be more accommodating, often out of a need for its very survival. Yet even in locations where a tradition was in the majority, one can find examples of true Christian inspiration, where individual clergy and laity functioned as effective agents of reconciliation. Illustrations of these positive and negative roles will be examined in each of the Christian traditions.

The Serbian Orthodox Church in Bosnia-Herzegovina

One of the characteristics of the Eastern Orthodox Church is its regionalization, the division into different autocephalous churches along territorial borders. Originally, the scope of regional synods coincided with the administrative divisions of temporal authority in the fourth century. When new churches, such as the Serbian Orthodox Church, started along the borders of the Roman Empire, the identity of these churches naturally developed primarily along cultural or ethno-linguistic lines.

When modern nationalism was introduced in western Europe in the eighteen century, it affected the Orthodox churches of eastern Europe. Faced with the status quo of Ottoman or Austro-Hungarian rule, the leadership of many Orthodox churches, sometimes enthusiastically, sometimes warily, subscribed to the sweeping nationalist movement. This nationalistic movement became intertwined with ethnic struggles for liberation in the Balkans, despite the fact that the ecumenical patriarch opposed the trend and the Synod of Constantinople in 1872 condemned ethnophyletism—the idea that nationalism should be the decisive factor in church organization.[18] Today, the Orthodox Church points to its historic opposition to ethnophyletism in order to question the establishment of autocephalous (independent of patriarchal authority) churches, as is the case today with some elements of the church in Montenegro and Macedonia. However, theologically, ethnophyletism questions the elevation of the national (understood as ethnic) group to a place of importance above that of God.[19] The current metropolitan of Montenegro, Amfilohije Radovic, defines this as "deification of the nation and transformation of the Living God into a tribal deity."[20] Given this definition, it is appropriate to apply the term to the emergence of religious nationalism within both the Orthodox and Catholic traditions of the former Yugoslavia. In fact, more than one Orthodox theologian has done so in recent times. Stanley Harakas, a Greek Orthodox theologian, identifies the ethnic division of the Orthodox Church as both a strength and a weakness. On the one hand, according to Harakas, it unites people; on the other hand it encourages overidentification with a particular ethnic heritage.[21] The Serbian Orthodox theologian Radovan Bigovic goes even further, saying that although the Orthodox Church condemned ethnophyletism as a heresy, it has, in reality, never abandoned secular nationalist romanticism, which he calls an "ecclesiological disease."[22]

Ethnic Captivity within the Serbian Orthodox Church in Bosnia-Herzegovina

During the 1980s, some segments of the Serbian Orthodox Church in Yugoslavia became a haven for the nationalist-oriented intelligentsia, offering them legal cover and moral legitimacy. This occurred because of the re-emergence of nationalism among the younger members of the hierarchy throughout the Church—an assessment made by a number of Serbian as well as foreign analysts. According to one Serbian journalist, this group of emerging church leaders functioned as a "clerical-political underground," striving to enhance the influence of the Church in Yugoslav society, advance the interests of the Serbian nation, and encourage the nationalist renaissance during the 1980s.[23] The interest in nationalism occurred in response to grievances that the Serbian community felt against other nationalities in the former Yugoslavia. But it derived its primary legitimacy from its self-understanding as the guardian of the Serbian people (or nation).[24] This heritage has its roots deep within Serbian history and tradition. Absent the Serbian Orthodox Church, it is unlikely that the Serbian people would have survived historically as a separate ethnic group. One indication of the strength of this religious-ethnic linkage can be gleaned from a statement that appeared in 1992 in *Pravoslavlje*, an official publication of the Serbian Orthodox Church, claiming that "Serbdom without Orthodoxy . . . is impossible; it is a mere abstraction."[25]

The aim of this resurgent nationalism was to provide a sense of belonging for the historically victimized Serbian people. This was depicted as especially important for those Serbs who lived in parts of Yugoslavia outside the borders of Serbia. Leading Serbian Orthodox theologians focused on the sufferings of the Serbian people, especially at the hands of Kosovar Albanians, Croats, and Bosnians. Serbian Orthodox journals have published accounts of Serbian victimization since the early 1980s, stressing the "uniqueness" of the genocide against the Serbs.[26] By May 1990, Serbian Orthodox clergy in Bosnia-Herzegovina were spreading the alarm that the resurrected Croatian Ustasha movement (a World War II fascist political party that was responsible for genocide committed against the Serbs) was again a grave threat and encouraging all Bosnian Serbs to vote in the coming elections for those who would guarantee and protect Serbian religious and national values.[27] At the same time, *Pravoslavlje* called for the defense of Serbs and Orthodoxy, if necessary by military means.[28] In all these cases, incidents of Serbian suffering, or a credible threat of suffering, did occur. The problem was that these were often exaggerated and used to justify repressive responses against others.

The cataloguing of Serb victimization, fed by theological interpretation, continued in numerous statements issued by the Serbian Orthodox Church throughout the war in Bosnia-Herzegovina. Although the Church hierarchy also recognized the suffering of other groups, at least in general terms, any specific itemization was usually limited to atrocities committed against Serbs. One example of both tendencies can be found in the "Memorandum of the Holy Assembly of Bishops of the Serbian Orthodox Church" issued early in the war (May 1992). On the one hand the statement called for recognizing the human rights of everyone and condemned the war, the displacement of civilians, and the destruction of religious buildings. On the other hand it itemized only Orthodox churches that had been destroyed and concentration camps where Serbs were imprisoned.[29]

There were also exceptions to the aforementioned inability to view the actions of one's own people with the same attitude of repentance that one requires of others. In April 1992, at the beginning of the ethnic cleansing campaign by Serb militias in Bosnia, Bishop Jefrem of the Serbian Orthodox Church in Banja Luka, Bosnia (together with Catholic bishop Franjo Komarica and Muslim leader Muftija Halilovic) signed an appeal condemning Chetnik (Serb nationalist) forces for slaughtering Muslim believers at worship in a mosque, attacking Catholic churches and attempting to create a "Greater Serbia."[30]

Such opinions, however, were not again heard from Serbian Orthodox leadership in Bosnia-Herzegovina once the propaganda machine pressured all Serb voices to defend against false accusations. By December of that year, the hierarchy of the Serbian Orthodox Church issued its "Communique Concerning the False Accusations against the Serbian Nation in Bosnia and Herzegovina." Despite careful documentation by internationally renowned organizations such as Amnesty International and Helsinki Watch, the bishops claimed that rape camps run by Serbian militias did not exist, while at the same time charging that Serbian women had suffered the same abuse. What had been seen by the whole world as an horrendous atrocity was depicted by the bishops as propaganda designed to satanize the Serbian people.[31] Even when the Belgrade government asked Atanasije Jevtic, the bishop of Herzegovina, for an explanation for the persecution of Muslims and destruction of the mosque in Trebinje in early 1993, the bishop responded that such a charge was an insult against the Serbian people. Bishop Atanasije went on to fault the government for allowing Serb villages and churches in Herzegovina to be destroyed by Croat forces.[32]

In addition to defending against the accusations of other people, there are instances where local Serbian Orthodox priests contributed directly to the fueling of hatred. For example, Father Djordje Ilica of Ilidza (a suburb of Sarajevo that was under Serbian control) said publicly that "the one who forgives is worse than the one who did the bad thing in the first place. . . . I would like us to live with any nationality except the Muslims and Croats. Even the children, they will grow up to kill Serbs again."[33] Furthermore, Serbian Orthodox priests and bishops actually blessed weapons and paramilitary units that were involved in executing the most brutal ethnic cleansing, including carving and burning signs of the cross into the bodies of Bosnian Muslims.[34] In the face of protests from antiwar protesters, one Serbian Orthodox bishop even accepted the support and protection of Arkan, one of the most infamous paramilitary commanders.[35] Another bishop claimed that the Bosnian Serb military acted in accord with Orthodox tradition and that General Mladic accepted all the suggestions of the metropolitan.[36]

The close linkage between church and ethnicity is also the best prism through which to understand the relationship between the Serbian Orthodox Church and the governments of both Serbia and the Bosnian Serb Republic. The fundamental position of the Church on church/state relations was given in *Pravoslavlje* at the beginning of the war in 1992:

> The Church is the sole moral arbiter in state-political matters. . . . The Church has no pretensions to replace the state government, but only that it has the right to control the government from the outside and to express its judgment—all for the well-being of the people.[37]

> If the government of the state and its highest leadership are not Orthodox, i.e. they do not have a spiritual relationship with the Serbian Orthodox Church . . . then they cannot be legitimate Serb representatives. . . . Fortunately, there are Serb lands that have all the features of a Serb state. Those are the Serbian Republic of Krajina and the Serbian Republic of Bosnia and Herzegovina. . . . Whether some day Serbia and Montenegro will become Serbian states only time will show.[38]

These quotations demonstrate the fact that the Serbian Orthodox Church considered only governments that accepted Orthodox tradition to be valid leaders of the Serbian people. This fundamental principle was to play a very large role in determining the stance that the Church would take vis-à-vis support for specific governments, for military action, and for peace treaties. All would be measured or legitimized on the basis of support for pro-Orthodox governing parties.

Initially, the Serbian Orthodox Church gave strong support to President Slobodan Milosevic. There were a number of reasons for this. First, Milosevic broke with previous communist policy and adopted a more nationalist stance toward the ethnic tensions in various parts of the former Yugoslavia. Both Milosevic and many Church leaders shared a common perspective regarding the grievances of the Serbian diaspora in Kosovo, Croatia, and Bosnia-Herzegovina. Patriarch German voiced support for Milosevic's change of attitude, in this regard, at the 600th anniversary of the Battle of Kosovo in 1989. Second, Milosevic took a more accommodating position toward the ecclesiastical goals and aspirations of the Serbian Orthodox Church. For example, he supported the completion of the Cathedral of St.

Sava in Belgrade, a project that had been halted by previous communist governments.[39] Third, Milosevic supported the right of all Serbs to live in one state. In addition to any political reasons, this was important to the Church because any other solution would mean the breakup of the Church's own administration, perhaps even removal of Orthodox churches in this new diaspora from the jurisdiction of the Patriarchate in Belgrade.[40]

The rapprochement between Milosevic and the Serbian Orthodox Church, however, was short-lived. Again, there were a number of reasons. The Church had always been suspicious of the socialist orientation of the regime. However, the failures of Milosevic to protect Serbs in Croatia and Bosnia-Herzegovina, together with the imposition of international sanctions against Yugoslavia, began to erode Serbian Orthodox support for his policies.[41] Consequently, in May 1992, the Holy Assembly of Bishops of the Serbian Orthodox Church, citing both political and religious reasons, publicly accused the Milosevic regime of staging elections, failing to "make possible equal rights for a democratic dialogue in society," failing to "heal the consequences of civil and fratricidal war," forbidding religious education in the schools, dispossessing and selling of Church property, and not allowing "the Church to assume her rightful place in society which belonged to her for centuries." The bishops concluded by distancing the Church from both the government and its constitution, calling for Milosevic's resignation and the creation of a "government of people's confidence, national unity, and salvation of all the people."[42] As Milosevic began to utilize increasingly authoritarian policies and to distance himself more from the Bosnian Serb government and from support for the idea that all Serbs should be allowed to live in the same state, the Serbian Orthodox leadership repeated this call for his resignation many times during the next eight years.[43] Although Patriarch Pavle clearly endorsed Serbian solidarity and self-determination, he also publicly supported anti-Milosevic demonstrations in 1997 and 2000 and condemned Serbia's political leaders for closing their eyes to the war crimes committed by Serbs in Bosnia-Herzegovina.[44]

In contrast to the conflicted relationship between the Church and Milosevic, the Church maintained a close and supportive relationship with the Bosnian Serb president, Radovan Karadzic, and the Bosnian Serb government.[45] Karadzic himself lauded the role of the Serbian Orthodox Church, saying:

> We think the Serbian Orthodox Church is the most important connecting tissue that has preserved the unity of the Serbian people through centuries. . . . We think that the Church should always be asked for advice. It is an honor for us that they are with us, that they

assess the steps we take and support us. . . . I have profited very much from my firm connections with the church. I have heard many useful pieces of advice, and received support for my decisions.[46]

In fact, in an interview published in *Svetigore*, the official monthly magazine of the Serbian Orthodox Church in Montenegro, Karadzic described the influence of the Church in even greater terms. He said: "What is most important we ask our Church; not a single important decision was made without the Church."[47] The Church itself confirmed its support for the Bosnian Serb government when Metropolitan Jovan of Tetovo said, in May 1993, that the Holy Synod of the Serbian Orthodox Church gave support to the efforts of the Bosnian Serbs to obtain their own state.[48] The same year, Father Dragomir Ubiparipovic writes,

> Church space and festivals were used for the promotion of leaders of the Serb Democratic Party and they were recommended to the people. In the limitless support, our tendency toward excess was clearly expressed. It went so far that even party leaders were confused by the support and the too flattering evaluations of these leaders—about their alleged God-given Messianic roles. And why not, when clerics . . . reminded them in front of the people "that God himself sent them to save the Serb clan." Therefore, one is to expect that the Church will be richly rewarded by the new government. But if one raises the question of responsibility for the outcome of the war (destruction and victims) in addition to the political and military leaders one should expect that the Church will also be mentioned.[49]

Later, Metropolitan Nikolaj of Dabro-Bosnia, Bishop Vasilije of Zvornik-Tuzla, and Bishop Atanasije of Zahum-Herzegovina were all present at the Bosnian Serb Assembly in Pale during the deliberations over acceptance of the Vance-Owen peace plan in 1994. Bishop Atanasije relayed the message of the Serbian Orthodox Church opposing the partitioning of Serb lands and people. After the Bosnian Serb Assembly decided to reject the peace plan, Metropolitan Amfilohije of Montenegro sent his support for the decision, saying: "Having revived in yourself the faith in God's justice, you renewed St. Lazar's loyalty to the people and raised the dignity of the Serb people."[50] Even after the war, in 1996, Bishop Jefrem of Banja Luka described Karadzic as one who demonstrated his faith in God before the whole world and as one ready to become a martyr who gives his life for justice, truth, and faith.[51]

From all these examples, it is clear that a significant number of leaders within the Serbian Orthodox Church, both within and outside Bosnia-

Herzegovina, allowed themselves to be associated with Karadzic's provocative ethnoreligious statements, political goals, and military policies. Some of these church leaders, out of the conviction that Karadzic represented a divinely blessed state leadership, went even further and gave Karadzic and his Bosnian Serb government their full support.

Agents of Reconciliation within the Serbian
Orthodox Church in Bosnia-Herzegovina

A few alternative voices have been heard within the Serbian Orthodox Church. Radovan Bigovic, theology professor at the Orthodox Theological Faculty in Belgrade, challenged the predominant understanding of church/state relations in an interview given shortly after the end of the war in Bosnia-Herzegovina. According to Bigovic, the Serbian Orthodox Church needs to "voluntarily, permanently repudiate their 'national' and 'state-established' roles. . . . No type of state can be based on the gospel of Christ. Only the church of God can be built on it. All attempts to create a 'Christian' or 'Orthodox' state were tragic and became the greatest blasphemy by Christians to the world."[52]

Challenges to a nationalist captivity of the Church have also been heard in other places. A variety of Serbian Orthodox participants, in seminars sponsored by the Center for Strategic and International Studies between 1995 and 2002, expressed concern over the close connection between religion and nationalism. Some called for the Serbian Orthodox Church to admit the sins committed against other peoples by Serbian military and police forces and to work to promote interfaith dialogue and reconciliation. The most significant comments came from Bishop Hrizostom of Bihac-Petrovac in Bosnia-Herzegovina. Speaking in a seminar held in Sabac, Serbia, in 1997, he called for the separation of religion and nationalism, opposition to the legitimation of war, and support of interfaith efforts to heal the hurts of society.[53] In 1998, the same bishop hosted a seminar in Bihac, Bosnia, during which he said that religion was still being manipulated by politicians in Bosnia-Herzegovina and called for the depoliticization of all religious communities. He specifically criticized the political authorities in the Bosnian Serb Republic for blocking the return of all displaced persons to their homes and participated in plans to accompany refugees in their efforts to return. In a concrete effort to bridge the religioethnic divide at that moment, the seminar concluded with Bishop Hrizostom leading the delegation of participants to visit the mufti of Bihac for the first time since the war.[54] Such actions since the end of the war have frequently placed Bishop Hrizostom in conflict with the other leadership of his own church and state, many of whom, according to Bishop Hrizostom, "do not accept the idea that . . . Muslims belong."[55]

In addition to Bishop Hrizostom, there are other examples of calls by Serbian Orthodox priests to admit the wrongs committed by their own people. One Serbian Orthodox priest who attended a seminar in Sarajevo during the war has frequently challenged aggression by all the ethnic groups, including Serbs. He criticized Serbian plans to take all Serbs out of Sarajevo during the war, stayed with his people who remained there, and participated in a variety of dialogue efforts with Catholics and Muslims.[56] At another seminar in Serbia, near the Bosnian border, a deputy to the bishop in Sabac raised the issue of acknowledgment of atrocities committed by Serbs during the war in Bosnia. He told a story of a Serb commander who had given a command to kill everyone in a Bosnian village, then watched as his troops carried out the order, and later came to this priest asking if he could ever be forgiven. The priest then confronted his fellow Orthodox priests with the reality that there were both victims and criminals among their people. Following the session, two other priests indicated the importance of Serbs in other places also acknowledging wrongs that had been committed by Serbs against other peoples. The local Serbian consultant for the seminar project claimed that sessions like this could enable the progressive elements of the Serbian Orthodox Church to face the Church's complicity in the Bosnian conflict.[57]

Finally, there are examples of efforts by local Serbian Orthodox priests and laypeople to care for people of other traditions. An Orthodox priest from Sokolac spoke on the occasion of the opening of a new mosque in Novoseoci in the autumn of 1991, calling for mutual respect, life together, and the overcoming of hatred and divisions in this "territory where Muslims and Serbs live together." The same priest, later serving as president of the local Red Cross, helped provide sanctuary in Sokolac, in the Bosnian Serb Republic, for 1,500 Croats fleeing from Vares at the time of Muslim/Croat fighting in 1993.[58] In another case of goodwill, a Muslim imam tells of Serbian Orthodox lay people assisting in the rebuilding of the mosque in Sanski Most just a few months prior to ethnic cleansing of that city's Muslims by Serbian troops.[59] Even if rare, these acts of love for neighbor and even the enemy further challenge the traditional linkage between religion and nationalism.

The Roman Catholic Church in Bosnia-Herzegovina

Any examination of the Catholic Church in Bosnia-Herzegovina must, like the case of the Serbian Orthodox Church, begin with the church's role in the fatherland, in this case Croatia. The Catholic hierarchy in Zagreb had great influence on political events in Bosnia-Herzegovina, especially in Herzegovina. At the same time, there are differences between the roles played by the Serbian Orthodox Church and the Catholic Church. Most important, Catholic ecclesiology does not advocate the formation of national churches, although it does allow ethnic parishes and national bishops' conferences. Therefore, the influence of religion in the development of nationalism took a different form in the Catholic Church in Croatia and Bosnia-Herzegovina. In the case of Croatia, there was a specific identification, on the part of the worldwide Catholic Church, with the justice of the Croatian cause during the wars in the former Yugoslavia. At the same time, this relationship has occasionally been expressed in overtly theological terms.

As with Serbian Orthodox theology, the war in Croatia was depicted as the Golgotha of the Croatian nation,[60] and the Croatian people are depicted as "chosen" by God while in the midst of great suffering. Josip Beljan, writing in the Catholic publication *Veritas*, amplifies this perspective:

> God has by way of his Church, by way of the Holy Father, looked at his faithful people, spoke out on their behalf, directly intervened in history, in the struggle, warring together with his people for their liberation. . . . With this war God also returned to his people, in its heart and home. [God] returned to the entire mass media, political, social, and state life of Croatia, from where he was driven out 45 years earlier. The cross of Christ stands next to the Croatian flag. . . . The Church is glad for the return of its people "from the twofold" slavery— Serbian and communist. This is a great "kairos" of God's grace for the entire Croatian people. . . . Here was not a battle for a piece of Croatian or Serbian land but a war between good and evil, Christianity and communism, culture and barbarity, civilization and primitivism, democracy and dictatorship, love and hatred. . . . Thank God, it all ended well, due to the Pope and Croatian politics.[61]

Ethnic Captivity within the Catholic Church in Bosnia-Herzegovina

Both the Vatican and the leadership of the Croatian Catholic Church played an important role in the quest for Croatian sovereignty.[62] Even in the late 1980s, Cardinal Kuharic and other Catholic bishops were advocates of Croatian national interests. Initially, they perceived a need to support ethnic political parties in order to counter communist rule. Later they were vocal in calling for national unity in response to what they saw as a national crisis precipitated by external aggression.[63] Even as late as 1996, Cardinal Kuharic proclaimed the Catholic Church's support for the Croatian state as a necessary guarantee of freedom for the Croatian people.[64] During the wars in Croatia and Bosnia-Herzegovina, this stance translated into strong support for Croatian nationalist symbols. For example, despite a considerable threat level to Serbs, the Church pressed for the exclusive use of the Croatian language and alphabet within Croatian society and for the creation of a Croatian Orthodox Church, independent from Serbian Orthodoxy.

After the Croatian Democratic Union (Hrvatska Democratska Zajednica, or HDZ) came to power in 1990, the Catholic Church, along with the nationalistic movement, were able to emerge from their opposition roles. Prior to this, the Croatian Catholic Church, because of its significant degree of support within the population, played the role of an informal, nonpublic "alternative authority structure," more effectively resisting communist influence on society than was the case elsewhere in the former Yugoslavia.

Following the elections in 1990, finally rid of this atheistic legacy, the Catholic leadership displayed almost unconditional support for the new Croatian government and its nationalistic policies. They were present at the opening of Parliament and appeared with state officials in the media.[65] As a result of this close relationship, Catholic catechism was reestablished in the public schools, giving the Church a powerful tool with which to reassert the linkage between religious and national identity. Until the first part of 1993, the actions of the Vatican, cardinal, and bishops clearly served to further solidify the Croat and Catholic identities. The Catholic bishop of Dubrovnik, Zelimir Puljic, summed up this perspective by saying that "to fight for Croatia is to fight for Catholicism."[66] Even a former communist politician, like Franjo Tudjman, began to refer to "all that is Croatian and Catholic," as though the two were inseparable.[67] To say "Crkva u Hrvata" (the Church among Croats) was as definitive a statement of linkage as was using the term "Srpska Crkva" (the Serbian Church).

To some extent it is understandable that the Catholic bishops gave such strong support to a new noncommunist government that restored the Catholic Church to legitimacy, promised to rebuild Croatian society after the era of communist malaise, and called for national unity at a time of crisis. The problem with the Church's response was that initially it embraced this new government uncritically. Furthermore, in their advocacy for the rights of the Croatian people, the Croatian Catholic bishops turned a deaf ear to legitimate concerns of the Serb minority, contributing to a major escalation of that population's threat level. One major concern that the bishops largely ignored was a plea by the Serbian Orthodox Church to condemn Croatian war crimes against Serbs during World War II, such as the incarceration and massacre of Serbs at the Croatian concentration camp at Jasenovac. In fact the Catholic bishops countered with charges of Serbian war crimes against

Croats (which were certainly much fewer in number during World War II) and vigorously promoted the cult of Cardinal Alojzije Stepinac, who was accused of complicity in forcible conversions and genocide against Serbs at that time. The only Croatian Catholic apology for these specific crimes was made by Bishop Pilher in 1963. The majority of the hierarchy of the Croatian Catholic Church has never admitted the role its predecessors played in legitimizing these atrocities.[68]

During the break-up of Yugoslavia, the Croatian Catholic Church's reaction to the expulsion of Serbs from the Krajina region of Croatia in 1995 typifies the ambiguity of many church officials. At first, they expressed joy at "Croatian liberation," supported their government's claim to have protected Serb rights, and charged the Serbs with orchestrating the exodus of their own people. Only when confronted with numerous media reports that Croatian troops had abused Serbian civilians did the church condemn this action as immoral.[69]

As with Serbia, this linkage between religion and nationality could be seen in the war effort through the presence of religious symbols, religious targets, and religious leaders. The symbols included soldiers, weapons, and vehicles being ornamented with rosaries and crosses.[70] Targets included places of worship and sacred objects, as well as other clergy. The Serbian Orthodox metropolitan bishop of Zagreb-Ljubljana received menacing letters from the Veterans Society of Croatia saying that the first to be attacked would be all Serbian bishops.[71] Finally, some Catholic priests, many of whom were refugees from occupied territories of Croatia, were sent as army chaplains to bless soldiers and weapons on the front lines. At least one priest, who later accepted a political office, and numerous former Catholic seminarians in Sarajevo carried guns and accompanied troops into battle. Perhaps most significantly, there was no censuring of this activity by the Catholic hierarchy.[72]

After succeeding in its attempt to influence the political process in Croatia, the Catholic leadership turned its attention to Bosnia and Herzegovina. In similar fashion to the Holy Synod of the Serbian Orthodox Church in Serbia, the Council of Croatian Bishops Conference of the Catholic Church issued statements that condemned the war in Bosnia-Herzegovina, but it only focused attention on the suffering of its own people.[73] As was the case with the Serbian Orthodox Church, much of the leadership of the Catholic Church sacralized a victimhood mentality. In October 1992 they noted that all citizens of Bosnia-Herzegovina (Muslim, Serb, and Croat) were suffering the consequences of war, but it was only the Catholics who were "going through great trial and martyrdom." Others were labeled as aggressors, but no Croats were condemned for criminal activities.[74] Furthermore, the Catholic bishops supported the activity of the HDZ, in violation of laws that forbade the existence of political parties formed exclusively on the basis of national or religious identity. The attempt on the part of the Catholic Church to change this law was a major factor in the division of Bosnian politics along religioethnic lines.[75]

With the onset of Muslim-Croat fighting in 1993, the depiction of Muslims in some Croat Catholic writing also became pejorative, referring to all Muslim combatants as mujahedins.[76] Finally, according to Franciscan priest Ivo Markovic of Sarajevo, the Catholic Church in Bosnia-Herzegovina not only supported nationalistic political parties as the only alternative to communism but also the establishment of a Bosnian Croat army.[77] As a result, the Croatian Catholic Church must bear its share of responsibility for the ensuing ethnic confrontation that led to such tragedy.

With political and ecclesiastical support from Zagreb, many of the Catholic clergy in Herzegovina gave unwavering assistance to the Croatian nationalists in that region. According to the vicar general of the Sarajevo Diocese of the Catholic Church, Mato Zovkic, most of the Catholic priests in Herzegovina, like most of the Croat population, "hoped in 1992–1993 that B & H [Bosnia-Herzegovina] would somehow disintegrate and that Western Herzegovina would be included into the Republic of Croatia." He went on to say that the aim was to create an ethnically pure Croatian territory in preparation for annexation.[78] It is no surprise, therefore, that many of the Catholic clergy of Herzegovina supported the creation of a Croat army in Herceg-Bosna. The staunchest supporters of this militant nationalist agenda were to be found among the Franciscans of Herzegovina. The Franciscan church in Bobani, for example, featured the portrait of a World War II Ustasha militiaman. Portraits of the leader of Ustasha Croatia, a war criminal named Ante Pavelic, were also present in the homes of local Franciscans. One of them, Father Vinko Mikulic, also stigmatized the Bosnian government by comparing it to the "Turkish occupiers." In Medjugorje, the site of a popular Catholic shrine commemorating an apparition of the Virgin Mary, statuettes of the Madonna were on sale next to Nazi regalia, while Franciscan priests provided a haven for the Herzegovinian mafia. The Croatian Defense Council (Hrvatsko Vijece Obrane, or HVO), in fact, promised to blow up the homes of anyone sheltering Muslims in that holy city.

In Mostar, the Franciscan provincial Tomislav Pervan, the head of 250 friars, opposed attempts by European mediators to reconcile the Catholic and Muslim populations of the city. In justification of this stand, he repeated the Tudjman propaganda that Muslims wanted an Islamic state, ignoring the fact that brutal atrocities against Muslims had been carried out by Croat and Serb nationalists in the name of creating Christian states.[79] In conclusion, one must agree with the assessment of the Catholic theologian Vjekoslav

Bajsic that many of the Catholic clergy of Herzegovina did not know how to work with outsiders (even non-Croat Catholics), perceiving them as dangerous and unfit for cooperation, thus giving allegiance to the most virulent form of religious nationalism.[80]

As fighting broke out between Croats and Muslims in 1993, Cardinal Kuharic began to criticize Tudjman's support of the Croat nationalists in Herzegovina and to warn the latter that they could be charged with war crimes against Muslims. Some have questioned the cardinal's motives, suggesting that he withdrew support because Herceg-Bosna's Croat leader, Mate Boban, had traded traditional Croat territory to Serb nationalists and had lost territory in his attacks on Muslims.[81] Furthermore, the Catholic leadership feared that the "greater Croatia" agenda of Herzegovina's Croat nationalists would provoke the Bosnian Muslims and therefore endanger the Catholic presence in Bosnia, where Catholics are a distinct minority.[82] Nonetheless, the new position of the Church did result in conflict with Tudjman and with the Croat leadership in Herzegovina, both of whom publicly denounced the Church as unpatriotic. Despite these threats, Cardinal Kuharic continued to criticize the Croatian nationalists and, in 1994, reiterated Pope John Paul II's warning to the Croatian people not to idolize the nation or the state.[83]

Agents of Reconciliation within the Catholic Church in Bosnia-Herzegovina

The Catholic bishops of Bosnia have a better record than do their Croatian counterparts of support for an end to the war and the maintenance of a multiethnic Bosnia-Herzegovina. For example, Cardinal Vinko Puljic of Sarajevo rejected a call to lift the arms embargo against Bosnia-Herzegovina and joined Pope John Paul II in calling for humanitarian intervention by the international community in order to disarm the aggressor and begin a process of demilitarization.[84] Yet even their record is mixed. In preparation for the 1990 elections, two of the Catholic bishops of Bosnia-Herzegovina sent pastoral letters encouraging Catholics to vote for parties that promised to protect the ethnic and religious interests of Croats. They did not tell their believers to vote for the HDZ, but that party was the only one promising to offer this protection. Once the war had started, they often followed the pattern of the Serbian Orthodox Church leaders, condemning crimes in general without mentioning concrete human rights violations by those from their own ethnic group.

At the same time, Cardinal Puljic of Sarajevo and Bishop Komarica of Banja Luka asked, in 1993, for the Croat political leaders in Zagreb and

Mostar to create a political program whereby all people in Bosnia-Herzegovina could live in their own homes. Bishop Komarica went even further than most of the other Catholic leadership, calling for the faithful to avoid using weapons, even for self-defense; to be prepared to suffer injustice rather than impose it on others; to love their neighbors and forgive their enemies. In fact, the civil authorities that favored the creation of ethnically secure territory for Croats reproached the bishops for insufficient support of the Croat cause and for too much criticism of criminal incidents involving HVO soldiers or local Croat leaders. Criminal actions by Croats have been specifically condemned by Mato Zovkic, vicar general of the Sarajevo Diocese. Zovkic writes that "Croats have prepared and partially caused the armed conflicts with Muslims by 'cleansing' Muslims from . . . localities under Croatian control in Herzegovina."[85]

The most open and tolerant stance among all the religious communities in Bosnia-Herzegovina, however, was that of the Bosnian Franciscans. Many members of that community consistently challenged the political instrumentalization of religion and emphasized, through both word and deed, the need for efforts at reconciliation between the various ethnoreligious communities. One of the earliest wartime efforts at interfaith dialogue was begun by a Franciscan from Sarajevo. In December 1991, Father Marko Orsolic was the primary impetus behind the formation of Zajedno ("Together"), an international multireligious and intercultural center. Since then Orsolic and his interfaith colleagues have held numerous joint prayer meetings and multireligious dialogues on reconciliation, church-state relations, and the role of religion in the peace process. They also provided assistance to refugees from all ethnic groups in Germany and Croatia during the war and in Sarajevo after the war.[86]

Another Franciscan, Father Mirko Majdandzic, ran a humanitarian aid organization, called Bread of St. Anton, during the siege in Sarajevo. These Franciscans not only fed poor people of all ethnic groups in the district of Dobrinja, but offered pastoral service to Serbian Orthodox laity who had no priests of their own living in that area.[87] Now living in Bugojno, on the border between Bosnia and Herzegovina, Father Majdandzic is working to encourage refugee return and interfaith dialogue between Muslims and Catholics.[88] The current provincial of the Franciscan Order in Bosnia, Father Mijo Dzolan, was a voice of reconciliation on the border of Bosnia and Herzegovina during the worst Croat-Muslim fighting in 1993 and 1994. As the head of the Franciscans' Rama Monastery in Scit, he spoke of how the Franciscans had stopped the Croat army from taking Bugojno. Father Mijo also sponsored spiritual retreats on reconciliation, served as mediator for numerous disputes between Muslims and Croats in the Prozor region, and was regularly consulted by UN peacemakers attempting to ease ethnic tensions in the region at that time.[89]

The most impressive example of such efforts among the Franciscans is that of Father Ivo Markovic, who is today the head of the Sarajevo-based organization Oci u Oci (Face to Face Interreligious Service). Before the war, in 1991, Father Markovic called on fellow Franciscans and others to support the prodemocracy protests in Sarajevo. During the war, he consistently challenged the religious leadership in all communities to separate themselves from the nationalistic aspirations of their ethnic political leaders. Furthermore, he demonstrated this spirit by working with Muslims in central Bosnia to allow humanitarian aid convoys access to all people. He also mediated an agreement between Muslim and Croat army commanders near Travnik in July 1992, playing a major role in helping to prevent these troops from participating in the Muslim/Croat fighting. As a result of his activities, some Franciscans and many other Catholic priests accused him of being a traitor to the Croat cause. After the war, Father Markovic was the guiding influence in the formation of the interreligious Pontanima Choir and Chamber Orchestra, a group that has brought a message of coexistence and reconciliation throughout Bosnia-Herzegovina. In addition, he was among the first religious leaders from Sarajevo to visit Serbian Orthodox people in Pale. He made fifty trips there during the year following Dayton, visiting whole neighborhoods of Serbian people, taking messages and letters back and forth between them and former Sarajevan neighbors, and taking Serbian young people into the city to visit. Within the first four months, he claimed that people's mentalities had begun to change because of personal interaction, despite ongoing brainwashing by the local media.[90] These efforts toward reconciliation on the part of numerous Bosnian Franciscans serve as one of the brightest models for constructive future peacemaking on the part of religious communities enmeshed in situations of deep-seated conflict.

The Role Played by the Churches in Kosovo

Between the end of the Bosnian war in November of 1995 and the beginning of the Kosovo war in March of 1999, a significant inter-church dialogue took place in Belgrade in February of 1997. Called an "Ecumenical Dialogue on Reconciliation" and sponsored by the Theological Faculty of the Serbian Orthodox Church and the Geneva-based Conference of European Churches, this event brought together thirty church delegates from all of the Christian confessions in Serbia, Croatia, Bosnia-Herzegovina, and Slovenia, together with another thirty from the rest of Europe and North America.

Patriarch Pavle opened the session by calling on all Christians "not to abide by narrow political or factional criteria but to see that the Church in any nation must raise that nation to the stature of the people of God." At the end of the session, a statement of "Actions for Reconciliation" was unanimously approved in which participants called for repentance and compassion, the promotion of interreligious dialogue, and the encouragement of religious media to counteract misrepresentations that propagate fear and hatred. With an eye toward transforming the churches' role in the future, these church leaders concluded their statement with a call to local Christian leaders to take a creative stand for reconciliation:

> Some of the most courageous and effective actions that Christians and their neighbors undertake begin at the local level, but these can be a powerful challenge to national and international leaders. Christian clergy and laity can be among those who help lead the way to reestablishing community. They can set an example through public confession of past failures and public criticisms of specific violations of human rights. Churches can play a vital role in the creation of democratic social structures, being vigilant in defense of social justice, and ready to challenge political and military leaders when necessary.[91]

The call for commitment to truth and conciliatory action that was apparent in this dialogue obviously had an influence on the role the churches were to play in the Kosovo conflict. To some extent this can be seen in the interreligious meetings and statements that occurred prior to the Kosovo war. Unlike their counterparts in the Croatian and Bosnian wars, the religious hierarchy in Kosovo saw more clearly the dangers of complicity and silence. They began to meet together prior to the outbreak of full-scale war, though not before the Albanian shift from President Ibrahim Rugova's strategy of nonviolence to the emergence of the Kosovo Liberation Army. The heads of Kosovo's three predominant religious communities—Serbian Orthodox bishop Artemije Radosavljevic, Roman Catholic bishop Mark Sopi, and the president of the Islamic Community of Kosovo, Dr. Rexhep Boja—met for the first time in Vienna in November of 1998.[92] Leaders of the three communities met for a second time in Vienna (just prior to the NATO bombing of Yugoslavia in March of 1999) where they called for an end to the polemics of hate, to all killing and acts of violence, and to all violations of basic human and religious rights.[93] Following the war, Bishop Artemije, Bishop Sopi, and Dr. Boja met again at the invitation of the Interreligious Council of Bosnia and Herzegovina. Meeting in Sarajevo in February of 2000, they agreed to a "Statement on Joint Moral Obligation." A couple of months later, they met in Pristina on the occasion of a visit to Kosovo by the Interreligious Council of Bosnia and Herzegovina. The Bosnian leaders, having formed their own council following the Bosnian war, helped the spiritual leaders of Kosovo to form the Interreligious Council of Kosovo and Metohija on April 13, 2000. In the statement issued to announce the formation of this council, the spiritual leaders reiterated their condemnation of all violence and any infringement on human rights and promised to continue the cooperation between themselves and their respective communities. In addition to these official meetings of the hierarchy, informal meetings organized by local representatives of the three religious communities have been held on a fairly regular basis in Pristina and Gjilan/Gnjilane.[94]

While, again, primarily addressing the role of the Christian churches in Kosovo, it is important to note the role played by the Islamic community, which is the largest religious community in Kosovo. At present, the Islamic Community has little influence on politics in Kosovo. The leadership of the official Sunni Islamic Community has, in fact, rejected a recent suggestion to form a Muslim political party.[95] Instead, the Presidency of the Islamic Community of Kosovo has called for the development of democratic process under the rule of law, justice for all citizens regardless of religion, ethnicity, or language, and the condemnation of all who commit crimes, including Albanian acts of revenge against Serb people or churches.[96]

At the same time, leaders within the Islamic Community have harshly criticized the Serbian Orthodox leadership for nurturing nationalistic propaganda.[97] While certainly true of many Serbian Orthodox leaders, this sentiment does not seem to adequately take into account a change in attitude, as documented hereafter, on the part of Serbian Orthodox leaders in Kosovo, one that was recognizable by early 1998, just as events were building toward war. Concomitant Serbian charges that Islamic fundamentalism has taken root within Kosovo are largely groundless. Most Kosovo Muslims look to the West for support rather than to traditional Muslim societies in the Middle East or Central Asia. However, in three specific arenas—the training of imams, distribution of Islamic literature, and some humanitarian aid efforts— there has been a growing Arab presence. Though the Kosovapress News Agency, founded by the former Kosovo Liberation Army, issued a statement in December 1999 opposing this fundamentalist presence, it remains to be seen whether this foreign effort will have any lasting influence within Kosovo society.[98]

Although the Islamic faith community now exerts little influence on political developments in Kosovo, this has not always been the case. Historically, the Sufi Muslims of the Dervish order in western Kosovo, Macedonia, and Albania have played a significant role in the development of Albanian nationalism, beginning in the nineteenth century. In particular, the heterodox Dervish sect of Bektashi attempted to present itself as a force for Albanian religious and national unity in the face of religious tension among Albanians and oppression by the Ottoman Turks. One of the most important Albanian nationalists in the late nineteenth century, Naim Frasheri, actually hoped to unite all Albanians around the Bektashi faith. He attempted to utilize the Kerbela myth, the founding event in Shi'ite Islam,[99] as a tool for triggering a revolt against Ottoman and Sunni hegemony. It is also clear that the Bektashi leadership at that time also desired this national leadership role, with their lodges functioning as places of worship for both Muslims and Christians, as well as being centers of nationalist activity. The Bektashi came much closer to accomplishing this aim in Albanian than they ever did in Kosovo, though its influence was still felt in the cultural resistance to both communism and the later Serbian nationalism. One of their leaders, Sheikh Myhedin, was tried twice as an Albanian nationalist by the communist Yugoslav government and was later killed by Serb nationalists during the ethnic cleansing in 1998.[100]

The Serbian Orthodox Church in Kosovo

In the early 1980s, some figures in the Serbian Orthodox Church took a leading role in nurturing the remembrance of the victimization of the Serbian people by focusing on the situation in Kosovo. The Church was especially disturbed by the exodus of Serbian people from Kosovo and by the destruction of Church property and shrines, phenomena that did, in fact, increase after 1981. In April 1982, twenty-one Serbian Orthodox priests, including three bishops, signed an appeal to the hierarchy, asking it to raise its voice "to protect the spiritual and biological existence of the Serb people in Kosovo and Metohija . . . and to write about the destruction, arson and sacrilege of the holy shrines of Kosovo."[101] One of the signatories, Bishop Atanasije Jevtic, former dean of the Orthodox Theological Faculty in Belgrade, responded to this challenge by accusing ethnic Albanians of raping adolescent girls and old women, mistreating monks and nuns in monasteries, and other drastic acts of psychological and physical terror against Serbs, including murder. He also accused them of nursing genocidal intentions.[102] This echoed accusations made thirteen years earlier by the Holy Synod of the Serbian Orthodox Church, in which it declared: "It is no exaggeration to say that planned *genocide* [emphasis in original] is being perpetrated against the Serbian people in Kosovo" and ordered its people to document the evidence of Albanian oppression.[103] The charge of genocide in these instances, however, was not accompanied by the kind of evidence necessary to fit with internationally accepted definitions of the term. Therefore, although there had been clear violations of the human rights of some Serbs by some Albanians, and although there was indeed an exodus of Kosovo Serbs for a variety of causal factors, the severity of these events was over-stated. While any degree of suffering deserves condemnation, exaggerating it to promote a national sense of victimhood, as took place in Kosovo in the 1980s and in which some of the leadership of the Serbian Orthodox Church actively participated, is both opportunistic and inappropriate.

During the early 1980s, the claim was made by some Serbian Orthodox clergy that the Church was the only institution that had not betrayed the Serbian nation. In particular, these church leaders drew a contrast between themselves and most Serbian communists, whom they accused of having "sold out" to the Kosovo Albanians. The cultivation of the theme of a suffering Serbian nation, however, was not totally attributable to the efforts of the Church. The same charge of genocide against the Serbian nation in Kosovo later appeared in the influential "Memorandum" of the Serbian Academy of Sciences.[104] Furthermore, key political leaders in Serbia also used the victimization theme to advance their political careers in the late 1980s. Most notable among these was Slobodan Milosevic. It is hardly surprising, then, to find both Milosevic and Serbian Orthodox Patriarch German, to-gether with other political, cultural and ecclesiastical elites, celebrating Ser-bian history and nationhood at the 600th anniversary of the Battle of Kosovo in 1989.[105]

Ethnic Captivity within the Serbian Orthodox Church in Kosovo

The Battle of Kosovo, where according to tradition the Muslim Turks de-feated the Orthodox Christian Serbs in June of 1389, has become one of the primary markers of Serbian identity. The initial folklore surrounding this event focused on the martyrdom of Serbian prince Lazar and on the moral decision attributed to him for choosing a heavenly kingdom over an earthly one. In this way, defeat was turned into a spiritual victory.[106]

It was not until the nineteenth century that the ancient Kosovo songs and folk tradition were finally collected and woven together into a cohesive Kosovo myth in order to support a Serbian nationalist quest for liberation from centuries of Ottoman rule. The resulting legacy was more than his-torical rendition since, like other myths, it sanctioned and enacted rites that marked the boundaries of the group, established links between the people's past, present, and future, formulated certain values and oppositions that rat-ified and endorsed a particular ideology or philosophy, and came to represent a transcendental importance within the culture. Furthermore, this Kosovo myth took on clear theological dimensions, identifying the death of the fourteenth-century Prince Lazar with the crucifixion of Christ and equating the vanquished Serb nation with the suffering of the chosen people of God. By the middle of the nineteenth century, the myth was used to justify territorial expansion in the pursuit of liberation and to define all perceived Serbian enemies, demonizing not only the Turks, but all Muslim people, identifying them with the anti-Christ. The epic drama *Gorski Vijenac* (The Mountain Wreath), written during that period by Petar Njegos, represents the first use of this myth to trigger political and military action to avenge the losses of Kosovo. The "Kosovo pledge" to work toward the institution of a "Heavenly Serbia" later motivated many Serbs to revolt against a variety of foreign dominations, including the Bosnian Peasant Insurrection of 1875; the Balkan wars of 1912–13; World War I, where it motivated Gavrilo Princep's assassination of Archduke Franz Ferdinand, and World War II, where the "spirit of Kosovo" ideologically shaped the coup that overthrew a pro-Axis government in Belgrade. Serbian Orthodox Patriarch Gavrilo proclaimed in March 1941 that the coup leaders had chosen the heavenly kingdom of truth, justice, national strength, and freedom.[107]

During all of the violence that erupted within the former Yugoslavia during the last decade, non-Serbs have frequently pointed to the Kosovo myth as one example of the ways in which religion has been used to enflame ethnic hatred. Although the actual use of the myth in the late twentieth century points more to the abuse of religion by literary elite and political players, it nevertheless has had its proponents within the Serbian Orthodox Church.[108]

Agents of Reconciliation within the Serbian Orthodox Church in Kosovo

Following the war in Bosnia and Herzegovina and the exodus of Croatian Serbs from the Krajina in 1995, the attitude of the Kosovo Serbs and of the Serbian Orthodox Church changed significantly. The Kosovo myth had called on Serbs to sacrifice earthly values for the sake of attaining a heavenly kingdom. It called on them to suffer in order to attain a moral perfection and spiritual legitimacy. When both Church and common people saw ordinary Serbs suffer while officials in Belgrade got rich, the Kosovo myth suddenly became hollow. It had become discredited by the very political elite who had used it to gain power.[109]

Some of the leadership within the Serbian Orthodox Church began to warn against ethnophyletism. Hieromonk Sava Janjic, from the Serbian Orthodox Monastery of Visoki Decani in Kosovo, has admitted the presence of individuals within the Orthodox Church who have preferred national interests to spiritual ones and thus fallen prey to ethnophyletism.[110] The ecumenical patriarchate of the Orthodox Church became concerned enough about the rise of this "nationalist fanaticism" that Ecumenical Patriarch Bartholomew convened a meeting of Orthodox bishops from around the world to address this issue in September 1996. Meeting on the island of Patmos, these bishops, including Patriarch Pavle of the Serbian Orthodox Church, condemned "national fanaticism" and insisted that the Orthodox understanding of nationalism "contained no elements of aggression and conflict among peoples."[111] Patriarch Pavle had, in fact, earlier that year personally exemplified the open spirit of this Orthodox statement when he sent a letter to protesting Kosovo Albanian students. Pavle expressed understanding for their peaceful protests and condemned the brutal use of force against them by Serbian police, calling it a grave sin.[112] The Serbian patriarch also repeatedly took a stand against the use of force to create a greater Serbia. At the close of the Kosovo war, at Gracanica Monastery on June 28, 1999, Patriarch Pavle said: "If the only way to create a greater Serbia is by crime, then I do not accept that and let that Serbia disappear. . . . And if all the Serbs had to die, and only I remained, and I could live only by crime, then I would not accept that; it would be better to die."[113]

At the same time, it is clear that the leadership of the Serbian Orthodox Church was still divided over the rightful place of nationalism within its circles. In November 1998, the Holy Synod issued a statement calling for Serb and Albanian populations to coexist in friendship. Yet, at the same time, the statement blamed only the Albanian separatists for the bloodshed in Kosovo and warned the international community that Kosovo was the "spiritual Jerusalem" of the Serbs, their spiritual source and national center.[114]

The most vigorous critique of Serbian nationalist chauvinism and oppression in Kosovo still came, however, from the leadership of the Serbian Orthodox Church in that region, namely from Father Sava and from Bishop Artemije of Raska-Prizren. Father Sava has challenged what he calls romantic myths, unrealistic ideas, and aggressive methods by which both Serbs and Albanians have promoted nationalism. Writing in prominent Albanian and Serbian newspapers, Father Sava challenged the fusion of nation and religion that "has impoverished and restricted the universal spiritual and missionary values which remained confined only within one people and one ethnic group" and has constituted an abuse of faith.[115] Referring specifically to Serbian nationalism, he charged that secularists had abused the symbols and myths of the Serbian Orthodox tradition. For example, when Father Sava saw the cross inscribed on the walls of a damaged Albanian village, he was appalled that the Serbian security forces would use a symbol of love and tolerance to communicate hate.[116] Furthermore, according to Father Sava, these nationalists talked about the Kosovo Covenant but failed to understand the true spiritual message of Prince Lazar. Father Sava claimed that the true believer would affirm the heavenly kingdom and heavenly virtues to which Lazar points but would not be deluded into believing that these can be achieved by means of violence or earthly power. In the end, Father Sava claimed that both Serbs and Albanians needed a "historical catharsis in which the ideas and the myths of the past would finally be left behind." A "policy of integration, democratization and peaceful life" should prevail, he said, over "the aggressive policy of blood and myths."[117]

Bishop Artemije and Father Sava were leading lights in the Serbian Resistance Movement, a political group that emerged in Kosovo after the end of the Bosnian war. Although committed to retaining Kosovo for Serbia, and even opposing the reinstatement of a pre-Milosevic level of local autonomy, the group did, as early as the beginning of 1998, condemn the violation of human rights of all people and call for dialogue between the ethnic groups.[118] Bishop Artemije and Father Sava went further and took a clear stand against repression of Albanians by Milosevic's police, ethnic cleansing of any people by any armed group, and the destruction of any property, including mosques.[119] Despite being attacked by state media and charged with being traitors to the Serbian people, they continually expressed their opposition to Milosevic's undemocratic rule and oppressive policies while at the same time condemning the actions of the Kosovo Liberation Army and later the NATO bombing of Yugoslavia.[120] Father Sava specifically accused Milosevic of exacerbating the crisis in Kosovo by refusing to introduce democratic reforms during the period when the Kosovo Albanian opposition movement was entirely nonviolent and by depriving the Albanians of their political rights when he reduced Kosovo's autonomy. The monk also charged Milosevic and the Serbian regime with using the fears of Kosovo Serbs to build their power base, and he further accused them of perpetrating xenophobia and paranoia among the people in order to serve their own selfish political interests.[121] Father Sava also called for Milosevic, along with Karadzic, Mladic, and Tudjman, to be indicted by the International Tribunal for the war crimes they committed in Bosnia-Herzegovina.[122] He strongly condemned the nationalists who committed barbarous acts against Muslims in Bosnia, but he defended the Serbian Orthodox Church in Kosovo against similar charges by Albanian Muslims.[123]

Father Sava and the other monks from the Decani monastery have also personally responded to the plight of displaced people of all ethnic groups, offering both aid and refuge. Father Sava insists that the monastery had a spiritual obligation toward the needy and unprotected people of all ethnic groups; according to him, he and those of his order had no moral right to respond on the basis of ethnicity or religion. Between May of 1998 and

March of 1999, therefore, they housed many displaced people in the monastery and assisted others by driving them to the hospital in Peja/Pec or by supplying food and medicine in cooperation with International Orthodox Christian Charities. Father Sava estimates that they assisted approximately 300 Serbs and 70 Albanians during this prewar period. During the period of bombing and ethnic cleansing (March–June 1999), the Decani monks took 150 Albanians into the monastery, an act that literally saved their lives, and helped them reestablish contact with their families. Furthermore, according to Father Sava, the monks urged the police to leave the people alone and continued to issue statements opposing the policies of Milosevic. Following the war, the Decani monastery has continued to be a sanctuary for any oppressed people, including waves of Roma, Slavic Muslims, and Serbs.[124]

Finally, Bishop Artemije and Father Sava have emerged as major political players in the Kosovo crisis. Since early 1998, they have been advocates of peaceful settlement, democratization, and a multiethnic Kosovo. Through attendance at international conferences, they met Kosovo Albanian politicians like Veton Surroj, publisher of *Koha Ditore,* and Adem Demaci, the prewar political representative of the Kosovo Liberation Army and the leader of the Kosovo Albanian Parliamentary Party. As a result, Surroj began to publish some of Father Sava's articles in his newspaper and Demaci visited the monks at Decani, thanking them for their aid to displaced people and for the balanced positions of the Serbian Orthodox Church.[125]

On numerous occasions before and after the war, Bishop Artemije and Father Sava also traveled to Washington, D. C., and to many European capitals in order to present their views and urge the international community to listen to both sides and refrain from imposing coercive solutions. Prior to and during the war, they were not able to gain a hearing for this agenda or have significant impact on decisionmaking. Although they were able to meet with dignitaries, they were kept out of the formal negotiation process by both the West and by Milosevic. Since the war, however, they have been perceived as the most able dialogue partners on the Serbian side. Father Sava advocated recognition of the atrocities committed by Serbian troops against the Albanian population. In an interview in Belgrade in July of 1999, he said that Milosevic supporters

> participated in forced expulsions of the [Albanian] population which otherwise would not have fled the province. In most cases they did not flee because of the bombardment, but because of systematic deportations, looting and other sorts of violence. We have been finding daily blood tracks of that violence.[126]

Both the bishop and Father Sava have been leaders of the postwar Serb National Council of Kosovo and Metohije, an organization that has pursued reconciliation among all ethnic groups, safety (especially for minorities), and recognition of human rights for all citizens of Kosovo. Bishop Artemije has, at times, participated in the Kosovo Transitional Council, a body of local leaders that the United Nations Mission in Kosovo (UNMIK) established to assist in governance of the province.

When the UN decided to restructure its mission in December of 1999, Bishop Artemije and Father Sava also agreed to serve on a similar body called the Interim Administrative Council. Although they resigned their positions in June 2000 because of the lack of progress on security issues for Kosovo Serbs, they quickly returned after a "Memorandum of Understanding" was signed governing security in the Serb enclaves. Their willingness to work with the international community, however, was not without its costs. In May of 2000, for example, at the meeting of the Holy Synod, Bishop Irinej Bulovic of Novi Sad presented a long list of accusations against Bishop Artemije because he had criticized Patriarch Pavle and Bishop Irinej for attending a "Republic Day" reception hosted by Milosevic. The majority of bishops refused to discuss the charges against Bishop Artemije, but the incident still serves as a reminder of the great differences within the Serbian Orthodox Church.[127]

The Roman Catholic Church in Kosovo

The Catholic Church in Kosovo was less involved in the political process than were any of the other three churches examined in this chapter. Bishop Sopi has, in fact, specifically encouraged the Church not to be involved in politics and has even been resistant to cooperation with a peacebuilding training program instituted by Catholic Relief Services since the end of the war. Part of the reason for this lesser political involvement may be due to the small size of the Catholic Church in Kosovo. There are now only 60,000 Albanian Catholics in Kosovo out of a population of two million. In addition, there are small numbers of Catholic Croats, Slovenes, and Roma. All told, there are only twenty-three parishes and thirty-five priests.[128]

During the early 1990s, Catholics did experience an increase in numbers resulting from the collective conversion of many Albanian Muslims. These converts brought with them a heightened political awareness as well. Muslims converting to Catholicism did so out of a desire to look toward the West, rather than the East, for help and political support. This crypto-Catholicism did not result in religious division within the Albanian community because of the new adherents having only a vague sense of religious belonging to the Catholic Church. Instead, their conversion helped to reinforce a common identity, purpose, and commitment to dialogue among Kosovo Albanians of both Christian and Muslim faiths.[129]

Ethnic Captivity within the Catholic Church in Kosovo

Alongside Dervish Muslim influence, there is a significant history of Catholic involvement in the Albanian nationalist movement that began in the mid–nineteenth century, including a Catholic-led movement to conduct a nationalist uprising against communist rule immediately following World War II. The leaders of this Catholic-led movement are still celebrated as heroes and martyrs by Kosovo Albanians.

During the 1980s and 1990s, the Albanian Catholic Church, under the leadership of former bishop Nikola Prela, continued to play a central role by working for Albanian rights within Kosovo. Early in that time period, it took the lead in publicizing human rights violations suffered by Albanians during communist rule. Later, when Albanian communists became dominant within the League of Communists of Kosovo, the Albanian Catholic Church in Kosovo entered into a better relationship with the governing authorities. This positive relationship led directly to the development of strong links between some of the Catholic clergy and the Democratic League of Kosovo (LDK), which rose to political prominence during the 1990s under the leadership of President Rugova and led the way in the development of an alternative social-political structure vis-à-vis the Milosevic regime. Other Albanian Catholics have been instrumental in establishing the Albanian Christian Democratic Party of Kosovo, a party that also welcomed Muslims into its membership and today has at least as many, or more, members from the Islamic community.

During the current crisis in Kosovo, some Albanian Catholic priests continue to play a major public role, but they do so primarily within the communities that have a large Catholic presence. For example, Father Ambroz Ukaj from Gjakove/Djakovica has remarked that the Catholics there view themselves as being obligated to act politically. The current political activism of these Albanian Catholics is primarily focused on the development of an independent, democratic Kosovo and therefore is still informed by the history of Catholic involvement in Albanian nationalism.[130]

The Croatian Catholic community in Kosovo has its own history and political orientation. Even more than their Albanian brethren, they became highly politicized in the early 1990s as war erupted in Croatia. The views of many of these Croatian Catholics were very pro-Tudjman and anti-Serb. Their use of Croatian symbols and their expressions of sympathy for Croatian nationalism led the Kosovo Serbs to label them as Ustasha. Because the conflict between Croatian Catholics and the Kosovo Serbs came to a head before that of the Albanians and Serbs, the small Croat community concluded that it had no choice but to leave. By December 1991, more than half the Croats from Janjevo had left for Croatia, and between July and December of 1992 a majority of the Croat population of Letnica had left as well. In addition to fearing the Serbs, the Croats were also concerned for their well-being in the event the Albanians obtained their independent republic, a fear that has proven to be well founded, given Albanian attacks on all Slavic communities since the end of the war in 1999.

When the Kosovo Croats left for Croatia in the early 1990s, it was the Catholic Church that enabled this migration. The Foundation of St. Isidorus helped evacuate the people to Croatia without passports or other documents because Croatian authorities only allowed ethnic Croats to enter Croatia. Priests handed out baptismal certificates in order to establish proof of Croatian Catholic identity. The result is that Croatian Catholicism has all but disappeared in Kosovo.[131]

Agents of Reconciliation within the Catholic Church in Kosovo

There is also a positive connection between Catholicism in Kosovo and Catholicism in Croatia and Bosnia. Most Kosovo Catholic priests, including Albanians, are either Franciscans themselves or were educated by Franciscans in Bosnia and Croatia.[132] In Sarajevo's Franciscan theological faculty, many aspiring priests have come under the influence of Father Ivo Markovic, Father Marko Orsolic, and other architects of Bosnia's interfaith dialogue and reconciliation efforts. In fact, Orsolic's international multireligious and intercultural center, called Zajedno, set up a project for reconstruction, multireligious dialogue, and reconciliation in Kosovo in 1999.[133] Initiatives involving interreligious and even interethnic dialogue have also been supported by local Catholic priests from Kosovo. One local Croatian priest who has been an active proponent of interfaith dialogue with local Serbian Orthodox priests is Father Matej Palic from Janjevo. Furthermore, Bishop Sopi, along with Bishop Artemije, participated in the Kosovo Transitional Council, the body of local leaders formed to assist the United Nations in its administration of Kosovo.[134]

The best example, though, of Catholic efforts at reconciliation can be seen in the work of Don Lush Gjergji, a priest from Binqa, Kosovo. Father Gjergji began his reconciliation efforts in 1990 when he brought together feuding Albanian families in an attempt to address the problem of blood vendettas. When leading these sessions, Father Gjergji told his fellow Albanians that revenge was equal to fratricide or suicide because, at that time, Albanians had suffered more from killing one another than they had suffered at the hands of the Serbs.[135] He also spoke of the power of God that could enable people to love and pardon even enemies.[136] He told them that Chris-

tianity cannot be embraced without forgiveness, without an end to the ven-
detta tradition. These efforts of Father Gjergji gave birth to the Mother
Teresa Humanitarian Association in Kosovo, an organization that has continued to work for peace and nonviolence and to provide humanitarian relief
for refugees.[137]

Since the war, Father Gjergji has continued to initiate humanitarian
efforts such as assisting widows to care for their children. He has also started
an informal effort of reconciliation by meeting alternatively with the Muslim
imam in the Vitina region and with Father Kyrilo Djurkovic, a Serbian
Orthodox priest from Gnjilane who has been active in peacemaking efforts.[138] When the Yugoslav army withdrew from Kosovo at the end of the
war, Father Gjergi recognized that this would threaten the security of Serbs
and therefore told his Serbian Orthodox colleague that, if anyone were to
threaten him, he could stay at his home. Father Gjergji has attempted to
represent everyone in the community; he has said: "As long as even one
citizen of Kosovo is threatened, I personally feel threatened. . . . As a Catholic cleric. . . . I am on the side of the little people, the persecuted, the
devastated. . . . As long as there is no love, we are all orphans, regardless [of
who kills whom]." Father Gjergji has firmly and consistently insisted on
condemning evil, wherever the source, and seeking to build the common
good. He concludes that "life, truth, justice, peace, love, forgiveness are
neither Serbian nor Albanian, but universal [values that must be re-
spected]."[139]

One final role played by the Catholic Church involved a non-Kosovo
Catholic community from Rome known as St. Egidio. St. Egidio is a lay
Catholic community that has a strong sense of compassion for the suffering
and the poor. Since the early 1990s, its members expressed this sense of
solidarity with the oppressed in Kosovo through humanitarian aid that was
distributed to both Serb and Albanian populations. This compassion, along
with St. Egidio's reputation for impartiality, opened the door to personal
contacts at high political levels on both sides. Believing that peacemaking is
an essential part of its mission and that peace comes through dialogue and
understanding, community members began, in 1993, a delicate shuttle dialogue between high-level officials over the question of the returning of
Albanian children to the educational system, one of many issues that divided
Serb and Albanian populations. Due to St. Egidio's preservation of confi-
dentiality and discretion, its use of a flexible approach in dialogue and negotiation, and its belief that it had nothing to lose in failure, its mediation
efforts succeeded. In September 1996, the Educational Agreement for Kosovo was signed by Milosevic and Rugova. This was the only agreement
ever signed by the Milosevic government and the Kosovo Albanians. Be-

cause of a number of difficulties, implementation of the agreement was delayed until March 23, 1998, when Albanian children finally returned to Kosovo's schools.[140]

Conclusion

It is clear that the churches of Bosnia-Herzegovina and Kosovo have played diverse roles in the conflicts. The Catholic Church in Kosovo had little political influence, while the Serbian Orthodox Church in Kosovo played a very important political role, forcefully challenging the Milosevic regime and cooperating with the United Nations administration. Many people from within both churches fell prey to ethnic captivity in Bosnia-Herzegovina, yet in Kosovo people in significant leadership positions challenged that same chauvinistic mentality. Much of the Catholic Church in Herzegovina, especially the Franciscans, also fell prey to a nationalist captivity; in Bosnia the opposite was generally true as many within the Catholic Church (especially the Franciscans) initiated creative efforts at reconciliation. Yet within each of these churches, in each context, it was possible to find numerous individuals who were able, under extremely difficult circumstances, to draw upon their faith in bringing healing and reconciliation to all people. Bishop Hrizostom called for courageous efforts at reconciliation and exemplified this by visiting the mufti of Bihac. The Franciscan priest Ivo Markovic challenged those within both church and politics who manipulated religion to their own political ends. He also traveled repeatedly to the Bosnian Serb capital of Pale during the first year after the Bosnian war to build bridges with Serbian Orthodox adherents. The Serbian Orthodox Father Sava challenged the "violence-prone" distortion of the Kosovo myth and condemned the atrocities committed by Serbian security forces against ethnic Albanians. At the same time, he and his fellow monks gave refuge and aid to Albanian, as well as Serbian, refugees. The Albanian Catholic Don Lush Gjergji has campaigned against acts of revenge and declared himself to be on the side of the persecuted, demonstrating this by opening his home to his Serbian Orthodox colleague when Albanian revenge attacks began after the Kosovo war. These Christian leaders have demonstrated the power of acting on basic precepts that are central to the Christian faith in any of its denominational expressions. One finds in these Christian leaders a balance between justice and reconciliation whereby injustice is cited and specific acts are condemned while at the same time efforts are made to reach out to the other side and to meet the needs of victimized people regardless of their ethnic identity.

A Christian Theological Basis for Reconciliation

The balance between justice and reconciliation finds its roots in the Old Testament term "shalom," usually translated as "peace" in English. This ancient Hebrew term literally means wholeness, fulfillment, completion, unity, and well-being.[141] Rightly understood, then, *shalom* refers to the realization of all the good that God has for the whole community of people. The vision of *shalom* is that of a just and reconciled community in which all adversarial relationships are unmasked and healed and where relationships are made right (or just) and restored (or reconciled).

In Christian ethics, one of the basic steps in the pursuit of shalom is the provision of hospitality to the stranger. The theologian Thomas Ogletree locates the commencement of moral consciousness in the readiness to welcome the stranger. For him, it is a response to the needs of the "other" that is the starting point for responsible Christian action.[142] This ethical precept also has its origins in the Semitic world of the Old Testament. According to the Pentateuch, a faithful follower of God must attempt a relationship of hospitality, even with a stranger from a hostile tribe. Furthermore, it is in fact inhospitality on the part of the citizens of Sodom that precipitates the crisis that leads to their doom (Genesis 19). In the New Testament, the teaching of Jesus is also heavily salted with expressions of hospitality. Jesus tells people to extend hospitality to Samaritans, the despised mixed-blooded ethnic group that shared the Holy Land with the Jews, and to tax collectors, the hated agents of Roman rule. In the Sermon on the Mount, Jesus even calls for the extension of this hospitality to one's enemy. Thus a truly Christian ethic will transcend the predictable, according to Croatian theologian Miroslav Volf, who points to Jesus' command to replace an "eye for an eye" mentality with "turn the other cheek."[143]

The call to this transcending ethic is a challenge to any Christian community. In the Balkans, however, it is especially difficult since the priestly role of the clergy has greatly overshadowed the prophetic. The primary role of the clergy in both the Catholic and Serbian Orthodox traditions is to nurture and protect the life of the community, despite its flaws. Acknowledgment of the prophetic call to self-examination of church leaders and whole church communities has been rare, as both traditions have tended to hide behind the theology of the church as the mystical bride of Christ and therefore beyond reproach.[144] Although one may rightly describe the "faithful" church in such terms, one must ask hard questions about the "unfaithful church."

Confusing the spiritual ideal with the institutional reality will not help the church to become a self-reflective agent of reconciliation. At the same time, the calls to prophetic self-examination and to hospitality toward the other have deeply resonated with many of the truly spiritual Christian people of Bosnia-Herzegovina and Kosovo. As previously noted, Prota Srecko Radosavljevic, a Serbian Orthodox priest serving in Serbia near the Bosnian border, has confronted his fellow Orthodox priests with evidence of Serbian complicity in the war in Bosnia-Herzegovina. Don Lush Gjergji has challenged Kosovo Albanians to emulate their national saint, the late Mother Theresa, by loving one's enemies and praying for those who persecute them rather than by taking revenge.[145] Bishop Komarica has done the same. On the other hand, as noted earlier, the Catholic theologian Vjekoslav Bajsic has lamented the fact that the Catholic clergy of Herzegovina did not know how to work with "outsiders," perceiving them as dangerous and unfit for cooperation. Turning the enemy into a friend, as proposed by St. Maximus the Confessor from the Orthodox tradition,[146] or into a partner, as proposed by the German theologian Juergen Moltman,[147] is a difficult but highly important task.

Putting Christian Principles into Practice

The willingness to reach out, at a grass-roots level, across the ethnic and religious divides is critical to the success of peacemaking in any conflicted society. Recent analysis of the resolution of the conflict in South Africa has indicated that the role of grass-roots efforts at conflict resolution was critical to the healing of that society. The lack of such efforts on so pervasive a level has also been identified as the critical factor in the failure of the Middle East peace process.

A relatively small group of highly motivated people can often have an impact that far outweighs their numbers. This was aptly demonstrated in a negative way as Bosnia-Herzegovina descended into war. The development of a small but critical mass for the pursuit of peacemaking and reconciliation can have just as much impact in a positive direction. As noted earlier, the "Actions for Reconciliation" adopted by participants in the Ecumenical Dialogue on Reconciliation that met in Belgrade in 1997 called on Christians to take effective action at the local level. Christians were urged to lead the way in establishing community beyond the ethnic divisions, set an example through public confession of wrongs, create democratic social structures, defend social justice, and challenge political leaders.

Holding Seminars for Religious People

Implementing the mandate from the Ecumenical Dialogue on Reconciliation in Belgrade appears to be a very tall order. However, the beginning of such a movement has begun to take shape in both Bosnia-Herzegovina and

Kosovo through the medium of reconciliation seminars. Most of these seminars, sponsored by the Center for Strategic and International Studies (CSIS) in Washington, D.C., have focused on community building among the ethnic/religious groups. A few of these seminars have been conducted for members of a single confession or ethnic group, since such homogeneous settings are more conducive to the kind of internal reflection that is most helpful in marginalizing extremist elements within the group.

Participants in all of the seminars have been led through a six-step process to help them transform their attitudes toward others. The first step is to listen to one another's stories. A mixed religious group of Bosnians listened as a Croatian woman from central Bosnia told of the incarceration of her and her two children in a Croat concentration camp because she was married to a Muslim man. Her faith in the midst of pain was a source of inspiration and bonding within the diverse group.

Second, as people feel heard and accepted across the ethnic divides, trust begins to build. People can begin to share their current fears and find more commonality than they expect. During the NATO bombing of Yugoslavia, a seminar was conducted in Bosnia that was attended by Serbs as well as Croats and Muslims. There was great tension among the participants because of their very different perspectives regarding the NATO campaign. However, the common fear that the war would spread to Bosnia brought some degree of solidarity within the group.

Third, identifying needs of the other group, the next step in the process, helps to rehumanize the enemy. During a seminar in Sarajevo in 1995, a young imam from Zepa surprised the Serbian Orthodox participants by telling how he had realized during the siege of his city that the Serb soldiers in the surrounding hills were acting out of the same basic need for survival that his Muslim people were experiencing.

Fourth, acknowledgment of wrongdoing by oneself or one's own group is a powerful and courageous act that can transform the relationships among participants. Usually someone can think of at least one wrong deed committed by someone in his or her ethnic group. When a Franciscan who had been detained and almost killed by Serbs confessed his bitterness toward all Serbs, it opened the way for a Serbian Orthodox priest to admit that Serbs had committed atrocities during the war in Bosnia-Herzegovina.

Fifth, forgiveness, defined as "giving up all hope of a better past," is a difficult process to undergo and often takes a great deal of time. Yet the young woman who began a seminar saying she could never forgive the Serbs ended by saying that she knew that someday she would be able to do so.

Sixth, participants are encouraged to envision a restorative justice that is bigger than punishment or revenge and is based on meeting the needs of people rather than enacting retribution. At a seminar in Kosovo, a number of young adults, representing most of the religious traditions, decided to meet together to examine what impact their combined efforts might have on organized crime. They are assessing ways in which the religious communities might develop programs to encourage other young people to turn away from drugs, prostitution, and the trading of weapons.

This whole progression is a part of the process of reconciliation. If a critical mass of people from different ethnic groups were to undergo such a process and begin to take effective action together, then the chance that reconciliation would begin to spread throughout the whole society would be greatly increased.

Building Indigenous Institutions

The prospect of extending the reach of such seminars throughout society is greatly enhanced now by the fact that the CSIS project in Serbia and in Bosnia-Herzegovina has become transformed into an indigenous initiative. The Center for Religious Dialogue (CRD) in Bosnia-Herzegovina was established in December 1998, with offices in Sarajevo and Banja Luka; and the Interreligious Center (IRC) in Serbia was established in April 2000, with an office in Belgrade. The mandate of both organizations is to further develop the work of training religious people in conflict resolution, reconciliation, and peacebuilding. As a result, the reach of these organizations now extends well beyond the religious communities. In Bosnia, for example, seminar participants have included members of the influential Academy of Sciences and Arts in Sarajevo, members of the Bosnian government, Bosnian staff from the Ombudsman Office operated by the United Nations, journalists from influential media in both entities of Bosnia, and other influential citizens for whom religious faith is a primary motivation.

Individual seminar alumni have been involved in creative peacebuilding projects such as alternative media programming and refugee return. As expressed by the director of the CRD in Sarajevo, Vjekoslav Saje:

> Thanks to the experience from our seminars, some religious figures
> became much more involved in decision making in their local com-
> munities, like Imam Mensur Pasalic from Fojnica, who encouraged
> the return of many Croat families from neighboring Kiseljak. . . . One
> of the goals of CRD is also . . . to introduce it [a dialogue process
> used in seminars with religious people] to the schools, firms and other
> institutions, apart from the religious ones. These are main activities by
> which people of different traditions, backgrounds and beliefs could ex-

pedite the change and help in making the shift [to a new way of living together]. CRD is more than willing to do a service of network-
ing with other agencies and help people in need . . . as well as initiate
different projects according to the ideas and proposals of local communities.[148]

The general secretary of the IRC in Belgrade, Marijana Ajzenkol, shares this
future vision of extending the role of the religious communities beyond just
interfaith dialogue. In August of 2001, at a conference sponsored by the IRC
and held at a Serbian Orthodox monastery in Soko, Serbia (just 7 kilometers
from Srebrenica, Bosnia), 170 educators and representatives from all religious
traditions met in order to show teachers firsthand the potential of effective
interreligious dialogue and cooperation. The IRC wants to repeat this kind
of activity with youth, politicians, and other groups in Serbian society. Following their sponsorship of the interfaith Pontanima Choir from Sarajevo at
a concert in Zemun (a Belgrade suburb), the IRC received an invitation
from the mayor to continue planning such interfaith events in his city.[149]

In addition to the activities sponsored by these two organizations, Saje
was also one of the team of people who assisted in facilitating the discussions
that produced the Interreligious Council of Bosnia-Herzegovina. This organization, which was formed through the combined efforts of the World
Conference on Religion and Peace, Mercy Corps International, and the
United States Institute of Peace, is composed of the religious hierarchy of
the four principal faith traditions in the area and has as its purpose the rebuilding of civil society through cooperative religious action. Thus far, the
Council, which is facilitating cooperative religious action designed to rebuild
civil society in Bosnia-Herzegovina, has built cooperative relationships with
agencies involved in postwar reconstruction, called for the return of refugees
from all ethnic and religious groups, and convened a legal task force to
examine the legal status of religious communities in the country.[150]

Supporting Faith-Inspired Individuals

In addition to the efforts of these new indigenous faith-based NGOs, various
efforts have been made by individuals who have been involved with the
interreligious seminars sponsored by the CSIS and its local partners like the
CRD and the IRC. Some of these persons have demonstrated significant
political reach within their own societies, a role that religious people there
have not had the opportunity to play until very recently. One example
involved Seid Hukovic, the president of the Academy of Sciences and Arts
in Sarajevo (which had hosted a CSIS seminar in 1995), who wrote a book

in Bosnian on conflict resolution, taught conflict resolution skills to Bosnian politicians, and was personally involved in the internal negotiations within the Bosnian government that led to its acceptance of the cease-fire that prepared the way for the Dayton peace process.[151]

A second, more influential example involved events surrounding the war in Kosovo. Aleksandar Vidojevic, a political advisor to Bishop Artemije of Kosovo and a participant in one of the CSIS seminars in Bogatic, Serbia, in June 1998, suggested that the CSIS project become the American counterpart in establishing a back-channel of communications between the governments of the United States and Yugoslavia. Through this process, ideas were generated regarding NATO deployment of a peacekeeping force in Kosovo that would potentially be acceptable to both sides. Various other influential actors within both the United States and Yugoslavia helped to take these ideas to the top levels of both governments. Although these ideas were not raised during the official Rambouillet negotiations,[152] the communications channel was kept open.

In April 1999, during the bombing of Yugoslavia, an American delegation met with Vidojevic and members of the Serbian and Yugoslav governments in order to propose to Milosevic an outline for possible agreement regarding the postwar deployment of NATO troops in Kosovo. Milosevic indicated that he would be willing to discuss this proposal. This response was shared with both the Albanian leadership of Kosovo and the State Department in Washington, D.C. Although the war continued for six more weeks, both the Yugoslav and American governments have indicated that these efforts helped bring the war to an end more quickly.[153] Despite numerous setbacks along the way, an effort that grew out of a conflict resolution training project for religious people had eventually helped to facilitate a termination of the conflict in Kosovo.

Moving beyond the Faith Communities

Beyond the efforts of indigenous faith-based NGOs and individuals, there is a third type of conflict resolution activity that is emerging, involving the use of faith-based approaches within a secular context. One example of this is the role played by World Vision International, a faith-based international NGO, in developing the Community Council for Peace and Tolerance of the City of Mitrovica (Kosovo). On November 8, 2000, World Vision staff initiated the first multiethnic, multireligious council meeting in this tense, very divided city. In subsequent months, the Council agreed to lay down any ethnic, religious, or gender-based prejudices, respect the rights and freedoms of all citizens, and set an example for interethnic, interreligious cooperation. At a Strategic Planning Workshop sponsored by World Vision and held in Caux, Switzerland, in October 2001, the Mitrovica Council for Peace and Tolerance, in a written declaration, committed themselves to "purge prejudice from our hearts," and "to unite our hearts" in order to "construct non-violent alternatives for dealing with our differences," and to propose "constructive solutions for common problems to both local Administration and to local and international non-governmental organizations."[154]

In another example where a faith-based approach has been used in a secular context, the CSIS project on religion and conflict resolution was invited to assist in training workshops sponsored by the United States Institute of Peace (USIP) and the Organization for Security and Cooperation in Europe (OSCE) in Kosovo. In each case, the CSIS was asked to focus on the same relationship building process that has proven so successful for religious people.

In the case of the OSCE workshops, the purpose was specifically to sensitize the staff of that organization, both domestic and international, to the potentially positive role that religion can play in the resolution of conflict. Utilizing religious belief systems and religious practices to empower people in working toward reconciliation was an overt aim of these workshops. According to Renata Korber, chief of training for the OSCE in Kosovo, this approach engendered greater openness and self-examination than she had ever previously witnessed.

Although not overtly expressed in the same way, the six steps of religious practices described earlier (processing grief, acknowledging fears, identifying needs, admitting wrongs done, forgiving others, and envisioning a restorative justice) were also used in the USIP workshops for municipal leaders and professional people. Used as a first step in the USIP workshops, this focus on relationship building, rooted in the religious traditions, was followed by skills training in communications and negotiations and by the facilitation of working groups on various justice issues. The success of this approach was readily apparent in the first USIP seminar, held in Gjilan/ Gnjilane, Kosovo, in May of 2000. Here, Serbs and Albanians who on the first day would barely talk to one another ended up working together in planning an irrigation system for southeastern Kosovo by the end of the fourth day.

The success of both of these ventures points to the value of utilizing practices developed in a religious context for other population groups. The fact that these efforts could succeed in a traditionally Muslim region like Kosovo further demonstrates the adaptability of the faith-based approach.[155] All of these examples demonstrate the potential impact that faith-based initiatives can have on the development of peacebuilding capacities both within and beyond the religious communities.

There are three basic roles that religious people have played in the efforts described in Bosnia-Herzegovina and Kosovo. Some of the seminar alumni have played the advocacy role, lobbying for refugee return, an end to corruption, or development of an irrigation system. Others have played a negotiation/mediation role—whether it is Bosnian Franciscan Ivo Markovic negotiating between Muslim and Croat commanders to keep their armies from fighting one another or an advisor to Bishop Artemije functioning as a back-channel of communications between the American and Yugoslav governments during the Kosovo War. The predominant role, however, has been that of education. Different types of educational environments have proven productive for different purposes. Multiconfessional seminars have helped people to break down their stereotypes of one another and begin to work on cooperative projects. Single-confessional seminars have helped people to confront the conflicts within their own community and, by providing a safe environment "within the faith," to assist those more prone to nationalistic tendencies to consider other alternatives.

In the future, the CRD in Bosnia-Herzegovina is planning to hold a seminar for those who live as minorities within their respective geographical locations. It is believed that such people, regardless of their religious confession, will be more open to dialogue because of their common tendency toward accommodation. It is conceivable that a coalition of minorities may well have a significant peacemaking influence on the members of their respective ethnic groups.

Ongoing support for such activities, at both the grass-roots and hierarchical levels in Bosnia-Herzegovina and Kosovo, is one of the more significant contributions that the international community can make to promote peace and stability in the Balkans. Further, grantmaking institutions, both governmental and private, would do well to consider including a conflict prevention/resolution dimension in their programs for postconflict intervention. Engaging staff from local or international NGOs involved in reconciliation work, such as those associated with the faith-based initiatives described in this chapter, could greatly benefit the peacebuilding process.

Whatever the context, people of faith often bring a depth of hope and inspiration that can energize an otherwise stagnant process. When freed from the nationalistic bondage that is all too often perpetuated within their own institutions, they can inspire politicians and bureaucrats to think "outside the box" in resolving intractable differences. There is no end to what might be accomplished, for as Jesus said, "with God, all things are possible" (Matthew 19:26).

NOTES

1. I wish to thank the many who assisted me in the writing of this chapter. Numerous people have contributed by giving invaluable feedback on earlier drafts. Some have helped in a long process of locating and translating primary source material. Listed alphabetically, these people include: Adisa Busuladic (staff member, International Relief and Development), Washington, D. C.; Jim Forest (director, Orthodox Peace Fellowship), Alkmaar, the Netherlands; Ivo Markovic (professor, Franciscan Theological Faculty), Sarajevo; Paul Mojzes (academic dean, Rosemont College), Rosemont, Pennsylvania; Suzana Mrgic (deputy chief executive, G17 Plus), Belgrade; Devin O'Shaughnessy (intern, Center for Strategic and International Studies), Washington, D. C.; Predrag P. Pajic (South Slav specialist in the European Division of the Library of Congress), Washington, D. C.; Heidi Paulson (coordinator, Program on Preventive Diplomacy, Center for Strategic and International Studies), Washington, D. C.; Ursina Pluss (intern, Center for Strategic and International Studies), Washington, D. C.; Rafaela Prifti (staff member, Radio Television of Kosova), New York and Pristina; Radomir Rakic (Office of the Patriarchate of the Serbian Orthodox Church), Belgrade; Vjekoslav Saje (director, Center for Religious Dialogue), Sarajevo; Aleksandar Vidojevic (former political advisor to the Serbian Orthodox bishop Artemije of Kosovo), Belgrade; and Fedja Zimic (staff member, Voice of America), Washington, D.C.

2. David Little and Kate McCann, "Religion and Peacebuilding in Bosnia," unpublished article, 1999 (United States Institute of Peace), pp. 1–2.

3. Standing Conference of Canonical Orthodox Bishops in the Americas, "Orthodox Bishops in Americas Condemn Violence and Intolerance in Kosovo," listserve: kosovo@egroups.com, June 21, 2000.

4. Srdjan Vrcan, "Religious Factor in the War in Bosnia and Herzegovina," in *Religion and the War in Bosnia*, ed. by Paul Mojzes (Atlanta: Scholars Press, 1998), p. 115.

5. Leonard Cohen, "Bosnia's 'Tribal Gods': The Role of Religion in Nationalist Politics," in Mojzes, *Religion and the War in Bosnia*, pp. 50–65.

6. "Message of Patriarch Pavle and Cardinal Kuharic following their Meeting in Geneva on 23 September 1992," in *Conference of European Churches* (CEC) *Documentation Service 17*, no. 34 (1992), pp. 22–24. It should be noted that this was the third meeting between the two leaders, the first having been held in May 1991 in Sremski Karlovici, Serbia, and the second in August 1991 in Slavonski Brod, Croatia.

7. "Appeal for Peace in Bosnia and Herzegovina," Appeal of Conscience Foundation, Zurich, November 26, 1992.

8. Pedro Ramet, "Religion and Nationalism in Yugoslavia," in *Religion and Nationalism in Soviet and East European Politics*, ed. by Pedro Ramet (Durham, N.C.: Duke University Press, 1989), pp. 299–311.

9. Patrick Moore, "Islamic Aspects of the Yugoslav Crisis," *Radio Free Europe/Radio Liberty Research Report* 1, no. 28, July 10, 1992, p. 38.

10. Some of the Bosnian Muslim leaders referred to include: Isma'il Balic, Halid Hajimulic, Halid Varatanovic, and Fadil Porca. (Khalid Duran, "Bosnia, The Other Andalusia: After the Evil Empire, An Evil New World Order," Gaithersburg, Maryland [n.d.], pp. 21–24).

11. Alija Izetbegovic, "The Islamic Declaration," *Balcanica: Storia, Cultura, Politica 9*, no. 3/4 (1992), pp. 103–4.

12. Dragoljub R. Zivojinovic, "Islam in the Balkans: Origins and Contemporary Implications," *Mediterranean Quarterly* 3, no. 4 (1992), pp. 62–64.

13. The charge was that the Party of Democratic Action was (1) pressuring Muslims, who had registered as Serbs, Croats, Yugoslavs, or "undecided" during the previous census, to now register as "Muslims" (Ivo Markovic, "Bosanski Muslimani," [Bosnian Muslims], trans. by Fedja Zimic, Zagreb, February 7, 1993 [original on file at Christian Information Service, Zagreb], p. 2), and (2) attempting to repatriate four million Bosnian Muslims from Turkey by passing a declaration in the Bosnian Parliament entitled "The Program of the Resettlement of the Bosnians from Turkey" (Zivojinovic, "Islam in the Balkans," pp. 62–64).

14. Izetbegovic specifically envisioned the creation of a great Islamic federation "from Morocco to Indonesia, from tropical Africa to Central Asia" (Izetbegovic, "The Islamic Declaration," pp. 119–20; and Zivojinovic, "Islam in the Balkans," pp. 58–60).

15. "Mr. Darko Lukic, Minister for Religious Affairs in the Bosnian Government: 'Building a State,' " *Vecernji List*, February 2, 1993, on file at the *Christian Information Service*, Zagreb.

16. Izetbegovic in "The Islamic Declaration," p. 89, writes "There can be neither peace nor coexistence between the Islamic religion and non-Islamic social and political institutions. . . . Islam obviously excludes the right or possibility of action on the part of any foreign ideology on that terrain."

17. Paul Mojzes, "The Camouflaged Role of Religion in the War in Bosnia and Herzegovina," in Mojzes, *Religion and the War in Bosnia*, pp. 74–75.

18. John Meyendorff, *The Byzantine Legacy in the Orthodox Church* (Crestwood, N.Y.: St. Vladimir's Seminary Press, 1982), pp. 220–29.

19. Basil Lourie, "Ecclesiology of a Refreshing Army," *Vertograd-Inform*, English Edition, *Orthodox Information Bulletin*, no. 3; available on-line at: www.private.peterlink. ru/alektor/v3.htm.

20. Metropolitan Amfilohije Radovic, "The Church as the Pillar and Stronghold of the Truth," available on-line at the web site of the Serbian Orthodox Church in Montenegro: www.rastko.org.yu/rastko-cg/duhovnost/the_church.html, February 21, 2001.

21. Stanley Samuel Harakas, *Living the Faith: The Praxis of Eastern Orthodox Ethics* (Minneapolis, Minn. Light and Life, 1992), p. 370.

22. Radovan Bigovic, *Crkva I Drustvo* (Church and Society), Hilandarski fond pri Bogoslovskom Fakultetu SPC (Beograd: Zajednica Sveti Nikola, Pariz, Beograd, 2000), p. 259.

23. Marinko Culic, "Pastir Svih Srba," *Danas*, no. 386, July 11, 1989, p. 25.

24. Radmila Radic, "Serbian Orthodox Church and the War in Bosnia and Herzegovina," in Mojzes, *Religion and the War in Bosnia*, pp. 161–67; and Leonard J. Cohen, *Serpent in the Bosom: The Rise and Fall of Slobodan Milosevic* (Boulder, Colo.: Westview Press, 2001), pp. 151–52.

25. Dragan Terzic, "Bez Pravoslavlja ne Postoji Srpstvo," *Pravoslavlje* (Serbian Orthodox publication), no. 608, July 15, 1992, p. 3.

26. One of the leading Serbian Orthodox theologians writing from this perspective was Bishop Atanasije Jevtic, the former dean of the Orthodox Theological Faculty in Belgrade (Geert van Dartel, "The Nations and the Churches in Yugoslavia," *Religion, State and Society* 20, nos. 3, 4 (1992), pp. 281–82; and Ivo Markovic, "Srpsko Pravoslavlje i Srpska Pravoslavna Crkva," [Serbian Orthodoxy and the Serbian Orthodox Church],

trans. by Fedja Zimic, Zagreb [n.d], p. 3). Some of Bishop Jevtic's writings about Kosovo are documented in note 102 hereafter.

27. Serbian Orthodox leaders making such warnings included Metropolitan Nikolaj of Sarajevo, Bishop Jefrem of Banja Luka and Bishop Vasilije of Tuzla. See "Vjerska Ravnoprravnot-temelj Demokratije: Tezak Polozaj Prvoslavne Crke u Bosni I Herce-govini," *Pravoslavlje* 24, no. 567, November 1, 1990, p. 1.

28. Paul Mojzes, *Yugoslavian Inferno: Ethnoreligious Warfare in the Balkans* (New York: Continuum, 1994), p. 137.

29. "Memorandum of the Holy Assembly of Bishops of the Serbian Orthodox Church, Issued at Its Regular Session Held from the 14th to the 27th of May, 1992," in Nicholas V. Trkla, "Position of the Serbian Orthodox Church Regarding the War in the Former Yugoslavia" (English language collection of Serbian Orthodox Church Statements), Chicago, September 1994. It should also be noted that Patriarch Pavle on numerous occasions condemned war crimes, though he defended the right of Serbs to conduct a defensive war, which he perceived as an active struggle against evil (Patriarch Pavle interviewed in *Pravoslavlje*, no. 603, 1992; *Pravoslavlje*, nos. 651, 652, 1994; *Politika*, June 22 and July 17, 1994; and *Svetigora*, no. 29, 1994).

30. "The War in Bosnia and Herzegovina: The Latest Appeal of the Religious Leaders in Banja Luka," April 4, 1992 (reported in *Christian Information Service*, KIS A.07.04.02, Zagreb, April 7, 1992).

31. "Communique Concerning the False Accusations against the Serbian Nation in Bosnia and Herzegovina," Belgrade, December 1992 (on file at the Conference of European Churches, Geneva).

32. Atanasije Jevtic, "Srpska Sramota," *Nedeljne Informativne Novine* (*NIN*), no. 2198, February 12, 1993, p. 20.

33. Barbara Demick, "Bosnian Serbs Nurture Anger," *Philadelphia Inquirer*, September 26, 1995, p. A9. Note, however, that Father Ilic is no longer serving as a parish priest (E-mail received from Radomir Rakic [editor of the Serbian Orthodox publication, *Pravoslavlje*, and faculty member of the Orthodox Theological Faculty in Belgrade], July 17, 2002).

34. Claims that Serbian guards carved signs of the cross into the bodies of Bosnian Muslims were made by Enes Denic from Vlasenica, Bosnia, during a personal inter-view at the Gasinci refugee camp, near Dakova, Croatia, March 11, 1993. Mr. Dedic claimed to have witnessed such incidents while he was held at concentration camps in Papraca and Batkovic, Bosnia, prior to arriving at the Gasinci refugee camp in Croatia. Claims that Serbian guards burned signs of the cross into the bodies of Bosnian Muslims were made by the Rijaset (leadership of the Islamic Community) and signed by Reis-ul-ulema Jakub Selimoski in a statement reported in "Muslim Leadership Proclaims," in *Christian Information Service*, KIS AG.23.01, Zagreb, [July 1992]. Claims that weapons and soldiers were blessed by Serbian Orthodox priests have been made in Tonci Kuzmanic, "Former Yugoslavia: The Religious War?" (revised version of an article published in *Religioni e Societa*, no. 4 [1992], Florence, Italy), p. 4, and Mojzes, "The Camouflaged Role of Religion in the War in Bosnia and Herzego-vina," p. 87.

35. Milka Tadic, "Arkan's Montenegro Link," Institute for War and Peace Reporting, Balkan Crisis Report, no. 108, January 18, 2000, available on-line at the web site of the Institute for War and Peace Reporting: www.iwpr.net; Cohen, *Serpent in the Bosom*, p. 155.

36. Interview of Metropolitan Nikolaj Mrdja in Nenad Stefanovic, "Lecicemo se Sto Godina od Komunizma" (We Are Going to Heal Ourselves from Communism over the Next 100 Years), *Duga*, no. 500, April 24–May 7, 1993, p. 59.

37. Dragan Terzic, "Zadaci Crkve u Novim Okolnostima," *Pravoslavlje*, no. 613, October 1, 1992, p. 3.

38. *Pravoslavlje*, no. 614, 1992, quoted in Radic, "Serbian Orthodox Church and the War in Bosnia and Herzegovina," pp. 173–74.

39. Cohen, "Bosnia's 'Tribal Gods': The Role of Religion in Nationalist Politics," pp. 55–56. See also note 105 hereafter for the specific content of Patriarch German's comments on this occasion.

40. Radic, "Serbian Orthodox Church and the War in Bosnia and Herzegovina," p. 162; and Patriarch Pavle, interviewed in *Conversations with the Epoch*, ed. by Milorad Vucelic (Belgrade: Ministry of Information of the Republic of Serbia, 1991), p. 13.

41. Cohen, *Serpent in the Bosom*, pp. 154–55.

42. "Memorandum of the Holy Assembly of Bishops of the Serbian Orthodox Church, Issued at Its Regular Session Held from the 14th to the 27th of May, 1992," p. 4.

43. One example can be found in the Holy Synod of Bishops of the Serbian Orthodox Church, "Appeal to the Serbian People," Belgrade, August 7, 1995, on file at the Conference of European Churches, Geneva.

44. Cohen, *Serpent in the Bosom*, p. 155.

45. Patriarch Pavle did attempt to mediate between Milosevic and Karadzic when Milosevic broke off political and economic relations with the Bosnian Serb Republic in August 1994 (Svetlana Djurdjevic Lukic, "Zavadjena Braca" [Brotherly Rift], *NIN*, August 12, 1994, p. 17). However, the Holy Synod met in an emergency session and issued a statement siding with the Bosnian Serbs (*NIN*, August 12, 1994, p. 15). Again in August 1995, Patriarch Pavle was a signatory to the agreement between Milosevic and Karadzic allowing Milosevic to represent the Bosnian Serbs at Dayton. However, again, Pavle's involvement agitated some of the other bishops, and at a meeting of the Holy Synod in December, Pavle's signature on the August 29 agreement was declared invalid, and the peace plan, though officially accepted, was declared to be unjust ("Slucaj Nevazeceg Potpisa" [The Case of the Invalid Signature], *NIN*, December 29, 1995, p. 18). It is noted that personal statements of the patriarch frequently sound more conciliatory than official statements of the Serbian Orthodox Church, which often reflect the views of more nationalist bishops (Peter Palmer, "Religions and Nationalism in Yugoslavia: A Tentative Comparison between the Catholic Church and the Other Communities" in *The Balkans: A Religious Backyard of Europe*, ed. by Mient Jan Faber [Ravenna, Italy: A. Longo, 1996], p. 155). Orthodox bishops, including patriarchs, do not have the same degree of power that Catholic bishops have. It is, therefore, very possible for even a patriarch to be publicly contradicted and opposed by other bishops in the Orthodox Church.

46. Interview with Radovan Karadzic by Drazenko Djukanovic, "Karadzic Summarizes Serbian Achievements," *Foreign Broadcast Information Service: Daily Report East Europe*, FBIS-EEU-95-009, January 13, 1995, p. 43.

47. Interview with Radovan Karadzic, entitled "The Resurrection of the Crouching Soul: A Conversation with Mr. Radovan Karadzic," by an anonymous author, in *Svetigora*, March 1995 (quoted and translated in Paul Mojzes, "Confessions of a Serb Leader," *Christian Century*, August 16–23, 1995, p. 766).

48. "Inaugural Speech of Bishop Jovan of Tetovo," *Pravoslavlje*, nos. 633–34, August 1–15, 1993, pp. 2–3.

49. Dragomir-Ubiparípovíc, "At the Dusk of War in Bosnia and Herzegovina," printed in both *Svecanik*, nos. 1–2, 1993, and *Hriscanska Misao*, no. 608, 1993, quoted in Radic, "Serbian Orthodox Church and the War in Bosnia and Herzegovina," pp. 176–77.

50. "Telegram Podrske Skupstini Republike Srpske-Metropolit Crnogorsko-Primorski Amfilohije, Cetinje, 5.8.1994" (Telegram sent from Metropolitan Amfilohije to the Assembly of Republika Srpska on August 5, 1994), *Svetigora*, nos. 30–31, August–September 1994, pp. 34–35.

51. Slavica Jovovic, "Srbi i Bog: Episkop Banjalucki Jefrem," *Intervju*, August 23–September 16, 1996 (English translation: Tatjana Peric, "Serbian Orthodox Church, Human Rights and War Crimes" [New York: Center for the Study of Human Rights, Columbia University, 1998], pp. 10–11).

52. Radovan Bigovic, interviewed in *Politika*, January 6, 1996, quoted in Radic, "Serbian Orthodox Church and the War in Bosnia and Herzegovina," p. 182.

53. Bishop Hrizostom, comments made during conflict resolution training workshop in Valjevo, Serbia, sponsored by the Center for Strategic and International Studies, Washington, D.C., December 13–15, 1997.

54. Bishop Hrizostom, comments made during conflict resolution training workshop in Bihac, Bosnia-Herzegovina, sponsored by the Center for Religious Dialogue, Sarajevo, and the Center for Strategic and International Studies, Washington, D. C., June 30–July 2, 1998.

55. Little and McCann, "Religion and Peacebuilding in Bosnia," pp. 4–5.

56. Father Krstan Bijeljac, comments made during conflict resolution training workshop in Sarajevo, sponsored by the Center for Strategic and International Studies, Washington, D. C., April 25–27, 1995.

57. Prota Srecko Radosavljevic and Zorica Josic, comments made during conflict resolution training workshop in Sabac, Serbia, sponsored by the Center for Strategic and International Studies, Washington, D. C., June 4–6, 1996.

58. Milorad Ljubinac, interview recorded in *Svjetla u Tunelu* (Lights in a Tunnel), ed. by Jezdimir Milosevic, trans. by Suzana Mrgic (Sarajevo: Protector); available on-line at: www.protector.com.ba.

59. Imam Husein Kovacevic from Sanski Most, comment made during conflict resolution training workshop in Sarajevo, sponsored by the Center for Religious Dialogue, Sarajevo, and the Center for Strategic and International Studies, Washington, D. C., April 3–5, 2001.

60. Van Dartel, "The Nations and the Churches in Yugoslavia," p. 281.

61. Josip Beljan, "Priznata Vjernost," (Recognition of Faithfulness) *Veritas*, nos. 9–10, September–October 1992, Zagreb, pp. 24–25 (trans. by Paul Mojzes, in *Yugoslavian Inferno*, p. 130.).

62. Following the declaration of Croatian independence in June 1991, the Vatican did call for some form of Yugoslav confederation, but by October the intensity and brutality of the war that followed convinced the Vatican that independence was essential (Statement of the Catholic Bishops of Yugoslavia, June 27, 1991, reprinted in *Catholic International*, 2, no. 16 (September 1991), p. 763; and "Holy See's Position on Yugoslav States," reprinted in *L'Osservatore Romane*, weekly English edition, January 1–8, 1992, p. 2).

63. Gerard F. Powers, "Religion, Conflict and Prospects for Peace in Bosnia, Croatia, and Yugoslavia," in Mojzes, *Religion and the War in Bosnia*, pp. 227–28.

64. *Catholic Press Agency—Zagreb*, account of interview with Cardinal Kuharic in the Catholic weekly *Glas Koncila*, January 3, 1996.

65. Mojzes, *Yugoslavian Inferno*, pp. 131–33; and Paul Mojzes, "The Role of the Religious Communities in the War in Former Yugoslavia," in *Religion in Eastern Europe*, 13, no. 3 (June 1993), pp. 18–19. It is also noteworthy that Cardinal Kuharic felt it necessary to assert that there was a distance between church and state, despite apparent linkages, in his interview with Marinko Culic, "Nismo u Narucju Vlasti" (We Are Not in the Arms of the Government), *Danas* 9, no. 461, December 18, 1990, pp. 20–23.

66. Gabriel Partos (Southeast Europe analyst with the BBC Service), "Religion and the Balkan Wars," Institute for War and Peace Reporting, 1996, available on-line at: www.demon.co.uk/iwpr/partos40.htm.

67. Franjo Tudjman, letter to Serbian Orthodox patriarch Pavle (reported in "Letter of Croatian President to Head of Serbian Orthodox Church," *Christian Information Service*, Zagreb, March 20, 1992).

68. Cardinal Kuharic did write in a letter to Serbian Orthodox Patriarch German, on November 12, 1990: "We regret and condemn all crimes that sons of the Croatian people, on whatever side or under whatever flag they were, have committed against the Serbian and other peoples." However, this was a very generalized apology without reference to specific atrocities, as requested by the Serbian Church and people (Van Dartel, "The Nations and the Churches in Yugoslavia," pp. 279–80 and 286–87; and Mojzes, *Yugoslavian Inferno*, pp. 131–34).

69. Powers, "Religion, Conflict, and Prospects for Peace in Bosnia, Croatia, and Yugoslavia," p. 230.

70. Kuzmanic, "Former Yugoslavia: The Religious War?" p. 4; and Mojzes, "The Camouflaged Role of Religion in the War in Bosnia and Herzegovina," p. 91.

71. "Serbian Orthodox Metropolitan Bishop Accuses Croatian Authorities—While Serbian Patriarch Paul Blesses the Foundation Stone of a New Orthodox Church on the Ruins of the Destroyed Catholic Church in Lovas" (reported in Christian Information Service, KIS AD3001, Zagreb, April 30, 1992).

72. Darko Pavacic, "Svecenik Nije Komesar" (A Priest Is Not a Commisssar), *Danas* 10, no. 503 (October 8, 1991), p. 28; Mojzes, "The Role of the Religious Communities in the War in the Former Yugoslavia," p. 17 (citing conversation with Marko Orsolic, a professor at the Franciscan Theological Fakulty in Sarajevo, who said that most of his students were using machine guns); and Franz K. Prueler, "Report on Caritas Europe Mission to Croatia and Serbia," September 9, 1991 (on file at Catholic Relief Services, Baltimore), p. 2.

73. Mato Zovkic, "War Wounds in Croatian Catholic Population of Bosnia-Herzegovina," in Mojzes *Religion and the War in Bosnia*, p. 212.

74. Council of the Croatian Bishops' Conference, "Statement of Croatian Bishops Regarding the Situation in Bosnia and Herzegovina," October 7, 1992 (reported in *Christian Information Service*, KIS AJ.12.01, Zagreb).

75. Jure Kristo, "The Catholic Church in Times of Crisis," p. 12 (cited by Paul Mojzes in "The Role of the Religious Communities in the War in Former Yugoslavia," p. 18). According to Mojzes, Kristo wrote, "The Catholic Church made offers to strike that provision (the law regarding nationalist political parties) from the books. At the

same time, the faithful were encouraged not to fear organizing themselves on the national and religious basis."

76. Mojzes, *Yugoslavian Inferno*, p. 135. This information is based on Mojzes claim to have found the term "Mujahedin" repeated in numerous references to Bosnian Muslims in the Catholic weekly *Glas Koncila*, between 1991 and 1993 (interview with Paul Mojzes, Reston, Virginia, November 18, 2001).

77. Ivo Markovic, "Uloga I Polozaj Katolicke Crkve u Ratu u Bosni I Hercegovini," (The Role and Place of the Catholic Church in the War in Bosnia and Hercegovina), trans. by Fedja Zimic (original published in *Christian Information Service*, Zagreb, January 26, 1993).

78. Zovkic, "War Wounds in Croatian Catholic Population of Bosnia-Herzegovina," p. 212.

79. The Croatian government also announced its independence on the tenth anniversary of the apparition in Medjugorje. This nationalization of the Virgin's appearance by Croatian politicians was a source of great pride to the Herzegovinian Franciscans (Michael Sells, *The Bridge Betrayed: Religion and Genocide in Bosnia* [Berkeley: University of California Press], pp. 106–7).

80. Mojzes, *Yugoslavian Inferno*, p. 135. The information is based on a series of personal interviews Paul Mojzes had in Zagreb with Vjekoslav Bajsic, a professor at the Catholic Theological Faculty in Zagreb (email from Paul Mojzes to me, October 23, 2001).

81. Gojko Beric, "Catholic Church: Setbacks in Bosnia Fuel Boban-Church Conflict," *Balkan War Report* 21 (August–September 1993), p. 15.

82. Mojzes, *Yugoslavian Inferno*, p. 135. This information is based on conversations Paul Mojzes had with Cardinal Puljic, Mato Zovkic, and Pero Sudar in Sarajevo (email from Paul Mozjes to this author, October 23, 2001). One can also find indications of this change in perspective in Zovkic, "War Wounds of Croatian Population of Bosnia-Herzegovina," pp. 208–13.

83. Powers, "Religion, Conflict and Prospects for Peace in Bosnia, Croatia, and Yugoslavia," pp. 227–29.

84. Cardinal Vinko Puljic, Archbishop of Sarajevo, address given at the Center for Strategic and International Studies, Washington, D. C., March 30, 1995, quoted in *Catholic News Service*, April 3, 1995, p. 7.

85. The reproach of the bishops by civil authorities was made during a meeting in Split, Croatia, between Catholic bishops and Croatian civil authorities from Bosnia-Herzegovina. Since the war, Zovkic (the vicar general of the Sarajevo Diocese) has been even more explicit in his condemnation of crimes by Croats. He writes that Croats had cleansed 50,000 Muslims from Herzegovina before the outbreak of Muslim-Croat fighting in March 1993. He also indicates that he became aware of the existence of Croatian concentration camps in Herzegovina as early as April of 1992 and that some priests who had previously been his students had defended the existence of these camps, charging that Muslims were an unreliable element. Yet he also claims that Cardinal Puljic made several pastoral visits to the region in an attempt to trace and calm down the ethnic tensions (Zovkic, "War Wounds in Croatian Catholic Population of Bosnia-Herzegovina," pp. 208–14). Zovkic has also admitted that the Catholic Church cannot say it had nothing to do with the terrible things Catholic soldiers did to Muslims during the war, referring to destruction of Muslim towns and killing of Muslim civilians (Jim Forest, "Belgrade Dialogue on Reconciliation," February 18–22, 1997, available on-

line at: http//ourworld.compuserve.com/homepages/jim_forest/Dialogue.htm, p. 1). For examples of Bishop Komarica's courageous positions, see Arthur Jones, "Croat Bishop Tells his Story, Wants Action," *National Catholic Reporter*, September 6, 1996, p. 5.

86. One of the joint prayer services sponsored by Zajedno took place in the Serbian Orthodox Church in Munich, where the priest, Father Slobodan Milunovic, organized a prayer service for the Muslims of Srebrenica (Marko Orsolic, interview recorded in *Svjetla u Tunelu* [Lights in a Tunnel] ed. by Jezdimir Milosevic, trans. by Suzana Mrgic [Sarajevo: *Protector*]; available on-line at: www.protector.com.ba; and "Zajedno: International Multireligious and Intercultural Center [IMIC]," program description available from Zajedno, Obala Kulina bana 39, Sarajevo, p. 1).

87. Mirko Majdandzic, interview recorded in Milosevic, *Svjetla u Tunelu* [Lights in a Tunnel].

88. Little and McCann, "Religion and Peacebuilding in Bosnia," p. 14; and Mirko Majdanzic, comments made during seminar conflict resolution training workshop in Bugojno, Bosnia-Herzegovina, sponsored by the Center for Religious Dialogue, Sarajevo, September 28–30, 1999.

89. Interview with Father Mijo Dzolan, Rama Monastery, Scit, Bosnia-Herzegovina, October 22, 1994. The next day, in a conversation with both the Muslim mayor of Prozor and an officer in the UN peacekeeping mission in Bosnia-Herzegovina, the latter indicated that Father Dzolan was the only person in the region who could speak and have both Croats and Muslims listen (Captain David Amos, NATO Implementation Force [IFOR] mission in Gorni Vakuf, Bosnia-Herzegovina, October 23, 1994).

90. Taped interview with Ivo Markovic, Tanenbaum Foundation, New York, April 1, 2000.

91. Forest, "Belgrade Dialogue on Reconciliation," p. 5.

92. "Religion in Kosovo," International Crisis Group (ICG), Balkan Report no. 105, Pristina/Brussels, January 31, 2001, p. 15.

93. Signatories on this document included Bishop Artemije, Bishop Sopi, the vice dean of the Faculty of Islamic Studies, Quemajl Morina, and the president of the Appeal of Conscience Foundation, Arthur Schneier ("Kosovo Peace and Tolerance: Vienna Declaration," sponsored by the Appeal of Conscience Foundation, New York, pp. 2–3).

94. "Religion in Kosovo," ICG Balkan Report, p. 15; and "Interreligious Council of Kosovo and Metohija: Statement to the Public," April 14, 2000, available on-line at: www.serbian-church.net/News/14-4-00_el.html, pp. 1–2. Note: "Gjilan" and "Gnjilane" are Albanian and Serbian spellings for the same Kosovo city. Use of such double spellings elsewhere in the text also refer to the Albanian and Serbian spellings for other Kosovo cities.

95. "Religion in Kosovo," ICG Balkan Report, pp. 2, 7.

96. "Statement of the Presidency of the Islamic Community of Kosovo: 26 August 1999," on file at the Office of External Affairs, Serbian Orthodox Church, Washington, D.C.

97. For example, Qemajl Morina, vice dean of the Faculty of Islamic Studies in Pristina, said that "the Serbs . . . always used religion when they needed to mobilize their forces for any holy 'Crusade' of cleansing 'Serb lands' of Muslims. . . . There is no doubt that the main force that sets this propaganda in motion is the Serbian Orthodox Church. . . . The Serbian Orthodox Church should be considered the mastermind be-

hind all these acts as long as it does not condemn them" (referring to destruction of forty mosques and the massacre of imams and other Kosovo Muslims). See Qemajl Morina, Hiermonk Sava Janjic, and Qemajl Morina, "Religion in Kosovo: A Christian and A Muslim View"; available on Decani listserve, at: www.egroups.com/list/decani, October 22, 1998, pp. 4–7.

98. "Religion in Kosovo," ICG Balkan Report, pp. 5–6.

99. In the Kerbela myth, Husayn, a beloved Shi'ite leader, is killed by a Sunni caliph and becomes a martyr whose death is to be avenged by his followers.

100. "Religion in Kosovo," ICG Balkan Report, pp. 4–5; and Ger Duizjings, *Religion and the Politics of Identity in Kosovo* (New York: Columbia University Press, 2000), pp. 81–83, 109–11, 122–24, 157–75.

101. An English translation of this petition can be found in *South Slav Journal* 5, no. 3 (1982), pp. 49–54.

102. Atanasije Jevtic, "Od Kosova do Jadovna" (From Kosovo to Jadovno), *Pravoslavlje*, no. 400, November 15, 1983, and no. 404, January 15, 1984; and Atanasije Jevtic, "Sa Kosova i oko Kosova" (From Kosovo and Around Kosovo), *Pravoslavlje*, no. 366, 1982, p. 3.

103. Appeal by the Holy Synod of Bishops of the Serbian Orthodox Church in 1969, quoted in Gordana Filipovic, *Kosovo: Past and Present* (Belgrade: Review of International Affairs, 1989), pp. 355–60.

104. For the section alleging genocide against the Serbs by Albanians in Kosovo, see the web site for the Serbian Unity Congress at: http://suc.suc.org/~kosta/tar/memorandum/memorandum.html#status.

105. On the evening before the celebration, Patriarch German commented that "the present changes in attitude of the Serbian [political] leadership toward the Serbian Church and its people . . . is the beginning of good cooperation that will benefit everybody." (Milo Gligorijevic, "Kosovo Lekcije iz Istorije" [Kosovo: a Lesson from History], *NIN*, no. 2008 [special supplement], June 25, 1989, p. 5).

106. Historically, some reports claim that the battle was actually a draw, or even a Serb victory. Furthermore, the final Ottoman victory over the Serbs did not take place until 1459 (Duizjings, *Religion and the Politics of Identity in Kosovo*, p. 182; and Tim Judah, *Kosovo: War and Revenge* [New Haven: Yale University Press, 2000], p. 8).

107. Duizjings, *Religion and the Politics of Identity in Kosovo*, pp. 182–93. Serb authors also referring to this Kosovo myth include Radic ("Serbian Orthodox Church and the War in Bosnia and Herzegovina," pp. 167–68); and Father Sava Janjic (see notes 114 and 116). Specific reference to the choice of a heavenly kingdom, as the central motif of the "Kosovo pledge," can be found in Milne Holton and Vasa D. Mihailovich, *Serbian Poetry from the Beginnings to the Present* (Columbus, Ohio: Slavica Publishers, 1988), p. 25. Reference to *Gorski Vijenac* can be found in P. P. Njegos, *The Mountain Wreath*, trans. and ed. by Vasa D. Mihailovich (Belgrade: Vajat, 1989), p. 2. References to the effect of the Kosovo myth on the Bosnian Peasant Insurrection can be found in Milorad Ekmecic, "The Emergence of St. Vitus Day as the Principal National Holiday for Serbs," in *Kosovo—Legacy of a Medieval Battle* ed. by Wayne S. Vucinich and Thomas Emmert (Minneapolis: University of Minnesota Press, 1991), p. 337. References to the effect of the Kosovo myth on the Balkan Wars of 1912–13 can be found in Mark Thompson, *A Paper House: The Ending of Yugoslavia* (London: Hutchinson Radius, 1992), p. 145. References to the effect of the Kosovo myth on World War I and World War II can be found in Tim Judah, *The Serbs: History, Myth*

and the Destruction of Yugoslavia (New Haven: Yale University Press, 1997), pp. 64, 97, and 113.

108. Some of the specific references by Serbian Orthodox priests include Atanasije Jevtic, "The Kosovo Pledge," references to the Kosovo pledge in Bishop Danilo Krstic and Amfilohije Radovic, "There Is No More Beautiful Faith Than the Christian," and Bozidar Mijac, "Escatology," in *Teoloski Pogledi* (Theological Views), no. 1–2 (1988), 8. All references are cited in Radic, "Serbian Orthodox Church and the War in Bosnia and Herzegovina," pp. 167–68.

109. Duizjings, *Religion and the Politics of Identity in Kosovo*, pp. 192–93, 205.

110. Hieromonk Sava Janjic, response to Qemajl Morina (vice dean of the Faculty of Islamic Studies in Pristina) in, Janjic and Morina, "Religion in Kosovo: A Christian and a Muslim View," pp. 3–7.

111. Steven P. Tsichlis, "Serbian Church Is Opposed to Brutal Regime," *Los Angeles Times*, May 15, 1999, available on Decani listserve at: www.egroups.com/group/decani, May 16, 1999, p. 2.

112. "Religion in Kosovo," ICG Balkan Report, p. 11.

113. Patriarch Pavle, "Several Statements, Prayers and Appeals of Patriarch Pavle," available on the web site of the Orthodox Peace Fellowship at www.incommunion. org/pavle.htm.

114. "Serbian Orthodox Church Asks for Part in Kosovo Talks," *Agence France Press*, November 13, 1998, available on Decani listserve at: www.egroups.com/group/decani, November 15, 1998, p. 1.

115. Father Sava, "Letter to *Koha Ditore* [Kosovo Albanian newspaper] on Kosovo Problem," June 30, 1998, available on Decani listserve at: www.egroups.com/list/ decani, June 30, 1998, pp. 2–3.

116. "Monk Fights Modern Battle in Medieval Kosovo Setting," *Reuters*, November 1, 1998, available on Decani listserve at: www.egroups.com/list/decani, pp. 1–3.

117. Hieromonk Sava, "The Interview to *Blic* Daily by Hiermonk Sava from Decani Monastery," July 6, 1998, available on-line at: www.decani.yunet.com/interview_ frsava.html, February 2, 2001, pp. 7–8.

118. "Conclusions of the Second All-Serbian Church-National Assembly," Pristina, Kosovo, January 24–25, 1998, available on-line at: www.kosovo.com/sabor_ conclusions.html, February 10, 1998, p.1; and Dusan Batakovic, Miodrag Jovicic, Zoran Lutovac, Caslav Ocic, Kosta Cavoski, and Dragoljub Popovic, "The Proposal for the Democratic Resolution of the Kosovo and Metohija Question", available on-line at www.kosovo.com/exp_group.html, February 10, 1998, pp. 2–6. Both these documents were distributed widely by Bishop Artemije and Father Sava during the first of five prewar trips to Washington, D.C., in March 1998.

119. "Conclusions of the Second All-Serbian Church-National Assembly," p. 1; Bishop Artemije, speech at the Current Issues Briefing of the United States Institute of Peace, September 15, 1998, available on-line at: www.usip.org/oc/cibriefing/artemije/ artemije_remarks.html, February 2, 2001, p. 2; and Father Sava, "The Interview to *Blic* Daily by Hiermonk Sava from Decani Monastery," July 6, 1998, p. 3.

120. Father Sava, "Kosovo Serb Orthodox Bishop Appeals against NATO Bombing of Yugoslavia," May 25, 1999, available on-line at: www.incommunion.org/soc.htm, May 27, 1999, p. 1.

121. Father Sava says all of this in an interview in the Belgrade newspaper *Blic*, where he also gives a very balanced history of the oppression experienced by both Albanians

and Serbs during the years since the collapse of the Ottoman Empire as they each have struggled to form a national identity ("The Interview to *Blic* Daily by Hieromonk Sava from Decani Monastery," July 7, 1998, pp. 3–7).

122. "Serb Monk in Ancient Church is a Thorn in Milosevic's Side," *New York Times*, October 12, 1998, available on Decani listserve at: www.egroups.com/list/decani, October 12, 1998, p. 1.

123. Hieromonk Sava Janjic, response to Quemajl Morina in Janjic and Morina, "Religion in Kosovo," p. 4.

124. Father Sava, "Letter to *Koha Ditore* on Kosovo Problem," p. 1; "The Public Statement by Decani Monastery," June 12, 1998, available on Decani listserve at: www.eGroups.com/list/decani, June 12, 1998, pp. 1–2; "The Interview to *Blic* Daily by Hieromonk Sava from Decani Monastery," July 7, 1998, p. 2; "Serbs Pushing for Kosovo Peace Say Their Views are Being Ignored," *Ohio Plain Dealer*, July 5, 1998, available on Decani listserve at: www.egroups.com/list/decani, July 7, 1998, p. 2; Scott Canon, "Decani Monks' Courage Saved the Lives of Many Kosovars," *Knight Rider Newspapers*, June 23, 1999, available on-line at www.decani.yunet.com/decanipeace. html; Andrew Wasley, "Heavenly Dispatches," in "Peace Journalism and the Kosovo Crisis"; available on Decani listserve at: www.egroups.com/list/decani, August 18, 2000, p. 6; Judah, *Kosovo: War and Revenge*, pp. 158–59; and interview with Father Sava by the author, Gracanica, Kosovo, May 10, 2000.

125. Judah, *Kosovo: War and Revenge*, pp. 160–61; "Mr. Demaci Visited Decani Monastery," *Kosovo News*, October 30, 1998, available on Decani listserve at: www. egroups.com/list/decani, October 30, 1998, p. 1.

126. Svetlana Djurdjevic-Lukic, "Krvavi Tragovi" (Bloody Tracks), *NIN*, July 8, 1999, pp. 13–14.

127. "Religion in Kosovo," ICG Balkan Report, pp. 11–13.

128. *Ibid.*, pp. 7–8.

129. Duijzings, *Religion and the Politics of Identity in Kosovo*, pp. 87, 104–5.

130. "Religion in Kosovo," ICG Balkan Report, pp. 7–8.

131. Duijzings, *Religion and the Politics of Identity in Kosovo*, pp. 38, 46–52.

132. "Religion in Kosovo," ICG Balkan Report, p. 9.

133. "Zajedno: International Multireligious and Intercultural Center," p. 2.

134. "Religion in Kosovo," ICG Balkan Report, pp. 7–9.

135. Nexhat Buzuku, "Attacks Harm Those Who Carry Them Out," *Koha Ditore*, August 20, 2000.

136. Email message received by author from Daniel Serwer (director of the Balkans program at the United States Institute of Peace), July 3, 2000.

137. Don Lush Gjergji, "Gjendja Aktuale Fetare Shqiptare: Shqyrtim Psikologjiko-shoqeror" (The Current State of Religion among the Albanians: A Psychosocial Examination), trans. by Rafeala Prifti, available on-line at: www.kosovo.de/phoenix/simpoziumi/simpoziumi_sek6_art09.html, p. 17.

138. "Religion in Kosovo," ICG Balkan Report, p. 8. Both Father Gjergji and Father Djurkovic, in fact, took part in a conflict resolution training program in Gjilan/Gnjilane, Kosovo, sponsored by the United States Institute of Peace, in May of 2000, in which the author served as a trainer.

139. Email from Daniel Serwer to the author, July 3, 2000.

140. Robert Morozzo della Rocca, "Community of St. Egidio in Kosovo," in *Private Peacemaking: USIP-Assisted Peacemaking Projects of Nonprofit Organizations*, Peaceworks no.

20, ed. by David Smock (Washington, D. C.: United States Institute of Peace, May 1998), pp. 13–16.

141. John I. Durham, "Shalom and the Presence of God," in *Proclamation and the Presence of God: Old Testament Essays in Honor of Gwynne Henton Davies*, ed. by John I. Durham and J. R. Porter (London: SCM Press, 1970), pp. 276–77.

142. Thomas W. Ogletree, *Hospitality to the Stranger: Dimensions of Moral Understanding* (Philadelphia: Fortress Press, 1985), pp. 35–58.

143. Cited in Alexa Smith, "Balkan Church Leaders Seek Reconciliation, Credibility," *Presbynews Note* 3195, 11 September 1995; available on-line at: www.lafayette.edu/milberg/bosnia.html.

144. Mojzes, "The Camouflaged Role of Religion in the War in Bosnia and Herzegovina," p. 77.

145. Gjergji, "Gjendja Aktuale Fetare Shqiptare," p. 17.

146. Stanley Samuel Harakas, *Toward Transfigured Life: The Origin of Eastern Orthodox Ethics* (Lewiston, N.Y.: Mellen Press, 1983), p. 165.

147. Juergen Moltmann, *The Experiment Hope*, ed. and trans. with a foreword by M. Douglas Meeks (London: SCM Press, 1975), p. 175.

148. Vjekoslav Saje, email message received by author on October 14, 2001.

149. Personal Interview with Marijana Ajzenkol, Bar, Montenegro, October 9, 2001.

150. World Conference on Religion and Peace, "The Interreligious Council of Bosnia-Herzegovina Promotes Collaborative Religious Action to Rebuild Civil Society," June 1998, available on-line at: www.wcrp.org/programs/bosbull4.html; World Conference on Religion and Peace, "A Statement by Religious Communities from Bosanska Krajina Region," December 14, 1998, available on-line at: www.wcrp.org/programs/bosstate.html; World Conference on Religion and Peace, "Religions for Peace in Bosnia," n.d., available on-line at: www.wcrp.org/programs/bosnia.html; and World Conference on Religion and Peace, "Building Religious Freedom in Bosnia," July of 1999, available on-line at: www.wcrp.org/programs/bosbull6.html.

151. Series of personal interviews with Seid Hukovic between April–November of 1995; and with Bishop Irinej Bulovic of Backa, in Novi Sad, Serbia, July of 1995.

152. According to Christopher Hill, chief United States negotiator at Rambouillet, during personal interview, Skopje, Macedonia, March 8, 1999.

153. Based on first-hand participation in these events.

154. "Community Council for Peace and Tolerance of the City of Mitrovica" (a brief history of the Council) and "Caux Declaration: Community Council for Peace and Tolerance," October 24, 2001. Both available from Civil Society Office, World Vision Kosovo.

155. Observations based on personal participation in both the OSCE and USIP workshops.

7 Khaled Abou El Fadl

Conflict Resolution as a Normative Value in Islamic Law
Handling Disputes with Non-Muslims

Reconciliation should be accompanied by justice, otherwise, it will not last.
While we all hope for peace, it shouldn't be peace at any cost, but peace based
on principle, on justice.

—CORAZON AQUINO

The causes of the ongoing, longstanding civil war that has raged off and on between the north and south of Sudan for thirty-five years are numerous and complex. Beyond the disparities between the economic and social development of the two regions, deep-seated ethnic and religious differences exist between the Muslim north and the predominately Christian and African traditionalist south. Further, Sudan's colonial experience effectively dismantled the country's traditional cultural and social institutions and introduced ill-suited government structures and nationalist ideologies. This, in turn, was exacerbated by postindependence Islamization policies, the most recent of which was precipitated by the rise to power of the National Islamic Front (NIF) in 1989.[1]

The civil war in Sudan points to a formidable problem confronting Muslim states in the modern age. Nations such as Sudan and Nigeria that have aspired to implement *Shari'ah* (Islamic law)[2] or to create a state modeled after an Islamic ideal have antagonized and alienated their non-Muslim citizenry. Torn by competing desires to assert Islamic identity, forge national unity, and provide equal treatment for their citizens, these nations have found themselves facing a serious dilemma. The attempt to create a Shari'ah-based state[3] raises the specter of irreconcilable conflicts with non-Muslims, partly because of fears that such a state will be founded on a belligerent and uncompromising system of thought. A social and political order modeled after the Shari'ah is, arguably, exclusionary and inaccessible to non-Muslims. Parties that do not believe in the divinity of the Shari'ah would have little reason to accept the legitimacy of a Shari'ah-based system of laws.

Assuming that the implementation of Shari'ah tends to aggravate conflicts with non-Muslims, to what extent are these conflicts resolvable? The

178

response will depend on the value that Shari'ah places on the peaceful resolution of conflicts with non-Muslims and on the extent to which Shari'ah
itself raises obstacles to the resolution of such conflicts. In making such an
assessment, it becomes appropriate to focus on Islamic normative doctrines
as they pertain to conflict resolution[4] and the degree to which they differentiate between conflicts that only involve Muslims and those that involve
both Muslims and non-Muslims. Thus, the issue to be addressed through
the medium of classical Islamic jurisprudence is whether or not the normative doctrines of Islam can be utilized to resolve conflicts such as the one
that plagues Sudan.

Some of the positions on conflict resolution delineated here have entered into mainstream Islamic discourses while others are either not generally
known or have not been integrated into contemporary discourse. The simple
fact that the precedents discussed in this chapter emerged from authoritative
sources in Islamic history, however, means that they carry normative weight
and offer the potential for transformative interpretation and action. Contrary
to the view of many contemporary Muslims, the Islamic tradition is not as
dogmatic and unitary as they seem to believe.

In fact, the Islamic tradition is rich and complex enough to offer flexible
paradigms that could be utilized to address the challenges posed to Islam by
the modern age. With this in mind, this chapter seeks to (1) challenge and
deconstruct some of the dogmatic positions often cited by Islamists as representing insurmountable obstacles to attaining peace with non-Muslims and
(2) explore some of the pronounced tensions that contemporary Muslims
confront, which demand more creative and daring approaches.

The Qur'anic Discourse on Conflict Resolution

The Qur'an was revealed over a span of about twenty-one years, mostly in
response to specific historical events. It is considered to be the fundamental
source of Islamic law because Muslims believe it to be the revealed, literal
word of God. Thus it carries considerable normative weight in all areas of
life, including the peaceful resolution of disputes.

It is important to note, however, that one cannot simplistically equate
the Qur'anic commandments with Islamic legal doctrine or Islamic historical
practice. This is not because Muslim juristic interpretations have necessarily
deviated from Qur'anic normative injunctions but because the meaning of
the Qur'an is determined within a human context that is susceptible to
numerous social and historical variations.

In many instances, the Qur'an commends *sulh* as the superior moral course of action to be taken by disputing parties. *Sulh* means conciliation or settlement; the active form, *islah,* means to make good, proper, or right, or to reconcile and settle. In general, the Qur'an equates the word *sulh,* or one of its variant forms, with the notion of an inherent good that is often juxtaposed against corruption and mischief (*ifsad*). Seeking to spread strife and prevent the resolution of conflicts is often equated with the sin of corruption and immorality.[5] At one point, the Qur'an formulates a general normative principle by pronouncing: "Reconciliation is the best course, even though people are often swayed by greed [from reaching an amicable resolution]."[6] Reconciliation refers not only to an amicable settlement involving a measure of compromise but also to the willingness to submit to a conflict resolution process involving the use of arbitrators (*hakam*). While such arbitrators are expected to assist the parties in a dispute to reach an amicable resolution, it is unclear if the Qur'an envisages the arbitrators rendering a decision that becomes binding and enforceable upon the parties in dispute.[7]

In more specific contexts, the Qur'an urges parties to reach amicable resolutions to marital disputes, disagreements over inheritance, personal injury cases, and in any case in which Muslims end up fighting one another.[8] Articulating a principle of brotherhood between all Muslims, the Qur'an says: "The believers are but a single brotherhood, so make peace and reconcile between your contending brothers, and fear God, so that God may have mercy upon you."[9]

Clearly the peaceful and amicable settlement of disputes is considered a commendable normative value in Islam.[10] But this begs the question of whether there are exceptions to this general rule. Are there situations where compromise and the peaceful settlement of disputes are not desirable? This question is of particular relevance to the case of conflicts between Muslims and non-Muslims.

While the Qur'anic discourse on Muslim/non-Muslim relationships is multifaceted and complex, emphasis will be placed on the verses that address the possibility of peaceful reconciliation between the two.[11] This task is complicated by the fact that most Qur'anic commands were articulated in response to a variety of specific historical circumstances, with each calling for a different message and tone. Depending on the circumstances, the Qur'an is at times conciliatory and at other times confrontational or even seemingly belligerent. As a result, the message can appear contradictory and conflicting but seems to suggest that non-Muslims may be granted protective status by Muslims if they agree to pay a poll tax, that Muslims may reconcile with hostile non-Muslims under certain conditions, and that peace and neutrality agreements with non-Muslims are permissible.[12]

Perhaps the most sweeping Qur'anic verse on the issue of fighting non-Muslims is the following:

> Fight those who believe not in God nor the Last Day nor hold that forbidden which hath been forbidden by God and His messenger nor acknowledge the religion of truth, from among the People of the Book until they pay the poll tax [*jizyah*] with willing submission and feel themselves subdued.[13]

According to this verse, non-Muslims are to be fought until they accept Muslim supremacy and submissively pay a poll tax levied on every adult male.

Muslim jurists, however, have argued that the tax is paid in return for Muslim protection. In theory, if the taxpayers' safety cannot be guaranteed against all threats, Muslim or non-Muslim, the tax is nullified.[14] While these specifications are not mentioned in the Qur'an, they were deduced by jurists on the basis of early Muslim practice.

In addition, the Qur'an leaves open the possibility that some day hostility between Muslims and non-Muslims could be replaced with friendship. The following verse is illustrative:

> It may be that God will grant love and friendship between you and those whom you now hold as enemies, for God has power over all things; and God is most forgiving, most merciful. God forbids you not, with regard to those who fight you not for your faith nor drive you out of your homes, from dealing kindly and justly with them, for God loveth those who are just. God only forbids you, with regard to those who fight you for your faith and drive you out of your homes, and support others in driving you out, from turning to them for friendship.[15]

Notably, this verse specifies that Muslims are not forbidden from reaching some kind of reconciliation with non-Muslims if these non-Muslims do not harm or oppress Muslims.

Other parts of the Qur'an explicitly address the issue of peace agreements between Muslims and non-Muslims. For instance:

> Against them make ready your strength to the utmost of your power including steeds of war to strike terror into the hearts of the enemies of God and your enemies. . . . But if the enemy inclines towards peace, you also should incline towards peace, and trust in God for God is the One that hears and knows all things.[16]

Further, the Qur'an addresses the appropriate course of conduct to be undertaken by Muslims toward non-Muslims who wish to remain neutral by not fighting with or against the Muslims. It says:

> Do not fight those who do not want to fight their own people and do not want to fight you either. If God had wished, He would have made them your enemies. Therefore, if they withdraw from you and do not fight you, and instead send you guarantees of peace, then God has not permitted you to war against them.[17]

Obviously, Qur'anic discourse does not support a simple conclusion. Further complicating matters is the fact that the chronology of the preceding verses is disputed. Muslim scholars debate whether these verses were intended to address specific situations or whether they were intended as progressive legislation—known as the specification-versus-abrogation debate. Scholars cannot agree on whether these verses are of continued validity and thus apply to different contexts or whether they represent an incremental articulation of a unified Islamic position. To the extent that they are treated as still being valid, the views of premodern scholars will continue to resonate (in much the same way as the pronouncements of Mohammed and other early figures from the formative period of Islam). A sense of what this debate entails is best conveyed by examining the scholarly debates on the Qur'anic notion of aggression in combat.

As noted here, the Qur'an commands Muslims to fight unbelievers, but in so doing, Muslims must not transgress.

> Fight in the cause of God those who fight you, but do not transgress, for God does not approve of transgressors. Slay them [the enemy] wherever you find them and expel them from the lands from which they expelled you. . . . But if they cease, let there be no hostility except against the tyrants and oppressors.[18]

This, however, raises a host of questions as to what constitutes a transgression. Most significantly, does the Qur'an permit aggressive warfare until the unbelievers submit to Muslim power and the poll tax? Does the Qur'an permit Muslims to enter into a relationship or treaty of peaceful coexistence with non-Muslims even if they do not pay the poll tax? These questions beg a further question: Why fight unbelievers? Are they fought because they are unbelievers or because they pose a danger to Muslims?

A line of argument pursued by many Muslim scholars asserts that the Qur'anic discourse must be understood in a progressive sense. At the beginning of the Islamic revelation, all forms of violence were forbidden, and then God later allowed Muslims to engage in defensive warfare. Muslims may fight if attacked but may not initiate combat. Eventually, however, God permitted Muslims to engage in aggressive warfare and to attack even if not attacked, provided that they first invite the enemy to convert to Islam. As such, these scholars argue that the Qur'anic verse mandating that non-Muslims be fought until they convert or pay the poll tax abrogated all other verses sanctioning peaceful coexistence or forbidding aggressive warfare. In short, only defensive warfare was permissible in the beginning, but this license was later broadened to include offensive warfare.[19]

This does not mean that all offensive wars waged by Muslims are necessarily just. Rather, a war must be fought in the cause of God; wars fought to defend or promote Islam are considered "just" wars. Conversely, wars fought for ethnic, tribal, nationalistic, or material reasons are not "just" wars and are thus not lawful.[20] In effect, transgression equates to fighting wars for non-Islamic or un-Islamic reasons. In addition, scholars who have advocated this position argue that transgression also refers to the means by which a war is conducted. By commanding Muslims not to transgress, God was instructing Muslims not to kill noncombatants, especially women, children, hermits, senior citizens, and, in the opinion of some, peasants.[21]

In contrast, a second line of argument professed by a considerable number of scholars rejects the notion that any of the Qur'anic verses can be abrogated. They argue that all verses were intended to apply to different situations and conditions. Building on positions adopted by Abu Bakr, the Prophet's Companion and the First Rightly Guided Caliph, and Ibn Abbas, also the Prophet's Companion, these scholars claim that the Qur'an forbade offensive warfare. Abu Bakr (r. 11–13/632–34)[22] held that pacifists who do not believe in violence, such as hermits, may not be fought.[23] Ibn Abbas (d. 68/686–687)[24] asserted that non-Muslims may not be fought if they cease fighting Muslims.[25] In addition, Abu Hanifah (d. 150/767), the eponym of the Hanafi school of law, argued that the reason for fighting non-Muslims is because of the threat that they may pose to Muslims, not because they are unbelievers.[26] Accordingly, disbelief in itself does not justify the waging of war against non-Muslims.

Consequently, when the Qur'an commands Muslims not to transgress, it mandates that Muslims not fight those who do not wish to fight them. Effectively, this means that if non-Muslims are sincere in seeking peace with Muslims, Muslims must accept. The only possible exception is if Muslims are trying to regain possession of their lost territory or homes.[27]

These two competing schools of thought center around the interpretation of Qur'anic discourse. At the heart of the debates lie competing visions of what God demands of Muslims. Does God demand that Muslims either convert all human beings to Islam or, in the alternative, subjugate them through payment of the poll tax? Can Muslims peacefully coexist with non-Muslims without either side being subjugated to the other?

Certainly, the spectacular military successes of early Islam gave credence to the idea that it is possible, and even desirable, that non-Muslims be given only one of three choices: convert to Islam, pay the poll tax, or fight. This position, however, was not universally accepted for a variety of reasons, among them the refusal to accept the doctrine of abrogation. In addition, the historical practice of early Muslims was complex and did not necessarily support the idea of unrestrained belligerence.

Regardless of whether or not Muslims are required to fight non-Muslims, the question remains as to whether warfare is the only legitimate means of resolving conflicts with non-Muslims. Even if certain non-Muslims do pay the poll tax, does this necessarily mean that any dispute between these non-Muslims and Muslims can only be resolved through conflict? Furthermore, assuming that Muslims are not obligated to wage war against non-Muslims, are there any guidelines governing the proper means for resolving conflicts? As already noted, the Qur'an sets out the general principle that conciliation (sulh) is morally desirable; but is this normative value limited by other considerations? Before addressing the juristic discourse on conflict resolution, it is important to get a sense of the early Muslim practice on this matter.

Conflict Resolution and Early Muslim Practice

As already mentioned, the peaceful resolution of conflict is a Qur'anic value, but the real challenge is to ascertain the weight it should be given. In terms of a hierarchy of values, where should conflict resolution be placed? On the one hand, if conflict resolution is a high-order value, then almost all compromise would appear to be justified so long as such compromise leads to resolution of the conflict and an affirmation of peace. On the other hand, if conflict resolution is not a higher-order value, then its pursuit should probably be constrained by the need to avoid compromising higher purposes. Hence one could say that there is a proportional relationship between the willingness to compromise and the possibility of conflict resolution.

The more one is willing to compromise, the greater the likelihood that a conflict can be resolved without a resort to force. The opposite is also true; the less the willingness to compromise, the lower the possibility of achieving a peaceful resolution. For instance, assuming that the Qur'an requires the collection of a poll tax from non-Muslims, what if a particular conflict is not resolvable as long as Muslims insist on this demand? Similarly, assuming that the Qur'an requires the application of particular criminal laws, what if a conflict is unresolvable unless Muslims are willing to compromise on this demand? Whether it is possible to resolve a conflict in each of these situations depends on the value that one places on conflict resolution regardless of the competing demands.

The tension between conflict resolution and other normative values is exemplified by the famous arbitration dispute between Ali and Mu'awiyah in early Islam. Shortly after Ali (r. 35–40/656–61), the Prophet's cousin and the Fourth Rightly Guided Caliph, took power, Mu'awiyah (d. 60/680) who was, at the time, governor of Syria, refused to recognize him. In this dispute, it is highly likely that both sides raised issues related to core Islamic values. After a bloody and indecisive confrontation, both sides agreed to resolve their differences through arbitration.[28]

Among Ali's supporters was a group of hard-liners, eventually known as the Khawarij, who vigorously protested Ali's decision to accept a process of arbitration. The Khawarij's logic was straightforward and simple: Ali was clearly the legitimate caliph, but his willingness to compromise indicated a lack of commitment to the truth. The truth cannot be compromised or negotiated, and according to the Khawarij, Ali was duty bound to defend righteousness regardless of the consequences. The Khawarij considered the willingness to arbitrate a grave sin that undermined Ali's rightful claim to power. As a result, the Khawarij, standing by principle, ended up waging war against both Ali and Mu'awiyah.[29]

The incident of the *tahkim* (arbitration) and the uncompromising position of the Khawarij were the subject of extensive debate in Islamic history. In Sunni and Shi'a Islam, a near consensus developed condemning the excessive intolerance of the Khawarij's position. In Sunni Islam, in particular, the historical precedent of the arbitration led to the development of doctrines emphasizing functionalism and expediency in political disputes.[30] Even more, Muslim jurists regularly cited the arbitration precedent in support of the desirability of negotiated settlements in political, commercial, and personal disputes. Although the arbitration incident sheds little light on recommended parameters of compromise, it does help to establish the normative value of compromise in Islamic political and legal discourse.

In this context, Muslim jurists often cite the following verse from the Qur'an.

If two parties among the believers fall into a quarrel, make peace between them. But if one of the parties transgresses against the other, then fight all against the transgressor until it complies with God's command. If it complies, then make peace between them with justice and fairness.[31]

Transgression, Muslim jurists argued, refers to the refusal to accept a peaceful resolution to conflict. If a party refuses to cooperate with a peaceful resolution, it must be compelled to do so, and only after compliance is obtained can a just and fair solution be sought. Therefore, as long as a party or both parties refuse to engage in a process of conflict resolution, it is not possible to reach justice or fairness. Justice and fairness are only possible within a process that aims to achieve those ends.[32]

It is important that the aforementioned arbitration incident was between two Muslim parties and the Qur'anic verse quoted addresses the case of a dispute between Muslims. Neither the incident nor the verse addresses the case of a conflict between Muslims and non-Muslims. Nevertheless, there is a connection between inter-Muslim conflicts and conflicts with non-Muslims.

Ali is reported to have cited the Prophet's conduct with non-Muslims in justification of his decision to accept arbitration with Mu'awiyah. Ali argued that the Prophet had sought a peaceful reconciliation (sulh) with non-Muslims. If Muslims are allowed to peacefully resolve their conflicts with non-Muslims, Ali contended, they ought to be able to do the same in inter-Muslim disputes.[33] Hence, interestingly enough, it was the Prophet's reconciliation with non-Muslims that is cited as justification for the permissibility of negotiated settlements between Muslims. This suggests that conflict resolution, as a value, carried the same normative weight for conflicts with non-Muslims as it does for Muslims.

Relying on this logic, some jurists have argued that the arbitration of disputes between Muslim states and non-Muslim states is permissible.[34] Furthermore, Muslim jurists have often said that an agreement of sulh is a binding contract and that it is among the most socially desirable of contracts.[35] The Qur'an says: "We have made you into tribes and nations so that you will come to know one another."[36] The persistence of conflicts, the jurists sensibly concluded, is not conducive to getting to "know one another." Some jurists added that the persistence of conflicts without adequate justification or cause is something that dignified people would find degrading.[37]

In this context, Muslim jurists list four types of sulh contracts, two of which refer to government disputes with rebels, and another to disputes between Muslims and non-Muslims.[38] Judging from a variety of texts, there is little doubt that Muslim jurists set a much higher value on the peaceful settlement of disputes among Muslims than they did with non-Muslims.

Nevertheless, it is important to note the fact that sulh with non-Muslims was considered a moral value in its own right.[39]

As already noted, a wealth of early Muslim practices support this conclusion. Early in Islamic history, when the Prophet became the governor of Medina (c. 1/622), he drafted what is known as the Constitution of Medina (*sulh al-Hudaybiyah*).[40] In this work he laid out a consensual social and political structure according to which Muslims and non-Muslims enjoyed reciprocal rights and obligations.[41] The Constitution emphasized that Muslims are to be considered a single polity distinct from all other tribes and groups living in Medina at the time. For instance, the document specifies: "To Jews their religion and to the Muslims their religion." In effect, Jews are to follow their own laws and bear their own expenses, as are Muslims. However, in the case of war, Muslims and Jews are to defend one another and equally bear the cost in doing so.[42]

Significantly, the Constitution makes no reference to a poll tax to be paid by non-Muslims. Moreover, it mandates that disputes between Muslims and non-Muslims are to be resolved peacefully and, in at least some reported versions, provides for arbitration to resolve all such disputes. Despite the moral weight of this precedent, it has not been fully developed. Muslim jurists often cite the precedent of the Constitution of Medina in arguing that Muslims and non-Muslims must share the burdens of the Islamic state. However, they do not thoroughly explore the implication of this precedent for the peaceful resolution of conflicts with non-Muslims or the inference that such conflicts should be resolved through an arbitration process of some sort.[43]

In addition to the so-called Constitution of Medina, the Prophet entered into a peace agreement, known as *sulh al-Hudaybiyah*, with the non-Muslims in Mecca. Scheduled to expire after ten years, it was breached by the Meccans after two years, and warfare ensued. The Prophet, however, entered into more successful peace arrangements with non-Muslim tribes[44] in Thaqif,[45] Ahl Najran, Yemen,[46] and Bahrain.[47]

After the Prophet's death, the early Muslims entered into agreements with what was then a predominately non-Muslim Egypt,[48] Sham, Jerusalem, and Damascus.[49] They also entered into peace treaties with Cyprusm,[50] Sudan, and Nubia. According to the terms of the treaty with Nubia, the Nubians were not subject to Muslim laws or jurisdiction and were not bound to pay the poll tax. Furthermore, there was a reciprocal agreement of safe conduct between Nubians and Muslims.[51] Significantly, 'Umar (r. 13–23/634–44), the Second Rightly Guided Caliph, entered into a peace settlement with Arab Christian tribes, which required them to pay the Islamic *zakah* (almsgiving), and not the poll tax. Reportedly, the Christians considered the *jizyah* (poll tax) degrading and insisted instead on paying the zakah, which was a yearly obligation.[52] In addition, Mu'awiyah (r. 41–60/661–80), the first Umayyad caliph, made a peace agreement with the Byzantines that he subsequently wanted to breach. Early Muslim juristic authorities are reported to have strenuously opposed the idea that Mu'awiyah would be free to breach his treaty obligations even with a non-Muslim state.[53]

These examples, however, were not conclusive in establishing the moral weight to be ascribed to peaceful settlements with non-Muslims. This is partly because most of the settlements recognized some form of Muslim supremacy and were not based on a reciprocal equality of rights and obligations. In most of these arrangements, non-Muslims were obligated to pay some form of tax in return for a guarantee of safe conduct and protection from external threats. In addition, the sulh agreements, except for ones like the Nubian arrangement, typically recognized the theoretical supremacy of Islamic law over customary and tribal laws.[54]

While conflict resolution involving inter-Muslim disputes was given serious weight, the value accorded to conflict resolution between Muslims and non-Muslims was more ambiguous. Much can be gleaned, however, from exploring technical rules that apply to dispute settlements between Muslims and non-Muslims. For instance, what, if any, are the restrictions and limitations on Muslims who seek to peacefully resolve their disputes with non-Muslims? Here it is important to review the main juristic discourses on this issue.

Conflict Resolution and the Juristic Discourse

As far as non-Muslims were concerned, Muslim jurists struggled in developing coherent rules for inclusion and exclusion from the Muslim community. There was no question that non-Muslims could belong to the Muslim community in one capacity or another. However, what was less clear were the factors differentiating the four categories of non-Muslims: *dhimmi* (a non-Muslim subject to the jurisdiction of Muslims), *mu'ahid* (a non-Muslim not subject to the jurisdiction of Muslims, but enjoying the protections of a treaty or agreement), *musta'man* (a non-Muslim who enjoys temporary residence in Muslim lands and is temporarily subject to Muslim laws), and *muharih* (a non-Muslim enemy who may be attacked as long as fair warning is given). These four categories were not mechanical or simply technical. Rather, they left considerable room for creative invention and negotiation.

As commonly understood, a dhimmi is a non-Muslim, usually from the

"People of the Book,"[55] who pays a poll tax and lives in Muslim territory. However, as simple as this may appear, the dhimmi category carries with it a number of complex implications. It is best to tackle these complexities by setting out three issues pertaining to dhimmis. First, are dhimmis distinguished by the fact that they are entitled to Muslim protection? Second, can non-Muslims enjoy the status of dhimmis without paying the poll tax? Third, can non-Muslims be dhimmis and yet not be subject to Muslim law?

Most jurists argued that the status of *dhimmah* is attained through a contractual relationship between non-Muslims and Muslims. A large number of jurists have concluded that instead of paying a poll tax, dhimmis may pay the same taxes paid by Muslims such as the zakah, *sadaqah* (alms other than the zakah), or the *kharaj* (land tax).[56] The issue of the poll tax, as opposed to other forms of taxes, is negotiable. The material issue for the status of dhimmah, however, is not the tax that is paid but the right to be considered a part of the Muslim state and to enjoy its protection. Therefore, some jurists have concluded that it is possible for a non-Muslim to become a subject of the Muslim state without paying either a poll tax or a land tax.[57]

If Muslims enter into a peace arrangement with non-Muslims who in turn do not commit themselves to the Muslim state, they then are not to be considered dhimmis. Even if these non-Muslims make a regular payment to or submit to Muslim legal jurisdiction, as long as there is no mutual agreement to defend one another's interests, they are not dhimmis.

Those who become dhimmis are considered subjects of *dar-al-Islam* (the abode of Islam or the Muslim nation). This would seem to imply that *dhimmis* are subject to the laws of the Muslim state without any special exemption. However, this is not the case. Muslim jurists disagree on exactly which laws apply to non-Muslim subjects of the state. In principle, Muslim jurists argue that non-Muslims are not bound by what in their own creed is lawful. They are only bound by what is unlawful in Islam and unlawful in their own creed as well.[58] For instance, non-Muslims may consume pork and drink alcohol as long as these items are not forbidden in their religion. A large number of jurists argue that, although lawful for non-Muslims, the consumption of such items should not take place in public.[59]

Some jurists argue that dhimmis are not bound by Muslim laws at all but must be governed by their own laws and courts.[60] Further, Muslim jurists disagree on whether dhimmis are subject to Muslim criminal laws (*hudud* penalties, involving the amputation of limbs).[61] Many argued that dhimmis are bound only by laws that regulate social dealings, such as commerce (*mu'amalat*), but not by religious laws.[62] Finally, Muslim jurists disagree on whether it is lawful for dhimmis to negotiate an agreement in which they purchase land for a sum of money and not be subject to Muslim laws.

Some jurists argued that dhimmis can be allowed to retain a kind of autonomous self-rule where they would not be subject to Muslim laws but are otherwise a part of the Muslim nation.[63] Other jurists, however, were concerned with the moral implications of allowing dhimmis to retain their own laws and therefore sought to place limits on the discretion of Muslim rulers in negotiating such arrangements. For example, Muslim jurists asserted that even if dhimmis retain their own laws, they should not be allowed to legalize immoral acts such as adultery or murder. In addition, if the non-Muslim rulers seek to negotiate an autonomous dhimmi status in order to freely oppress and exploit their people, Muslims must not accept this arrangement because it effectively means supporting injustice. In this situation, Muslims must either refuse to grant the non-Muslim rulers dhimmi status or insist on the application of Muslim public laws.[64]

It would seem that what distinguishes dhimmis from other non-Muslims are the obligations that bind them to Muslims. As noted earlier, it is not a particular set of laws or the nature of taxes that apply to non-Muslims that is fundamental to creating dhimmi status. Rather it is the set of obligations or commitments that form a bond between non-Muslims and Muslims that is the determining factor in creating this status. It ought to be recalled that dhimmis are considered insiders to the Muslim state. In support of this point, one finds an extensive literature forbidding Muslims from oppressing the dhimmis, treating them unjustly, or levying oppressive taxes against them.[65] There is also an often-quoted report attributed to the Prophet that states that a Muslim who murders a dhimmi will not enter Heaven regardless of his level of piety.[66]

This is not to say the dhimmis, as subjects of the Muslim state, are equal in status to Muslims. There are many laws that would appear today to treat dhimmis as second-class citizens. Thus there is tension between the rules of inclusion that consider dhimmis to be part of the world of Islam and the laws of exclusion that set them apart from Muslims. Paradoxically, it is the rules of exclusion that permit dhimmis to exempt themselves from the regular laws of the state or to negotiate an autonomous status within a Muslim nation (the south of Sudan comes to mind).

It is important to note that traditional Islamic theory mandates that non-Muslims can become dhimmis only if they pay the poll tax and submit to Muslim laws and hence become entitled to Muslim protection. Yet, if that is so, what motivated Muslim jurists to accept the arrangements that allow non-Muslims an exemption from the poll tax and Muslim law?

The answer lies in the fact that Muslim jurists themselves emphasize that all special arrangements with non-Muslims are justified by considerations of practical necessity and public interest. This is an indication that such exemptions were necessary to resolve or avoid conflicts with non-Muslims. This, perhaps, is most clear in 'Umar's decision to allow the Christian tribes to pay the Muslim zakah instead of the poll tax and in the special status that was negotiated with Nubia. Therefore, traditional Islamic conflict resolution theory does not necessarily enjoy a higher normative value than that of conflict resolution with non-Muslims. The rules regulating how Muslims are to deal with non-Muslims are not necessarily set in stone; rather, they are necessarily weighed against other Islamic values, and conflict resolution is an Islamic value that receives serious consideration in Islamic jurisprudence.

Everything said thus far relates to dynamics between Muslims and non-Muslims who are subjects of the Muslim state. However, Muslims could arguably maintain a belligerent attitude toward non-Muslims who remain outside the jurisdiction of Muslims and maintain a conciliatory attitude with non-Muslims who formally submit to Muslim sovereignty. There is little doubt that early Muslim jurists tended to see peace treaties as of temporary duration. This, however, was the result of a belligerent attitude toward non-Muslims as well as a product of historical circumstances.

Typically, Muslim jurists would say that a peace treaty is binding, even if it turns out to be disadvantageous to Muslims.[67] However, a peace treaty was not seen as a vehicle for establishing a friendship or long-term relationship but rather as an expedient for temporarily ending hostilities. Thus, early Muslim jurists seemed to assume that a long-term peace commitment denied Muslims the necessary flexibility for dealing with changing circumstances and interests.

The majority of the early authorities argued that it is preferable that peace treaties be of a short duration, one to five years, and not exceed a ten-year term. The ten-year limit was inspired by the terms of the Treaty of Hudaybiyah, which was entered into by the Prophet. Usually, the early jurists cited two reasons for the ten-year limit: (1) a permanent peace treaty is bound to weaken Muslims because they would become lax and uninterested in *jihad* (struggle and perseverance),[68] and (2) a permanent peace treaty would cripple Muslims and deny them the capacity to react to changing circumstances.[69] If peace continued to be advantageous, Muslims could always renew the treaty once it expired.[70] Importantly, however, an increasing number of jurists after the fifth/eleventh century[71] rejected the ten-year limit, with many of them arguing either that the Muslim ruler may continue to renew a peace treaty for ten-year periods indefinitely, or that permanent peace treaties are lawful in Islam.[72] A prominent jurist such as Ibn Taymiyyah (d. 728/1328) argued that there is no evidence supporting a particular term limit on peace treaties.[73] Other jurists argued that permanent treaties are lawful as long as they incorporate conditions that safeguard the interests of Muslims.[74]

Interestingly, Muslim jurists also grudgingly accepted the possibility that under certain conditions, Muslims might have to pay a poll tax to non-Muslims if they were too weak to enter into a peace treaty with non-Muslims. This was largely driven by the historical circumstances in which pre-modern Muslim jurists lived. Whether paid by Muslims or non-Muslims, a poll tax was considered a surety for nonaggression, and Muslims might find themselves in a position where they needed to secure peace even at a financial price.[75] Importantly, Muslim jurists exhibited increasing pliancy in handling external relations with non-Muslim polities. For instance, a large number of jurists, citing an incident in which the Prophet provided humanitarian aid to the unbelievers of Mecca, argued for liberal trade relations with non-Muslims even in the absence of a treaty.[76] Although the exact historical circumstances that induced the shift in the juristic discourse from distrust to acceptance of long-term treaty commitments are unclear, it is clear that Muslim jurists tended to base their determinations on their understanding of what was in the best interest of the Muslim state. This may be due in part to Muslim jurists recognizing that matters of foreign affairs would be best left to the discretion of the political authorities.

Muslim jurists, however, continued to insist on asserting moral parameters not subject to considerations of political expediency. For example, jurists, even those writing after the fifth/eleventh century, continued to insist that even if the enemy tortured or murdered Muslim hostages, Muslims are forbidden from doing the same.[77] Furthermore, Muslim jurists continued to prohibit treaties that were revocable at will by either the Muslim or non-Muslim party. Such treaties, they argued, were immoral and unlawful.[78]

Territory, Secession, and Conflict Resolution

If one were to take Islamic theory to its logical conclusion, it would seem that non-Muslims are free to enter or not to enter into a contractual relationship with Muslims. If dhimmis do not want the protection of Muslims they are, in theory, free to opt out of the arrangement and become *mu'ahids* (a non-Muslim not subject to the jurisdiction of Muslims but enjoying the protections of a treaty or agreement) instead of dhimmis.

Other than the case of holy sites such as Mecca, Medina, and Jerusalem, territorial integrity is treated somewhat ambiguously in Islamic thought. Therefore, it would stand to reason that, if logistically feasible, dhimmis ought to be free to terminate their dhimmi status, and, if they wish to do so, secede with their own territory from the Muslim polity. This raises the question of the nature of the abode of Islam (dar-al-Islam). In order to address this issue, a bit of background is appropriate.

The Qur'an insists that all lands belong to God, and that God has delegated the earth to humankind, as a whole, and made all of humanity God's deputies (khulafa).[79] Furthermore, the Qur'an exhibits considerable hostility toward the ethos of blind loyalty to a tribe, clan, family, or even a piece of land. The Qur'an, for instance, commands Muslims to commit themselves to justice, even if that means testifying against their own families, clans, or tribes.[80] It also condemns the moral corruptness of blind loyalty to ancestral practices and calls such loyalties the "cant of ignorance [hamiyat al-jahiliyyah]."[81] In fact, the Qur'an does not show much regard for formal territorial boundaries and calls on Muslims to reside wherever they may be able to worship God freely.[82] Territory in Qur'anic discourse thus serves two distinct functions: (1) it provides a place where God's laws may be enforced, and (2) it serves as a homeland where one finds safety and security.

The Qur'an consistently calls on Muslims to implement God's laws; this mandate presumes the existence of a territorial jurisdiction where the laws may be implemented.[83] In addition, the Qur'an frequently speaks of territory in a functional sense—as the place where people find shelter, security, and a livelihood. Further, as alluded to earlier, the Qur'an treats the expulsion of Muslims from their homes as a sin worse than murder and commands Muslims to fight to regain their rights over their homeland. In general, the Qur'an speaks of the fundamental right that one has to one's home, and it recognizes that people have a basic right to regain their lost homes, even if they have to use force.[84] Although the Qur'an does not sanctify official borders, in juristic thinking, borders, often called thugh'r, do acquire the functional significance of defining the jurisdiction of the Shari'ah and the parameters of the homeland.

Nevertheless, there is a tension between the role of territory as a place where God's laws may be enforced and a territory that one considers to be home. It is possible for Muslims to find safety, security, and a home in a place where God's law is not the law of the land. Further, territory may acquire a powerful symbolic significance representing political power and sovereignty. For example, although Muslim jurists were willing, under certain circumstances, to concede considerable autonomy to dhimmis in the conduct of their own affairs, they were far more reluctant to allow dhimmis to sever themselves completely from the Islamic state.

It is important to note that these various conceptions of territory in Islamic thought have generated considerable ambiguity in the definition of *dar-al-Islam* (the abode of Islam). At the most straightforward level, the abode of Islam is a place where Islamic law is in force and where Muslims live. But beyond that, the juristic discourse tends to focus on the tension between the formal character of a territory and the substantive quality of life that a specific territory is able to support. Some jurists, for example, argue that regardless of the formal association of a territory, wherever safety (*amn*) and justice (*'adl*) can be found, that territory is part of the abode of Islam. As a result, a territory could be predominately non-Muslim and could be governed by non-Muslims, but if it offers Muslims safety and justice, it is to be considered part of the abode of Islam.

On the other hand, some jurists argue that any territory that has ever been ruled by Muslims remains forever a part of the abode of Islam. When Muslim territory was conquered by the Crusaders and Mongols, Muslim jurists were reluctant to conclude that since these territories were no longer governed by Shari'ah, they ceased to be within the abode of Islam. Rather, a large number of jurists argued that since these conquered territories once served as a homeland for Muslims, they remain a part of the abode of Islam.[85]

In summary, the notion of the abode of Islam is flexible and symbolic. It connotes a commitment to a moral community not necessarily bounded by space or territory. Wherever Muslims resided and could express their commitment to the concept of justice elicited by Shari'ah was considered a part of the Muslim moral community and thus part of the abode of Islam. This did not mean that Muslim jurists failed to display a commitment to territorial affiliations or recognize the effectiveness of legal jurisdictions. In fact, one of the four major Sunni schools of law, the Hanafis, were meticulous in articulating a sophisticated theory of legal jurisdiction based on territorial boundaries.[86]

However, in identifying the essential nature of the abode of Islam, it was the qualitative nature of the moral commitment that determined the rules of exclusion and inclusion in the Muslim community (known as *ummah*). Be that as it may, the question remains: What happens if a group of individuals wishes to secede or break off from Muslim territory to create its own distinct moral community?

Premodern jurists had an easier time dealing with the conceptual challenges posed by Muslim rebels and secessionists. They argued that such rebels should not be treated as unbelievers or even criminals but instead should be treated leniently. There was a condition attached, however. For Muslim secessionists or rebels to be treated leniently, their rebellion or secession must be based on a *ta'wil* (an ideology, cause, or principled reason that motivates the rebels or secessionists). If their rebellion was, in fact, based on a *ta'wil*, they acquired a protected status known as the *bughah*. However, those who rebelled or attempted to secede because of tribal, ethnic, or nationalistic reasons were denied this status.[87]

In all cases, Muslim jurists strongly emphasized the imperative of compromise and conflict resolution with the *bughah*. In this process, the rebels or secessionists had to be asked about the reason for their dissatisfaction, and if they mentioned a grievance or injustice, it had to be addressed. Further, every effort was to be made to reconcile the rebels or secessionists and to resolve the situation peacefully. In the view of most premodern jurists, the bughah were not to be fought unless they resorted to violence first or at least prepared to do so. Once defeated, the bughah could not be executed, tortured, or imprisoned, nor could their properties be confiscated. Importantly, most premodern jurists went further and argued that if the rebels or secessionists established a government and enforced Shari'ah, their legal acts and adjudications were to be recognized and enforced by all Muslims. This is the case whether the rebels or secessionists were defeated or not.[88]

This underscores the prevalence of principled, or moral, communities over territorial associations. Muslim jurists did not give exclusive consideration or deference to the territorial integrity of the Muslim state. Rather, they accepted, or at least tolerated, the legitimacy of divergent views of Shari'ah and the notion of transformability of territory. In other words, a competing view of Shari'ah, or justice, may challenge the prevailing view and may even motivate its adherents to secede with a particular piece of territory in order to effectuate that view. Notably, the Shari'ah remains the core value worthy of deference and consideration, and not territory or allegiance to political boundaries.

Muslim jurists had a more difficult time dealing with the issue of secession or rebellion by dhimmis. In the case of Muslim rebels, even if the rebels achieved a level of autonomy, they remained a part of the abode of Islam, and thus the geographic plot representing the Islamic world would not shrink or contract in any sense. Although in theory dhimmis are bound to Muslims through a contract (*'aqd al-dhimmah*) and in theory they are free to reject Muslim protection and opt to become either *muharibs* (enemies not enjoying a treaty with Muslims) or *mu'ahids* (non-Muslims bound by a treaty of nonaggression with Muslims), it was not deemed practical to accept this inferred divisibility of Islamic territory.

The response of the jurists was to argue as persuasively as possible that the contract of dhimmah is not breached by acts of aggression on the part of the dhimmis. Furthermore, if the dhimmis escape to enemy territory or rebel against Muslims because of an injustice that has befallen them, this is not considered a violation of their contract with Muslims. Rather, Muslims must investigate their grievances and address the injustice.[89] If the dhimmis join Muslim rebels who enjoy the status of the bughah, the dhimmis are to be afforded the same lenient treatment afforded to the Muslim rebels or secessionists. In addition, dhimmi rebellions against unjust Muslim rulers were not considered a violation of their status.[90] In short, Muslim jurists struggled to maintain the fiction of community with the dhimmis and presumed that all conflicts could be fairly and justly resolved.

It is as if the jurists believed that the only reason dhimmis would want a divorce from the Muslim community was because they suffered some injustice. If so, they presumably believed that the injustice could and should be addressed, thus eliminating the need for divorce. If, however, dhimmis did seek a divorce from the Muslim community for tribal, ethnic, or nationalistic reasons, these were considered illegitimate motivations or causes. As with Muslim rebels or secessionists, tribal, ethnic, or nationalistic causes were considered part of the "cant of ignorance."

Effectively, Muslim jurists ended up with a set of counterintuitive doctrines on conflict resolution. As far as non-Muslims not subject to Muslim jurisdiction were concerned (i.e., mu'ahids and muharibs), there was greater flexibility in achieving successful dispute resolution. While there is a set of moral constraints that apply to these groups, the jurists ultimately exhibited considerable flexibility and deference to the demands of political interest. Other than the case of Muslims being expelled from their homeland by non-Muslims, Islamic law did not pose an obstacle to making peace with non-Muslims. The contractual theory behind the relationship of dhimmah offered unlimited opportunities for conflict resolution. Practical concerns about the territorial and sovereign integrity of the abode of Islam, however, complicated issues considerably and forced Muslim jurists to resort to legal fictions of a continuing community with non-Muslims.

The Nation-State and Modern Dilemmas

The modern nation-state poses unprecedented challenges to the Islamic juristic tradition. These challenges do not relate to the ability of Muslims to maintain peaceful relations with non-Muslim nations, as many seem to believe. The Islamic juristic heritage itself provides a wealth of precedents that support treaties of nonaggression and cooperation with non-Muslim polities. Rather, the nation-state poses a fundamental challenge to Islamic notions of the Shari'ah-state and of a cross-territorial Islamic community (ummah). Shari'ah represents the commitment of the state to a religiously based communal bond. The implementation of Shari'ah means the implementation of a divine will, not necessarily the implementation of the will of the collective citizenry. Such an implementation of Islamic law therefore presumes a Muslim citizenry. The idea that the state could be comprised of Muslims who might not want to submit to the divine law is without precedent in premodern Islamic thought. Until the modern age, Islam, as a religion, was inseparable from its law—Islamic law was the core and kernel of being a Muslim.[91]

Moreover, the very idea of citizenship in a community that is defined by territorial boundaries is inconsistent with the very rationale of a contractually based dhimmah status. In theory, the dhimmah are citizens of the state as long as they wish to remain so. The logic of dhimmah implied that non-Muslims must be willing to commit to a Muslim community, but non-Muslims remained outsiders to that community by virtue of the fact that, in theory, they retained the choice of opting out of the arrangement if they so wished.

Of course, it is quite possible to take the territorial boundaries of the state as a given, and then opt for a legal pluralism within the state. In other words, it is possible to adapt the traditional Islamic paradigm to the realities of the nation-state by allowing for a complex legal reality. According to this adaptation, Muslims would be governed by Islamic law, Jews would be governed by laws of their choice, and the same logic would apply to each convictional group. The jurisdictional complexities that would result from this kind of legal pluralism would be cumbersome, to say the least. A coherent approach would have to be found for determining which groups within society would qualify for their own legal jurisdiction and which would not. However, the more polarized and dichotomous such legal jurisdictions are, the more difficult it becomes to justify the idea of a single state.

Most important, the traditional Islamic approach was founded on a presumption of the existence of an empire that was territorially semidivisible, with specific tribes and clans living in particular territories. Each tribe or clan, as a whole, adopted a set of religious convictions that were often intermingled with its customary practices and rituals. In this setting, it was more feasible to recognize different legal jurisdictions based on territory. Modern urbanization and population mobility have made such a well-ordered and settled social structure difficult to sustain.

Although it is difficult to invoke the symbolism of popular sovereignty, democracy, and national unity while at the same time insisting on a traditional Shari'ah state, this does not mean that Islamic law has no role to play in the modern age. In fact, it is impractical and undesirable for Muslim societies to ignore their religious and moral convictions or to attempt to create an artificial division between those convictions and their laws. But Muslim societies do need to reevaluate the traditional paradigms that have guided Shari'ah discourses in light of the difficult challenges posed by the modern nation-state. For instance, it is important to recognize that public laws of the state, if they are Islamically based, cannot simply be presented to a non-Muslim minority as the law of the land and then be justified by reference to the divine will. The desirability and implementation of these laws must be debated and negotiated, not assumed. Concessions to a non-Muslim minority will need to be made and institutional guarantees created in order to persuade them that the application of Islamic laws do not condemn them to a second-class status.

Moreover, Muslim societies should not dogmatically assume that a particular paradigm is necessarily Islamic. For instance, many Muslims in the contemporary age overlook the fact that the very idea of a state law that is Islamic is problematic. Historically, state or governmental law in Muslim societies was considered merely regulatory and administrative. The state or government was not the source of Shari'ah law. Islamic law consisted of the totality of juristic discourses, but state-generated and enforced law was not considered divine or immutable. Sunni Islam, in particular, rejected the idea of an institutionalized church that has the power to speak for God. As one well-known slogan puts it, "there is no church in Islam."

However, since Islam rejects the idea of a church having the power to define divine law, the very notion of the state acting as a church and becoming God's executor on earth is highly problematic. This means that the law enforced by the state is considered the state's own, not God's, and is therefore impeachable and changeable. God's law and the divine will remain ideal and aspirational in nature. Therefore, the state cannot legitimately seek sanctification for its laws and policies by claiming that they are an expression of divine will. They are simply an attempt to express laws that are consistent with the divine will, and they must be justified on their own terms. Thus, when a Muslim or non-Muslim criticizes the law, they are criticizing the state's law—the attempt at the divine ideal, but not the divine ideal itself.

This is important to understand in light of modern attempts to create Islamic states that implement so-called Islamic legal codes. The idea of a centralized-codified law that is applied by the state as God's law is a modern phenomenon and something of an anathema in Islamic jurisprudence. In fact, it is primarily the product of Islam's coming into contact with and being influenced by the system of civil law.

Historically, Muslims developed several legal schools of thought, all of which were considered equally orthodox.[92] In addition, Muslim jurists actively resisted attempts by the state to codify the law or give supremacy to one legal school of thought over all others.[93] In theory, Shari'ah was the core value that society must serve, but there was pronounced tension between the obligation to live by God's law and the fact that this law is manifested only through subjective interpretive determinations. This tension was somewhat resolved by distinguishing between Shari'ah and *fiqh*.

Shari'ah, it was argued, is the divine ideal, standing as if suspended in midair, unaffected and uncorrupted by the vagaries of life. The *fiqh* is the human attempt to understand and apply the ideal. Therefore, Shari'ah is immutable, immaculate, and flawless; fiqh is not.[94] Shari'ah stood as a symbolic construct for the divine perfection that is unreachable by human effort. It is the epitome of justice, goodness, and beauty as conceived and retained by God. Its perfection is preserved, so to speak, in the mind of God, but anything that is channeled through a human agency is necessarily marred by human imperfection. Under this theory, the various schools of thought were equally legitimate because they all represented imperfect attempts at understanding God's perfection. As such, Shari'ah was a work-in-progress that would never be completed. In historical application, Islamic law enjoyed a rather amorphous, constantly evolving, and growing quality, akin to the tradition of the classical common law.[95]

Although Sunni jurists insisted that rulers should consult with them on all matters pertaining to the affairs of the state, the jurists themselves never demanded the right to rule the Islamic state directly. In fact, Sunni jurists never assumed direct rule in the political sphere.[96] Throughout Islamic history, the ulama (jurists) performed a wide range of economic, political, and administrative functions, but, most important, they acted as mediators between the ruling class and the laity. As Afaf Marsot says: "[The ulama] were the purveyors of Islam, the guardians of its tradition, the depository of ancestral wisdom, and the moral tutors of the population."[97] While they legitimated and often interpreted the actions of the rulers to the masses, they also used their moral weight to thwart tyrannous measures and, at times, led or sanctioned rebellions against the ruling classes.[98] As Marsot points out, "to both rulers and ruled they were an objective haven which contending factions could turn to in times of stress."[99] They played the role of interpreters of the divine word, custodians of the moral conscience of the community, and curators reminding and pointing the community towards the ideal that is God.

Modernity and the onslaught of colonialism, however, dismantled the traditional institutions of the ulama and turned them from "vociferous spokesmen of the masses" into salaried state functionaries who played a primarily conservative, legitimizing role for the ruling regimes.[100] The erosion of the ulama's role and its cooption by the modern praetorian state, with its hybrid practices of secularism, has diminished the significance of Islamic normative determinations.[101] Moreover, the institutional processes, the hermeneutic methodologies, and the epistemological assumptions of classical Islamic jurisprudence have been deconstructed in the modern age. Muslim states have increasingly turned to the civil law model of codified laws that provides a centralized and uniform set of laws for the nation-state as a whole.

With the marginalized role of the traditionally educated jurists and the large-scale borrowing of the civil law model, it is hardly surprising that many of the contemporary Islamic legal reformers, such as Hasan al-Turabi and 'Abd al-Razzaq al-Sanhuri, are firmly grounded in a French legal education. Their epistemological understanding of law and its role in society is far more rooted in the continental legal tradition than in Islamic historical processes. But the fact remains that this civil law model, when adopted and implemented by a purportedly Islamic government, empowers the state to centralize, coopt, and monopolize the discourse on the divine will. Thus the codification and implementation of a unitary, purportedly Islamic law is conducive to making the state the virtual divine representative on earth.

Thus part of the problem with the application of Islamic laws in the contemporary age is that the state often cites the purported divine origin of these laws as a way of insulating itself from criticism. Since the state claims to act on behalf of the divine will, negotiating or reasoning with it is difficult, to say the least. Furthermore, if the state wishes to claim that it legitimately represents all of its citizens, then it cannot invoke God's authority as a way of marginalizing or ignoring some part of its citizenry. Since the state cannot possibly represent God, then there is no alternative but for the state to take its representation of the citizenry very seriously. Simply put, the state must be able to justify its laws and policies to its full citizenry, Muslim and non-Muslim alike.

If countries like Sudan insist on a dogmatic application of Shari'ah law to situations in which a sizable non-Muslim population is involved, this will only aggravate tensions with these populations. Non-Muslim populations, quite reasonably, are adverse to becoming second-class citizens in their own countries. Premodern Muslim jurists innovatively responded to the historical challenges that confronted their societies in their own time and age. Modern Muslim jurists would be well advised to do the same.

Whether the Islamic heritage stands as an obstacle to the resolution of conflicts with non-Muslims in the modern age depends on the normative weight that contemporary Muslims are willing to assign to conflict resolution as a value. It is reassuring that there is considerable support in the Islamic heritage for making conflict resolution a prime and essential normative value.

In every conflict over territory, there is a risk of achieving a territorial victory at the expense of suffering a moral defeat in terms of suffering and oppression on the part of a non-Muslim minority. This does not mean that

Muslim nations must accept the divisibility and fracturing of their territories in order to fulfill the ideal of a consensual community committed to the fulfillment of Shari'ah values. But it is imperative for Muslims to rise to the challenge of negotiating flexible and innovative models of statehood with their non-Muslim citizenry that effectively address their legitimate concerns. After all, the Shari'ah itself aspires to create communities founded on the ideal of consensual commitments. It is impossible to even approach this ideal without vigilantly pursuing all available avenues for the peaceful resolution of disputes.

Conclusion

As is evident from the foregoing, there is considerable flexibility and variation in how Shari'ah is implemented from one culture to the next, from one country to the next—indeed, from one generation to the next. The following chapter attempts to show how this flexibility and variance can be brought to bear in addressing longstanding grievances that have been feeding the civil war in Sudan off and on for the past forty-five years.

NOTES

1. See Edgar O'Balance, *Sudan, Civil War and Terrorism 1959–99* (New York: St. Martin's Press, 2000), pp. 132–33; Girma Kebbede, "Sudan: The North-South Conflict in Historical Perspective," in *Sudan's Predicament: Civil War, Displacement and Ecological Degradation*, ed. by Girma Kebbede (Aldershot, England: Ashgate, 1999), pp. 20–21; Sally Ann Baynard, "Democratic Republic of Sudan," in *The Government and Politics of the Middle East and North Africa*, ed. by David E. Long and Bernard Reich, 3rd ed. (Boulder, Colo.: Westview Press, 1995), p. 332.

2. For the purposes of this section of the chapter, *Shari'ah* is equated with Islamic law. But as delineated later, this is not entirely accurate. *Shari'ah* literally means "the way" or "water source." It refers to the divine sources, principles, and values that guide the formulation of Islamic law. Islamic legal commandments are known as *ahkam*, or "the rules." The *ahkam* are a product of a process known as *fiqh* (the understanding). Therefore, through the application of *fiqh* to the divine sources, principles and values, the jurists generate *ahkam*. Effectively, this means that the Shari'ah is divine, immutable, and unchangeable. The rules, or *fiqh*, are not divine and are thus fallible and subject to change.

3. A Shari'ah-based state is a state that purports to model its legal and political system after what it believes to be the imperatives of Islamic law. For the purposes of this chapter, it is not assumed that such a state will necessarily be a theocracy or any other system of government. The characteristics and nature of a theocratic system of government is a disputed matter. Furthermore, it is not clearly apparent whether nations such as Sudan or Pakistan are theocratic states, despite their heavy reliance on Islamic law.

4. The term "conflict resolution" used in this sense refers to the notion of pursuing and reaching a peaceful resolution to disputes. The resolution could be reached through negotiation, mediation, arbitration, or formal adjudication. In all cases, a binding and final resolution to a dispute is sought without a resort to armed force.

5. Qur'an 2:220; 2:11; 4:114; 8:1; 11:88; 11:117.

6. Qur'an 4:128. Muslim jurists often cite this verse in their discussions on the resolution of conflicts.

7. There is some evidence that at least some of the Prophet's Companions understood the Qur'anic discourse to provide for such a binding process of arbitration. Reportedly, Ali, the Prophet's cousin and the fourth Rightly Guided Caliph, considered the decision of an arbitrator in a marital dispute to be binding on the parties. Abu al-Qasim Jar Allah Mahmud b. 'Umar al-Zamakhshari, al-Kashshaf 'an Haqa'iq al-Tanzil wa 'Uyun al-Aqawil fi Wujuh al-Ta"wil (n.p.: Dar al-Fikr, n.d.), 1:525.

8. See Qur'an 2:178; 2:182; 2:228; 4:35; 4:128; 5:95.

9. Qur'an 49:10.

10. For instance, one of the complexities raised by the Qur'anic commands is the effect of denials of liability, or the refusal to recognize the other party's right, on legal settlements. Some jurists argued that legal settlements are recognized only if there are disputed claims of right. These jurists argued that if a party to a dispute admits fault, then full liability has been established against the admitting party and thus settlements ought not be allowed. Other jurists argued that the Qur'an places a nearly absolute value on the desirability of peaceful settlements. Therefore, they argued, legal settlements ought to be allowed even if there is an admission of fault or liability by one of the parties to the dispute. Some jurists insisted that legal settlements ought to be recognized only if there is an admission of fault or liability by one of the parties. This debate is indicative of the normative weight that different jurists ascribed to conflict resolution and peaceful settlements. According to certain schools of thought, the admission of fault does not detract from the desirability of conflict resolution. Regardless of who is right or wrong, and under all conditions, conflict resolution remains desirable. See Nasir al-Din Muhammad b. Yusuf al-Samarqandi, al-Fiqh al-Nafi', ed. by Ibrahim al-'Abbud (Riyadh: Maktabat al-'Ubaykan, 2000), 3:1265–68; Abu Bakr b. Mas'ud al-Kasani, Bada'i' al-Sana'i' fi Tartib al-Shara'i', ed. by 'Ali Muhammad Mu'awwad and 'Adil Ahmad 'Abd al-Mawjud (Beirut: Dar al-Kutub al-'Ilmiyyah, 1997), 7:466–67; Abu al-Qasim b. 'Ubayd Allah Jallab al-Basri, al-Tafri', ed. by Husayn b. Salim al-Dahmani (Beirut: Dar al-Gharb al-Islami, 1987), 2:288–89; Abu al-Walid Muhammad b. Ahmad al-Qurttubi Ibn Rushd I, al-Muqaddimat al-Mumahhidat, ed. by Muhammad Hujji (Beirut: Dar al-Gharb al-Islami, 1988), 2:518–19; Shihab al-Din Ahmad al-Qarafi, al-Dhakhirah, ed. by Muhammad Abu Khubrah (Beirut: Dar al-Gharb al-Islami, 1994), 5: 352–55; Abu Ishaq Ibrahim b. 'Ali b. Yusuf al-Shirazi al-Fayruzabadi, al-Muhadhdhab fi Fiqh al-Imam al-Shafi'i (Beirut: Dar al-Kutub al-'Ilmiyyah, 1995), 2:135–37; Shams al-Din Muhammad b. Abi al-'Abbas Ahmad b. Hamzah b. Shihab al-Din al-Ansari al-Ramli, Nihayat al-Muhtaj ila Sharh al-Minhaj fi al-Fiqh 'ala Madhhab al-Imam al-Shafi'i, 3rd ed. (Beirut: Dar Ihya' al-Turath al-'Arabi, 1992), 4:387; Abu Muhammad 'Abd Allah b. Ahmad b. Muhammad Ibn Qudamah, al-Mughni (Beirut: Dar Ihya' al-Turath al-'Arabi, n.d.), 4:530–33; Abu Muhammad b. Sa'id b. Hazm, al-Muhalla, ed. 'Abd al-Ghaffar al-Bandari (Beirut: Dar al-Kutub al-'Ilmiyyah, n.d.), 6:464–65. Of course, certain legal settlements are against public policy and are unlawful, such as a settlement that requires one of the parties to give false testimony or lie. See Ibn Qudamah, al-Mughni, 4:550–51.

11. On the Qur'anic discourse on the relationship between Muslims and non-Muslims, see Fazlur Rahman, *Major Themes of the Qur'an* (Minneapolis: Bibliotheca Islamica, 1989), pp. 162–70; Farid Esack, *Qur'an, Liberation and Pluralism: An Islamic Perspective of Interreligious Solidarity against Oppression* (Oxford: Oneworld Press, 1997), pp. 146–76; Abdulaziz Abdulhussein Sachedina, *The Islamic Roots of Democratic Pluralism.* (Oxford: Oxford University Press, 2001), pp. 22–62.

12. See, on this issue, Reuven Firestone, *Jihad: The Origins of Holy War in Islam* (Oxford: Oxford University Press, 1999), pp. 47–65.

13. Qur'an 9:29.

14. Abu al-Hasan 'Ali b. Muhammad b. Habib al-Mawardi, *al-Hawi al-Kabir fi Fiqh Madhhab al-Imam al-Shafi'i*, ed. by 'Ali Muhammad Mu'awwad and 'Adil Ahmad 'Abd al-Mawjud (Beirut: Dar al-Kutub al-'Ilmiyya, 1994), 14:370–71, 386–87; Abu Hamid Muhammad b. Muhammad al-Ghazali, *al-Wajiz fi Fiqh al-Imam al-Shafi'i*, ed. by 'Ali Mu'awwad and 'Adil 'Abd al-Mawjud (Beirut: Dar al-Arqam, 1997), 2:200–201; Abu Zakariyya Muhyi al-Din b. Sharaf al-Nawawi, *Rawdat al-Talibin wa 'Umdat al-Muftin,* ed. by Zuhayr al-Shawish, 3rd ed. (Beirut: al-Maktab al-Islami, 1991), 10:320–21; Ibn Qudamah, *al-Mughni,* 8:462–63; Mansur b. Yunus al-Bahuti (d. 1051/1641), *Kashshaf al-Qina' 'an Matn al-Iqna',* ed. by Abu 'Abd Allah Muhammad Hasan Muhammad Hasan Isma'il (Beirut: Dar al-Kutub al-'Ilmiyyah, 1997), 3:130–31.

15. Qur'an 60:7–9.

16. Qur'an 8:60–61.

17. Qur'an 4:90.

18. Qur'an 2:191–92.

19. 'Imad al-Din b. Muhammad al-Kiyya al-Harrasi, *Ahkam al-Qur'an,* ed. by Musa Muhammad 'Ali and 'Izzat 'Ali 'Id 'Atiyyah (Cairo: Dar al-Kutub al-Haditha, 1974), 1: 120–21, 124–25; al-Zamakhshari, *al-Kashshaf,* 1:341;, Abu 'Abd Allah Muhammad b. Ahmad al-Ansari al-Qurtubi, *al-Jami' li Ahkam al-Qur'an* (Beirut: Dar al-Kutub al-'Ilmiyyah, 1993), 2:231–32; 'Imad al-Din Abu al-Fida' b. 'Umar Ibn Kathir, *Mukhtasar Tafsir Ibn Kathir,* ed. by Muhammad 'Ali al-Sabuni, 7th ed. (Beirut: Dar al-Qur'an al-Karim, 1981), 1:170; Abu Bakr Ahmad b. 'Ali al-Razi al-Jassas, *Ahkam al-Qur'an* (Beirut: Dar al-Kutub al-'Ilmiyya, 1994), 1:312–15.

20. Al-Qurtubi, *al-Jami',* 2:233; Sayyid Qutb, *Fi Zilal al-Qur'an,* 10th ed. (Beirut: Dar al-Shuruq, 1981), 2:187; Ahmad Ibn Hanbal, *Musnad al-Imam Ahmad b. Hanbal,* ed. by 'Ali Hasan al-Tawil, Samir Taha al-Majdhub, and Samir Husayn Ghawi (Beirut: al-Maktab al-Islami, 1993), 2:390, 403, 646; Shihab al-Din Ahmad b. 'Ali Ibn Hajar al-'Asqalani, *Fath al-Bari: Sharh Sahih al-Bukhari* (Beirut: Dar al-Ma'rifah, n.d.), 14:530–31; Muhyi al-Din Abi Zakariyya Yahya b. Sharaf al-Nawawi, *Sharh Sahih Muslim,* ed. by Khalil al-Mis (Beirut: Dar al-Qalam, n.d.), 12:480, 482; al-Jassas, *Ahkam,* 3:400–401; Shams al-Din Muhammad b. Ahmad Abi Sahl al-Sarakhsi, *Kitab al-Mabsut* (Beirut: Dar al-Kutb al-'Ilmiyya, 1993),10:124; Ibn Hazm, *al-Muhalla,* 11:335; al-Qarafi, *al-Dhakhira,* 12:10; Ahmad Ibn Taymiyya, *Majmu' Fatawa Sayyid al-Islam Ahmad b. Taymiyya,* ed. by 'Abd al-Rahman b. Muhammad b. Qasim al-'Asimi al-Najdi al-Hanbali et al (n.p.: n.p., n.d.), 4:440–41, 452, *Minhaj al-Sunna al-Nabawiyya* (Beirut: al-Maktaba al-'Ilmiyya, n.d.), 2:232, and *al-Siyasa al-Shar'iyya fi Islah al-Ra'i wa al-Ra'iyya* (Beirut: Dar al-Afaq, 1983), pp. 70, 83; al-Kiyya al-Harrasi, *Ahkam al-Qur'an,* 3:382; Ibn Qudama, *al-Mughni,* 10:72–73, and *al-Kafi fi Fiqh al-Imam Ahmad b. Hanbal,* ed. by Zuhir al-Shawish (Beirut: al-Maktab al-Islami, 1982), 4:154; Shams al-Din Abi 'Abd Allah Muhammad b. Abi Bakr Ibn Qayyim al-Jawziyya, *AhkamAhl al-Dhimma,* ed. by Subhi Salih (Beirut: Dar al-'Ilm li al-Malayin, 1983), 2:469–70.

21. Abu Bakr Muhammad b. 'Abd Allah Ibn al-'Arabi, *Ahkam al-Qur'an*, ed. by 'Ali Muhammad al-Bajawi (Beirut: Dar al-Ma'rifah, n.d.), 1:104–5; al-Qurtubi, *al-Jami'*, 2: 234; Muhammad b. 'Ali b. Muhammad al-Shawkani, *Fath al-Qadir. al-Jami' bayn Fannay al-Riwayah wa al-Dirayah min 'Ilm al-Tafsir* (Beirut: Dar al-Ma'rifah, 1996),1:243; Abu Ja'far Muhammad b. Jarir al-Tabari, *Tafsir al-Tabari min Kitabihi Jami' al-Bayan 'an Ta'wil Ayat al-Qur'an*, ed. by Bashshar 'Awwad Ma'ruf and 'Isam Faris al-Harastani (Beirut: Mu'assasat al-Risalah, 1994), 1:516.

22. "R. 11–13/632–34" indicates that Abu Bakr ruled from years 11 to 13 in the Islamic era and from 632 to 634 AD in the Christian era.

23. Al-Kiyya al-Harrasi, *Ahkam al-Qur'an*, 1:122–23.

24. The year that Ibn Abbas died; depending on the month, either year 68 in the Islamic era or 686/687 AD in the Christian era.

25. Fakhr al-Din Muhammad b. 'Umar b. al-Husayn al-Razi, *al-Tafsir al-Kabir li al-Imam Fakhr al-Din al-Razi*, 3rd ed. (Beirut: Dar Ihya' al-Turath al-'Arabi, 1999), 5:291.

26. Ibn al-'Arabi, *Ahkam al-Qur'an*, 1:108–9.

27. Al-Zamakhshari, *al-Kashshaf*, 1:342; Muhammad Mahmud al-Hijazi, *al-Tafsir al-Wadih* (Beirut: Dar al-Kitab al-'Arabi, 1982), 1:54–55; Hud b. Muhkam al-Huwwariyy, *Tafsir Kitab Allah al-'Aziz* (Beirut: Dar al-Gharb al-Islami, 1990), 1:180–81; al-Razi, *al-Tafsir al-Kabir*, 5:288; Muhammad Rashid Rida, *Tafsir al-Qur'an al-Hakim al-Mashhur bi Tafsir al-Manar*, ed. by Ibrahim Shams al-Din (Beirut: Dar al-Kutub al-'Ilmiyyah, 1999), 2:170; Athir al-Din Muhammad b. Yusuf Abu Hayyan al-Andalusi, *Tafsir al-Bahr al-Muhit*, ed. by 'Adil Ahmad 'Abd al-Mawjud and 'Ali Muhammad Mu'awwad (Beirut: Dar al-Kutub al-'Ilmiyyah, 1993),2:73, 3:331.

28. In the end, the arbitration effort was a failure.

29. Hisham Ja'it, *al-Fitna: Jadaliyyat al-Din wa al-Siyasa fi al-Islam al-Mubakkir*, 2nd ed. (Beirut: Dar al-Tali'a, 1993), pp. 207–35.

30. See Khaled Abou El Fadl, *Rebellion and Violence in Islamic Law* (Cambridge: Cambridge University Press, 2001).

31. Qur'an 49:9.

32. In the context of discussing this Qur'anic verse, Muslim jurists also cited numerous occasions where the Prophet sought to reconcile disputing Muslims with each other. Shams al-Din Abi 'Abd Allah Muhammad b. Abi Bakr Ibn Qayyim al-Jawziyyah, *'Awn al-Ma'bud Sharh Sunan Abi Dawud*, ed. by 'Abd al-Rahman Muhammad 'Uthman, 2nd ed. (Medina: al-Maktabah al-Salafiyyah, 1968/69), 9:516–17; Ibn Hajar al-'Asqalani, *Fath al-Bari*, 5:297, 299, 306, 307; Ibn Hanbal, *Musnad*, 1:104; al-Ramli, *Nihayat al-Muhtaj*, 4:382, 384, 387; Muhammad b. Isma'il al-Amir al-Yamani al-San'ani, *Subul al-Salam Sharh Bulugh al-Maram min Jam' Adillat al-Ahkam*, ed. by Khalil Ma'mun Shiha (Beirut: Dar al-Ma'rifa, 1996), 3:92–93; Ibn Qudama, *al-Mughni*, 4:542–43; al-Bahuti, *Kashshaf*, 3:456–57; Ibn Rushd I, *al-Muqaddimat al-Mumahhidat*, 2:516–17; Abu al-Walid Muhammad b. Ahmad b. Muhammad b. Ahmad al-Qurtubi Ibn Rushd II, *Bidayat al-Mujtahid wa Nihayat al-Muqtasid* (Beirut: Dar al-Kutub al-'Ilmiyyah, 1997), 2:440–41; Abu 'Abd Allah Muhammad b. Muhammad b. 'Abd al-Rahman al-Maghribi al-Hattab al-Ra'ini, *Mawahib al-Jalil li Sharh Mukhtasar Khalil* (Beirut: Dar al-Kutub al-'Ilmiyyah, 1995), 7:3.

33. Ibn Hanbal, *Musnad*, 1:426; 3:638.

34. It is obligatory to abide by the arbitration agreement unless the arbitrators' holding is clearly contrary to Islamic law. See Muhammad Hasan al-Najafi, *Jawahir al-Kalam fi Sharh Shara'i' al-Islam*, ed. by 'Abbas al-Quchani, 7th ed. (Beirut: Dar Ihya' al-Turath al-'Arabi, n.d.), 21:114–15.

35. For instance, see Al-Bahuti, Kashshaf, 3:456–57.

36. Qur'an 49:13.

37. Ibn Qudama, al-Mughni, 4:528–29.

38. Al-Ramli, Nihayat al-Muhtaj, 4:382; Ibn Qudama, al-Mughni, 4:527; al-Kasani, Bada'i' al-Sana'i',7:466–67; Abu Ishaq Burhan al-Din Ibrahim b. Muhammad b. 'Abd Allah b. Muhammad Ibn Muflih, al-Mubdi' fi Sharh al-Muqni', ed. by 'Ali b. 'Abd Allah Al Thani (Beirut: al-Maktab al-Islami, 1973), 4:278; Ahmad b. Yahya al-Wansharisi, al-Mi'yar al-Mu'rib wa al-Jami' al-Maghrib 'an Fatawa 'Ulama' Ifriqiyah wa al-Andalus wa al-Maghrib, ed. by Muhammad Hujji (Beirut: Dar al-Gharb al-Islami, 1981), 6:344–45; al-Hattab al-Ra'ini Mawahib al-Jalil, 7:3. Some divided sulh into an agreement in or between: (1) Muslims and non-Muslims; (2) the government and rebels; (3) marital disputes; (4) debtors and creditors; (5) personal injury cases; and (6) property disputes. Al- San'ani, Subul al-Salam, 3:92–93.

39. See for instance, al-Kasani, Bada'i' al-Sana'i', 7:466–67.

40. On the Constitution of Medina, see Frederick Denny, "Ummah in the Constitution of Medina," Journal of Near Eastern Studies 36, no. 1 (1977), pp. 39–47; Moshe Gil, "The Constitution of Medina: A Reconsideration," Israel Oriental Studies 4 (1974), pp. 44–65; Akira Goto, "The Constitution of Medina," Orient: Report of the Society for Near Eastern Studies in Japan 18 (1982), pp. 1–17; Husayn Mu'nis, Dustur Ummat al-Islam: Dirasa fi Usul al-Hukm wa Tabi'atihi wa Ghayatihi 'inda al-Muslimin (Cairo: Dar al-Irshad, 1993); Uri Rubin, "The 'Constitution of Medina': Some Notes," Studia Islamica 62 (1986), pp. 5–23; R. B. Serjeant, "The 'Constitution of Medina,' " Islamic Quarterly 8, nos. 1, 2 (1964), pp. 3–16, and "The Sunnah Jami'ah, Pacts with the Yathrib Jews, and the Tahrim of Yathrib: Analysis and Translation of the Documents Comprised in the So-Called 'Constitution of Medina,' " Bulletin of the School of Oriental and African Studies 61, no. 1 (1978), pp. 1–42. A translation of the Constitution of Medina is also found in Montgomery Watt, Islamic Political Thought (Edinburgh: Edinburgh University Press, 1968), pp. 130–34.

41. The document reads more like a treaty or political settlement than a constitution in the modern sense of the word.

42. See Watt's translation in Islamic Political Thought, p. 132.

43. Part of the reason for this juristic failure is that the constitutional experiment in Medina was confronted with many obstacles. Allegedly, the Jewish tribes violated the terms of the Constitution by refusing to help defend Muslims against their enemies and by actively lending support to such enemies. This led to the expulsion of the Jewish tribes from Medina. Arguably, contributing to the dispute between the Jewish tribes and Muslims was the fact that the Jewish tribes refused to accept the Prophet as an arbitrator. However, there are numerous reports that purportedly neutral individuals arbitrated disputes between the Jewish tribes and Muslims. Furthermore, some scholars have challenged the claim that the Jewish tribes were ever expelled from Medina. See Arent Jan Wensinck, Muhammad and the Jews of Medina, trans. and ed. by Wolfgang Behn (Freiburg im Breisgau: Klaus Schwarz Verlag, 1975), pp. 122–23; Barakat Ahmad, Muhammad and the Jews: A Re-Examination (New Delhi: Vikas, 1979), p. 59.

44. Ibn Qayyim al-Jawziyyah, 'Awn al-Ma'bud, 7:446–47, 8:192–93.

45. Ibid., 8:266–67.

46. Ibid., 8:272–73, 290–91; Ibn Hajar al-'Asqalani, Fath al-Bari, 6:259, 6:264, 7:500; al-Najafi, Jawahir al-Kalam, 21:294–95.

47. Ibn Hajar al-'Asqalani, Fath al-Bari, 6:258; Ibn Hanbal, Musnad, 4:441.

48. Ibn Hajar al-'Asqalani, Fath al-Bari, 6:265.

49. Ibid., 7:509. Islam quickly spread in Sham and Jerusalem.

50. Ibid., 6:269; 6:281, 7:510. Armenia remained predominantly non-Muslim.

51. Ibid., 6:268. According to the safe conduct agreement, Nubians were obligated to allow Muslims to worship and conduct business without persecution in Nubia, and Muslims were obligated to do the same with Nubians entering into Muslim territories.

52. Al-Nawawi, *Rawdat al-Talibin,* 10:316–17.

53. Ibn Qayyim al-Jawziyyah, *'Awn al-Ma'bud,* 7:438–39; Ibn Hajar al-'Asqalani, *Fath al-Bari,* 6:275.

54. With Islamic expansion in the first/seventh century into Egypt and Persia, religious groups fell under the sovereignty of Muslim rule. However, these groups often received a much more favorable economic and political position than under their former rulers, whether Sassanian or Greek. Marshall G. S. Hodgson, *The Classical Age of Islam,* vol. 1 of *The Venture of Islam: Conscience and History in a World Civilization* (Chicago: University of Chicago Press, 1977), pp. 305–8. For example, after the Muslim conquest of Egypt in the first/seventh century, Coptic Christians received security at home and from foreign invasion upon payment of the *jizya* (poll tax). This imposition during the early conquest does not seem to have limited the Coptic community's religious rights or expression, especially in light of the continued construction of Coptic churches in the region. Alfred J. Butler, *The Arab Conquest of Egypt and the Last Thirty Years of the Roman Dominion,* 2nd ed. (Oxford: Clarendon Press, 1998), pp. 449–50. On the other hand, it is suggested that while religious freedom was secured for Copts, the imposition of the jizya may have served as an incentive to conversion, thereby shadowing claims to religious freedom (Butler, *Arab Conquest,* p. 463).

55. Non-Muslim "People of the Book" are Christians and Jews. In traditional theology, only Christians and Jews could qualify for dhimmah status. Atheists and the followers of non-Abrahamic faiths could not be a part of the Muslim community and were not granted any legitimate status in a Muslim state. However, the historical practice of Muslim jurists was not so dogmatic; adherents to other religions, such as Buddhists and Hindus, were treated as dhimmis. Atheists were presumed to belong to the religion of their family; no independent inquiry was made into the details of their convictions.

56. Al-Nawawi, *Rawdat al-Talibin,* 10:316–17, 320–21.

57. Ibn Taymiyya, *Majmu' Fatawa,* 29:208–9.

58. Al-Nawawi, *Rawdat al-Talibin,* 10:328–29; Ibrahim b. Muhammad b. Salim b. Duwayyan, *Manar al-Sabil fi Sharh al-Dalil,* ed. by Muhammad 'Id al-'Abbasi (Riyad: Maktabat al-Ma'arif li al-Nashr wa al-Tawzi', 1996), 2:24–25.

59. Al-Ghazali, *al-Wajiz,* 2:200–201; al-Nawawi, *Rawdat al-Talibin,* 10:320–21; Ibn Duwayyan, *Manar al-Sabil,* 2:28–29; al-Najafi, *Jawahir al-Kalam,* 21:300–301; al-Tusi, *al-Mabsut,* 2:44–45, 60–61.

60. Al-Mawardi, *al-Hawi al-Kabir,* 14:298–99, 386–87.

61. Abu 'Abd Allah Muhammad b. Idris al-Shafi'i, *al-Umm* (Beirut: Dar al-Fikr, 1990), 8:388.

62. Al-Sarakhsi, *Kitab al-Mabsut,* 5:86, 89.

63. Al-Tusi, *al-Mabsut,* 2:52–53, 56–57; al-Najafi, *Jawahir al-Kalam,* 21:174–75; Shams al-Din Muhammad b. Ahmad Abi Sahl al-Sarakhsi, *Sharh Kitab al-Siyar al-Kabir* (by Muhammad b. al-Husayn al-Shaybani [d. 189/805]), ed. by Abu 'Abd Allah Muhammad Hasan Muhammad Hasan Isma'il al-Shafi'i (Beirut: Dar al-Kutub al-'Ilmiyya, 1997), 3:24–25; al-Sarakhsi, *Kitab al-Mabsut,* 5:88.

64. Al-Sarakhsi, *Kitab al-Mabsut,* 5:85.

65. Ibn Qayyim al-Jawziyyah, *'Awn al-Ma'bud*, 8:302–5.

66. Al-San'ani, *Subul al-Salam*, 4:108–9; Ibn Qayyim al-Jawziyyah, *'Awn al-Ma'bud*, 7:440–41.

67. For instance, see al-Nawawi, *Rawdat al-Talibin*, 10: 338–39; Ibn Hajar al-'Asqalani, *Fath al-Bari*, 6:275; Ibn Taymiyya, *Majmu' Fatawa*, 29:138–39; al-Najafi, *Jawahir al-Kalam*, 21:294–95.

68. "Jihad" is erroneously translated as "holy war" in Western sources. Holy war, which in Arabic would read "*al-úarb al-muqadasah*," is unknown in the Islamic tradition. "Jihad" means to struggle or persevere in the pursuit of a just cause. In Islamic theology, there are three types of jihad: (1) to struggle against the inner self, and purify oneself from evil; (2) to enjoin the good and forbid the evil in society, and resist social corruptions (3) To fight, in the cause of God, to protect Islam and Muslims from harm. The most worthy and esteemed jihad is the first. See Rudolph Peters, *Jihad in Classical and Modern Islam* (Princeton: Markus Wiener, 1996), pp. 103–48.

69. Al-Shafi'i, *al-Umm*, 8:386; Muhammad b. Ibrahim b. al-Mundhir al-Nisaburi, *al-Iqna'*, ed. by Muhammad Hasan Muhammad Hasan Isma'il al-Shafi'i and 'Ala' 'Ali 'Ali Gharib (Beirut: Dar al-Kutub al-'Ilmiyya, 1997), 400–401; Abu al-Hasan 'Ali b. Muhammad b. Habib al-Mawardi, *al-Ahkam al-Sultaniyya wa al-Wilaya al-Diniyya* (Beirut: Dar al-Kutub al-'Ilmiyyah, 1985), pp. 62–63; al-Shirazi al-Fayruzabadi, *al-Muhadhdhab*, 3:322–23; al-Najafi, *Jawahir al-Kalam*, 21:296–97; Abu Hanifa al-Nu'man b. Muhammad b. Mansur b. Ahmad b. Hayyun al-Tamimi al-Maghribi, *Da'a'im al-Islam wa Dhikr al-Halal wa al-Haram wa al-Qadaya wa al-Ahkam*, ed. by Asif b. 'Ali Asghar Fayzi (Cairo: Dar al-Ma'arif, n.d.), 1:378–79.

70. Al-Mawardi, *al-Hawi al-Kabir*, 14:296–97.

71. The Islamic calendar begins with the death of Mohammed in 632 CE, thus setting it apart from the Gregorian calendar by five centuries.

72. Al-Nawawi, *Rawdat al-Talibin*, 10: 334–35; Abu Bakr Muhammad b. Ahmad al-Shashi al-Qaffal, *Hulyat al-'Ulama' fi Ma'rifat Madhahib al-Fuqaha'* (Amman, Jordan: Maktabat al-Risala al-Haditha, 1988), 7:718–21; al-Ramli, *Nihayat al-Muhtaj*, 8:107; Ibn Qudama, *al-Mughni*, 8:460–61; al-Najafi, *Jawahir al-Kalam*, 21:298–99; al-Sarakhsi, *Sharh*, 3:46–47; Abu al-Hasan 'Ali b. Abi Bakr b. 'Abd al-Jalil al-Marghinani, *al-Hidayah Sharh Bidayat al-Mubtadi* (Egypt: Mustafa al-Babi al-Halabi, 1975), 1:138–39; Abu Ishaq Burhan al-Din Ibrahim b. Muhammad b. 'Abd Allah b. Muhammad Ibn Muflih, *al-Mubdi' fi Sharh al-Muqni'*, ed. by 'Ali b. 'Abd Allah Al Thani (Beirut: al-Maktab al-Islami, 1973), 3:398–99.

73. Ibn Taymiyyah, *Majmu' Fatawa*, 29:140–41.

74. Al-Mawardi, *al-Hawi al-Kabir*, 14:352–53.

75. Sarakhsi, *Sharh Kitab al-Siyar*, 5:5; al-Marghinani, *al-Hidayah*, 1:138–39; Al-Nawawi, *Rawdat al-Talibin*, 4:194; Ibn Qudamah, *al-Mughni*, 8:460; al-Najafi, *Jawahir al-Kalam*, 21:293.

76. For instance, see Sarakhsi, *Kitab al-Mabsut*, 10:92. Reportedly, the Prophet sent 500 dinars to the poor of Mecca during a serious drought in Mecca. This took place when Mecca was still the avowed enemy of Muslims.

77. Al-Sarakhsi, *Sharh*, 3:54–55; al-Mawardi, *al-Hawi al-Kabir*, 14:354–55; al-Ramli, *Nihayat al-Muhtaj*, 8:108; al-Najafi, *Jawahir al-Kalam*, 21:300–301.

78. Al-Bahuti, *Kashshaf*, 3:128–29.

79. Qur'an 35:39; 27:62; 6:12.

80. Qur'an 4:135.

81. Qur'an 48:26.

82. For instance, see Qur'an 4:97, 7:10; 11:61; 16:112; 106:4.

83. For instance, see Qur'an 5:42; 4:58–59; 4:105; 2:213; 3:23; 5:44–47; 38:26; 6:57; 42:10.

84. Qur'an 2:190–93; 60:8–9. Also see Qur'an 2:246; 3:195; 22:40; 59:8.

85. These various positions are discussed in greater detail in Khaled Abou El Fadl, "Islamic Law and Muslim Minorities: The Juristic Discourse on Muslim Minorities from the Second/Eighth to the Eleventh/Seventeenth Centuries," *Islamic Law and Society* 1, no. 2 (1994), pp. 141–87, esp. 153–64, "Striking a Balance: Islamic Legal Discourse on Muslim Minorities," in *Muslims on the Americanization Path?* ed. by Yvonne Yazbeck Haddad and John L. Esposito (Oxford: Oxford University Press, 2000), 47–65, esp. 58–63; and "Legal Debates on Muslim Minorities: Between Rejection and Accommodation," *Journal of Religious Ethics* 22, no. 1 (1994), pp. 127–62, esp. 131–32.

86. For the Hanafis position, see Abou El Fadl, "Islamic Law and Muslim Minorities," pp. 164–81.

87. Al-Nawawi, *Sharh*, 12:480, 482; al-Jassas, *Ahkam*, 3:400–401; al-Sarakhsi, *Kitab al-Mabsut*, 10:124; Ibn Hazm, *al-Muhalla*, 11:335; al-Qarafi, *al-Dhakhira*, 12:10; Ibn Taymiyya, *Majmu' Fatawa*, 4:440–41, 452, *Minhaj*, 2:232, and *al-Siyasa*, 70, 83; al-Kiyya al-Harrasi, *Ahkam al-Qur'an*, 3:382; Ibn Qudama, *al-Mughni*, 10:72, and *al-Kafi*, 4:154; Ibn Qayyim, *Ahkam*, 2:469–70.

88. For a lengthy study on this matter, see Abou El Fadl, *Rebellion and Political Violence in Islamic Law*.

89. For instance, see Abu al-Walid Ibn Rushd, *al-Bayan wa al-Tahsil wa al-Sharh wa al-Tawjih wa al-Ta'lil fi al-Masa'il al-Mustakhrajah*, ed. by Muhammad Hujji (Beirut: Dar al-Gharb al-Islami, 1988), 3:18–19.

90. Abu al-Hasan 'Ali b. Muhammad b. Habib al-Mawardi, *Kitab Qital Ahl al-Baghy min al-Hawi al-Kabir*, ed. by Ibrahim b. 'Ali Sandaqji (Cairo: Matba'at al-Madani, 1987), 147–49; For a much more extensive treatment see Abou El Fadl, *Rebellion and Political Violence in Islamic Law*.

91. See Joseph Schacht, *An Introduction to Islamic Law* (Oxford: Oxford University Press, 1964), p. 1.

92. The four surviving Sunni schools of law and legal thought are the Hanafi, Maliki, Shafi'i, and Hanbali schools. On the history of these schools, as well as those that are now extinct, such as the Tabari and Zahiri schools, see Christopher Melchert, *The Formation of the Sunni Schools of Law, Ninth–Tenth Centuries* C.E. (Leiden: Brill, 1997). On the organization, structure, and curriculum of legal learning, see George Makdisi, *The Rise of Colleges: Institutions of Learning in Islam and the West* (Edinburgh: Edinburgh University Press, 1981).

93. See Yasin Dutton, *The Origins of Islamic Law* (Richmond, England: Curzon Press, 1999), p. 29; Sherman Jackson, *Islamic Law and the State: The Constitutional Jurisprudence of Shihab al-Din al-Qarafi* (Leiden: Brill, 1996).

94. This sophisticated doctrine is simplified in order to make a point. Muslim jurists engaged in lengthy attempts to differentiate between the two concepts of Shari'ah and fiqh. See Mahmasani, *Falsafat al-Tashri'*, pp. 21–24, 199–200; Weiss, *Spirit*, pp. 119–21; Abu Zahrah, *Usul al-Fiqh*, p. 291; Mustafa Zayd, *al-Maslahah fi al-Tashri' al-Islami wa Najm al-Din al-Tufi*, 2nd ed. (Cairo: Dar al-Fikr al-'Arabi, 1964), p. 22; Yusuf Hamid al-'Alim, *al-Maqasid al-'Ammah li al-Shari'ah al-Islamiyyah* (Herndon, Va.: International Institute of Islamic Thought, 1991), p. 80; Muhammad b. 'Ali b. Muhammad al-

Shawkani, *Talab al-'Ilm wa Tabaqat al-Muta'allimin: Adab al-Talab wa Muntaha al-'Arab* (n.p.: Dar al-Arqam, 1981), pp. 145–51.

95. On the historical processes of Shari'ah and the extent to which they differ from modern processes, see Khaled Abou El Fadl, *Speaking in God's Name: Islamic Law, Authority and Women* (Oxford: Oneworld Press, 2001); Wael Hallaq, *Authority, Continuity and Change in Islamic Law* (Cambridge: Cambridge University Press, 2001), and *A History of Islamic Legal Theories* (Cambridge: Cambridge University Press, 1997).

96. After the evacuation of the French from Egypt in 1801, 'Umar Makram, with the assistance of the jurists, overthrew the French agent left behind. Instead of assuming power directly, the jurists offered the government to the Egyptianized Albanian Muhammad 'Ali. See Afaf Lutfi al-Sayyid Marsot, "The Ulama of Cairo in the Eighteenth and Nineteenth Century," in *Scholars, Saints, and Sufis,* ed. by Nikki Keddi (Berkeley: University of California Press, 1972), pp. 149–65,162–63.

97. Ibid., p. 149.

98. Ibid., p. 150. For an exhaustive study on the role of the ulama in legitimating rulers and rebellions through the use of their moral weight, see Abou El Fadl, *Islamic Law.* On the social and political roles played by the ulama, see Edward Mortimer, *Faith and Power: The Politics of Islam* (New York: Vintage Books, 1982), pp. 299–307; Malcolm H. Kerr, *Islamic Reform: The Political and Legal Theories of Muhammad 'Abduh and Rashid Rida* (Berkeley: University of California Press, 1966), p. 196; Louis J. Cantori, "Religion and Politics in Egypt," in *Religion and Politics in the Middle East,* ed. by Michael Curtis (Boulder, Colo.: Westview Press, 1981), pp. 77–90.

99. Marsot, "The Ulama," p. 159.

100. Daniel Crecelius, "Egyptian Ulama and Modernization," in *Scholars,* pp. 167–209, 168. Crecelius makes this point about the ulama of Egypt in the modern age. However, see Fouad Ajami, "In the Pharaoh's Shadow: Religion and Authority in Egypt," in *Islam in the Political Process,* ed. by James Piscatori (London: Cambridge University Press, 1983), p. 18; Mortimer, *Faith,* pp. 91, 95; Malise Ruthven, *Islam in the World* (Oxford: Oxford University Press, 1984), p. 179. Of course, there are notable exceptions in the contemporary Islamic practice. Many clerics become prominent opponents of the present Muslim regimes and suffer enormously for their troubles.

101. On the idea of the praetorian state see Amos Perlmutter, *Egypt: The Praetorian State* (New Brunswick, N.J.: Transaction Books, 1974).

Conflict Resolution as a Normative Value in Islamic Law
Application to the Republic of Sudan

Since acquiring independence from Britain in 1956, the Republic of Sudan has been ravaged off and on by protracted conflict between the Arab, Islamic north, and the rebellious Christian/African traditionalist south. The latest incarnation of the struggle, a nineteen-year ongoing civil war, has already led to more than two million deaths and 4.5 million people being displaced. The struggle, while fundamentally about political power and an inequitable distribution of resources, is cloaked in religious overtones. To date, neither military action nor diplomacy has been able to achieve a lasting peace.

As the largest state in Africa, the Republic of Sudan borders nine African countries and bridges the Arabic-speaking world with the African world of the Nilotic, Bantoid, and Sudanic peoples. The country itself is as complex as it is large. The intent of this chapter is to develop a guide for achieving peace and stability in the Sudan that both incorporates the peacemaking tenets of Islam and builds upon the intellectual touchstones of Islamic law. It begins with the historical evolution of Sudan and then explores how the scholarly insights of students of Islamic thought and history can help create a new framework for peace and coexistence.

Historical Roots of the Sudanese Problem

In its broadest terms, the Sudan represents an amalgamation of diverse ethnic and religious groups that intermingled with one another slowly and peacefully over the centuries. This gradual process of assimilation (coupled with the country's unique blend of Arabic and African cultures) served to create a pluralistic spirit and sense of natural inclusiveness among the Sudanese people that still prevails in those sections of the country not wracked by war.

Sudan first became a focal point of political interest in the early nineteenth century, when Muhammed Ali, the Ottoman viceroy of Egypt, "turned his eyes southward to the Sudan, the still unknown land from whence came slaves and which was rumored to contain gold and ivory in plenty."[1] This image of natural wealth became a magnet for colonial expansion on the part of the Turks, the Egyptians, and later the British. Egyptian interests, however, transcended those of the others. From then until the present, Egypt has had a deep and abiding interest in who controls the headwaters of the Nile.

After World War II, when the British were divesting their colonies, the Arabic, Islamic north petitioned for both its independence and that of the Christian and African traditionalist south, over which it claimed sovereignty. In a clear break with their established policy of treating the north and south as two different entities (indeed, going to great lengths to keep them separate in order to maintain the south as a bulwark against the further advance of Islam and to one day incorporate the south into a future federated British East Africa) and despite the wishes of many in the south to become a part of Uganda or Kenya, the British decided to grant independence to both as a single entity under a central government. This was due in large measure to Egyptian pressures to safeguard the headwaters of the Nile by unifying Sudan under Arab leadership and—it is alleged—by eventually annexing both the north and the south.[2] With the south underdeveloped and northerners dominating the intellectual, governmental, and military hierarchies during the colonial period, control of the unified state fell by default to the north.[3]

Elected representatives from the south reluctantly voted for a unified Sudan, but only because of a provision in the plan for independence that called for the new Constituent Assembly to give serious consideration to a federal system in which the south would enjoy considerable autonomy. Southern scholars, however, have since concluded that the conference at which the south approved the plan was really not intended to address "the southern question" in an honest manner but rather to serve "as a rubber stamp to give legitimacy to a decision [to incorporate the south into Sudan] which had been made by the colonial officials in Khartoum."[4]

By the mid-1950s, it had become clear to many in the south that the north was not only ignoring the southern question but was actively suppressing southern attempts to address it. Southern fears were inflamed by the imposition of Arabic as the only language of administration, which effectively deprived the predominantly English-speaking southerners of any opportunity to take part in public service. Although the north's policy of "Arabization" may have been prompted by a perceived need to keep the south from joining a British-controlled East African federation, it effectively pushed the south into a corner from which its only escape was armed resistance.[5] In 1955, several units in the Sudanese army loyal to the south mutinied, sparking a civil war that has lasted off and on until the present.

Over the years, the southerners' fear of having Islam forcibly imposed on them has fueled multiple opposition movements and made compromise exceedingly difficult. Failed attempts by the north to do precisely that have created deep suspicions of any northern gestures toward peaceful compromise. In 1972, however, a significant breakthrough occurred when mediation efforts by the World Council of Churches (WCC) and the All-Africa Council of Churches (AACC) led to ratification of the Addis Ababa Accords, which ended the conflict, at least for a time. In his highly acclaimed analysis of these negotiations, Ethiopian scholar and conflict resolution practitioner Hizkias Assefa notes that the religious nature of the mediators played a crucial role in gaining the trust of both sides and making diplomatic progress possible:

> In a conflict where religion is an important factor in the intercommunal life of the parties, like that of the Sudan, the intermediaries were better off if they were considered as "people of religion" rather than politicians, even if they were from a competing or different faith. This is because people of religion are allowed to raise moral questions and concerns. . . .In view of this, the fact that the third parties were ecumenical bodies rather than political organizations may have made credible their concern for reconciliation and the alleviation of human suffering, and made readily acceptable their offer for mediation.[6]

This agreement failed in 1983, when growing political pressures on then-president Gaafar Muhammed Nimeiri induced him to back out of the agreement, thus sparking renewed hostilities. One of the key reasons for the agreement's failure was the fact that it was an agreement between elites without any accompanying attempt to strengthen north-south relationships at the grass-roots level. The agreement essentially became little more than a personal triumph for Nimeiri and Joseph Lagu, the southern signatory.[7] As Mahgoub Kurdi, a Muslim scholar, argues in *The Encounter of Religions: An Analysis of the Problem of Religion in Southern Sudan, 1899–1983*, "instead of considering the Addis Ababa Agreement as a beginning for further processes of economic development, political stability, and national integration, Nimeiri's regime committed the mistake of conceiving the Agreement in itself as the great achievement."[8]

In early 1985, discontent with the regime reached the breaking point when Nimeiri was deposed in a coup led by Lt. Gen. Swar Al Dahab. Later that year, Dahab facilitated the installment of a civilian government headed by Sadiq Al Mahdi. Al Mahdi's new government renewed negotiations with the southern rebels; and in February of 1989, agreement was reached on a peace plan that included provisions to abolish military alliances with Egypt and Libya and to freeze the imposition of Islamic law. In June of 1989, however, this democratically elected government was overturned by the National Islamic Front (NIF), headed by then-colonel Omar al-Bashir, leader of the Revolutionary Command Council for National Salvation. Upon taking power, the NIF repudiated its predecessor's peace agreement and launched a program of "Islamization," which imposed Shari'ah on the north in 1991 and, until recently, sought to do so in the south as well.

As can be seen from this brief encapsulation of Sudan's history, Sudanese society has struggled mightily with questions of identity stemming from the ongoing tension between its determination to assert the lost glories of Islam and Arabism[9] on the one hand and to participate fully in sub-Saharan Africa on the other.[10] As expressed by Mansour Khalid, a northern Sudanese intellectual and politician:

> The external factors, if anything, are only a reflection of Sudan's crisis of national identity and the inability of northern Sudanese, particularly the ruling elite, to come to terms with themselves, face realities, and articulate a genuine vision of Sudanese national identity to the outside world. . . .The Sudanese conflict is about national self-identification. It is a cultural problem that affects all Sudanese, from all regions, which has disturbed the peace and unity of Sudan for over 30 years. There is still no consensus among Sudanese about what kind of country Sudan is. Are we Arabs? Are we Africans? Are we Afro-Arabs? Are we Muslims? What is Sudan and what does it mean to be Sudanese?[11]

Sudanese nationalism since independence has leaned heavily toward Arab nationalism. Like Baathists in Iraq and Syria who attempted to stretch the cultural identity of their respective populations to fit a mold of Arab nationalism, the Sudanese elite have tried to remake their non-Arabic-speaking populations in the image of Sudanese Arabism. But unlike their Arabic-speaking neighbors across the Red Sea, Sudanese Arab nationalists live in a country whose multicultural, multireligious, and multiethnic forms are without parallel. Not only is Sudan inhabited by diverse ethnic and tribal groups speaking dozens of languages, but the northern heartland of Sudan itself is the home of a number of linguistic rivals to the Arabic language.

A good example of the Sudanese situation at the micro level is illustrated by the plight of the Nuba people. Living in the Nuba Mountains, which encompass less than a third of the 30,000 square miles within the state of South Kordofan, the Nuba people consist of fifty ethnic groups that share a common experience of persecution and oppression. Their history is a microcosm of Sudanese history as it has been experienced from one cultural zone to another. Anthropologists who have studied this segment of the Sudanese population indicate that among the Nuba, there are "grave differences in settlement patterns, expressions of kinship, religious orientation, ties to secular urban centers, types of economic activities, and the organization of work."[12] The languages spoken among the Nuba, which number more than a hundred, are divided into three major categories: Sudanic, Bantoid, and Nubian.[13] Beyond this, the Nuba people illustrate the complexities and ambiguities of Sudanese identity in yet another way: their habitat lies just north of the internal north-south divide. Because of their location, the Nuba have become a heavily contested pawn between the warring factions in the civil war.

The anthropological data on the complexity and diversity of the Nuba peoples underscore the ethnographic question wrapped in a larger Sudanese riddle: If the Nuba people themselves do not enjoy the kind of linguistic and cultural unity conducive to state-building (and nation-building), how can one expect the Sudan to take shape as a moral agency in the world of nation-states? Is Sudan a state only because it enjoys, in the Weberian sense, an internal monopoly of violence and a corresponding right to domestic jurisdiction? A case can be made that Sudan's identity has developed as it has over the forty-seven years since independence largely because the northern elites have not only assumed the imperial power of the British but because they have replicated politically what their predecessors had articulated socially and culturally.

The Internal and External Influence of Religion

Because Christianity and Islam in Sudan preceded the modern Turko-Egyptian and British demarcation of Sudan as a country, one could argue that both Christianity and Islam (in the form of the Coptic Orthodox Church and the popular Sufi orders respectively) are more indigenous to Sudan than is the concept of a modern nation-state. It was the introduction of Western Christianity by the colonists (in the form of missionary organizations) and of official Islam by the Turko-Egyptians (in the form of Shari'ah judges and scholars) and the collaborative use of both by the central colonial government that introduced an external dimension to religion in Sudan.

The political situation of Sudan, caught in the historical competition between Islam and Christianity and presently divided along racial, ethnic, regional, and religious lines, is aggravated by an inability to resolve fundamental issues related to nation-building.[14] These issues relate to the fact that Sudan has been under continual contestation since the end of colonial rule; and, like a number of other states in the international system, does not enjoy the universal approval of those living within its "jurisdiction." This is due in large measure to the general absence of widely shared principles by which the state is to be governed, such as the principle of political equality for all citizens. Much of Sudanese history has involved rule by a military strongman who has either embraced a radical secular ideology or clothed himself in the garments of political Islam. The few moments in which democracy has flowered have been too brief for any kind of democratic consolidation to take hold.[15]

In exploring the root causes of Sudan's problems and how religion relates to them, it is also helpful to note the internal factors that have contributed to the religious character of the current crisis. They are both historical and sociological. First, one can argue that the Arab takeover of northern Sudan not only transformed the religious landscape of the region but also led to the gradual and eventual triumph of the Arabic language and Arab culture. These processes of Islamization and Arabization have, in turn, led the offspring of the native peoples of northern Sudan to redefine themselves as Arabs. Through these acts of self-definition, northern Sudanese have projected themselves, and continue to project themselves, as custodians of an Arab-Islamic heritage.

The foregoing feelings and attitudes contributed to the political and cultural differences between the northern Sudanese and the British in the nineteenth century, when the latter tried to impose its imperial order on the country. One cannot understand the Mahdi (who dealt the British a disastrous defeat at the battle of Omdurman) and his struggle to create an Islamic state in the Sudan if one fails to recognize the precolonial internalization of Arabic/Islamic cultural values. What these processes of Arabization and Islamization did for the Sudan was to create a real or imagined marriage of ethnicity with religion. That is to say, the fusion of religion and ethnicity made it possible for Sudanese of varying hues and colors to think of themselves as Arabs, not because of any impeccable genealogical connection to the original Arabs who migrated to the Sudan centuries earlier but because of their command of the Arabic language and mastery of the cues and codes of Muslim society.

It is important to note that this self-definition of the northern Sudanese as Arabs is consistent with the Prophet Mohammed's defining statement that "whoever speaks Arabic is an Arab." Not only did this approach make it possible for the northern Sudanese to identify themselves as Arabs, but it also—and perhaps more significant—enabled them to identify with the larger Muslim *ummah* (or community) that extends beyond the ethnic and cultural boundaries of Arabia.

This pattern of self-definition helped to extend Arabic and Islamic influence in the Sudan through the influence of the ruling elites of northern Sudan. The coming of the Europeans and the new elitism that they brought effectively challenged this status quo. However, there were other more far-reaching implications of colonialism's impact on Sudanese society, such as the deliberate attempt by British colonial authorities to separate the south from the north, thereby precluding the development of any sense of national unity. Despite the best efforts of British colonial authorities to keep the two separate, precolonial trade linkages between the north and south were somehow kept alive.[16]

Related to this colonial policy of divide and rule in the Sudan was the enthronement of English as the dominant language in the country. By imposing English as the language of the ruling colonial circles, the colonizers created a rival to Arabic. This, in turn, led to the creation of a new breed of elites, who found power and prestige not because of their mastery of the Arabic language and their competency in Islamic affairs but because of their command of the English language and the culture it promoted. In the special case of Sudan, this language policy of the colonial administration had several immediate implications. First, it made it categorically clear to young Sudanese that the road to success in the colonial system would be through learning and mastering English. By establishing English as the new language of prestige, the British devalued Arabic in the north and empowered the babelized Africans living in the south (who showed some command of this imported language). It is important to note, though, that Arabic, or a southernized version of it called "Juba Arabic," remains the lingua franca among many tribes of southern Sudan, particularly those that have not had any formal education. This is the case even among troops of the Sudan Peoples' Liberation Army (SPLA).

The use of English, however, conferred on these Africans a language that was inherently more powerful than Arabic and brought with it Christianity as an alternative religion (especially in the south, where missionaries were given free reign to ply their trade). This proved to be a critical transition for southerners, as many of them converted to Christianity, and consciously or unconsciously imbibed the prejudices and stereotypes associated with the English language. This process of change would later translate negatively in future dialogue between northern and southern leaders. Ironically, this European tongue has become the neutral international language that binds the warring factions, especially in the south, where different ethnic languages make it impossible for southern leaders to speak to one another in the absence of an English or Arabic medium. Because of their sense of deprivation in comparison with their Arabic-speaking neighbors, southern Sudanese are generally resistant to speaking in Arabic. This alienation constitutes one of several cultural and psychocultural inpediments to national unity.

As implied earlier, the language question is very related to the religious question. Although most of the peoples of the Sudan cannot and do not speak English, the fact that their leaders now appropriate this borrowed tongue to serve their respective causes abroad has effectively provided regional, religious, and "racial" dimensions to the conflict. Through a combination of language and religious factors, northern Sudanese came to view English speakers as part and parcel of the Anglo-Christian caravan, even if the speakers were members of their own clans and families. This is a somewhat common phenomenon throughout formerly colonized parts of the Muslim world.

The cultural and political history of the Muslim world in general and of the Sudan in particular can be explained by this culture war between secularly minded Muslims, who see European languages as vehicles of culture and knowledge beyond the pale of Islam and therefore deserving of appropriation wherever helpful, and their more fundamentalist rivals, who view these languages as nicotine, designed to seduce and subdue those faithful Muslims who embrace it. When looked at in this manner, one begins to understand how religious extremists on both sides of the divide are able to cause the havoc that they do.[17]

Conflict Resolution as a Value under Islamic Law

In seeking to understand how one can resolve conflicts between Muslims and non-Muslims under Shari'ah, the insights offered by Khaled Abou El Fadl in the previous chapter become very helpful. As he suggests, the Islamic tradition is rich and sufficiently complex to offer contemporary Muslims flexible paradigms for addressing the challenges of modernity. In his treatment of this important area, he challenges and deconstructs dogmatic positions often cited by Islamists as representing insurmountable obstacles to resolving conflict peacefully with non-Muslims.[18]

In addressing conflicts between Muslims and non-Muslims in the modern era, one should not simplistically equate Qur'anic commandments with Islamic legal doctrines or historic practice. Scholars who share this view—

and many Muslim thinkers are increasingly moving in this direction—tend to argue that the meaning of the text is determined within a subjective human context that is susceptible to wide social and historical variations.[19] The point of departure for this discussion, therefore, is to examine *sulh*, the Qur'anic word for reconciliation or settlement, and its various usages in the holy text.

Experts on Qur'anic terminology indicate that various forms of *sulh* convey the notion of an inherent good that is often juxtaposed against corruption and mischief. This interpretation helps one appreciate the Qur'anic advice to Muslims that reconciliation is the preferred course, even though people are often swayed by greed from reaching an amicable resolution (Qur'an 4:128). Given this injunction, what then can be said about the limits of Muslim receptivity to reconciliation? What specific situations can be identified in which compromise and peaceful settlement of a dispute are deemed unacceptable? Is Sudan one of these?

As revealed by a careful examination of Qur'anic and hadith[20] sources, and the opinions of hundreds of learned jurists over the years, the answers to the foregoing questions are multifaceted and complex in nature. A number of Muslim legal thinkers and scholars of Islamic thought, such as Khaled Abou El Fadl, Taha Jaber, Abdulaziz Sachedina, Fazlur Rahman, Farid Essack, and Abdullah an-Na'im, have focused a great deal of attention on this issue. To these scholars, the most telling verse from the Qur'an regarding conflict with non-Muslims is to be found in surah 9, verse 29:

> Fight those who do not believe in Allah nor the Last Day, nor hold that forbidden which has been forbidden by Allah and his Messenger, nor acknowledge the Religion of Truth, (even if they are) People of the Book, until they pay the jizya with willing submission, and feel themselves subdued.[21]

This Qur'anic verse has been used, and continues to be used, by many Islamists to justify their use of violence. In the present world system, though, few Muslim jurists (*fuqaha*) would invoke it as justification for the establishment of an Islamic state. Today, jurists who are concerned with the welfare of their communities would not apply this verse to the maintenance of Muslim societies in an age of modernization and globalization. Rather, they would dwell on the need for Muslims to create political and social systems that promote conflict prevention and resolution.

Conflicts are an inevitable part of life and are fully recognized in the Qur'an as such. In suratul Balad (chapter 90, verse 4), the Holy Qur'an reminds the fledgling but growing Muslim community in Mecca that the

essence of life is toil and struggle. This characterization of the human condition makes it necessary, in the Qur'anic view, for each individual to promote peace both in his or her own life and in the social universe that he or
she inhabits with others. Thus, there is a two-pronged approach to peace.
One is the jihad (struggle) against the *nafs* (the spirit within the human body
that needs purification) and the other is the jihad against anyone or anything
that tries to destabilize the collective peace and security of the *ummah*. The
first jihad is the greater struggle; for without it, civilized society would soon
disappear. The second, in turn, is very dependent on the first.

With the foregoing as a baseline, how then can conflict between Mus-
lims and non-Muslims be addressed? In his treatment of this issue, Abou El
Fadl offers some useful insights. First, he suggests that the Holy Prophet
Muhammad sanctioned conflict resolution between Muslims and non-
Muslims as well as between Muslims themselves. Similarly, both he and other
Muslim authors on Islamic law have argued that in Sunni Islam, in particular,
the historical precedent of the earlier mentioned arbitration between Ali Ibn
Abi Talib and Muawiyah Ibn Abu Sufyan at the Battle of Siffin in 657 CE
led to the development of doctrines that emphasize functionalism and expediency in political disputes. Moreover, Muslim jurists have regularly cited
the arbitration precedent in support of negotiating settlements in political,
commercial, and personal disputes. While the arbitration example did not
provide parameters of possible compromise, it did serve to establish compromise as a normative value in Islamic political and legal discourse.[22]

In this context, it becomes appropriate to reference the critical passage
in the Qur'an that not only reflects the divine plan of appointing humans
to different tribes and nations but also sets forth the goal for this intended
diversity, namely, that human beings must "know one another" as a way of
acknowledging the common moral wisdom of the human race:

> O humankind, We have created you male and female, and ap-
> pointed you
>   races and tribes, so that you may know one another. Surely the
> noblest
>   among you in the sight of God is the most spiritually and morally
> conscious of you. God is all-knowing, All-aware. (Qur'an 49:13)

This verse, which is found in a section of the Holy Book that includes a
series of warnings to Muslims and the human community more generally,
expounds on the damaging effects of gossip, backbiting, name-calling, and
the exhibition of any form of superiority over others. It makes clear in the
process that mutual understanding is the sine qua non for human solidarity

beyond the narrow circle of family and tribe. This Qur'anic admonition contains a number of moral inferences on the nature and origins of human conflict. In addition to offering insights on the basis of conflicts, the Qur'an also focuses on the qualities needed to resolve them. As mentioned earlier, the individual is admonished to wage jihad against his or her baser animal instincts and is told to develop piety because the best among the different tribes and nations are those people who have developed *taqwa* (God-consciousness). Similarly, the Qur'an reminds Muslims that the diversity of human beings must serve to encourage mutual understanding. This idea has received attention among some Muslim jurists who link establishment of civil order to the development of effective interpersonal communications among human beings.

Muslim jurists who have studied these Qur'anic injunctions, in tandem with the rulings of the eminent jurists of the past, have identified four different types of contracts, one of which includes reconciliation with non-Muslims. Examples of the latter that are usually cited include the treaties with non-Muslims in Egypt, Sham (Syria), Jerusalem, Armenia, Cyprus, Sudan, and Nubia before the Western imperial era. Policymakers and scholars interested in fashioning new approaches to reconciliation and peacemaking between Muslims and non-Muslims in countries like the Sudan should pay heed to these fragments scattered across the pages of Islamic history. Contemporary Muslim jurists, working hand-in-hand with Muslim politicians, can formulate new relationships with non-Muslims by cultivating the numerous warrants and examples that exist within that history for the resolution of contemporary conflict. This is particularly the case in light of the rulings of a number of Muslim jurists of the past that non-Muslims can live in a Muslim society, paying taxes that all citizens pay for the upkeep and benefit of everyone, Muslims and non-Muslims alike. Hence non-Muslims need not pay either the poll tax or the land tax that was levied in times past under different political and social systems. Today Muslims and non-Muslims live together in many nation-states where they are treated as equal citizens. This is totally consistent with the Qur'anic teachings of some fourteen centuries ago to the effect that humanity was effectively one community (Qur'an 5:48).

Shari'a and the Sudan

In the seventh century in the Sudan, the dominant influence of Christianity was slowly displaced by Islam through the peaceful and gradual migration of Muslims from North Africa, many of them under the influence of Sufism, with its emphasis on tolerance toward (and peaceful interaction with) the traditional religious beliefs and practices of the region. Over time, however, Islam in the Sudan came to acquire a hardened edge, first as a liberating force in reaction to the oppressive ways of conquering colonial powers and later as a seal of legitimacy for regimes that had seized power by force. This latter aspect manifested itself most dramatically in 1983 with the wholesale enactment of Shari'a law under then president Nimeiri. In one fell swoop, the pervasive influence of English common law was displaced by a set of laws that effectively accords second-class citizenship (or worse) to non-Muslims. It also discriminates against Muslim women in several important areas.

Both inside and outside of Sudan, this widescale adoption of Shari'a generated considerable controversy with regard to (1) the motives for its introduction, (2) the substance of the laws themselves and whether they reflected the true spirit of Islam and, (3) most acutely, whether or not they should be applied to non-Muslims. It also polarized political forces in the North, aggravated the civil war in the South, and led to the isolation of Sudan internationally. Shari'a itself, however, has been characteristically perceived by most Sudanese Muslims as a symbol of religious freedom and political independence. Its application was thus seen by many as an expression of the political will to be free—legally from British criminal and civil law, politically from secular imperatives, and economically from usury and an interest-based financial system. Although Shari'a had been applied to personal matters for Muslims since the days of British colonialism, its more sweeping application to civil law represented a radical departure from that earlier legacy, a departure that resulted in a new legacy which is still unfolding.

For non-Muslims, the introduction of Shari'a was an onerous development. As reflected in its most recent expression, the March 1991 Penal Code of Sudan, Shari'a contains five controversial features: (1) defining women as legal minors, (2) limiting the citizenship status of non-Muslims, (3) implementing traditional Islamic *hudud* penalties—that is, stoning for adultery, amputation for theft, and flogging for numerous other offenses, (4) defining apostasy as a capital offense, and (5) instituting the lex talionis ("an eye for an eye, a tooth for a tooth") as a legal principle.

It is particularly difficult for Westerners who have been infused from an early age with a strong sense of separation of church and state to understand the desire to implement Islamic law. In a 1992 address at the Washington-based Center for Strategic and International Studies, Sudanese ideologue Hasan al-Turabi provided additional insights into the underlying motives behind its introduction:

> We do not have a basis in Muslim culture or ethics for morality except in religion. And our society has been experiencing so much communication, people are being displaced, moved from one place to another. . . . Once you go to urban areas or you move to other places because of economic transformation, or war or drought or whatever, the customs cannot serve you. You need more universal values, more human norms, so to speak. But also in the field of political power and political institutions, especially after the Shari'a was disestablished by colonialists, we lost completely a sense of a higher law or we lost the idea that politics is part of religion and part of morality. . . . The Shari'a for many centuries provided us with a higher law than any other functions of government.[23]

Following the move to Shari'a in 1983, the country descended into civil unrest as noncompliant citizens were beaten, dispossessed, and even—in one case—executed for apostasy. In March of 1985, when Nimeiri realized that the imposition of Shari'a weakened his position both domestically and internationally, he accused Islamic hard-liners of treason and imprisoned them as a means of distancing himself from his former policy.

After Nimeiri was deposed in a bloodless coup, his democratically elected successor, Sadiq al-Mahdi, continued the process of "Islamization" through the adoption of "alternative laws" that legally enshrined a conservative and traditional version of Shari'a into official statutes. In June of 1989, Islamist forces led by the National Islamic Front (NIF) staged a coup against the al-Mahdi government. Once in power, it redefined the civil war against the Christian and African traditionalist south as a holy war, a move that gave a new sense of urgency to both sides and dramatically increased the scope and magnitude of the violence.

Why Shari'a Is Offensive to Non-Muslims

Aside from the seemingly draconian *hudud* punishments (from which non-Muslims are theoretically exempt), two aspects of Shari'a are especially offensive to non-Muslims: rules governing marriages between Muslims and Christians and the discriminatory handling of religious conversion. In the first issue, Muslim men are allowed to take non-Muslim wives, but non-Muslim men are not allowed to take Muslim wives; the reasoning here is that the children of the match will adopt the religion of their father, and thus this policy "protects" the Islamic majority while slowly whittling away at the non-Muslim minorities.

The second and more important issue is that of permitting religious conversion both to and from Islam. According to Islamic tradition, conversion to Islam is encouraged but conversion from Islam is apostasy, an offense worthy of death in some countries—a practice which has been amply documented throughout the Islamic world. Despite such fundamental challenges, there may be a constructive way of getting at these problems without a counterproductive confrontation with the proponents of Shari'a.

Shari'a Revisited

Shari'a, as it is known today, was developed by Muslim jurists who interpreted the Qur'an and Sunna in the historical context of the eighth and ninth centuries, when discrimination on grounds of sex and religion was the universal norm. In contrast to that norm, Shari'a was a liberalizing influence that modified and lightened the harsh consequences of slavery and discrimination—and remained that way through the nineteenth century. (Indeed, it led the way in making it obligatory for the state and wealthier citizens to look after the poor and weaker members of society.) By the middle of the twentieth century, however, it began to fall behind an evolving global norm based on universal human rights.

A legal text must be read with an eye to what it was attempting to accomplish in its original context, not necessarily as if it were written with explicit reference to today's world. Specifically, a law crafted to reform an objectionable practice will, through the need to sell it to elements more supportive of the status quo, most likely err on the side of "not going far enough" rather than "going too far"; it therefore should not be automatically construed as forbidding further movement in the direction of reform once such a move becomes politically viable.

As noted Sudanese scholar Abdullah An-Na'im persuasively argues: "Shari'a evolved through human agency over several centuries following the Prophet's death in 632. In other words, Shari'a is not divine law, but a human understanding of divine sources."[24] This same case was made thirty years earlier by the Sudanese reformer Ustadh Mahmoud Taha, when he proposed an effective methodology for closing the gap with modernity. In his 1967 book *The Second Message of Islam,* he notes that the process by which early Muslim jurists decided which texts should be considered legally binding and which should be considered inapplicable (based on the social mores of the time in which sexual and religious discrimination were accepted practice) was fundamentally a process of human choice. He goes on to argue that this same process should be revisited by modern jurists in order to accommodate the radically different norms of the day. He further concludes that all inequalities and discriminatory practices under Shari'a could easily be reversed by selecting alternative Qur'anic and sunna texts as legally binding;[25] or as An-Na'im puts it: "Muslims today can reinterpret the same divine sources used in the original formulation of Shari'a—the Qur'an and the sunna—to construct a modern version, which would validate their right to self-determination in Islamic terms without violating the rights of others."[26]

Just as there are differing models of Islamic states—Sudan, Saudi Arabia, Iran, Afghanistan—so too are there variations in how Shari'a is interpreted and applied. As another notable Sudanese scholar, Al-Tayib Zein al-Abdin, points out, "there is no conformity amongst scholars about the system, functions, powers, and methods of decision-making in a state based on Shari'ah law."[27] In short, how Shari'a is implemented, particularly in relation to non-Muslims, varies according to location and circumstances, such as the political, economic, and security conditions prevailing at the time. As Al Tayib Al-Abdin further notes, "Contemporary ulama and scholars may reach different rulings according to the conditions of their own times."[28]

Although Sudan's latest constitution (1998) specifies that all Sudanese are to be equal in their rights and duties relating to public life; that there is to be no discrimination according to race, sex, or religion; that every sect or group has the right to retain its particular culture, language, or religion and to bring up their children according to its traditions, in reality, there is a considerable gap between theory and practice. Non-Muslims do not enjoy the same privileges as Muslims, they do not have equal access to political power, nor do they enjoy a fair share of the resources. These are the realities that have fueled two civil wars and untold suffering, especially in the South.

The north's recently expressed willingness to forego Shari'a in the south and to support a referendum on self-determination in the south following a six-year transition period will go far to ease the difficulties. The redistribution of political power and resources that will take place during the transition period reform process will go even further—perhaps even far enough to hold the country together. Left unaddressed as of this writing is the lingering plight of the non-Muslims in the North, many of whom fled the South because of the war and related famine. Their religious freedom and general well-being are of serious concern. Christians feel discrimination in such areas as education, employment, access to the national media, and the right to build new churches. The challenges confronting African traditionalists as "unbelievers" are even greater. In short, effective measures need to be developed that can alleviate the second-class status of minorities in a Shari'a context.

Once peace takes hold, the government of Sudan would do well to emulate the example set by the Prophet when he led the return of the Muslims to Mecca in 630 AD. The exercise of forgiveness and absence of retributive justice that followed are often cited as inspiring examples of Islamic tolerance and compassion. It is unlikely that this will be a problem in any event. The war aside, one of the truly distinctive characteristics of Sudanese culture is its natural inclusiveness, which most observers attribute to its unique blend of Arabic and African influence. On a personal level in those parts of the country not wracked by war, relations between Muslims and Christians are quite amicable. Problems only arise in relation to government attempts to impose an Islamic template on all of its citizens.

Because the Islamic movement in the Sudan is politically oriented and Western educated, it is inherently pragmatic and capable of compromise. Recent concessions in the peace process suggest that the government may have concluded that a settlement of the conflict will enable a rising tide of oil exports to benefit everyone, north and south alike. If so, this realization coupled with an alternative formulation of Islamic public law that fits more naturally with the tolerant predisposition of the Sudanese people and that eliminates existing limitations on human rights could one day enable Sudan to become a model for the entire continent.

Conclusion

In concluding this brief examination of how the peacemaking tenets of Islam might be usefully applied to the conflict in Sudan, one should note and capitalize on the fact that Islamic civilization has given rise to numerous schools of thought over time. The survival of Islamic societies in an age of globalization will rest on the ingenuity of Muslim leaders and their ability to respond to new ideas on how the past can be harnessed to serve the future. The example of Moorish Spain—perhaps the high-water mark of interreligious cooperation and peaceful coexistence between Muslims, Christians, and Jews—comes to mind.

Yet another example deserving of modern replication was that set by the Prophet after vanquishing the monks of St. Catherine near Mount Sinai in 631 AD. In an act similar to granting the charter to the Christians of Najar (cited in chapter 2) and in keeping with the Qur'anic principle that there be no compulsion in religion (2:256), he struck the following terms with the monks:

> They were not to be unfairly taxed; no bishop was to be driven out
> of his bishopric; no Christian was to be forced to abandon his religion;

no monk was to be expelled from his monastery; no pilgrim was to be detained from his pilgrimage; no churches were to be pulled down for the sake of building mosques or houses for Muslims; Christian women married to Muslims were to enjoy their own religion; if the Christians were in need of assistance for the repair of their churches or for any other matter pertaining to their religion, the Muslims were to assist them.[29]

In other words, conflict-ridden Muslim countries like the Republic of Sudan should revisit their Islamic heritage more creatively by drawing on the moral building blocks that a new generation of Islamic scholarship is bringing to the forefront. In Abdulaziz Sachedina's recent work, *The Islamic Roots of Democratic Pluralism*, for example, he makes a thoughtful and compelling case for why Islam, if it is to remain relevant in the twenty-first century, must reopen its doors of religious interpretation, examine and correct any interpretations that are questionable, replace outdated laws, and formulate new doctrines that will be responsive to a rapidly changing, interdependent world. This will be no small challenge; thirty-four years of conflict out of forty-seven years of independence in the Sudan suggest the magnitude of the need. Consideration of the foregoing by Sudan's Ulama Council[30] would represent a solid beginning.

NOTES

1. Edgar O'Ballance, *The Secret War in the Sudan, 1955–1972* (Hamden, Conn.: Archon Books, 1977), pp. 19–20.

2. Hizkias Assefa, *Mediation of Civil Wars: Approaches and Strategies—The Sudan Conflict* (Boulder, Colo.: Westview Press, 1987), pp. 50–51.

3. As Assefa notes, "In accordance with the strict traditions of British civil service, seniority, experience, and academic qualifications were to be used as criteria for selection. Out of the 800 positions filled, only six were given to the Southerners, and the highest of those six was that of an Assistant District Commissioner" (ibid., p. 51).

4. Abel Alier, "The Southern Sudan Question," in *The Southern Sudan: The Problem of National Integration*, ed. by Dunstan Wai (London: Frank Cass, 1973), pp. 16–17.

5. Foreign Area Studies, The American University, *Sudan: a Country Study*, 3rd ed. (Washington: U.S. Government Printing Office, 1983), p. 43

6. Assefa, *Mediation of Civil Wars*, pp. 165–66.

7. Mahgoub Kurdi, "The Encounter of Religions: An Analysis of the Problem of Religion in Southern Sudan, 1899–1983" (Ph. D. diss., Temple University, 1985), p. 220.

8. Ibid., p. 221.

9. Because Islam is the only world religion whose founder inspired far-reaching territorial conquest during his lifetime, there is a sense of triumphalism that reverberates in Muslim religious discourse.

10. For a historical account of the origins of the contemporary state of Sudan, see P. M. Holt and M. M. Daly, *History of Sudan: From the Coming of Islam to the Present Day* (Boulder, Colo.: Westview Press, 1990).

11. Cited in Francis Deng, *War of Visions: Conflict of Identities in the Sudan* (Washington, D.C.: Brookings Institution, 1995), pp. 347–48.

12. Andrew P. Davidson, *In the Shadow of History: The Passing of Lineage Society* (London: Transaction, 1996), p. 2.

13. S. F. Nadel, *The Nuba* (New York: Oxford University Press, 1947), p. 2.

14. Donald Petterson, *Inside Sudan: Political Islam, Conflict, and Catastrophe* (Boulder, Colo.: Westview Press, 1999).

15. Jay Spaulding and Stephanie Beswick, *White Nile, Black Blood: War, Leadership and Ethnicity from Khartoum to Kampala* (Lawrenceville, N.J.: Red Sea Press, 1999).

16. Petterson, *Inside Sudan*; Francis Deng and Abdullah an-Naim, *Human Rights in Africa: Cross Cultural Perspectives* (Washington, D.C.: 1990); Francis Deng and I. W. Zartman, eds., *Conflict Resolution in Africa* (Washington, D.C.: Brookings Institution, 1991); Abdullah An-Naim, "Reforming Islam: Sudan and the Paradox of Self-Determination," *Harvard International Review* 19, no. 2 (1997), p.24.

17. Girma Kebbede, *Sudan's Predicament: Civil War, Displacement and Ecological Degradation* (Aldershot, England:Ashgate, 1999); Edgar O'Balance, *Sudan, Civil War and Terrorism 1959–99* (New York: St. Martin's Press, 2000).

18. Ibid.

19. Ibid.

20. The hadith are the sayings of the Prophet.

21. Abdullah Yusuf Ali, *Holy Qur'an Translation* (Elmhurst, N.Y.: Tahrike Tarsile Qur'an, 1998), p. 116.

22. Khaled Abou El Fadl, *Rebellion and Violence in Islamic Law* (Cambridge: Cambridge University Press, 2001).

23. Hasan al-Turabi, address at the Center for Strategic and International Studies, Washington, D. C., May 12, 1992.

24. Abdullahi An-Naim, "Reforming Islam: Sudan and the Paradox of Self-Determination," *Harvard International Review* 19, no. 2 (1997), p. 25.

25. Ibid., p. 64.

26. Ibid., p. 25.

27. Al-Tayib Zein Al-Abdin, "A State Based on Shari'ah and the Right of Non-Muslims" in *Self-Determination, the Oil and Gas Sector and Religion and the State in the Sudan,* Consultation Report no. 3 of the Sudan Peace-Building Programme sponsored by the African Renaissance Institute (ARI) and Relationships Foundation International (RFI), London, January 2002, p. 196.

28. Ibid., p. 198.

29. Ibid.

30. The Ulama Council is a highly select group of Islamic scholars who provide religious guidance in relation to state decisions.

III

Closure

9 R. Scott Appleby

Retrieving the Missing Dimension of Statecraft
Religious Faith in the Service of Peacebuilding

Peace, no less than war, requires idealism and
self-sacrifice and a righteous and dynamic faith.

—JOHN FOSTER DULLES

Close to three thousand people from four dozen nations died on September 11, 2001, in the terrorist attacks that destroyed the New York World Trade Center and damaged the Pentagon. Shortly thereafter, it became apparent that Osama bin Laden, a self-proclaimed Muslim freedom fighter, and his extensive Al-Qaeda network had engineered the attacks as an act of holy war against the United States and its allies. As a result of the attacks, the United States and Great Britain, among other nations of the West, finally and fully came to grips with the fact of religious violence. Now manifested on a truly global scale, the astonishing power of religious faith is undeniable, even within those policymaking circles accustomed to formulating secular explanations for a range of acts and operations that have been engineered and enacted by self-styled "true believers."

The Western myopia on this subject of religious power has been astounding. Christians of the United States, long accustomed to living in a religiously plural society governed by the principles of religious freedom, church-state separation, and the rule of law, seemed to have forgotten the death-defying roots of their own tradition. Christians, like Muslims, have considered martyrdom a prime opportunity for holiness and, indeed, a direct ticket to heaven. Consider the early second century example of Ignatius, bishop of Antioch, whose letters, written while he was traveling under armed guard to his death in Rome, pleaded with fellow Christians not to rescue him from his fate—to be eaten by lions. "What a thrill I shall have from the wild beasts that are ready for me! I hope that they will make short work of me," (Saint) Ignatius exults. "I shall coax them on to eat me up at once and not to hold off, as sometimes happens, through fear. And if they are reluctant, I shall force them to it. Forgive me—I know what is good for me. Now is the moment I am beginning to be a disciple."[1] One need not reach back to the early church fathers, however, to glimpse the self-sacrificing intensity of the religious imagination. Roman Catholic school-children as recently as the early 1960s were still being taught to prepare themselves to die for their faith rather than to renounce Jesus—in this case, the setting was the Cold War and the enemy the communist "pagans" of the Soviet Union.[2]

When pagan Rome gave way to the "Holy Roman Empire" of medieval Christendom, the tables were turned. Christian crusaders and inquisitors were on the giving end of lethal violence. The religious imagination of millions of contemporary Muslims is shaped in part by the vividly preserved cultural memory of these brutal encounters with the so-called followers of the "Prince of Peace." Thus President George W. Bush inadvertently confirmed Arab and Muslim suspicions about "Christian statecraft" when he described "Operation Infinite Justice" (as the U.S. military response to the September 11 terrorist attacks was initially named) as a "crusade."

Contemporary American Christians, however, safe to practice their faith openly, tend not to think of Christianity as a source of lethal violence. Until recently they have also failed to recognize the religious nature of much of the political violence in the world. Remarkably but typically, Americans expressed surprise upon reading the letter of instruction sent by Mohamed Atta, one of bin Laden's confederates, to his fellow doomed hijackers. Attorney General John Ashcroft called the document's prayers and exhortations to martyrdom "a disturbing and shocking view into the mindset of these terrorists." "Chilling," "eerie," and "haunting," effused the journalist Bob Woodward. Like other major news organizations on September 28, 2001, ABC News led with the story, portraying the letter as a minor revelation, a confirmation that the United States faces an unconventional war against an irrational enemy.

Such stunned reactions to evidence that Muslim extremists seem actually to believe in God, pray to him, and even invoke his assistance are baffling. Even a cockeyed glance in the direction of world events beyond U.S. borders since, say, the Shi'ite revolution in Iran twenty-three years ago would have prepared the arbiters of American public opinion to anticipate the possibility that the young Muslim suicide hijackers would be willing, even eager, to sacrifice their lives in support of a cause they judged to be sacred. Did we somehow overlook the televised images of Iranian women sending their young sons across land-mined fields to certain death in the protracted war against Iraq? Have we forgotten the 241 U.S. Marines killed in October of 1983 at the hands of faceless Shi'ite "self-martyrs" who drove explosive-laden trucks into their barracks? Did we assume that the suicide bombers of

Hamas and Islamic Jihad of Palestine were an aberration—or, worse, a problem for the Israelis and the Middle East alone?

The Displacement of Religion:
From Care of Souls to Cradle of Ideology

This book acknowledges the hard fact of contemporary religious violence. The range of cases makes it clear that Christianity and Islam enjoy no monopoly on religious extremism: Israel's Jewish provocateurs, India's Hindu nationalists, and Sri Lanka's Sinhalese Buddhist agitators provide sobering examples of religiously motivated intolerance, rioting, torture, and murder. The rate of killing accelerates, in fact, when the combatants on both sides claim religion as their motivation. "Holy wars" tend to drag on interminably.[3] The transcendent cause—the battle in service of a reality "greater than ourselves"—is a source of renewal for warriors who otherwise might abandon a struggle that becomes protracted, exhausting, and ambiguous in its political consequences.

The case of Kashmir in this regard is typical. While the current armed conflict began in 1989, its roots go back to the million lives lost in the Hindu-Muslim bloodshed that accompanied the partition of India in 1947. India's occupation of Muslim-majority Kashmir, as Ainslie Embree relates, has alienated Kashmiris who suspect that Hindu prejudice lurks behind India's failure to address the dire economic conditions of the region, including its staggering levels of unemployment. The sadly predictable radical Muslim response has been the influx of mujahedin (self-styled "freedom fighters") armed by Pakistan and trained in guerrilla warfare. Like religious extremists elsewhere,[4] the mujahedin target their "lukewarm" coreligionists, fellow Muslims whom they suspect of neutrality or, worse, collusion with the Indian security forces. The suffering of the local civilian population, on whose behalf the battles are supposedly being fought, is not ameliorated but only intensifies as the violence assumes a life of its own.

Meanwhile, the decade-long transformation of Indian political culture at the hands of Hindu nationalists—a transformation that can be described as a creeping desecularization—has strengthened the religious underpinnings of India's policies toward Pakistan and its surrogates in Kashmir. The undeniable religious element in the conflict not only raises the stakes for the Muslim warriors and intensifies their zeal and brutality; it also provides India a pretext for abandoning the internationally recognized rules of military engagement. The result is consistent and egregious violation of human rights.

On display are the unfortunate dynamics of "antifundamentalism"—the cynical and indiscriminate use of the label "fundamentalist" or "religious terrorist" to justify the demonization of the enemy and to legitimate state terror.[5] There is a sad irony in the fact of India, "the world's largest democracy" and a nation that has championed pluralism and religious freedom, being reduced to such tactics by religious extremism on both sides of the conflict.

In the spirit of Embree's shrewd assessment of the situation in Kashmir, each author describes and deplores religious violence in the setting he analyzes. H. L. Seneviratne traces the Buddhist elements of the war in Sri Lanka to what he terms "modern Buddhism," which is infatuated with the ethnic nationalism of the Sinhalese movement. In the political empowerment of the Buddhist monk, who was designated by the reformer Angarika Dharmapala to lead a national program of sociomoral regeneration, one sees a process of displacement that is regrettably familiar to the student of religion in the twentieth century.

In both classical textual Buddhism and pluralism-fostering syncretistic Buddhism, the monk is a religious figure dedicated exclusively to the accumulation of merit. But in so many modern conflicts the space for religion *qua* religion shrinks, and the religious leader is summoned to the political stage. The reduction of religion to ideology brings with it wrenching demands on the traditional religious figure. The monk—or, *mutatis mutandis,* the rabbi, priest, or imam—is coaxed, recruited, or required to step out of his customary roles as leader of prayer and public ritual, nonpartisan interpreter of scripture or religious law, and agent of hospitality, forgiveness, and reconciliation. Under pressure from the roiling forces of sectarian and ethnic conflict, driven by "identity crises" that are fabricated or exaggerated for the purpose of drawing sharp battle lines, the monk (priest, rabbi, imam) becomes an agent provocateur, a spokesperson for and mobilizer of ordinary believers who can be convinced that the source of their poverty or "relative deprivation" lies not in corrupt and despotic regimes, or in political elitism, but in the designs and plots of the ethnic or religious "other."

Dharmapala did not intend such displacement to occur, but his attempt to restore a utopian Buddhist past while simultaneously adapting Buddhism to meet the requirements of a modern industrial society made the politicization of the monks inevitable. The "inner-worldly asceticism" of the great tradition gave way to a merely worldly program of reform. The monks he recruited from the monastic college of Vidyodaya, Seneviratne explains, interpreted Dharmapala as advocating their involvement in the political and social welfare of the laity—a radical reversal of the traditional pattern of lay-monk relations. Meanwhile, the monks of Vidyalankara became embroiled in the 1956 election campaign, lobbying successfully to make Sinhala the official language of the country and to create a department of cultural affairs that would in effect give official status to Buddhism. Buddhism was accorded a "special place" in the new constitution of 1972; a Ministry of Buddhism was established by the constitution of 1977.

The resulting ethnoreligious majoritarianism led to the alienation of the minorities, including the Hindu-oriented Tamils, and to the rise of separatist movements. Economic stagnation followed, along with the dismantling of democratic institutions, including the independent judiciary and free press. Today, the nationalist monks are among the most aggressive proponents of the war against the Tamils. For their part, the Tamils have a loose affiliation with Hinduism, which in any case does not deter them from conducting outrageous and indiscriminate acts of terror against the Sri Lankan population as well as the government that Dharmapala's monks helped to create.

The conflict between Israelis and Palestinians, explored in these pages by Marc Gopin, also features "displaced" believers and their leaders acting as surrogates for secular interests. Religious Zionist rabbis of Gush Emunim have taken to issuing binding religious rulings on matters of state policy, such as their fateful declaration that Prime Minister Itzhak Rabin could be considered a "rodef," or traitor, for "trading holy land for peace." Fundamentalist Jews who call for the expulsion of Palestinian Arabs from "the greater land of Israel" provide political space for the uncompromising policies of the Israeli right wing. The self-martyrs of Hamas and Islamic jihad also see themselves as defending holy land. And their self-sacrificial zeal also carves political space for other rejectionists who long ago resolved to oppose any peace agreement that would not lead to the weakening and eventual destruction of Israel.

The study of Sudan provided by Sulayman S. Nyang and Douglas Johnston illustrates another dimension of religious violence, namely, the utility of religion for binding together previously scattered groups and constructing ethnic identity as both a sacred patrimony and a political force. Nyang and Johnston rightly underscore the priority of language, perhaps the most durable mark of ethnicity, as the bearer of religion, culture, and political loyalties in the Sudan. The Arab conquest of northern Sudan led to an intertwined process of Arabization and Islamization; the culture that emerged from this process enabled natives of various tribal backgrounds to see themselves as "Arab Muslims" and to define Sudan in such ethnoreligious terms, despite the fact that some territorial groups of the north, and most of the south, neither spoke Arabic nor adopted Islam. The colonial presence of the British, and the Christianization of parts of the south, assured that English would compete with Arabic, as well as the hundreds of indigenous dialects, as the linguistic carrier of national culture.

Stalemate between these language groups and their cultural canopies led to the failure of every national project and to the fragmentation of peoples that continues to characterize the Sudan. Ironically, the complete victory of religious absolutism may have better served national "unity" and a "negative peace" (a minimalist definition of peace as the absence of violence). Violent conflict, such as the civil war that has ravaged the country intermittently for forty-seven years, occurs when the construction and imposition of ethno-religious identity is a partial rather than a complete success. Neither religious absolutism nor imposed ethnic identity can serve as the social foundation for an enduring peace, of course, which has to be based on the principles of political self-determination, economic justice, respect for and enforcement of human rights, and other elements of "positive peace."[6]

While religion has been used in the Sudan to unify previously disparate groups, in the former Yugoslavia it has been used to separate and differentiate the Slavic people into hostile—and at times, murderous—ethnoreligious groups. The Serbian Orthodox Church has been essential not only to the preservation of Serbian identity, David Steele notes, but also, sadly, to construction of a sense of grievance matched by a blindness to the sufferings of other Yugoslavians and to the atrocities committed by Serbian armies and militias against Bosnian Muslims. The Roman Catholic Church has played a similar role with regard to the creation of a belligerent Croatian national identity.

Both Christianity and Islam encompass a variety of lingual and cultural expressions. If the peacemaking capacity of religion is to contribute to nonviolent conflict transformation in the Sudan and the former Yugoslavia, religious as well as political leaders must draw on and celebrate this transcultural religious openness that is typical of both faiths. Indeed, the cultural capaciousness of Islam and Christianity is a woefully underdeveloped resource in conflict resolution in general.

At this turn in the narrative of religious violence, religious peacemaking makes its entry. "Peace" is a term elusive in its meaning and therefore uncertain in its application. It is perhaps more precise to speak of the social conditions that make for peace. These conditions include, but are not limited to, sustained economic development based on access to education and jobs; increasing levels of participation in the processes of political self-determination in developing nations around the world; the extension and protection of human rights; and the development of nonviolent and culturally specific methods of conflict transformation. Peace is also defined by the obstacles to its realization, including the burgeoning world market in arms and technologies of destruction; unjust economic practices by both developed and underdeveloped nations; gross imbalances in the distribution of resources and educational opportunity; the weakness or lack of democratic political cultures and institutions of civil society in much of the world; and the persistence of ethnic, religious, and economically driven hatreds and civil wars.

Peacebuilders, according to this logic, are agents of social change who "prefer peace to war," that is, they seek nonviolent solutions to social problems, oppose all forms of discrimination on the basis of gender, race, religion or ethnicity, and seek to end unjust economic, political, and social practices.

Religious traditions, of course, complicate these definitions in constructive as well as unsettling ways. On the constructive side, religions have a keen awareness of injustice and the subtle workings of prejudice and evil. From centuries of service, reflection, and prayer, religious communities possess a profound understanding of the psychological and social as well as the spiritual needs of the human person and of human communities. For proponents of "universal human rights," as they are generally defined in the 1948 Universal Declaration of Human Rights and other United Nations and international covenants and treaties, however, certain religious attitudes and values can be unsettling. Some religions, or movements within them, officially reject a rights-based definition of justice, for example, in favor of a system that privileges communal authority (often meaning the authority of religious or tribal elites) and emphasizes the obligations or duties incumbent on the individual. Moreover, some religious texts, traditions, and leaders provide legitimation for certain forms of discrimination based on religion, gender, race, or ethnicity. Accordingly, religious and secular traditions of wisdom and practice are often in tension, and on some important points they seem incommensurable.

Religious peacemakers refuse to leave the field to the ideologues who would place religion in the service of ethnic politics or of bloody antimodernist revolutions like those envisioned by religious terrorists such as Osama bin Laden. Lost in the rush to defend sacred space, fuse religion with ethnicity, and annihilate the enemy is the practice of the faith itself, the peacemakers remind their coreligionists. Faith-based diplomacy and religious peacebuilding are nurtured in the spaces where the actual practice of the religious tradition in all its multivalence still remains possible. This is perhaps the greatest tragedy of contemporary deadly conflicts that reach into the inner sanctum: they rob younger believers of the opportunity to become grounded in the vast, spiritually enriching depths of the great tradition itself. In such depths one finds alternatives to the spiritually deadening, morally pulverizing lethal violence of today's religious, ethnic, and ethnoreligious wars.

Religious Faith as a Source of Diplomacy and Peacebuilding

In light of the insurmountable evidence that religious intolerance and religiously motivated violence are a prevalent and enduring source of conflict
across the globe, it seems fair to ask how right-minded people could possibly
consider religion also to be a source of diplomacy, nonviolent conflict transformation, and peacebuilding. Answering this question, indeed, is the burden
of this book.

The beginning of an answer lies in the willingness of the editor and
authors—along with an increasing if still small number of scholars, journalists, educators, religious and civic leaders, policy analysts, and government
officials in the United States and Europe—to explore the dynamics of religious violence and intolerance in order to consider alternative approaches
to conflict resolution that are based on the peacemaking tenets within religious traditions. This is precisely the accomplishment of Khaled Abou El
Fadl's finely calibrated discussion of the Shari'ah, the practices of the early
caliphs, and the Muslim juristic tradition, all of which together serve as the
cumulative framework within which conflicts in the Sudan and other Muslim states unfold and take on meaning. Following the defeat of the Ottoman
Empire and the abolishment of the caliphate in the early twentieth century,
modern Islamists have attempted to establish a nation-state based on Shari'ah.
Thus the relevant question in settings such as Sudan, Algeria, Tunisia, Saudi
Arabia, Jordan, and Syria is that addressed by Abou El Fadl: To what extent
can conflicts between Muslims and non-Muslims be peacefully resolved
through resort to Islamic law? Conversely, in which areas does the Shari'ah
pose an obstacle to such resolution?

"Faith-based diplomacy" turns on precisely such questions. Its relevance
to actual conflict in today's world depends, however, on how strongly the
combatants, as well as third-party mediators such as the United States, hold
to three underlying convictions. First, faith-based diplomacy makes sense
where religion is seen to be a genuine and in some cases a decisive factor
in the conflict, rather than a dispensable sidebar, artifact, or instrument of
propaganda. This first conviction is shared by the authors of this book—as
well as by the authors of dozens of other scholarly and policy-oriented books
treating post–Cold War conflicts, who argue that religion indeed plays either
a central or supporting role in the conflicts in the Middle East, Kashmir,
Sudan, the former Yugoslavia, Sri Lanka, Afghanistan, Indonesia, and elsewhere. The importance of the second conviction is conditional upon the
truth of the first. Where religion is a determining or supporting factor in

conflict, faith-based diplomacy can make a difference if the religion is simultaneously a way of life, an intellectual heritage, and a social tradition, all of which are constantly being contested and reinterpreted. Finally, faith-based diplomacy can also play an important role in certain conflicts where there is no religious involvement, normally in a third-party mediating capacity.

Referring to Islam, Abou El Fadl makes this point by explaining the logic behind his approach to Islamic conflict resolution: Muslims believe that the Qur'an is "the revealed, literal word of God." Although the Qur'an was revealed over a span of twenty-one years, mostly in response to specific historical events, "it carries considerable normative weight among Muslims." Thus, Abou El Fadl continues, "it would be useful to explore the Qur'anic commandments regarding the peaceful resolution of disputes." Then comes the expression of the second conviction, regarding the interpretive fluidity of religion:

> It is important to note, however, that it would be a mistake to simplistically equate the Qur'anic commandments and Islamic legal doctrine or Islamic historical practice. This is not because Muslim juristic interpretations have necessarily deviated from the Qur'anic normative injunctions, but because the meaning of the Qur'an is determined within a subjective human context that is susceptible to numerous social and historical variations.

Specifically with regard to the teaching on the peaceful resolution of conflicts with non-Muslims, Abou El Fadl observes, the Qur'an is "at times conciliatory and at other times confrontational or even seemingly belligerent."

In consequence of the shifting but not unstable set of meanings that attach themselves to the Qur'anic discourse at any particular time in history, the art of interpretation and argumentation stands at the heart of Islam as a lived religion. This means that conflict mediation and resolution within the abode of Islam is also an art and a skill that must be practiced by informed—and religiously formed—practitioners. Faith-based diplomacy, therefore, is the work, at least in part, of insiders with expertise in the religious tradition(s) whose meaning and relevance for the contemporary conflict is being contested.

What is true of contemporary Islam is also true of Judaism, Christianity, Buddhism, and Hinduism, the other religious traditions examined in this book. The contested nature of these religions—of *all* religions, one might venture—provides both the opportunity and the challenge for faith-based diplomats and religious mediators. The legal, theological, and spiritual resources of a religious tradition, that is, are their stock-in-trade. But these resources are relevant only to the extent that they shape religion as it is lived on the ground, where text and tradition transform, and are transformed by, the concrete realities of daily life.

Understanding "lived religion," therefore, is the key both to countering the tendency to religious extremism within a given religious community and to enhancing the potential for moderation, compromise, and the tolerance of outsiders: religious communities repeatedly demonstrate that they contain both orientations. Members of a religious community who understand themselves as being called to a self-sacrificing, "everything for the Lord" mode are quite capable of channeling militant energies into coalition building and peacemaking—if such behavior is shown: (1) to be in the interests of the community; and (2) to accord with the divine law or the teaching of the religious leader. Faith-based diplomats work in collaboration with other third-party mediators in ensuring that moderation will have its economic, security, and other rewards; they must lead the effort, however, in demonstrating that the give-and-take of negotiation is consistent with the sacred duty of the combatants.

This latter task is achievable, if difficult, because the range of legitimate and thus acceptable religious attitudes toward conflict and violence are located within the religion itself. Ideas about and images of God—of the sacred—vary significantly even within a single religious tradition, as do the meaning and application of ethical teachings, including norms governing the acceptable uses of violence (if any), the conduct of war, and the establishment of a just peace. The ethics, beliefs, and way of life of a religious community are embedded in voluminous and internally contradictory sacred texts, and they are instilled in believers by ritual, catechism, and other spiritual practices that change over time. Sacred texts, practices, and precepts are always subject to interpretation and adaptation. Religion and religious or communal identity is always being contested, always "up for grabs" in the day-to-day negotiations of life. Touchstones and boundaries and dogmatic lines in the sand are regularly reinforced, but even these can shift under the pressure of circumstances and crisis.

One finds in the abode of Islam, for an example, the kind of opening and opportunity that conflict and contestation can provide for the religious peacemaker (as well as for the extremist). A staple of the discourse of Islamic extremists is the claim that the traditional religious leaders of the Islamic world, such as the sheikhs of Cairo's al-Azhar seminary and university—the center of the Sunni educational and religious "establishment"—have been coopted by dictatorial and compromising rulers such as Egyptian president Hosni Mubarak or the monarchy of Saudi Arabia. These traditional Muslim religious leaders, as a result, have been marginalized and delegitimated in many circles of the Islamic world, leaving the field open to religiously un-schooled but disgruntled "lay" men, many of whom come from educational backgrounds in engineering, applied science, or business.

In the late 1990s, Osama bin Laden, for example, began to refer to himself as "Sheikh" Osama Bin-Muhammad bin-Laden, as he did in the "fatwa" he issued on February 23, 1998, announcing his legal "ruling" that every Muslim now has the individual duty to "kill the Americans and their allies—civilians and military." In attempting to launch a holy war against the West, bin Laden sought to rally Muslims to his highly tendentious reading of the Qur'an and the Shari'ah. In so doing, he recognized implicitly that Islam—like Christianity, Judaism, Hinduism, and Buddhism—is a living tra-dition, the meaning of its sacred texts and moral laws ever awaiting a new and compelling *ijtihad* ("personal effort," that is, "the right of a qualified scholar to go back to the primary sources and work out from them what he thought were the Islamic principles involved").[7]

The automatic expertise of bin Laden and his comrades, such as Ayman al-Zawahiri, formerly the chief of Egypt's Islamic Jihad, has not gone un-contested in the Islamic world, however. Religious leaders as well as heads of state within the Sunni Muslim world have denounced the "kill all Amer-icans" fatwa, the attacks of September 11, and, indeed, the violent approach to redressing Islamic grievances. Strikingly, Mohammad Khatami, the Shi'ite president of Iran, an Islamic state often associated with extremism, joined his Sunni colleagues in condemning what he calls "a new form of active nihilism [that] assumes various names, [some of which] bear a semblance of religiosity and some proclaim spirituality." Khatami denigrated religious ex-tremists as "superficial literalists clinging to simplistic ideas," and he called for the development of a crossreligious language that would allow religious communities "to be understood and [provided with] a capacity to listen and understand."[8] President Khatami also proposed an alliance of religiously rooted moderates, from across faith lines, who could offer a vision for their respective societies that uses "neither materialistic secularism nor religious fundamentalism as a starting point."[9] Significantly, his condemnation of ter-rorism was accompanied by strong advocacy of the notion of religious plu-ralism and tolerance of religious and ethnic minorities.

Such global statements by high-profile leaders are important because they help to establish the sociomoral context and the interreligious atmo-sphere within which faith-based diplomacy and religious peacebuilding may thrive. Indeed, Khatami made his remarks at a forum on "The Role of Religion in the Dialogue among Civilizations," held at the Cathedral of St. John the Divine in New York City and organized by religious peacebuilders of the World Conference on Religion and Peace.

Important as they are, however, such grand calls to moderation are no substitute for the detailed and disciplined work that must be undertaken at what El Fadl in chapter 7 has called "the level of the microdiscourses of each religious community." This, too, is a way of stating the expertise of the faith-based diplomat. "Getting religion right" requires erudition of a particular type: deep knowledge of religious practices and teachings; intimate familiarity with the ethical traditions (e.g., "just war") and schools (especially important in the Christian, Buddhist, Jewish, and Islamic cases); and, where appropriate, advanced training in religious law (especially important in the Islamic and Jewish cases).

Can the faith-based diplomat be seen, therefore, as a technical consultant, a member of a new class of religious experts, one who could serve, for example, as a cultural attaché assigned to an embassy or a ministry of foreign affairs? Yes—but that is not enough. While the faith-based diplomat should fit each of these functional descriptions, and while expertise—specialized knowledge, as well as skill in mediation—assuredly should be at the heart of the discipline of faith-based diplomacy, something more is required of this type of mediator. The faith-based diplomat, that is, should be a person of faith, one who understands the psychodynamics of religion and spirituality because he or she has experienced them personally and has meditated or reflected on them and on their relevance to conflict transformation. This will no doubt be a controversial recommendation for Americans who reject religious tests for office, but it seems unavoidable to those who have been in the field attempting to build bridges to religiously inspired combatants and their political leaders.

The faith-based diplomat must find and widen the narrow path between religious extremism and religious commitment that exists within a threatened religious community—a religious or ethnoreligious community, that is, which is engaged in deadly conflict. The extremist elements in the community may claim to be "radical," rooted in and renewing the fundamental truths of their religious traditions, but they also exalt violence as a religious prerogative or even as a spiritual *imperative* in the quest for justice. Yet the community also contains members who renounce violence as an acceptable extreme and would restrict the war against oppressors and injustice to noncoercive spiritual, cultural, political, and psychological means.[10]

The salient difference between these two broadly sketched expressions of religious militance is found not in the use of violence per se but in the religious actor's attitude toward violence and his or her understanding of its role in conflict. The faith-based diplomat must understand this spectrum and engage it as fully as possible. Committed to the cessation of violence and the resolution of conflict, this new breed of diplomat must identify and help to empower or privilege those elements within the community who embrace *reconciliation or peaceful coexistence with the enemy* as their goal. By contrast, the extremist is committed primarily to *victory over the enemy,* whether by gradual means or by the direct and frequent use of violence.

It should be clear that the potential peacemakers within a religious community are no less passionate, no less "radical," than the extremists; indeed, one could argue that the militant peacemaker's rejection of violence as a means of achieving political goals is the more strenuous and radical path. The faith-based diplomat is challenged to negotiate these psychodynamics, imbedded as they are in the social relations of the religious community, and to evoke the peacemaking option within that community.[11]

Faith-Based Resources for Peacebuilding

In addition to his or her own religious expertise, faith life, mediation training and experience, professional networks, and personal friendships, what resources may the faith-based peacebuilder draw upon? The answer depends on the peacebuilder's skill in invoking or evoking resources that lie dormant or partly concealed within the histories and religious traditions of the communities in conflict. In chapter 2, Douglas Johnston and Brian Cox discuss precisely this need for the articulation, development, and concrete application of the moral warrants for peacemaking found in all of the major religious traditions of the world. This important task falls squarely within the domain of the faith-based diplomat.

The case studies suggest at least five resources for conflict transformation, diplomacy, and peacebuilding that are available within religious traditions, religious communities, and religious actors. Where these resources are to be found within religions, and how they are to be retrieved and brought forward in the service of conflict transformation, is the subject of the following recommendations.

1. *Identify the genius of each religious tradition and cultivate ways to evoke its distinctive strengths in conflict resolution and peacebuilding.*

Thus far, the observations of this chapter have addressed the peacemaking resources of religious traditions in rather general terms. It is true, as noted, that there are many similarities shared across religious traditions: the contested nature of sacred texts and traditions; the inevitablilty of interpretation and competition for authority in this arena of hermeneutics; the simultaneous presence of extremist and moderate elements—if not within a particular cell, militia, or faction, then within the larger host community from which such smaller units are recruited; the necessity of confronting and reacting to secular modernity and its expressive forms, from pluralism to liberalism to globalization; the felt need of religious communities, perhaps deeply psychological as well as spiritual, to resist assimilation into alien but superficially appealing secular or plural milieus; the "emergency clause" texts that suspend ethical norms of war and peace in order to preserve the religious tradition or homeland by whatever means necessary; and so on.

While these similarities are important and instructive in themselves, the faith-based diplomat must know several religious traditions, not only his or her own, in such a way as to perceive and command the particular internal dynamics, historical experiences, and unique peacebuilding resources of each.

Merely for illustrative purposes, the following paragraphs indicate one distinctive resource for peacebuilding found within Judaism, one within Christianity, and one within Islam. These fundamental observations are necessary but insufficient elements of the kind of religious inventory and map that is being recommended. The "religious map" to be included in the repertoire of an experienced faith-based diplomat would build on these resources, identify others, and create an extraordinarily detailed religious and cultural topography, nuanced according to the specific religious, political, and social conditions of the site of the conflict being mediated or resolved. And as all religion is local, the map of religious resources for peacebuilding will vary in its specific contents as the site of conflict changes.

• *Jewish resources for peacebuilding: conflict transformation rooted in practices derived from rabbinic commentary, ritual and mitzvot (religious-ethical obligations).*

Marc Gopin's chapter focuses in part on the Jewish notion of teshuva, a term that encompasses the process of repentance, transformation, and restoration. Gopin underscores the centrality of the concept of teshuva for a successful peace process in the Middle East. For the process to be effective over the long term, he argues, Jewish-Israeli engagement must begin with the confrontation of a past filled with profound suffering and injustice.

The Jewish mind perceives the inherent relationship between the past and the present, justice and mercy, repentance and the possibility of forgiveness. The Jewish soul is prepared, gradually and painstakingly, for the offering and receiving of forgiveness through rituals of mourning and the practices of atonement.

Gopin understands that durable peace is impossible unless sustained attention is paid to cultural values and spiritual dynamics that are deeply rooted in the Jewish religious consciousness. Significantly, such cultural values have been absorbed and internalized by secular Jews as well.

Tracing the historically given meanings and capturing the nuances of teshuva is nonetheless an intricate task. The concept is developed in multiple, overlapping rabbinic commentaries on disparate Talmudic passages; in pre-scribed prayers; through the performance of religious obligations, or mitzvot; and in biblical verses that reveal the various dimensions of teshuva (e.g., the Psalmist's reference to *seliha*, "the power to forgive"). Moreover, teshuva becomes possible only through mastery of a web of ethical obligations, such as the call to imitate God by overlooking sin (over al pesah) and by bearing the burden of sin (noseh avon).

As this discussion suggests, Judaism offers distinctive conceptual re-sources for peacebuilding, but it would be inaccurate to consider these "con-cepts" to be in any way abstract or merely theoretical; rather, they are em-bodied in ritual and brought to life in the everyday moral practices cited by Gopin and other authorities on Judaism. While Jewish thought and practice with respect to teshuva is indeed intricate, it is not forbidding. In chapter 5, as well as in his other writings, Gopin demonstrates that the values, rituals, and practices associated with teshuva are analogous in many respects to val-ues, rituals, and practices found in secular as well as other religious com-munities.

It is the "ethical obligation" of the faith-based diplomat, Gopin's work suggests, to become fluent in these competing and overlapping discourses of "transformation toward forgiveness and peace."

- *Christian resources for peacebuilding: The role of churches
  and "the church"*

Christianity is distinctive among the religions under consideration in that its basic form of social organization is ecclesial (the "ecclesia" is "the sacred assembly," known popularly as the church). Churches are individual units, and in some polities (religious organizational structures) they are autonomous and independent of all other churches. Even in evangelical or "low church" structures, however, the churches tend to form networks of affiliation, bound together by common cause if not by theological imperatives. In "high church" forms of Protestantism such as the Anglican Church, as well as in Roman Catholicism, the church is hierarchical—present *as ecclesia* locally, regionally, nationally, internationally, and transnationally or "universally."

The interconnectedness of these units is a potentially enormous resource for any political or religious leader who would seek to mobilize "the people" in support of a campaign. In the same way, the grass-roots presence of the churches constitutes an invaluable opportunity for the faith-based diplomat who seeks to develop broad-based local support for negotiations and peace-building initiatives. At the same time, the regional and transnational presence of the churches can be useful for diplomats who find it necessary to transcend the narrowly ethnic or nationalist tendencies of some local churches and call their members to a higher religious loyalty.

Because they are primarily, if not exclusively, local—and surpassingly human—institutions, churches seldom fail to acquire the benefits of local knowledge or to escape the debilitating effects of local prejudice. Churches, in other words, their ideals and doctrines notwithstanding, are not unambiguous forces for tolerance, forgiveness, and peacemaking. However, the sheer ubiquity of churches in the Christian regions of the world creates space for alternative voices and empowers a critical minority of religious leaders in most settings who are willing to denounce extremist violence and to promote truth-telling and reconciliation. These courageous religious leaders command the resources of the local churches that they pastor; they may exercise influence within the larger church community; and they have been known to reach out to like-minded religious leaders in the so-called enemy camp.

David Steele dramatically illustrates the dynamics of churches caught in deadly conflict in his judicious account of the multidimensional roles of the Serbian Orthodox and Roman Catholic churches in the wars in Bosnia-Herzegovina and Kosovo. No one reading Steele's chapter would conclude that the Christian churches of the region represent unambiguous resources for the reduction of violent conflict. To the contrary, the churches and many of their leaders in the priesthood and the episcopacy seemed determined to outdo one another in reinforcing uncritical and morally outrageous Serbian or Croatian ultranationalism and in legitimating violence against the ethnic and religious "other."

Yet Steele's narrative contains several striking counterexamples of church-based delegitimation of violence, confession of religious and nationalist sins, and advocacy of forgiveness and reconciliation. These efforts came not only from individual religious figures, such as the Bosnian Fransciscan priest Ivo Markovic, the Serbian Orthodox Bishop Hrizostom, and Father Sava, the Serbian Orthodox monk of Kosovo. Entire religious communities, such as the Franciscans of Bosnia, continually engaged in creative efforts at peace education and reconciliation, as well as opposition to ethnophiletism.

Perhaps the most heartening aspect of the story is the evidence that the churches and their leaders may have learned valuable lessons from their general misconduct in the Bosnian war. During the aftermath of the war and continuing through the war in Kosovo, Serbian Orthodox as well as Croatian Catholic bishops, priests, and lay leaders tempered their ultranationalist rhetoric, condemned atrocities and attitudes within their own communities, sponsored or participated in a series of local reconciliation seminars, and entered more readily and frequently into ecumenical collaboration, including participation in the promising Interreligious Councils established in Bosnia and Kosovo. The peacebuilding potential of the transnational dimension of the Christian churches was also demonstrated in various ways, not least through the constructive intervention of Catholic Relief Services and the mediation of the international lay Catholic community of St. Egidio, which brokered the Educational Agreement that allowed Albanian children to return to Kosovo schools in 1998.

Faith-based diplomats working in Christian zones must study the patterns of church involvement in such conflicts, set against the backdrop of the intricate relationships between local parishes; communities of religious, national episcopal conferences, or councils of ministers; faith-based nongovernmental organizations; and universalizing agencies such as the Vatican or the World Council of Churches. Within and across these levels, faith-based diplomats will be able to identify and employ experienced as well as previously dormant advocates of negotiation, nonviolent conflict resolution, and the long-term building of cultures of tolerance. The development of indigenous Christian peacemakers is essential not only for conflict reduction and transformation efforts but also for the prevention of future deadly conflicts that are based, even in part, on religious and ethnic grievances.

- *Islamic resources for peace-building: Contesting the legal traditions on war and peace*

Islam is more than the sum of its religious law and legal discourses. As is the case for Jews, Christians, Hindus, and Buddhists, the faith of Muslims is powerfully expressed in particular beliefs, rituals, practices, observance of ethical obligations, and distinctive forms of social organization. In addition, as indicated hereafter, Islam has given life to the rich mystical tradition known as Sufism. All of these dimensions of Islam constitute resources for peacebuilding.

One expert in this book, however, makes the case for Islamic legal discourse as the sine qua non for effective conflict resolution in conflicts involving Muslim combatants. Legal discourse can become exceedingly technical very quickly, of course; but Khaled Abou El Fadl is concerned not with the details of the "microdiscourse" but rather with the principles and values that it upholds, augments, and enforces. Within Sunnism in particular, he explains, the practical, expeditious, and nonviolent resolution of conflict became a central, unifying value as a result of the successful arbitration of political disputes between Muslim factions. Negotiated settlements subsequently became the religiously sanctioned means of limiting conflict and preventing the outbreak or spread of deadly violence. Abou El Fadl thus extols "the normative value of compromise in Islamic political and legal discourses." He cites the Qur'anic verse that calls for Islamic authorities to compel "transgressors"—those who refuse to accept a mediated, peaceful resolution to the conflict—to return to the negotiating table. Muslims go to war with fellow Muslims, tradition dictates, only when they refuse to make peace according to the Word of God.

Abou El Fadl notes that different rules obtain when the conflict occurs between Muslims and non-Muslims, but he argues that nonviolent conflict transformation remains the norm in these disputes as well. Indeed, he explains, the Prophet's reconciliatory attitude toward non-Muslims was cited by Muslim legal scholars as justification for the permissibility of negotiated settlements between Muslims. Conflict resolution, as a value, therefore carries the same normative weight whether it is sought with Muslims or non-Muslims. Abou El Fadl also endorses the opinion of jurists who argued in favor of the peaceful arbitration of disputes between Muslim and non-Muslim states.

In a conflict setting, when parties are attempting to prevent the outbreak of violence or to end violence, arguments based on historical precedents and textual exegesis are always "heard" in these specific social contexts. Abou El Fadl acknowledges, with regret, the modern collapse of the traditional institutions of the *ulama*, which once provided a forum for interaction with the Muslim masses in the determination of Islamic norms. In the absence of such forums, "official" Islamic practices and attitudes are developed "from above" by clerics who have become salaried state functionaries that never stray far, in their rulings and preaching, from the "orthodoxy" espoused by the self-interested, antidemocratic regimes in the Islamic world. The disintegration of the role of the ulama and its cooption by the secularized modern state, Abou El Fadl laments, has made Islamic normative determinations "all the less rich." The Islamic world awaits—and desperately needs—a renewal of the institutional processes, interpretive strategies, and epistemological assumptions of classical Islamic jurisprudence.

What is most striking about Abou El Fadl's essay, however, is its method of argumentation. Awareness of the present challenges facing the believing community consciously informs the retrieval and presentation of historical-legal precedents, as well as the interpretation of the Qur'an. Abou El Fadl openly acknowledges that he is advancing a kind of religious accommodation to the contemporary emphasis on nonviolent conflict transformation. Speaking authoritatively the first-order discourse of a religious jurist, he has crafted a second-order discourse that reaches beyond the expertise of a legal scholar to engage, first, the Muslim community at large and, second, the non-Muslim interlocutors who are also devoted to fashioning crossreligious and crosscultural modes of conflict resolution.

In the intellectual example set by Professor Abou El Fadl, the faith-based diplomat discovers an important lesson. Expertise in Islamic law and the classical tradition of jurisprudence, grounded in a deep knowledge of and respect for the normative sources of Islam, is the surest foundation for those who would venture to mediate disputes and peacefully transform conflicts involving Muslims.

2. Provide access to the mystical, experiential, and syncretistic dimensions of the faith traditions

Each of the world's major religions features a tradition or way of life shaped by direct religious experience of the holy. Mysticism provides an enriching alternative vision within religions otherwise defined by law, ethics, doctrines, and polities; the mystical traditions are exceedingly relevant to the practical problem of peacemaking. The Sufi brotherhoods of Islam and the Jewish practitioners of kabbalah provide space and impetus for the useful transgression of religious and cultural boundaries, which mystics tend to perceive as artifical in any case. The great Christian mystics such as Julian of Norwich and St. John of the Cross journeyed along a *via negativa,* or path of renunication, that empowered them to be wholly indifferent to self-interest while remaining remarkably open to the "other"; the present-day exemplars of Christian mysticism are by temperament and training mediators.

These mystical, experience-based dimensions of the major religions are fluid and syncretistic: they penetrate beyond the formal expressions of organized religion, such as religious law, dogma, doctrine, and other boundary-setting instruments, to perceive the unity-in-diversity of the sacred and all its manifestations. Often considered marginal or even heretical by the mainstream religious establishment, especially in the monotheistic faiths, the upholders of the mystical traditions are natural pluralists and peacemakers. They feel free to borrow liberally from what is good and loving in the surrounding culture and in other religious traditions. Far from being irrelevant, the custodians of these traditions of mysticism and charismatic power guide and inspire the lived religion of the people; they help shape the actual or operative beliefs and practices of the people, that is, in contrast to the formal, professed, text-based religious systems fostered and preserved in the seminary, yeshiva, or madrassa.

Mystical traditions play a significant role in the case studies of this book relating to Asian religions. Syncretistic Buddhism has incorporated deities as well as patterns of ritual and worship from Hinduism, the predominant religion of the Tamil minority of Sri Lanka. The intimate historical relationship between Sri Lankan Buddhism and Hinduism in the matter of worship— ritual at the major Buddhist shrines is modeled on the Hindu puja, and Hindus participate in major Buddhist festivals—constitutes a promising basis for an ethos of inclusivism that could conceivably be extended to the political culture of Sri Lanka. Already, H. L. Seneviratne notes, it forms the basis for increasingly cordial relations between the majority Buddhists and all minority religious groups—Hindus, Muslims, and Christians. Even Roman Catholics, inspired by the world theology and interreligious dynamism of the Second Vatican Council, interact in significant ways with the Buddhist majority.

A similar potential exists in Kashmir, Ainslie Embree observes, where the spiritual traditions of Bhakti (Hinduism) and Sufism (Islam) share a kind of outsider status vis-à-vis the conventional orthodoxy of their respective mainstreams, as well as common spiritual principles that could help bridge the differences that underlie the conflict. In its emphasis on intense love and devotion to a particular deity or deities, Bhakti, the devotional tradition of Hinduism, intersects theologically and experientially with the Sufi tradition, which paved the way for and continues to characterize much of the Islamic presence in the region. Neither Bhakti nor Sufism thrives on traditional learning or theology; both traditions locate the heart of their devotion in the building of relationships of love and loyalty. These common insights and priorities, Embree suggests, may represent an effective path to authentic dialogue on the conflict in Kashmir.

For the purposes of introducing culturally authentic voices to the process of dialogue and conflict mediation, then, Embree and Seneviratne recommend drawing on the mystical/experiential/sapiential traditions and their representatives. The largest single obstacle to this incorporation of Sufis, monks, devotional priests, and other religious virtuosi into the diplomatic process is their vulnerability to ideological and theological attacks from the mainstream representatives of the tradition—as well as the possibility in some conflict settings of actual physical attacks. A third recommendation for incorporating faith-based resources into diplomacy and peacebuilding attempts to address this concern.

3. *Engage scholars, theologians, hierarchs or other officials, and prominent lay leaders who believe conflict resolution to be a normative commitment of their religious communities*

Religious traditions, as already mentioned, are internally plural arguments about the meaning and proper application of the sacred teachings, texts, and practices that serve as the foundation and framework for the lived religion. These meanings and applications are constantly being contested from within.

The experience of deadly conflict tends to mobilize and amplify the range of interpretive voices speaking from within a religious tradition, each of which hopes to use the crisis as an occasion to advance a particular set of interests, school of thought, or interpretive line.

In this regard, crises occasioned by deadly conflicts represent opportunities for the evolution of the religious tradition in a particular direction. The experience of the world wars of the twentieth century, for example, profoundly affected Christian interpretations of the just war tradition, as did the onset of the nuclear arms race, in a quite different direction. The Gulf War of 1990–91 had a transformative effect on Muslim as well as Christian attitudes toward, and doctrines addressing, "just war" in an age of scud missiles and biochemical weapons. Thus there are tactical reasons for incorporating mainstream voices—or those aspiring to the mainstream—into mediation and peacebuilding processes.

Proponents of faith-based diplomacy are well advised to invite and honor the first-order discourse spoken by jurists, sages, gurus, bishops, theologians, and ethicists who elicit the concrete language of "diplomacy" not from the conflict resolution textbooks and traditions of the West but from the vernacular of the religious and ethnic communities they represent. It is necessary to avoid a "one size fits all" approach to dialogue and mediation; universalizing concepts such as "human rights" should be made to resonate with the sensibilities of religious and ethnic communities. (Gopin notes, as mentioned, that a notion like "forgiveness" has its own complex—and irreducible—connotations in Jewish law, exegesis, culture, and tradition.) The concept as expressed must include connotations if it is to resonate with the Israeli public, much less with rabbinic councils who will pronounce "authoritatively" on the orthodoxy of peace accords.

Strategy for the long term also recommends the prominent incorporation into peacemaking processes of religious leaders who see nonviolent conflict transformation as a religiously sanctioned moral imperative, as a "good" that gives expression to the deepest values of the tradition. Within each of the religious communities represented in this book, one can identify religious agents who are intent on moving the tradition toward accommodation with international law, human rights conventions, and pluralism. These aspirants are poised to help their communities develop and refine "second-order" or "bridging" discourses, through which primary religious symbols, practices, and values are translated into a public idiom that reaches beyond the boundaries of the faith community in order to engage in mutually fruitful dialogue with others. Often these agents of religious evolution are contesting for positions of authority and leadership within the mainstream community. Enhancing their status by including them prominently in faith-based diplomacy may risk the possibility of backlash and obstructionism on the part of threatened elites; but in light of the stakes involved, it is a risk worth taking.

4. *Within religious communities, develop experts and expertise in culturally derived methods of conflict resolution and other skills essential to effective faith-based diplomacy*

Each of the authors offers recommendations for advancing the inchoate field of faith-based diplomacy. Embree, for example, recommends that religious leaders take an active and interventionist role in resolving the conflict by exploiting their influence over believers and their control of local institutions whose resources and social spaces could be placed in the service of peace-building. In addition, he suggests that local communities of believers in India, Pakistan, and the disputed territories could be mobilized to demand an end to the conflict and thus to delegitimate the actions of both the "jihadi" warriors and the Indian security forces. Finally, Embree proposes that the warring parties, or the populations that support them, could be brought closer together by the building of crosscultural solidarity grounded in the fundamental values of human dignity and compassion shared by all the religions of South Asia. "What is needed for peace in Jammu and Kashmir, and for the region as a whole," he concludes, "is a dialogue in which both official and unofficial representatives of the groups concerned participate. It is only after such a dialogue has taken place that negotiations can be expected to bear fruit."

Marc Gopin, one might reasonably conclude, would find Embree's recommendations relevant to the Arab-Israeli conflict but premature. Most religious leaders in the Middle East as well as Africa and South Asia are insufficiently prepared to contribute to faith-based diplomacy and religious peacebuilding. The principles and practices of peacemaking embedded in Jewish, Christian, Islamic, Hindu, and Buddhist texts and traditions, for the most part, remain an open secret. It is also true, however, that religious leaders draw daily on precepts and scriptures that command tolerance and forgiveness and renounce revenge, hatred, and brutality. Nor are the examples of Gandhi, King, Badshah Khan,[12] and other religious advocates of peace unknown in their respective religious communities, where they succeeded in identifying their religion closely with nonviolent—and effective—practices of conflict transformation.[13]

Those highly visible religious leaders who have changed the face of some modern conflicts have generally been representatives of a particular faith community, a multinational religious body such as the Roman Catholic Church or a transdenominational religious organization such as the World

Council of Churches. The authors invoke their names and records (see, for example, Embree's discussion of the interesting but ambiguous figure the Shankaracharaya of Puri, Swami Adhokshayananda). Such charismatic individuals will continue to accomplish a great deal of good in the area of religiously motivated conflict transformation.

What is needed, however, in order to make faith-based diplomacy a viable reality are trained religious actors who reside in, or are available to, local communities that are besieged by deadly conflict or facing early warnings of conflict. These men and women must practice the "mediator virtues"—humility, openness to the "other," vast reserves of patience. Leaders in their faith communities, they should undergo training in the skills of mediation, reconciliation, interfaith or intrafaith dialogue, and the like. Local knowledge and specialization is the key to long-term success in this arena. David Steele's essay documents the complexity of the postwar reality in the Balkans and testifies to the depth of passion as well as misunderstanding that defines the enormous challenges faced by any humanitarian agent. In Steele's own reconciliation workshops, conducted by and for the victims of the Bosnian war, there was no long-term substitute for local religious and civic leadership capable of guiding the long and tortuous process of remembering, naming, and ultimately moving beyond the atrocities that occurred at the hands of both Croatian Catholic and Serbian Orthodox adherents.

5. In developing the field of faith-based diplomacy, draw on the range
of actors, networks, institutions, and nongovernmental organizations
working in related areas

By this point, the reader may reasonably conclude that faith-based diplomacy and religious peacebuilding require an enormous religious and cultural infrastructure, the building of which is an unrealistic goal. It is true that faith-based diplomacy becomes operational only to the extent that such an infrastructure is in place. Developments in the 1980s and 1990s, however, provide reasons for hope. These developments include the appearance of dozens of new nongovernmental organizations dedicated to conflict resolution (including faith-based NGOs), as well as a remarkable growth in the capacity of previously existing NGOs dedicated to conflict resolution. This activity has resulted in, among other things, the multiplication of sites of religiously motivated conflict transformation.[14]

In its broadest definiton, religious peacebuilding includes Christian ethicists who are refining just war and pacifist traditions in light of contemporary military and political circumstances; Muslim jurists and theologians who are upholding the integrity and priority of Islamic law while demonstrating its relevance to nonviolent conflict resolution; Jewish, Buddhist, and

Hindu scholars who are studying and "translating" into second-order, broadly accessible language the insights and values of their respective traditions, especially as they address the question of human rights; courageous religious officials who join crosscultural and interreligious dialogues, often in the face of internal opposition from their coreligionists; transnational religious movements, such as the Community of St. Egidio, that are engaging in conflict transformation through the provision of good offices, mediation, and social services in nations gripped by civil or regional wars; and local religious leaders who work for genuine reconciliation among aggrieved parties.

Related to these efforts and operating on a global level are a host of religious and secular-humanitarian NGOs, some originating in the early years of the United Nations and working within its auspices, others active as independent agents of peace and development. Such organizations and agencies as the Mennonite Central Committee, the World Conference on Religion and Peace, the Society of Engaged Buddhists, and Catholic Relief Services foster ecumenical cooperation in communities riven by ethnic and religious violence, conduct workshops and courses in religious resources for conflict transformation, and facilitate communication and dialogue between communities that are historically divided over competing ethnic or religious claims. Other NGOs such as the Appeal of Conscience Foundation, depend on the international status of individual religious leaders whose personal prestige and integrity gain them access to high government officials.

Finally, the major religious traditions of the world themselves continue to evolve; one finds evidence, for example, of the internal transformation of international religious communities, including the Roman Catholic Church, which has in recent decades reevaluated the purposes and methods of its missions and relief work in light of the imperatives of dialogue and inculturation rather than proselytism. In the 1990s, several denominations and religious or multireligious bodies have been preparing themselves for, and assuming, proactive peacemaking roles. The expanded range of institutionally affiliated religious actors include lay and clerical human rights advocates, development and relief workers, missionaries, denominational structures, ad hoc commissions and delegations, and interdenominational and multireligious bodies such as the World Council of Churches.

Of course, these agencies and movements have their own agendas and priorities; only a handful contribute directly to the development of faith-based diplomacy. Nonetheless there have been serious and partly successful efforts to mount sustained and coordinated faith-based reponses to the crises and conflicts afflicting the world, especially those with a religious dimension.

Perhaps the most promising of the recent developments is the emergence of faith-based actors and agencies who work effectively with secular individuals and agencies and nongovernmental and intergovernmental organizations. In this emerging model, which might be described as "religious-secular" in its orientation, the faith-based diplomat rarely draws explicitly on his (or her) own religious identity, although his faith—in the possibilities for peace, as well as in his particular religious creed—subtly shapes his attitudes and informs his approach to mediation. But the key to the success of this model is the building of strong secular and religious networks and coalitions.

Faith-based actors have much to contribute in building such networks and coalitions. Typically they have contacts within several religious communities in addition to their own; they can rely on the good offices of their coreligionists around the world; and frequently they have earned the trust of secular officials and coworkers in the arena of conflict transformation. They offer their secular and governmental collaborators a wealth of cultural knowledge and insight, hard earned from proximity to the peoples in conflict, that can prove invaluable in constructing productive dialogues across cultural and religious boundaries and battle lines.

Faith-based diplomats, in turn, have much to learn from the secular "veterans" of conflict management. Effective interaction with governmental and intergovernmental agencies, for example, is fundamental to the success of faith-based (and secular) diplomacy. Access to, and prudent use of, the resources of such agencies is a skill honed over time. Faith-based diplomats know that they must rely on an array of partners who possess the technical expertise, media connections, financial means, intelligence data, logistical capabilities, and other resources essential to bringing warring parties to the negotiating table, securing an agreement, and implementing the agreement.

This is the kind of activity in which the earlier-mentioned International Center for Religion & Diplomacy is engaged in the Sudan and Kashmir. Perhaps the most instructive example of successful "religious-secular" diplomacy, though, is the role that was played by the Community of St. Egidio in mediating the end of the civil war in Mozambique. In this effort, the Community, which is composed of laypersons who are professionals in many walks of life, received assistance of various kinds from friends in the Italian government; the Vatican; the U. S. government, including the Central Intelligence Agency; the government of Mozambique; the government of Portugal; the rebel movement in Mozambique; and the Communist Party of Italy! It is instructive to note that St. Egidio mediators do not hide their identity as Roman Catholics but neither do they publicize it—unless and until it may prove useful in their work. Another example of the Community's work was the Agreement on Education that they brokered between the Serbian government and the Albanian community of Kosovo, an accomplishment that was made possible through prior relationships of trust that they had established with Yugoslavia's president Slobodan Milosevic and Ibrahim Rugova, the Albanian Muslim leader.[15]

Conclusion

The terrorist attack against the United States on September 11, 2001, triggered a global conflict that seemed, in part, to pit religious extremists against religious peacebuilders. In the aftermath, mainstream "realist" policymakers developed a deeper understanding of religion's powerful role in legitimating the kind of violence that characterizes post–cold war conflicts. At this writing, however, they remain insufficiently familiar with faith-based actors who are working to reduce violence and to prevent or resolve conflicts through intrareligious, interreligious, and secular-religious dialogue and mediation.

This lapse is unfortunate, for religious actors and religious communities will become ever more prominent in the campaign for a sustainable and just peace in the many troubled regions of the world. Whether religious energies will be channeled toward constructive means of resolving conflict will depend, in no small part, on the intervention, mediation, and leadership of people of faith who are dedicated to militant but nonviolent peacebuilding. A strategy of reinforcing and building on their efforts, as was done so effectively in Mozambique,[16] would seem shrewd, wise, and highly appropriate.

NOTES

1. Ignatius of Antioch, "To the Romans," in Cyril C. Richardson, ed., *Early Christian Fathers* (New York: Macmillan, 1975), pp. 104–5. "I am corresponding with all the churches and bidding them all realize that I am voluntarily dying for God—if, that is, you do not interfere. I plead with you, do not do me an unreasonable kindness. Let me be fodder for wild beasts—that is how I can get to God. I am God's wheat and I am being ground by the teeth of the wild beasts to make a pure loaf for Christ," writes Ignatius. "Come fire, cross, battling with wild beasts, wrenching of bones, mangling of limbs, crushing of my whole body—only let me get to Jesus Christ!"

2. Jay P. Dolan, *The American Catholic Experience* (Notre Dame, Ind.: University of Notre Dame Press, 1985), p. 422.

3. Mark Juergensmeyer, *Terror in the Mind of God* (Berkeley: University of California Press, 2000), pp. 122–46.

4. For documentation from several religious traditions, see Martin E. Marty and R. Scott Appleby, "An Interim Report on a Hypothetical Family," in *Fundamentalisms Observed,* ed. by Martin E. Marty and R. Scott Appleby (Chicago: University of Chicago Press, 1991), pp. 814–42.

5. Mark Juergensmeyer, "Anti-Fundamentalism," in *Fundamentalisms Comprehended,*

ed. by Martin E. Marty and R. Scott Appleby (Chicago: University of Chicago Press, 1995), pp. 353–66.

6. The concepts of negative peace and positive peace are fundamental to the discipline of peace studies. For a discussion of their usage, see David Barash, "Negative Peace" and "Positive Peace," in *Approaches to Peace: A Reader in Peace Studies,* ed. by David Barash (New York: Oxford University Press, 2000).

7. W. Montgomery Watt, *Islamic Fundamentalism and Modernity* (London: Routledge, 1988), p. 29.

8. Gustav Niehbuhr, "Iranian Contrasts Faith and Nihilism," *New York Times,* November 17, 2001, p. A10.

9. William F. Vendley, quoted in ibid.

10. The true believer's life finds meaning only in relation to God's commands; the authority of the sacred far outweighs mundane considerations. In this context, extremism—which implies the explicit rejection of moderation or compromise in the pursuit of justice—operates as a religious norm. As the political scientist Charles Liebman argues, "a propensity to religious extremism does not require explanation since it is entirely consistent with basic religious tenets and authentic religious orientations." Extremism is thus "a tendency to which every religiously oriented person is attracted." Charles Liebman, "Extremism as a Religious Norm," *Journal for the Scientific Study of Religion* 22, no. 1 (1985), pp. 75–86.

11. The dreadful record of religiously inspired violence and intolerance notwithstanding, history paints a more complicated picture of religious agency. Religious radicals of the Christian Reformation condemned coercion in matters of religion and were prominent among the early modern proponents of religious liberty and freedom of speech; Baptists, original advocates of religious autonomy, were champions of church-state separation. In the twentieth century Hindu and Christian religious leaders, including martyrs for peace such as Mahatma Gandhi and Martin Luther King, Jr., were perhaps the most influential pioneers of nonviolence as both a spiritual practice and a political strategy. Islam, Judaism, and Buddhism have produced their own nonviolent religious militants and peacemakers. Brian Tierney, "Religious Rights: An Historical Perspective," in *Religious Human Rights in Global Perspective: Religious Perspectives,* ed. by John Witte, Jr., and Johan D. van der Vyver (The Hague: Martinus Nijhoff, 1996), 35. Max Weber famously identified the religious roots of modern human rights: "The transition to the conception that every human being as such has certain rights was mainly completed through the rationalistic enlightenment of the seventeenth and eighteenth centuries with the aid, for a time, of powerful religious forces, particularly Anabaptist influences. . . . Sects [such as the Quakers or Baptists] gave rise to an inalienable personal right of the governed as against any power, whether political, hierocratic, or patriarchal." Weber, *Economy and Society,* vol. 2 (New York: Bedminster Press, 1968), 868.

12. Badshah Khan was a Muslim and Pashtun warrior who, under the influence of Gandhi, adopted a strict code of nonviolence that his followers adopted as well. See Eknath Easwaran, *A Man to Match His Mountains: Badshah Khan, Nonviolent Soldier of Islam* (Petaluma, Calif.: Nilgiri Press, 1984).

13. On Mahatma Gandhi's legacy among nonviolent religious activists in Hinduism, Buddhism, Christianity, and Islam, see Catherine Ingram, *In the Footsteps of Gandhi: Conversations with Spiritual Social Activists* (Berkeley, Calif.: Parallax Press, 1990). On King as a nonviolent religious leader consult, inter alia, Albert J. Raboteau, "Martin Luther King, Jr., and the Tradition of Black Religious Protest," in *Religion and the Life of the*

Nation: American Recoveries, ed. by Rowland A. Sherrill (Urbana, Ill.: University of Illinois Press, 1990), pp. 46–63; Daniel L. Buttry, *Christian Peacemaking: From Heritage to Hope* (Valley Forge, Penn.: Judson Press, 1994), pp. 45–59. For a comparative overview of peacemakers in Islam, Judaism and Christianity, see Marc Gopin, "Religion, Violence, and Conflict Resolution," *Peace and Change* 22, no. 1 (January 1997), pp. 1–31.

14. Loramy C. Conradi Gerstbauer, "Having Faith in NGOs? A Comparative Study of Faith-based and Secular NGOs Engaged in International Peacebuilding," Ph.D dissertation, University of Notre Dame, 2001.

15. The 1996 Agreement on Education restored the teaching of Albanian in Kosovo's schools and university and created a joint educational administrative team whose members were to be drawn from Kosovo's Albanian and Serb communities. Andrea Riccardi, founder of the St. Egidio movement, said that he hoped to build on the progress toward resolving this "highly explosive and contentious issue" by negotiating agreements to restore peaceful relations to the health and recreation sectors. Albanian Muslims constituted 90 percent of the population and enjoyed a statute granting them autonomy within the Yugoslav Federation. That year, however, the Yugoslav government in Belgrade abolished the statute and imposed the mandatory teaching of the Serbian language in the schools of Kosovo. In vehement response, the Albanian-speaking majority abandoned the public school and university system and created their own parallel educational institutions. In September 1996, as tensions reached a flashpoint, the Community of St. Egidio, active as a provider of social services in Albania since 1990, mediated the Agreement. On March 23, 1998, Serbian and Albanian officials endorsed a measure which gave St. Egidio significant responsibility for implementing the provisions of the Agreement. It appointed St. Egidio representatives to a joint Serbian-Albanian committee charged with reintegrating the elementary and high schools of Kosovo, as well as the faculty and students of Pristina University, and with overcoming the remaining obstacles to the normalization of the educational system (e.g., funding, administration, languages, programs, diplomas, and employee status questions). For details, see R. Scott Appleby, *The Ambivalence of the Sacred: Religion, Violence and Reconciliation* (Lanham, Md.: Rowman and Littlefield, 2000), pp. 155–65, 209–10.

16. See chapter 2, note 21.

Index